Frank McCourt

is a retired New York schoolteacher. *Angela's Ashes* is his first book.

Praise for *Angela's Ashes:*

'I was moved and dazzled by the sombre and lively beauty of this book; it is a story of survival and growth beyond all odds; a chronicle of surprising triumphs, written in language that is always itself triumphant.'

MARY GORDON, author of *The Shadow Man*

'This book is absolutely extraordinary and incredibly touching and powerful.'

LYNDA MYLES, director of *The Commitments*

'[A] masterly and at times heartrending account . . . pro-digiously detailed and frequently poetic. McCourt, a retired schoolmaster, is a fully paid-up subscriber to the sub-Joycean school of Irish letters . . . he also possesses the gift of humour. The suffering and intermittent joys McCourt recounts have produced an unexpected classic of reminiscence, brilliantly evoking a world that was sour and hostile to change.' WALTER ELLIS, *Sunday Times*

'Outstanding . . . a bittersweet and grimly comic narrative of growing up dirt-poor in rain-sodden, priest-ridden Limerick.' BOYD TONKIN, *New Statesman*

'The unbearable bleakness of this haunting childhood memoir is redeemed by the author's generosity of vision and the vibrant quality of his writing.'

TERENCE BLACKER, *Mail on Sunday*

'A story as sad as this one should make hard reading. But the younger Frank's resilience, and the older Frank's ability to weave a yarn that contains not a few threads of humour, urge the reader on. This is a jewel of a book.'

GRANIA MCFADDEN, *Belfast Telegraph*

'Sombre, funny, unnerving, buoyant, *Angela's Ashes* is a treat to read and an undoubted feat to have written.'

GEORGE O'BRIEN, *Irish Times*

'Our first Irish Dickens . . . Big strong, unashamed sentiment . . . the thing Irish people run away from, afraid of their own hearts . . . But in some hands sentimentality is powerful and an instrument of the truth. I think the sentiment in *Angela's Ashes* is something the reader will be the richer for opening towards.'

NUALA O'FAOLAIN, *Irish Times*

'Frank McCourt's Irish childhood may have been a bleak affair, but his memoir is something else – unexpectedly exuberant, impressionistic and funny. Despite McCourt's litany of the indignities he suffered, *Angela's Ashes* is a joy to read. The poverty is relentless, and McCourt's account of it would be unbearable were it not for the resilience of the people and the music of their language. Whatever else happened to McCourt, we can be thankful that he always had the words.'

ALIX MADRIGAL, *San Francisco Chronicle*

'The reader of this stunning memoir can only hope that Mr McCourt will set down the story of his subsequent adventures in America in another book. *Angela's Ashes* is so good it deserves a sequel.'

MICHIKO KAKUTANI, *New York Times*

FRANK McCOURT

Angela's Ashes

A Memoir of a Childhood

Flamingo

An Imprint of HarperCollinsPublishers

This book is dedicated to my brothers,
Malachy, Michael, Alphonsus.
I learn from you, I admire you and I love you.

Flamingo
An Imprint of HarperCollins*Publishers*
77–85 Fulham Palace Road,
Hammersmith, London w6 8jb

Published by Flamingo 1997
3 5 7 9 8 6 4

First published in Great Britain by
HarperCollins*Publishers* 1996

Author photograph © Jerry Bauer

isbn 0 00 651034 5

Set in Bembo by
Rowland Phototypesetting Ltd,
Bury St Edmunds, Suffolk

Printed and bound in Great Britain by
Caledonian International Book Manufacturing Ltd, Glasgow

ACKNOWLEDGEMENTS

This is a small hymn to an exaltation of women.

R'lene Dahlberg fanned the embers.
Lisa Schwarzbaum read early pages and encouraged me.
Mary Breasted Smyth, elegant novelist herself, read the first
third and passed it on to
Molly Friedrich, who became my agent and thought that
Nan Graham, Editor-in-Chief at Scribner, would be just the
right person to put the book on the road.
And Molly was right.

My daughter, Maggie, has shown me how life can be
a grand adventure, while exquisite moments with
my granddaughter, Chiara, have helped me recall
a small child's wonder.
My wife, Ellen, listened while I read and cheered me
to the final page.

I am blessed among men.

My father and mother should have stayed in New York where they met and married and where I was born. Instead, they returned to Ireland when I was four, my brother, Malachy, three, the twins, Oliver and Eugene, barely one, and my sister, Margaret, dead and gone.

When I look back on my childhood I wonder how I survived at all. It was, of course, a miserable childhood: the happy childhood is hardly worth your while. Worse than the ordinary miserable childhood is the miserable Irish childhood, and worse yet is the miserable Irish Catholic childhood.

People everywhere brag and whimper about the woes of their early years, but nothing can compare with the Irish version: the poverty; the shiftless loquacious alcoholic father; the pious defeated mother moaning by the fire; pompous priests; bullying schoolmasters; the English and the terrible things they did to us for eight hundred long years.

Above all—we were wet.

Out in the Atlantic Ocean great sheets of rain gathered to drift slowly up the River Shannon and settle forever in Limerick. The rain dampened the city from the Feast of the Circumcision to New Year's Eve. It created a cacophony of hacking coughs, bronchial rattles, asthmatic wheezes, consumptive croaks. It turned noses into fountains, lungs into bacterial sponges. It provoked cures galore; to ease the catarrh you boiled onions in milk blackened with pepper; for the congested passages you made a paste of boiled flour and nettles, wrapped it in a rag, and slapped it, sizzling, on the chest.

From October to April the walls of Limerick glistened with the damp. Clothes never dried: tweed and woolen coats housed living things, sometimes sprouted mysterious vegetations. In pubs, steam rose from damp bodies and garments to be inhaled with cigarette and pipe smoke laced with the stale fumes of spilled stout and whiskey and tinged with the odor of piss wafting in from the outdoor jakes where many a man puked up his week's wages.

The rain drove us into the church—our refuge, our strength, our only dry place. At Mass, Benediction, novenas, we huddled in great damp clumps, dozing through priest drone, while steam rose again from our clothes to mingle with the sweetness of incense, flowers and candles.

Limerick gained a reputation for piety, but we knew it was only the rain.

My father, Malachy McCourt, was born on a farm in Toome, County Antrim. Like his father before, he grew up wild, in trouble with the English, or the Irish, or both. He fought with the Old IRA and for some desperate act he wound up a fugitive with a price on his head.

When I was a child I would look at my father, the thinning hair, the collapsing teeth, and wonder why anyone would give money for a head like that. When I was thirteen my father's mother told me a secret: as a wee lad your poor father was dropped on his head. It was an accident, he was never the same after, and you must remember that people dropped on their heads can be a bit peculiar.

Because of the price on the head he had been dropped on, he had to be spirited out of Ireland via cargo ship from Galway. In New York, with Prohibition in full swing, he thought he had died and gone to hell for his sins. Then he discovered speakeasies and he rejoiced.

After wandering and drinking in America and England he yearned for peace in his declining years. He returned to

Belfast, which erupted all around him. He said, A pox on all their houses, and chatted with the ladies of Andersontown. They tempted him with delicacies but he waved them away and drank his tea. He no longer smoked or touched alcohol, so what was the use? It was time to go and he died in the Royal Victoria Hospital.

My mother, the former Angela Sheehan, grew up in a Limerick slum with her mother, two brothers, Thomas and Patrick, and a sister, Agnes. She never saw her father, who had run off to Australia weeks before her birth.

After a night of drinking porter in the pubs of Limerick he staggers down the lane singing his favorite song,

> *Who threw the overalls in Mrs. Murphy's chowder?*
> *Nobody spoke so he said it all the louder*
> *It's a dirty Irish trick and I can lick the Mick*
> *Who threw the overalls in Murphy's chowder.*

He's in great form altogether and he thinks he'll play a while with little Patrick, one year old. Lovely little fella. Loves his daddy. Laughs when Daddy throws him up in the air. Upsy daisy, little Paddy, upsy daisy, up in the air in the dark, so dark, oh, Jasus, you miss the child on the way down and poor little Patrick lands on his head, gurgles a bit, whimpers, goes quiet. Grandma heaves herself from the bed, heavy with the child in her belly, my mother. She's barely able to lift little Patrick from the floor. She moans a long moan over the child and turns on Grandpa. Get out of it. Out. If you stay here a minute longer I'll take the hatchet to you, you drunken lunatic. By Jesus, I'll swing at the end of a rope for you. Get out.

Grandpa stands his ground like a man. I have a right, he says, to stay in me own house.

She runs at him and he melts before this whirling dervish with a damaged child in her arms and a healthy one stirring

3

inside. He stumbles from the house, up the lane, and doesn't stop till he reaches Melbourne in Australia.

Little Pat, my uncle, was never the same after. He grew up soft in the head with a left leg that went one way, his body the other. He never learned to read or write but God blessed him in another way. When he started to sell newspapers at the age of eight he could count money better than the Chancellor of the Exchequer himself. No one knew why he was called Ab Sheehan, The Abbot, but all Limerick loved him.

My mother's troubles began the night she was born. There is my grandmother in the bed heaving and gasping with the labor pains, praying to St. Gerard Majella, patron saint of expectant mothers. There is Nurse O'Halloran, the midwife, all dressed up in her finery. It's New Year's Eve and Mrs. O'Halloran is anxious for this child to be born so that she can rush off to the parties and celebrations. She tells my grandmother: Will you push, will you, push. Jesus, Mary and holy St. Joseph, if you don't hurry with this child it won't be born till the New Year and what good is that to me with me new dress? Never mind St. Gerard Majella. What can a man do for a woman at a time like this even if he is a saint? St. Gerard Majella my arse.

My grandmother switches her prayers to St. Ann, patron saint of difficult labor. But the child won't come. Nurse O'Halloran tells my grandmother, Pray to St. Jude, patron saint of desperate cases.

St. Jude, patron of desperate cases, help me. I'm desperate. She grunts and pushes and the infant's head appears, only the head, my mother, and it's the stroke of midnight, the New Year. Limerick City erupts with whistles, horns, sirens, brass bands, people calling and singing, Happy New Year. Should auld acquaintance be forgot, and church bells all over ring out the Angelus and Nurse O'Halloran weeps for the waste of a dress, that child still in there and me in me finery. Will you come out, child, will you? Grandma gives a great push

4

and the child is in the world, a lovely girl with black curly hair and sad blue eyes.

Ah, Lord above, says Nurse O'Halloran, this child is a time straddler, born with her head in the New Year and her arse in the Old or was it her head in the Old Year and her arse in the New. You'll have to write to the Pope, missus, to find out what year this child was born in and I'll save this dress for next year.

And the child was named Angela for the Angelus which rang the midnight hour, the New Year, the minute of her coming and because she was a little angel anyway.

> Love her as in childhood
> Though feeble, old and grey.
> For you'll never miss a mother's love
> Till she's buried beneath the clay.

At the St. Vincent de Paul School, Angela learned to read, write, and calculate and by her ninth year her schooling was done. She tried her hand at being a charwoman, a skivvy, a maid with a little white hat opening doors, but she could not manage the little curtsy that is required and her mother said, You don't have the knack of it. You're pure useless. Why don't you go to America where there's room for all sorts of uselessness? I'll give you the fare.

She arrived in New York just in time for the first Thanksgiving Day of the Great Depression. She met Malachy at a party given by Dan MacAdorey and his wife, Minnie, on Classon Avenue in Brooklyn. Malachy liked Angela and she liked him. He had a hangdog look, which came from the three months he had just spent in jail for hijacking a truck. He and his friend John McErlaine believed what they were told in the speakeasy, that the truck was packed to the roof with cases of canned pork and beans. Neither knew how to drive and when the police saw the truck lurch and jerk along Myrtle Avenue they pulled it over. The police searched the truck and wondered why anyone would hijack a truck containing, not pork and beans, but cases of buttons.

With Angela drawn to the hangdog look and Malachy lonely after three months in jail, there was bound to be a knee-trembler.

A knee-trembler is the act itself done up against a wall, man and woman up on their toes, straining so hard their knees tremble with the excitement that's in it.

That knee-trembler put Angela in an interesting condition and, of course, there was talk. Angela had cousins, the Mac-Namara sisters, Delia and Philomena, married, respectively, to Jimmy Fortune of County Mayo, and Tommy Flynn, of Brooklyn itself.

Delia and Philomena were large women, great-breasted and fierce. When they sailed along the sidewalks of Brooklyn lesser creatures stepped aside, respect was shown. The sisters knew what was right and they knew what was wrong and any doubts could be resolved by the One, Holy, Roman, Catholic and Apostolic Church. They knew that Angela, unmarried, had no right to be in an interesting condition and they would take steps.

Steps they took. With Jimmy and Tommy in tow they marched to the speakeasy on Atlantic Avenue where Malachy could be found on Friday, payday when he had a job. The man in the speak, Joey Cacciamani, did not want to admit the sisters but Philomena told him that if he wanted to keep the nose on his face and that door on its hinges he'd better open up for they were there on God's business. Joey said, Awright, awright, you Irish. Jeezoz! Trouble, trouble.

Malachy, at the far end of the bar, turned pale, gave the great-breasted ones a sickly smile, offered them a drink. They resisted the smile and spurned the offer. Delia said, We don't know what class of a tribe you come from in the North of Ireland.

Philomena said, There is a suspicion you might have Pres-

6

byterians in your family, which would explain what you did to our cousin.

Jimmy said, Ah, now, ah, now. 'Tisn't his fault if there's Presbyterians in his family.

Delia said, You shuddup.

Tommy had to join in. What you did to that poor unfortunate girl is a disgrace to the Irish race and you should be ashamed of yourself.

Och, I am, said Malachy. I am.

Nobody asked you to talk, said Philomena. You done enough damage with your blather, so shut your yap.

And while your yap is shut, said Delia, we're here to see you do the right thing by our poor cousin, Angela Sheehan.

Malachy said, Och, indeed, indeed. The right thing is the right thing and I'd be glad to buy you all a drink while we have this little talk.

Take the drink, said Tommy, and shove it up your ass.

Philomena said, Our little cousin no sooner gets off the boat than you are at her. We have morals in Limerick, you know, morals. We're not like jackrabbits from Antrim, a place crawling with Presbyterians.

Jimmy said, He don't look like a Presbyterian.

You shuddup, said Delia.

Another thing we noticed, said Philomena. You have a very odd manner.

Malachy smiled. I do?

You do, says Delia. I think 'tis one of the first things we noticed about you, that odd manner, and it gives us a very uneasy feeling.

'Tis that sneaky little Presbyterian smile, said Philomena.

Och, said Malachy, it's just the trouble I have with my teeth.

Teeth or no teeth, odd manner or no odd manner, you're gonna marry that girl, said Tommy. Up the middle aisle you're going.

Och, said Malachy, I wasn't planning to get married, you

know. There's no work and I wouldn't be able to support . . .

Married is what you're going to be, said Delia.

Up the middle aisle, said Jimmy.

You shuddup, said Delia.

Malachy watched them leave. I'm in a desperate pickle, he told Joey Cacciamani.

Bet your ass, said Joey. I see them babes comin' at me I jump inna Hudson River.

Malachy considered the pickle he was in. He had a few dollars in his pocket from the last job and he had an uncle in San Francisco or one of the other California Sans. Wouldn't he be better off in California, far from the great-breasted MacNamara sisters and their grim husbands? He would, indeed, and he'd have a drop of the Irish to celebrate his decision and departure. Joey poured and the drink nearly took the lining off Malachy's gullet. Irish, indeed! He told Joey it was a Prohibition concoction from the devil's own still. Joey shrugged. I don't know nothing. I only pour. Still, it was better than nothing and Malachy would have another and one for yourself, Joey, and ask them two decent Italians what they'd like and what are you talking about, of course, I have the money to pay for it.

He awoke on a bench in the Long Island Railroad Station, a cop rapping on his boots with a nightstick, his escape money gone, the MacNamara sisters ready to eat him alive in Brooklyn.

On the feast of St. Joseph, a bitter day in March, four months after the knee-trembler, Malachy married Angela and in August the child was born. In November Malachy got drunk and decided it was time to register the child's birth. He thought he might name the child Malachy, after himself, but his North of Ireland accent and the alcoholic mumble con-

8

fused the clerk so much he simply entered the name Male on the certificate.

Not until late December did they take Male to St. Paul's Church to be baptized and named Francis after his father's father and the lovely saint of Assisi. Angela wanted to give him a middle name, Munchin, after the patron saint of Limerick but Malachy said over his dead body. No son of his would have a Limerick name. It's hard enough going through life with one name. Sticking on middle names was an atrocious American habit and there was no need for a second name when you're christened after the man from Assisi.

There was a delay the day of the baptism when the chosen godfather, John McErlaine, got drunk at the speakeasy and forgot his responsibilities. Philomena told her husband, Tommy, he'd have to be godfather. Child's soul is in danger, she said. Tommy put his head down and grumbled. All right. I'll be godfather but I'm not goin' to be responsible if he grows up like his father causin' trouble and goin' through life with the odd manner for if he does he can go to John McErlaine at the speakeasy. The priest said, True for you, Tom, decent man that you are, fine man that never set foot inside a speakeasy. Malachy, fresh from the speakeasy himself, felt insulted and wanted to argue with the priest, one sacrilege on top of another. Take off that collar and we'll see who's the man. He had to be held back by the great-breasted ones and their husbands grim. Angela, new mother, agitated, forgot she was holding the child and let him slip into the baptismal font, a total immersion of the Protestant type. The altar boy assisting the priest plucked the infant from the font and restored him to Angela, who sobbed and clutched him, dripping, to her bosom. The priest laughed, said he had never seen the likes, that the child was a regular little Baptist now and hardly needed a priest. This maddened Malachy again and he wanted to jump at the priest for calling the child some class of a Protestant. The priest said, Quiet, man, you're in God's house, and when Malachy said, God's house, my arse, he was thrown out on Court Street because you can't say arse in God's house.

After baptism Philomena said she had tea and ham and cakes in her house around the corner. Malachy said, Tea? and she said, Yes, tea, or is it whiskey you want? He said tea was grand but first he'd have to go and deal with John McErlaine, who didn't have the decency to carry out his duties as godfather. Angela said, You're only looking for an excuse to run to the speakeasy, and he said, As God is my witness, the drink is the last thing on my mind. Angela started to cry. Your son's christening day and you have to go drinking. Delia told him he was a disgusting specimen but what could you expect from the North of Ireland.

Malachy looked from one to the other, shifted on his feet, pulled his cap down over his eyes, shoved his hands deep in his trouser pockets, said, Och, aye, the way they do in the far reaches of County Antrim, turned, hurried up Court Street to the speakeasy on Atlantic Avenue where he was sure they'd ply him with free drink in honor of his son's baptism.

At Philomena's house the sisters and their husbands ate and drank while Angela sat in a corner nursing the baby and crying. Philomena stuffed her mouth with bread and ham and rumbled at Angela, That's what you get for being such a fool. Hardly off the boat and you fall for that lunatic. You shoulda stayed single, put the child up for adoption, and you'd be a free woman today. Angela cried harder and Delia took up the attack, Oh, stop it, Angela, stop it. You have nobody to blame but yourself for gettin' into trouble with a drunkard from the North, a man that doesn't even look like a Catholic, him with his odd manner. I'd say that . . . that . . . Malachy has a streak of the Presbyterian in him right enough. You shuddup, Jimmy.

If I was you, said Philomena, I'd make sure there's no more children. He don't have a job, so he don't, an' never will the way he drinks. So . . . no more children, Angela. Are you listenin' to me?

I am, Philomena.

A year later another child was born. Angela called him Malachy after his father and gave him a middle name, Gerard, after his father's brother.

The MacNamara sisters said Angela was nothing but a rabbit and they wanted nothing to do with her till she came to her senses.

Their husbands agreed.

I'm in a playground on Classon Avenue in Brooklyn with my brother, Malachy. He's two, I'm three. We're on the seesaw.

Up, down, up, down.

Malachy goes up.

I get off.

Malachy goes down. Seesaw hits the ground. He screams. His hand is on his mouth and there's blood.

Oh, God. Blood is bad. My mother will kill me.

And here she is, trying to run across the playground. Her big belly slows her.

She says, What did you do? What did you do to the child?

I don't know what to say. I don't know what I did.

She pulls my ear. Go home. Go to bed.

Bed? In the middle of the day?

She pushes me toward the playground gate. Go.

She picks up Malachy and waddles off.

My father's friend, Mr. MacAdorey, is outside our building. He's standing at the edge of the sidewalk with his wife, Minnie, looking at a dog lying in the gutter. There is blood all around the dog's head. It's the color of the blood from Malachy's mouth.

Malachy has dog blood and the dog has Malachy blood.

I pull Mr. MacAdorey's hand. I tell him Malachy has blood like the dog.

Oh, he does, indeed, Francis. Cats have it, too. And Eskimos. All the same blood.

Minnie says, Stop that, Dan. Stop confusing the wee fellow. She tells me the poor wee dog was hit by a car and he crawled all the way from the middle of the street before he died. Wanted to come home, the poor wee creature.

Mr. MacAdorey says, You'd better go home, Francis. I don't know what you did to your wee brother, but your mother took him off to the hospital. Go home, child.

Will Malachy die like the dog, Mr. MacAdorey?

Minnie says, He bit his tongue. He won't die.

Why did the dog die?

It was his time, Francis.

The apartment is empty and I wander between the two rooms, the bedroom and the kitchen. My father is out looking for a job and my mother is at the hospital with Malachy. I wish I had something to eat but there's nothing in the icebox but cabbage leaves floating in the melted ice. My father said never eat anything floating in water for the rot that might be in it. I fall asleep on my parents' bed and when my mother shakes me it's nearly dark. Your little brother is going to sleep a while. Nearly bit his tongue off. Stitches galore. Go into the other room.

My father is in the kitchen sipping black tea from his big white enamel mug. He lifts me to his lap.

Dad, will you tell me the story about Coo Coo?

12

Cuchulain. Say it after me, Coo-hoo-lin. I'll tell you the story when you say the name right. Coo-hoo-lin.

I say it right and he tells me the story of Cuchulain, who had a different name when he was a boy, Setanta. He grew up in Ireland where Dad lived when he was a boy in County Antrim. Setanta had a stick and ball and one day he hit the ball and it went into the mouth of a big dog that belonged to Culain and choked him. Oh, Culain was angry and he said, What am I to do now without my big dog to guard my house and my wife and my ten small children as well as numerous pigs, hens, sheep?

Setanta said, I'm sorry. I'll guard your house with my stick and ball and I'll change my name to Cuchulain, the Hound of Culain. He did. He guarded the house and regions beyond and became a great hero, the Hound of Ulster itself. Dad said he was a greater hero than Hercules or Achilles that the Greeks were always bragging about and he could take on King Arthur and all his knights in a fair fight which, of course, you could never get with an Englishman anyway.

That's my story. Dad can't tell that story to Malachy or any other children down the hall.

He finishes the story and lets me sip his tea. It's bitter, but I'm happy there on his lap.

For days Malachy's tongue is swollen and he can hardly make a sound never mind talk. But even if he could no one is paying any attention to him because we have two new babies who were brought by an angel in the middle of the night. The neighbors say, Ooh, Ah, they're lovely boys, look at those big eyes.

Malachy stands in the middle of the room, looking up at everyone, pointing to his tongue and saying, Uck, uck. When the neighbors say, Can't you see we're looking at your little brothers? he cries, till Dad pats him on the head. Put in your tongue, son, and go out and play with Frankie. Go on.

13

In the playground I tell Malachy about the dog who died in the street because someone drove a ball into his mouth. Malachy shakes his head. No uck ball. Car uck kill dog. He cries because his tongue hurts and he can hardly talk and it's terrible when you can't talk. He won't let me push him on the swing. He says, You uck kill me uck on seesaw. He gets Freddie Leibowitz to push him and he's happy, laughing when he swings to the sky. Freddie is big, he's seven, and I ask him to push me. He says, No, you tried to kill your brother.

I try to get the swing going myself but all I can do is move it back and forth and I'm angry because Freddie and Malachy are laughing at the way I can't swing. They're great pals now, Freddie, seven, Malachy, two. They laugh every day and Malachy's tongue gets better with all the laughing.

When he laughs you can see how white and small and pretty his teeth are and you can see his eyes shine. He has blue eyes like my mother. He has golden hair and pink cheeks. I have brown eyes like Dad. I have black hair and my cheeks are white in the mirror. My mother tells Mrs. Leibowitz down the hall that Malachy is the happiest child in the world. She tells Mrs. Leibowitz down the hall, Frankie has the odd manner like his father. I wonder what the odd manner is but I can't ask because I'm not supposed to be listening.

I wish I could swing up into the sky, up into the clouds. I might be able to fly around the whole world and not hear my brothers, Oliver and Eugene, cry in the middle of the night anymore. My mother says they're always hungry. She cries in the middle of the night, too. She says she's worn out nursing and feeding and changing and four boys is too much for her. She wishes she had one little girl all for herself. She'd give anything for one little girl.

I'm in the playground with Malachy. I'm four, he's three.

He lets me push him on the swing because he's no good at swinging himself and Freddie Leibowitz is in school. We have to stay in the playground because the twins are sleeping and my mother says she's worn out. Go out and play, she says, and give me some rest. Dad is out looking for a job again and sometimes he comes home with the smell of whiskey, singing all the songs about suffering Ireland. Mam gets angry and says Ireland can kiss her arse. He says that's nice language to be using in front of the children and she says never mind the language, food on the table is what she wants, not suffering Ireland. She says it was a sad day Prohibition ended because Dad gets the drink going around to saloons offering to sweep out the bars and lift barrels for a whiskey or a beer. Sometimes he brings home bits of the free lunch, rye bread, corned beef, pickles. He puts the food on the table and drinks tea himself. He says food is a shock to the system and he doesn't know where we get our appetites. Mam says, They get their appetites because they're starving half the time.

When Dad gets a job Mam is cheerful and she sings,

> *Anyone can see why I wanted your kiss,*
> *It had to be and the reason is this*
> *Could it be true, someone like you*
> *Could love me, love me?*

When Dad brings home the first week's wages Mam is delighted she can pay the lovely Italian man in the grocery shop and she can hold her head up again because there's nothing worse in the world than to owe and be beholden to anyone. She cleans the kitchen, washes the mugs and plates, brushes crumbs and bits of food from the table, cleans out the icebox and orders a fresh block of ice from another Italian. She buys toilet paper that we can take down the hall to

the lavatory and that, she says, is better than having the headlines from the *Daily News* blackening your arse. She boils water
on the stove and spends a day at a great tin tub washing our
shirts and socks, diapers for the twins, our two sheets, our three
towels. She hangs everything out on the clotheslines behind
the apartment house and we can watch the clothes dance in
wind and sun. She says you wouldn't want the neighbors to
know what you have in the way of a wash but there's nothing
like the sweetness of clothes dried by the sun.

When Dad brings home the first week's wages on a Friday
night we know the weekend will be wonderful. On Saturday
night Mam will boil water on the stove and wash us in the
great tin tub and Dad will dry us. Malachy will turn around
and show his behind. Dad will pretend to be shocked and
we'll all laugh. Mam will make hot cocoa and we'll be able
to stay up while Dad tells us a story out of his head. All we
have to do is say a name, Mr. MacAdorey or Mr. Leibowitz
down the hall, and Dad will have the two of them rowing
up a river in Brazil chased by Indians with green noses and
puce shoulders. On nights like that we can drift off to sleep
knowing there will be a breakfast of eggs, fried tomatoes and
fried bread, tea with lashings of sugar and milk and, later in
the day, a big dinner of mashed potatoes, peas and ham, and
a trifle Mam makes, layers of fruit and warm delicious custard
on a cake soaked in sherry.

When Dad brings home the first week's wages and the
weather is fine Mam takes us to the playground. She sits on
a bench and talks to Minnie MacAdorey. She tells Minnie
stories about characters in Limerick and Minnie tells her
about characters in Belfast and they laugh because there are
funny people in Ireland, North and South. Then they teach
each other sad songs and Malachy and I leave the swings and
seesaws to sit with them on the bench and sing,

A group of young soldiers one night in a camp
Were talking of sweethearts they had.

16

All seemed so merry except one young lad,
And he was downhearted and sad.
Come and join us, said one of the boys,
Surely there's someone for you.
But Ned shook his head and proudly he said
I am in love with two, Each like a mother to me,
From neither of them shall I part.
For one is my mother, God bless her and love her,
The other is my sweetheart.

Malachy and I sing that song and Mam and Minnie laugh till they cry at the way Malachy takes a deep bow and holds his arms out to Mam at the end. Dan MacAdorey comes along on his way home from work and says Rudy Vallee better start worrying about the competition.

When we go home Mam makes tea and bread and jam or mashed potatoes with butter and salt. Dad drinks the tea and eats nothing. Mam says, God above, How can you work all day and not eat? He says, The tea is enough. She says, You'll ruin your health, and he tells her again that food is a shock to the system. He drinks his tea and tells us stories and shows us letters and words in the *Daily News* or he smokes a cigarette, stares at the wall, runs his tongue over his lips.

When Dad's job goes into the third week he does not bring home the wages. On Friday night we wait for him and Mam gives us bread and tea. The darkness comes down and the lights come on along Classon Avenue. Other men with jobs are home already and having eggs for dinner because you can't have meat on a Friday. You can hear the families talking upstairs and downstairs and down the hall and Bing Crosby is singing on the radio, Brother, can you spare a dime?

Malachy and I play with the twins. We know Mam won't sing Anyone can see why I wanted your kiss. She sits at the kitchen table talking to herself, What am I going to do? till it's late and Dad rolls up the stairs singing Roddy McCorley.

He pushes in the door and calls for us, Where are my troops? Where are my four warriors?

Mam says, Leave those boys alone. They're gone to bed half hungry because you have to fill your belly with whiskey.

He comes to the bedroom door. Up, boys, up. A nickel for everyone who promises to die for Ireland.

> Deep in Canadian woods we met
> From one bright island flown.
> Great is the land we tread, but yet
> Our hearts are with our own.

Up, boys, up. Francis, Malachy, Oliver, Eugene. The Red Branch Knights, the Fenian Men, the IRA. Up, up.

Mam is at the kitchen table, shaking, her hair hanging damp, her face wet. Can't you leave them alone? she says. Jesus, Mary and Joseph, isn't it enough that you come home without a penny in your pocket without making fools of the children on top of it?

She comes to us. Go back to bed, she says.

I want them up, he says. I want them ready for the day Ireland will be free from the center to the sea.

Don't cross me, she says, for if you do it'll be a sorry day in your mother's house.

He pulls his cap down over his face and cries, My poor mother. Poor Ireland. Och, what are we going to do?

Mam says, You're pure stone mad, and she tells us again to go to bed.

On the morning of the fourth Friday of Dad's job Mam asks him if he'll be home tonight with his wages or will he drink everything again? He looks at us and shakes his head at Mam as if to say, Och, you shouldn't talk like that in front of the children.

Mam keeps at him. I'm asking you, Are you coming home so that we can have a bit of supper or will it be midnight with no money in your pocket and you singing Kevin Barry and the rest of the sad songs?

He puts on his cap, shoves his hands into his trouser pockets, sighs and looks up at the ceiling. I told you before I'll be home, he says.

Later in the day Mam dresses us. She puts the twins into the pram and off we go through the long streets of Brooklyn. Sometimes she lets Malachy sit in the pram when he's tired of trotting along beside her. She tells me I'm too big for the pram. I could tell her I have pains in my legs from trying to keep up with her but she's not singing and I know this is not the day to be talking about my pains.

We come to a big gate where there's a man standing in a box with windows all around. Mam talks to the man. She wants to know if she can go inside to where the men are paid and maybe they'd give her some of Dad's wages so he wouldn't spend it in the bars. The man shakes his head. I'm sorry, lady, but if we did that we'd have half the wives in Brooklyn storming the place. Lotta men have the drinking problem but there's nothing we can do long as they show up sober and do their work.

We wait across the street. Mam lets me sit on the sidewalk with my back against the wall. She gives the twins their bottles of water and sugar but Malachy and I have to wait till she gets money from Dad and we can go to the Italian for tea and bread and eggs.

When the whistle blows at half five men in caps and overalls swarm through the gate, their faces and hands black from the work. Mam tells us watch carefully for Dad because she can hardly see across the street herself, her eyes are that bad. There are dozens of men, then a few, then none. Mam is crying, Why couldn't ye see him? Are ye blind or what?

She goes back to the man in the box. Are you sure there wouldn't be one man left inside?

No, lady, he says. They're out. I don't know how he got past you.

We go back through the long streets of Brooklyn. The twins hold up their bottles and cry for more water and sugar. Malachy says he's hungry and Mam tells him wait a little, we'll get money from Dad and we'll all have a nice supper. We'll go to the Italian and get eggs and make toast with the flames on the stove and we'll have jam on it. Oh, we will, and we'll all be nice and warm.

It's dark on Atlantic Avenue and all the bars around the Long Island Railroad Station are bright and noisy. We go from bar to bar looking for Dad. Mam leaves us outside with the pram while she goes in or she sends me. There are crowds of noisy men and stale smells that remind me of Dad when he comes home with the smell of the whiskey on him.

The man behind the bar says, Yeah, sonny, whaddya want? You're not supposeta be in here, y'know.

I'm looking for my father. Is my father here?

Naw, sonny, how'd I know dat? Who's your fawdah?

His name is Malachy and he sings Kevin Barry.

Malarkey?

No, Malachy.

Malachy? And he sings Kevin Barry?

He calls out to the men in the bar, Youse guys, youse know guy Malachy what sings Kevin Barry?

Men shake their heads. One says he knew a guy Michael sang Kevin Barry but he died of the drink which he had because of his war wounds.

The barman says, Jeez, Pete, I didn't ax ya to tell me history o' da woild, did I? Naw, kid. We don't let people sing in here. Causes trouble. Specially the Irish. Let 'em sing, next the fists are flying. Besides, I never hold a name like dat Malachy. Naw, kid, no Malachy here.

The man called Pete holds his glass toward me. Here, kid, have a sip, but the barman says, Whaddya doin', Pete? Tryina get the kid drunk? Do that again, Pete, an' I'll come out an' break y'ass.

Mam tries all the bars around the station before she gives

up. She leans against a wall and cries. Jesus, we still have to walk all the way to Classon Avenue and I have four starving children. She sends me back into the bar where Pete offered me the sip to see if the barman would fill the twins' bottles with water and maybe a little sugar in each. The men in the bar think it's very funny that the barman should be filling baby bottles but he's big and he tells them shut their lip. He tells me babies should be drinking milk not water and when I tell him Mam doesn't have the money he empties the baby bottles and fills them with milk. He says, Tell ya mom they need that for the teeth an' bones. Ya drink water an' sugar an' all ya get is rickets. Tell ya Mom.

Mam is happy with the milk. She says she knows all about teeth and bones and rickets but beggars can't be choosers.

When we reach Classon Avenue she goes straight to the Italian grocery shop. She tells the man her husband is late tonight, that he's probably working overtime, and would it be at all possible to get a few things and she'll be sure to see him tomorrow?

The Italian says, Missus, you always pay your bill sooner or later and you can have anything you like in this store.

Oh, she says, I don't want much.

Anything you like, missus, because I know you're an honest woman and you got a bunch o' nice kids there.

We have eggs and toast and jam though we're so weary walking the long streets of Brooklyn we can barely move our jaws to chew. The twins fall asleep after eating and Mam lays them on the bed to change their diapers. She sends me down the hall to rinse the dirty diapers in the lavatory so that they can be hung up to dry and used the next day. Malachy helps her wash the twins' bottoms though he's ready to fall asleep himself.

I crawl into bed with Malachy and the twins. I look out at Mam at the kitchen table, smoking a cigarette, drinking tea, and crying. I want to get up and tell her I'll be a man soon and I'll get a job in the place with the big gate and I'll come home every Friday night with money for eggs and toast and jam and she can sing again Anyone can see why I wanted your kiss.

The next week Dad loses the job. He comes home that Friday night, throws his wages on the table and says to Mam, Are you happy now? You hang around the gate complaining and accusing and they sack me. They were looking for an excuse and you gave it to them.

He takes a few dollars from his wages and goes out. He comes home late roaring and singing. The twins cry and Mam shushes them and cries a long time herself.

We spend hours in the playground when the twins are sleeping, when Mam is tired, and when Dad comes home with the whiskey smell on him, roaring about Kevin Barry getting hanged on a Monday morning or the Roddy McCorley song,

> Up the narrow street he stepped
> Smiling and proud and young
> About the hemp-rope on his neck
> The golden ringlets clung,
> There's never a tear in the blue eyes
> Both glad and bright are they,
> As Roddy McCorley goes to die
> On the bridge of Toome today.

When he sings he marches around the table, Mam cries and the twins howl with her. She says, Go out, Frankie, go out, Malachy. You shouldn't see your father like this. Stay in the playground.

We don't mind going to the playground. We can play with the leaves piling up on the ground and we can push each other on the swings but then winter comes to Classon Avenue and the swings are frozen and won't even move. Minnie MacAdorey says, God help these poor wee boys.

They don't have a glove between them. That makes me laugh because I know Malachy and I have four hands between us and one glove would be silly. Malachy doesn't know what I'm laughing at: He won't know anything till he's four going on five.

Minnie brings us in and gives us tea and porridge with jam in it. Mr. MacAdorey sits in an armchair with their new baby, Maisie. He holds her bottle and sings,

> *Clap hands, clap hands,*
> *Till Daddy comes home,*
> *With buns in his pocket*
> *For Maisie alone.*
> *Clap hands, clap hands,*
> *Till Daddy comes home,*
> *For Daddy has money*
> *And Mammy has none.*

Malachy tries to sing that song but I tell him stop, it's Maisie's song. He starts to cry and Minnie says, There, there. You can sing the song. That's a song for all the children. Mr. MacAdorey smiles at Malachy and I wonder what kind of world is it where anyone can sing anyone else's song.

Minnie says, Don't frown, Frankie. It makes your face dark and God knows it's dark enough. Some day you'll have a little sister and you can sing that song to her. Och, aye. You'll have a little sister, surely.

Minnie is right and Mam gets her wish. There's a new baby soon, a little girl, and they call her Margaret. We all love Margaret. She has black curly hair and blue eyes like Mam and she waves her little hands and chirps like any little bird in the trees along Classon Avenue. Minnie says there was a holiday in heaven the day this child was made. Mrs. Leibowitz says the world never saw such eyes, such a smile, such happiness. She makes me dance, says Mrs. Leibowitz.

When Dad comes home from looking for a job he holds Margaret and sings to her:

> In a shady nook one moonlit night
> A leprechaun I spied.
> With scarlet cap and coat of green
> A cruiskeen by his side.
> 'Twas tick tock tick his hammer went
> Upon a tiny shoe.
> Oh, I laugh to think he was caught at last,
> But the fairy was laughing, too.

He walks around the kitchen with her and talks to her. He tells her how lovely she is with her curly black hair and the blue eyes of her mother. He tells her he'll take her to Ireland and they'll walk the Glens of Antrim and swim in Lough Neagh. He'll get a job soon, so he will, and she'll have dresses of silk and shoes with silver buckles.

The more Dad sings to Margaret the less she cries and as the days pass she even begins to laugh. Mam says, Look at him trying to dance with that child in his arms, him with his two left feet. She laughs and we all laugh.

The twins cried when they were small and Dad and Mam would say Whisht and Hush and feed them and they'd go back to sleep. But when Margaret cries there's a high lonely feeling in the air and Dad is out of bed in a second, holding her to him, doing a slow dance around the table, singing to her, making sounds like a mother. When he passes the window where the streetlight shines in you can see tears on his cheeks and that's strange because he never cries for anyone unless he has the drink taken and he sings the Kevin Barry song and the Roddy McCorley song. Now he cries over Margaret and he has no smell of drink on him.

Mam tells Minnie MacAdorey, He's in heaven over that

child. He hasn't touched a drop since she was born. I should've had a little girl a long time ago.

Och, they're lovely, aren't they? says Minnie. The little boys are grand, too, but you need a little girl for yourself.

My mother laughs, For myself? Lord above, if I didn't nurse her I wouldn't be able to get near her the way he wants to be holding her day and night.

Minnie says it's lovely, all the same, to see a man so charmed with his little girl for isn't everyone charmed with her?

Everyone.

The twins are able to stand and walk and they have accidents all the time. Their bottoms are sore because they're always wet and shitty. They put dirty things in their mouths, bits of paper, feathers, shoelaces, and they get sick. Mam says we're all driving her crazy. She dresses the twins, puts them in the pram, and Malachy and I take them to the playground. The cold weather is gone and the trees have green leaves up and down Classon Avenue.

We race the pram around the playground and the twins laugh and make goo-goo sounds till they get hungry and start to cry. There are two bottles in the pram filled with water and sugar and that keeps them quiet for awhile till they're hungry again and they cry so hard I don't know what to do because they're so small and I wish I could give them all kinds of food so that they'd laugh and make the baby sounds. They love the mushy food Mam makes in a pot, bread mashed up in milk and water and sugar. Mam calls it bread and goody.

If I take the twins home now Mam will yell at me for giving her no rest or for waking Margaret. We are to stay in the playground till she sticks her head out the window and calls for us. I make funny faces for the twins to stop their crying. I put a piece of paper on my head and let it fall and they laugh and laugh. I push the pram over to Malachy playing on the swings with Freddie Leibowitz. Malachy is trying to tell Freddie all about the way Setanta became Cuchulain. I tell him stop telling that story, it's my story. He won't stop. I push him and he cries, Waah, waah, I'll tell Mam. Freddie pushes me and everything turns dark in my head and I run at him with fists and knees and feet till he yells, Hey, stop, stop, and I won't because I can't, I don't know how, and if I stop Malachy will go on taking my story from me. Freddie pushes me away and runs off, yelling, Frankie tried to kill me. Frankie tried to kill me. I don't know what to do because I never tried to kill anyone before and now Malachy, on the swing, cries, Don't kill me, Frankie, and he looks so helpless I put my arms around him and help him off the swing. He hugs me. I won't tell your story anymore. I won't tell Freddie about Coo, Coo. I want to laugh but I can't because the twins are crying in the pram and it's dark in the playground and what's the use of trying to make funny faces and letting things fall off your head when they can't see you in the dark?

The Italian grocery shop is across the street and I see bananas, apples, oranges. I know the twins can eat bananas. Malachy loves bananas and I like them myself. But you need money, Italians are not known for giving away bananas especially to the McCourts who owe them money already for groceries.

My mother tells me all the time, Never, never leave that playground except to come home. But what am I to do with the twins bawling with the hunger in the pram? I tell Malachy I'll be back in a minute. I make sure no one is looking, grab a bunch of bananas outside the Italian grocery shop and run down Myrtle Avenue, away from the playground, around the block and back to the other end where there's a hole in the fence. We push the pram to a dark corner and peel the bananas for the twins. There are five bananas in the bunch and we feast on them in the dark corner. The twins slobber and chew and spread banana over their faces, their hair, their clothes. I realize then that questions will be asked. Mam will want to know why the twins are smothered in bananas, where did you get them? I can't tell her about the Italian shop on the corner. I will have to say, A man.

That's what I'll say. A man.

Then the strange thing happens. There's a man at the gate of the playground. He's calling me. Oh, God, it's the Italian. Hey, sonny, come 'ere. Hey, talkin' to ya. Come 'ere.

I go to him.

You the kid wid the little bruddas, right? Twins?

Yes, sir.

Heah. Gotta bag o' fruit. I don' give it to you I trow id out. Right? So, heah, take the bag. Ya got apples, oranges, bananas. Ya like bananas, right? I think ya like bananas, eh? Ha, ha. I know ya like the bananas. Heah, take the bag. Ya gotta nice mother there. Ya father? Well, ya know, he's got the problem, the Irish thing. Give them twins a banana. Shud 'em up. I hear 'em all the way cross the street.

Thank you, sir.

Jeez. Polite kid, eh? Where ja loin dat?

My father told me to say thanks, sir.

Your father? Oh, well.

Dad sits at the table reading the paper. He says that President Roosevelt is a good man and everyone in America will soon have a job. Mam is on the other side of the table feeding Margaret with a bottle. She has the hard look that frightens me.

Where did you get that fruit?

The man.

What man?

The Italian man gave it to me.

Did you steal that fruit?

Malachy says, The man. The man gave Frankie the bag.

27

And what did you do to Freddie Leibowitz? His mother was here. Lovely woman. I don't know what we'd do without her and Minnie MacAdorey. And you had to attack poor Freddie.

Malachy jumps up and down. He din't. He din't. Din't try to kill Freddie. Din't try to kill me.

Dad says, Whisht, Malachy, whisht. Come over here. And he takes Malachy on his lap.

My mother says, Go down the hall and tell Freddie you're sorry.

But Dad says, Do you want to tell Freddie you're sorry?

I don't.

My parents look at one another. Dad says, Freddie is a good boy. He was only pushing your little brother on the swing. Isn't that right?

He was trying to steal my Cuchulain story.

Och, now. Freddie doesn't care about the Cuchulain story. He has his own story. Hundreds of stories. He's Jewish.

What's Jewish?

Dad laughs. Jewish is, Jewish is people with their own stories. They don't need Cuchulain. They have Moses. They have Samson.

What's Samson?

If you go down and talk to Freddie I'll tell you about Samson later. You can tell Freddie you're sorry and you'll never do it again and you can even ask him about Samson. Anything you like as long as you talk to Freddie. Will you?

The baby gives a little cry in my mother's arms and Dad jumps up, dropping Malachy to the floor. Is she all right? My mother says, Of course she's all right. She's feeding. God above, you're a bundle of nerves.

They're talking about Margaret now and I'm forgotten. I don't care. I'm going down the hall to ask Freddie about Samson, to see if Samson is as good as Cuchulain, to see if

Freddie has his own story or if he still wants to steal Cuchulain. Malachy wants to go with me now that my father is standing and doesn't have a lap anymore.

Mrs. Leibowitz says, Oh, Frankie, Frankie, come in, come in. And little Malachy. And tell me, Frankie, what did you do to Freddie? Tried to kill him? Freddie is a good boy, Frankie. Reads his book. Listens to radio with his papa. He swinks you brother on swink. And you try to kill him. Oh, Frankie, Frankie. And you poor mother and her sick baby.

She's not sick, Mrs. Leibowitz.

Sick she is. Zat is one sick baby. I know from sick babies. I work in hoztipal. Don't tell me, Frankie. Come in, come in. Freddie, Freddie, Frankie is here. Come out. Frankie won't kill you no more. You and little Malachy. Nice Chewish name, have piece cake, eh? Why they give you a Chewish name, eh? So, glass milk, piece cake. You boys so thin, Irish don't eat.

We sit at the table with Freddie, eating cake, drinking milk. Mr. Leibowitz sits in an armchair reading the paper, listening to the radio. Sometimes he speaks to Mrs. Leibowitz and I don't understand because strange sounds come from his mouth. Freddie understands. When Mr. Leibowitz makes the strange sounds Freddie gets up and takes him a piece of cake. Mr. Leibowitz smiles at Freddie and pats his head and Freddie smiles back and makes the strange sounds.

Mrs. Leibowitz shakes her head at Malachy and me. Oy, so thin. She says Oy so much Malachy laughs and says Oy and the Leibowitzes laugh and Mr. Leibowitz says words we can understand, When Irish oyes are smiling. Mrs. Leibowitz laughs so hard her body shakes and she holds her stomach and Malachy says Oy again because he knows that makes everyone laugh. I say Oy but no one laughs and I know Oy belongs to Malachy the way Cuchulain belongs to me and Malachy can have his Oy.

Mrs. Leibowitz, my father said Freddie has a favorite story. Malachy says, Sam, Sam, Oy. Everyone laughs again but

29

I don't because I can't remember what comes after Sam. Freddie mumbles through his cake, Samson, and Mrs. Leibowitz tells him, Don't talk wiz you mouse full, and I laugh because she's grown-up and she says mouse instead of mouth. Malachy laughs because I laugh and the Leibowitzes look at each other and smile. Freddie says, Not Samson. My favorite story is David and the giant, Goliath. David killed him dead with a slingshot, a stone in his head. His brains was on the ground.

Were on the ground, says Mr. Leibowitz.

Yes, Papa.

Papa. That's what Freddie calls his father and Dad is what I call my father.

My mother's whisper wakes me. What's up with the child? It's still early and there isn't much morning in the room but you can see Dad over by the window with Margaret in his arms. He's rocking her and sighing, Och.

Mam says, Is she, is she sick?

Och, she's very quiet and she's a wee bit cold.

My mother is out of the bed, taking the child. Go for the doctor. Go for God's sake, and my father is pulling on his trousers over his shirt, no jacket, shoes, no socks on this bitter day.

We wait in the room, the twins asleep at the bottom of the bed, Malachy stirring beside me. Frankie, I want a drink of water. Mam rocks in her bed with the baby in her arms. Oh, Margaret, Margaret, my own little love. Open your lovely blue eyes, my little leanv.

I fill a cup of water for Malachy and me and my mother wails, Water for you and your brother. Oh, indeed, Water, is it? And nothing for your sister. Your poor little sister. Did you ask if she had a mouth in her head? Did you ask if she'd like a drop of water? Oh, no. Go on and drink your water, you and your brother, as if nothing happened. A regular day for the two of you, isn't it? And the twins sleeping away as if they didn't have a care and their poor little sister sick here in my arms. Sick in my arms. Oh, sweet Jesus in heaven.

Why is she talking like this? She's not talking like my mother today. I want my father. Where is my father?

I get back into bed and start to cry. Malachy says, Why you cry? Why you cry? till Mam is at me again. Your sister is sick in my arms and you're there whining and whinging. If I go over to that bed I'll give you something to whinge about.

Dad is back with the doctor. Dad has the whiskey smell. The doctor examines the baby, prods her, raises her eyelids, feels her neck, arms, legs. He straightens up and shakes his head. She's gone. Mam reaches for the baby, hugs her, turns to the wall. The doctor wants to know, Was there any kind of accident? Did anyone drop the baby? Did the boys play too hard with her? Anything?

My father shakes his head. Doctor says he'll have to take her to examine her and Dad signs a paper. My mother begs for another few minutes with her baby but the doctor says he doesn't have all day. When Dad reaches for Margaret my mother pulls away against the wall. She has the wild look, her black curly hair is damp on her forehead and there is sweat all over her face, her eyes are wide open and her face is shiny with tears, she keeps shaking her head and moaning, Ah, no, ah, no, till Dad eases the baby from her arms. The doctor wraps Margaret completely in a blanket and my mother cries, Oh, Jesus, you'll smother her. Jesus, Mary and Joseph, help me. The doctor leaves. My mother turns to the wall and doesn't make a move or sound. The twins are awake, crying with the hunger, but Dad stands in the middle of the room, staring at the ceiling. His face is white and he beats on his thighs with his fists. He comes to the bed, puts his hand on my head. His hand is shaking. Francis, I'm going out for cigarettes.

Mam stays in the bed all day, hardly moving. Malachy and

I fill the twins' bottles with water and sugar. In the kitchen we find a half loaf of stale bread and two cold sausages. We can't have tea because the milk is sour in the icebox where the ice is melted again and everyone knows you can't drink tea without milk unless your father gives it to you out of his mug while he's telling you about Cuchulain.

The twins are hungry again but I know I can't give them water and sugar all day and night. I boil sour milk in a pot, mash in some of the stale bread, and try to feed them from a cup, bread and goody. They make faces and run to Mam's bed, crying. She keeps her face to the wall and they run back to me, still crying. They won't eat the bread and goody till I kill the taste of the sour milk with sugar. Now they eat and smile and rub the goody over their faces. Malachy wants some and if he can eat it, so can I. We all sit on the floor eating the goody and chewing on the cold sausage and drinking water my mother keeps in a milk bottle in the icebox.

After we eat and drink we have to go to the lavatory down the hall but we can't get in because Mrs. Leibowitz is inside, humming and singing. She says, Wait, children, wait, darlinks. Won't be two seconds. Malachy claps his hands and dances around, singing, Wait, chiltren, wait, darlinks. Mrs. Leibowitz opens the lavatory door. Look at him. Little actor awready. So, chiltren, how's you mother?

She's in bed, Mrs. Leibowitz. The doctor took Margaret and my father went for cigarettes.

Oh, Frankie, Frankie. I said that was one sick child.

Malachy is clutching himself. Have to pee. Have to pee.

So, pee awready. You boys pee and we see you mother.

After we pee Mrs. Leibowitz comes to see Mam. Oh, Mrs. McCourt. Oy vey, darlink. Look at this. Look at these twins. Naked. Mrs. McCourt, what is mazzer, eh? The baby she is sick? So talk to me. Poor woman. Here turn around, missus. Talk to me. Oy, this is one mess. Talk to me, Mrs. McCourt.

She helps my mother sit up against the wall. Mam seems

smaller. Mrs. Leibowitz says she'll bring some soup and tells me get some water to wash my mother's face. I dip a towel in cold water and pat her forehead. She presses my hand against her cheeks. Oh, Jesus, Frankie. Oh, Jesus. She won't let my hand go and I'm frightened because I've never seen her like this before. She's saying Frankie only because it's my hand she's holding and it's Margaret she's thinking about, not me. Your lovely little sister is dead, Frankie. Dead. And where is your father? She lets my hand drop. I said where is your father? Drinking. That's where he is. There isn't a penny in the house. He can't get a job but he finds money for the drink, money for the drink, money for the drink, money for the drink. She rears back, knocks her head on the wall and screams, Where is she? Where is she? Where is my little girl? Oh, Jesus, Mary and Joseph, help me this night. I'll go mad, so I will, I'll go pure mad.

Mrs. Leibowitz rushes in. Missus, missus, what is it? The little girl. Where is she?

My mother screams again, Dead, Mrs. Leibowitz. Dead. Her head drops and she rocks back and forth. Middle of the night, Mrs. Leibowitz. In her pram. I should have been watching her. Seven weeks she had in this world and died in the middle of the night, alone, Mrs. Leibowitz, all alone in that pram.

Mrs. Leibowitz holds my mother in her arms. Shush, now, shush. Babies go like that. It happens, missus. God takes them.

In the pram, Mrs. Leibowitz. Near my bed. I could have picked her up and she didn't have to die, did she? God doesn't want little babies. What is God going to do with little babies?

I don't know, missus. I don't know from God. Have soup. Good soup. Make you strong. You boys. Get bowls. I give you soup.

What's bowls, Mrs. Leibowitz?

Oh, Frankie. You don't know bowl? For the soup, darlink.

You don' have a bowl? So get cups for the soup. I mix pea soup and lentil soup. No ham. Irish like the ham. No ham, Frankie. Drink, missus. Drink you soup.

She spoons the soup into my mother's mouth, wipes the dribble from her chin. Malachy and I sit on the floor drinking from mugs. We spoon the soup into the twins' mouths. It is lovely and hot and tasty. My mother never makes soup like this and I wonder if there's any chance Mrs. Leibowitz could ever be my mother. Freddie could be me and have my mother and my father, too, and he could have Malachy and the twins for brothers. He can't have Margaret anymore because she's like the dog in the street that was taken away. I don't know why she was taken away. My mother said she died in her pram and that must be like getting hit by a car because they take you away.

I wish little Margaret could be here for the soup. I could give it to her with a spoon the way Mrs. Leibowitz is giving it to my mother and she'd gurgle and laugh the way she did with Dad. She wouldn't cry anymore and my mother wouldn't be in the bed day and night and Dad would be telling me Cuchulain stories and I wouldn't want Mrs. Leibowitz to be my mother anymore. Mrs. Leibowitz is nice but I'd rather have my father telling me Cuchulain stories and Margaret chirping and Mam laughing when Dad dances with two left feet.

Minnie MacAdorey comes in to help. Mother o' God, Mrs. Leibowitz, these twins smell to the high heavens.

I don't know about Mother o' God, Minnie, but these twins need a wash. They need clean diapers. Frankie, where are the clean diapers?

I don't know.

Minnie says, They're just wearing rags for diapers. I'll get some of Maisie's. Frankie, you take off those rags and throw them out.

Malachy removes Oliver's rag and I struggle with Eugene. The safety pin is stuck and when he wriggles it comes loose, sticks him in the hip, and starts him screaming for Mam. But Minnie is back with a towel and soap and hot water. I help her wash away the caked shit and she lets me shake talcum powder on the twins' raw sore skin. She says they're good little boys and she has a big surprise for them. She goes down the hall and brings back a pot of mashed potatoes for all of us. There is plenty of salt and butter in the potatoes and I wonder if there's any chance Minnie could be my mother so that I could eat like this all the time. If I could have Mrs. Leibowitz and Minnie for mothers at the same time I'd have no end of soup and mashed potatoes.

Minnie and Mrs. Leibowitz sit at the table. Mrs. Leibowitz says something has to be done. These children are running wild and where is the father? I hear Minnie whisper he's out for the drink. Mrs. Leibowitz says terrible, terrible, the way the Irish drink. Minnie says her Dan doesn't drink. Never touches the stuff and Dan told her that when the baby died that poor man, Malachy McCourt, went mad all over Flat-bush Avenue and Atlantic Avenue, that he was thrown out of all the bars around the Long Island Railroad Station, that the cops would have thrown him in jail if it was anything else but the death of that lovely little baby.

Here he has four lovely little boys, says Minnie, but it's no comfort to him. That little girl brought out something in him. You know he didn't even drink after she was born and that was a miracle.

Mrs. Leibowitz wants to know where Mam's cousins are, the big women with the quiet husbands. Minnie will find them and tell them the children are neglected, running wild, sore arses and everything.

Two days later Dad returns from his cigarette hunt. It's the middle of the night but he gets Malachy and me out of the bed. He has the smell of the drink on him. He has us stand at attention in the kitchen. We are soldiers. He tells us we must promise to die for Ireland.

We will, Dad, we will.

All together we sing Kevin Barry,

> *On Mountjoy one Monday morning,*
> *High upon the gallows tree,*
> *Kevin Barry gave his young life*
> *For the cause of liberty.*
> *Just a lad of eighteen summers*
> *Sure there's no one can deny*
> *As he marched to death that morning*
> *How he held his head on high.*

There's a knock at the door, Mr. MacAdorey. Och, Malachy, for God's sake, it's three in the morning. You have the whole house woke with the singing.

Och, Dan, I'm only teaching the boys to die for Ireland.

You can teach them to die for Ireland in the daytime, Malachy.

'Tis urgent, Dan, 'tis urgent.

I know, Malachy, but they're only children. Babies. You go to bed now like a dacent man.

Bed, Dan! What am I to do in bed? Her little face is there day and night, her curly black hair and her lovely blue eyes. Oh, Jesus, Dan, what will I do? Was it the hunger that killed her, Dan?

Of course not. Your missus was nursing her. God took her. He has his reasons.

One more song, Dan, before we go to bed.

Good night, Malachy.

Come on, boys. Sing.

> *Because he loved the motherland,*
> *Because he loved the green*

He goes to meet a martyr's fate
With proud and joyous mien;
True to the last, oh! true to the last
He treads the upward way;
Young Roddy McCorley goes to die
On the bridge at Toome today.

You'll die for Ireland, won't you, boys?

We will, Dad.

And we'll all meet your little sister in heaven, won't we, boys?

We will, Dad.

My brother is standing with his face pressed against a leg of the table and he's asleep. Dad lifts him, staggers across the room, places him in the bed by my mother. I climb into bed and my father, still in his clothes, lies beside me. I'm hoping he'll put his arms around me but he goes on singing about Roddy McCorley and talking to Margaret, Oh, my little curly-haired, blue-eyed love, I would dress you in silks and take you to Lough Neagh, till day is at the window and I fall asleep.

That night Cuchulain comes to me. There's a big green bird on his shoulder that keeps singing about Kevin Barry and Roddy McCorley and I don't like that bird because there's blood dripping from his mouth when he sings. In one hand Cuchulain carries the gae bolga, the spear that is so mighty only he can throw it. In the other hand he carries a banana, which he keeps offering to the bird, who just squawks and spits blood at him. You'd wonder why Cuchulain puts up with a bird like that. If the twins ever spat blood at me when I offered them a banana I think I'd hit them on the head with it.

In the morning my father is at the kitchen table and I tell him my dream. He says there were no bananas in Ireland in the old times and even if there were Cuchulain would never offer one to that bird because that was the one that came over from England for the summer and perched on his shoulder when he was dying and propped up against a stone and when the men of Erin which is Ireland wanted to kill him they were afraid till they saw the bird drinking Cuchulain's blood and then they knew it was safe to attack him, the dirty bloody cowards. So you have to be wary of birds, Francis, birds and Englishmen.

Most of the day Mam lies in bed with her face to the wall. If she drinks tea or eats anything she throws up in the bucket under the bed and I have to empty it and rinse it in the lavatory down the hall. Mrs. Leibowitz brings her soup and funny bread that is twisted. Mam tries to slice it but Mrs. Leibowitz laughs and tells her just pull. Malachy calls it pull bread but Mrs. Leibowitz says, No, it's challah, and teaches us how to say it. She shakes her head. Oy, you Irish. You'll live forever but you'll never say challah like a Chew.

Minnie MacAdorey brings potatoes and cabbage and sometimes a piece of meat. Och, times are hard, Angela, but that lovely man, Mr. Roosevelt, will find a job for everyone and your husband will have work. Poor man, it's not his fault there's a Depression. He looks for work day and night. My Dan is lucky, four years with the city and he don't drink. He grew up in Toome with your husband. Some drink. Some don't. Curse of the Irish. Now eat, Angela. Build yourself up after your loss.

Mr. MacAdorey tells Dad there's work with the WPA and when he gets the work there's money for food and Mam leaves the bed to clean the twins and to feed us. When Dad comes home with the drink smell there's no money and Mam screams at him till the twins cry, and Malachy and I run out to the playground. On those nights Mam crawls back into bed and Dad sings the sad songs about Ireland. Why doesn't he hold her and help her sleep the way he did with my little sister who died? Why doesn't he sing a Margaret song or a song that will dry Mam's tears? He still gets Malachy and me out of bed to stand in our shirts promising to die for Ireland. One night he wanted to make the twins promise to die for Ireland but they can't even talk and Mam screamed at him, You mad oul' bastard, can't you leave the children alone?

He'll give us a nickel for ice cream if we promise to die for Ireland and we promise but we never get the nickel.

We get soup from Mrs. Leibowitz and mashed potatoes from Minnie MacAdorey and they show us how to take care of the twins, how to wash their bottoms and how to wash diaper rags after they get them all shitty. Mrs. Leibowitz calls them diapers and Minnie calls them nappies but it doesn't matter what they call them because the twins get them shitty anyway. If Mam stays in the bed and Dad goes out looking for a job we can do what we like all day. We can put the twins in the small swings in the park and swing them till they get hungry and cry. The Italian man calls to me from across the street, Hey, Frankie, c'mere. Watch out crossing da street. Dem twins hungry again? He gives us bits of cheese and ham and bananas but I can't eat bananas anymore after the way the bird spat blood at Cuchulain.

The man says his name is Mr. Dimino and that's his wife, Angela, behind the counter. I tell him that's my mother's name. No kiddin', kid. Your mother is Angela? I didn't know the Irish had any Angelas. Hey, Angela, his mother's name is Angela. She smiles. She says, Thatsa nice.

Mr. Dimino asks me about Mam and Dad and who cooks for us. I tell him we get food from Mrs. Leibowitz and Minnie MacAdorey. I tell him all about the diapers and the nappies and how they get shitty anyway and he laughs. Angela, you listenin' to this? Thank God you're Italian, Angela. He says, Kid, I gotta talk to Mrs. Leibowitz. Ya gotta have relations can take care of you. Ya see Minnie MacAdorey, tell her come in see me. You kids runnin' wild.

Two big women are at the door. They say, Who are you?

I'm Frank.

Frank! How old are you?

I'm four going on five.

You're not very big for your age, are you?

I don't know.

Is your mother here?

She's in the bed.

What is she doing in the bed on a fine day in the middle of the day?

She's sleeping.

Well, we'll come in. We have to talk to your mother.

They brush past me into the room. Jesus, Mary and Joseph, the smell of this place. And who are these children?

Malachy runs smiling to the big women. When he smiles you can see how white and straight and pretty his teeth are and you can see the shiny blue of his eyes, the pink of his cheeks. All that makes the big women smile and I wonder why they didn't smile when they talked to me.

Malachy says, I'm Malachy and this is Oliver and this is Eugene, they're twins, and that's Frankie over there.

The big woman with the brown hair says, Well, you're not a bit shy, are you? I'm your mother's cousin, Philomena, and this is your mother's cousin, Delia. I'm Mrs. Flynn and she's Mrs. Fortune and that's what you call us.

Good God, says Philomena. Those twins are naked. Don't you have clothes for them?

Malachy says, They're all shitty.

Delia barks. See. That's what happens. A mouth like a sewer, and no wonder with a father from the North. Don't use that word. That's a bad word, a curse word. You could go to hell using a word like that.

What's hell? says Malachy. You'll know soon enough, says Delia.

The big women sit at the table with Mrs. Leibowitz and Minnie MacAdorey. Philomena says it's terrible what happened to Angela's little baby. They heard all about it and you'd wonder, wouldn't you, what they did with the little body. You might wonder and I might wonder but Tommy Flynn didn't wonder. Tommy said that Malachy from the North got money for that baby. Money? says Mrs. Leibowitz. That's right, says Philomena. Money. They take bodies any age and do experiments on them and there's not much left to give back nor would you want back bits of baby when they can't be buried in consecrated ground in that condition.

That's terrible, says Mrs. Leibowitz. A father or mother would never give the baby for something like that.

They would, says Delia, when they have the craving for the drink. They'd give their own mothers when they have the craving so what's a baby that's dead and gone in the first place?

Mrs. Leibowitz shakes her head and rocks in her chair. Oy, she says, oy, oy, oy. The poor baby. The poor mother. I thank God my husband don' have no what you call it? Craving? Right, craving. It's the Irish have the craving.

Not my husband, says Philomena. I'd break his face if he came home with the craving. Of course, Delia's Jimmy has the craving. Every Friday night you see him slipping into the saloon.

You needn't start insulting my Jimmy, says Delia. He works. He brings home his wages.

You'd want to keep an eye on him, says Philomena. The craving could get the better of him and you'd have another Malachy from the North on your hands.

Mind your own bloody business, says Delia. At least Jimmy is Irish, not born in Brooklyn like your Tommy.

And Philomena has no answer for that.

Minnie is holding her baby and the big women say she's

a lovely baby, clean, not like this pack of Angela's running around this place. Philomena says she doesn't know where Angela got her dirty habits because Angela's mother was spotless, so clean you could eat your dinner off her floor.

I wonder why you'd want to eat your dinner off the floor when you had a table and a chair.

Delia says something has to be done about Angela and these children for they are a disgrace, so they are, enough to make you ashamed to be related. A letter has to be written to Angela's mother. Philomena will write it because a teacher in Limerick told her once she had a fine fist. Delia has to tell Mrs. Leibowitz that a fine fist means good handwriting.

Mrs. Leibowitz goes down the hall to borrow her husband's fountain pen, paper and an envelope. The four women sit at the table and make up a letter to send to my mother's mother:

Dear Aunt Margaret,

I take pen in hand to write you this letter and hope this finds you as it leaves us in the best of health. My husband Tommy is in fine form working away and Delia's husband Jimmy is in fine form working away and we hope this finds you in fine form. I am very sorry to tell you that Angela is not in fine form as the baby died, the little girl that was called Margaret after yourself, and Angela has not been the same since lying in the bed with her face to the wall. To make matters worser we think she's expecting again and that's too much altogether. The minute she losses one child there is another one on the way. We don't know how she does it. She's married four years, five children and another on the way. That shows you what can happen when you marry someone from the North for they have no control over themselves up there a bunch of Protestands that they are. He goes out for work every day but we know he spends all his

42

time in the saloons and gets a few dollars for sweeping floors and lifting barrels and spends the money right back on the drink. It's terrible, Aunt Margaret, and we all think Angela and the children would be better off in her native land. We don't have the money to buy the tickets ourselves for times is hard but you might be able to see your way. Hopping this finds you in fine form as it leaves us thank God and His Blessed Mother.

I remain your loving neice
Philomena Flynn (what was MacNamara)
and last but not least your neice
Delia Fortune (what was MacNamara, too, ha ha ha)

Grandma Sheehan sent money to Philomena and Delia. They bought the tickets, found a steamer trunk at the St. Vincent de Paul Society, hired a van to take us to the pier in Manhattan, put us on the ship, said Good-bye and good riddance, and went away.

The ship pulled away from the dock. Mam said, That's the Statue of Liberty and that's Ellis Island where all the immigrants came in. Then she leaned over the side and vomited and the wind from the Atlantic blew it all over us and other happy people admiring the view. Passengers cursed and ran, seagulls came from all over the harbor and Mam hung limp and pale on the ship's rail.

II

In a week we arrived at Moville, County Donegal, where we took a bus to Belfast and from there another bus to Toome in County Antrim. We left the trunk in a shop and set out to walk the two miles up the road to Grandpa McCourt's house. It was dark on the road, the dawn barely stirring on the hills beyond.

Dad carried the twins in his arms and they took turns crying with the hunger. Mam stopped every few minutes to sit and rest on the stone wall along the road. We sat with her and watched the sky turn red and then blue. Birds started to chirp and sing in the trees and as the dawn came up we saw strange creatures in the fields, standing, looking at us. Malachy said, What are they, Dad?

Cows, son.

What are cows, Dad?

Cows are cows, son.

We walked farther along the brightening road and there were other creatures in the fields, white furry creatures.

Malachy said, What are they, Dad?

Sheep, son.

What are sheep, Dad?

My father barked at him, Is there any end to your questions? Sheep are sheep, cows are cows, and that over there is a goat. A goat is a goat. The goat gives milk, the sheep gives wool, the cow gives everything. What else in God's name do you want to know?

And Malachy yelped with fright because Dad never talked like that, never spoke sharply to us. He might get us up in the middle of the night and make us promise to die for Ireland but he never barked like this. Malachy ran to Mam and she said, There, there, love, don't cry. Your father is just worn out carrying the twins and 'tis hard answering all those questions when you're carting twins through the world.

Dad set the twins on the road and held out his arms to Malachy. Now the twins started to cry and Malachy clung to Mam, sobbing. The cows mooed, the sheep maaed, the goat ehehed, the birds twittered in the trees, and the beep beep of a motor car cut through everything. A man called from the motor car, Good Lord, what are you people doing on this road at this hour of an Easter Sunday morning?

Dad said, Good morning, Father.

Father? I said. Dad, is that your father?

Mam said, Don't ask him any questions.

Dad said, No, no, this is a priest.

Malachy said, What's a—? but Mam put her hand over his mouth.

The priest had white hair and a white collar. He said, Where are you going?

Dad said, Up the road to McCourts of Moneyglass, and the priest took us in his motor car. He said he knew the McCourts, a fine family, good Catholics, some daily communicants, and he hoped he'd see us all at Mass, especially the little Yankees who didn't know what a priest was, God help us.

At the house my mother reaches for the gate latch. Dad says, No, no, not that way. Not the front gate. They use the front door only for visits from the priest or funerals.

We make our way around the house to the kitchen door. Dad pushes in the door and there's Grandpa McCourt drinking tea from a big mug and Grandma McCourt frying something.

Och, says Grandpa, you're here.

Och, we are, says Dad. He points to my mother. This is Angela, he says. Grandpa says, Och, you must be worn out, Angela. Grandma says nothing, she turns back to the frying pan. Grandpa leads us through the kitchen to a large room with a long table and chairs. He says, Sit down and have some tea. Would you like boxty?

Malachy says, What's boxty?

Dad laughs. Pancakes, son. Pancakes made with potatoes.

Grandpa says, We have eggs. It's Easter Sunday and you can have all the eggs you can hold.

We have tea and boxty and boiled eggs and we all fall asleep. I wake up in a bed with Malachy and the twins. My parents are in another bed over by the window. Where am I? It's getting dark. This is not the ship. Mam snores hink, Dad snores honk. I get up and poke at Dad. I have to pee. He says, Use the chamber pot.

What?

Under the bed, son. The chamber pot. It has roses on it and maidens cavorting in the glen. Pee in that, son.

I want to ask him what he's talking about for even if I'm bursting I feel strange peeing into a pot with roses and maidens cavorting, whatever they are. We had nothing like this in Classon Avenue where Mrs. Leibowitz sang in the lavatory while we clutched ourselves in the hall.

Now Malachy has to use the chamber pot but he wants to sit on it. Dad says, No, you can't do that, son. You have to go outside. When he says that I have to go, too, to sit. He leads us downstairs and through the big room where Grandpa is sitting reading by the fire and Grandma is dozing in her chair. It's dark outside, though the moon is bright enough for us to see where we're going. Dad opens the door of a little house that has a seat with a hole in it. He shows Malachy and me how to sit on the hole and how to wipe ourselves with squares of newspaper stuck on a nail. Then he tells us wait while he goes inside, closes the door and grunts. The moon is so bright I can look down the field and see the things called cows and sheep and I wonder why they don't go home.

In the house there are other people in the room with my grandparents. Dad says, These are your aunts: Emily, Nora, Maggie, Vera. Your aunt Eva is in Ballymena with children like you. My aunts are not like Mrs. Leibowitz and Minnie MacAdorey, they nod their heads but they don't hug us or smile. Mam comes into the room with the twins and when Dad tells his sisters, This is Angela and these are the twins, they just nod again.

Grandma goes to the kitchen and soon we have bread and sausages and tea. The only one who speaks at the table is Malachy. He points his spoon at the aunts and asks their names again. When Mam tells him eat his sausage and be quiet his eyes fill with tears and Aunt Nora reaches over to comfort him. She says, There, there, and I wonder why everyone says there there when Malachy cries. I wonder what there there means.

It's quiet at the table till Dad says, Things are terrible in America. Grandma says, Och, aye. I read it in the paper. But they say Mr. Roosevelt is a good man and if you stayed you might have work by now.

Dad shakes his head and Grandma says, I don't know what you're going to do, Malachy. Things are worse here than they are in America. No work here and, God knows, we don't have room in this house for six more people.

Dad says, I thought I might get work on some of the farms. We could get a small place.

Where would you stay in the meantime? says Grandma. And how would you support yourself and your family?

Och, I could go on the dole, I suppose.

You can't get off a ship from America and go on the dole, says Grandpa. They make you wait a while and what would you do while you're waiting?

Dad says nothing and Mam looks straight ahead at the wall.

You'd be better off in the Free State, says Grandma. Dublin is big and surely there's work there or in the farms around.

You're entitled to money from the IRA, too, says Grandpa. You did your bit and they've been handing out money to men all over the Free State. You could go to Dublin and ask for help. We can loan you the bus fare to Dublin. The twins can sit on your lap and you won't have to pay for them.

Dad says, Och, aye, and Mam stares at the wall with tears in her eyes.

After we ate we went back to bed and next morning, all the grown-ups sat around looking sad. Soon a man came in a motor car and took us back down the road to the shop which had our trunk. They lifted the trunk up on the roof of a bus and we got into the bus. Dad said we were going to Dublin. Malachy said, What's Dublin? but no one answered him. Dad held Eugene on his lap and Mam held Oliver. Dad looked out at the fields and told me this is where Cuchulain liked to go for a walk. I asked him where Cuchulain hit the ball into the dog's mouth and he said a few miles away.

Malachy said, Look, look, and we looked. It was a great silvery sheet of water and Dad said it was Lough Neagh, the largest lake in Ireland, the lake where Cuchulain used to swim after his great battles. Cuchulain would get so hot that when he jumped into Lough Neagh it boiled over and warmed the surrounding countryside for days. Some day we'd all come back and go swimming like Cuchulain himself. We'd fish for eels and fry them in a pan not like Cuchulain, who would pluck them from the lough and swallow them, wriggling, because there's great power in an eel.

Is that right, Dad?

'Tis.

Mam didn't look out the window at Lough Neagh. Her cheek rested on top of Oliver's head and she stared at the floor of the bus.

Soon the bus is rolling into a place where there are big houses, motor cars, horses pulling carts, people on bicycles and hundreds walking. Malachy is excited. Dad, Dad, where's the playground, the swings? I want to see Freddie Leibowitz.

Och, son, you're in Dublin now, far from Classon Avenue. You're in Ireland, a long way from New York.

When the bus stops the trunk is lifted down and set on the floor of the bus station. Dad tells Mam she can sit on a bench in the station while he goes to see the IRA man in a place called Terenure. He says there are lavatories in the station for the boys, he won't be long, he'll have money when he returns and we'll all have food. He tells me go with him and Mam says, No, I need him to help. But when Dad says, I'll need help carrying all that money, she laughs and says, All right, go with your Pop.

Your Pop. That means she's in a good mood. If she says your father it means she's in a bad mood.

Dad holds my hand as I trot along beside him. He's a fast walker, it's a long way to Terenure and I'm hoping he'll stop and carry me the way he did with the twins in Toome. But he lopes along and says nothing except to ask people where Terenure is. In awhile he says we're in Terenure and now we have to find Mr. Charles Heggarty of the IRA. A man with a pink patch on his eye tells us we're on the right street, Charlie Heggarty lives at number fourteen, God blast him. The man tells Dad, I can see you're a man that did his bit. Dad says, Och, I did my bit, and the man says, I did me bit, too, and what did it get me but one eye less and a pension that wouldn't feed a canary.

But Ireland is free, says Dad, and that's a grand thing.

Free, my arse, the man says. I think we were better off under the English. Good luck to you anyway, mister, for I think I know what you're here for.

A woman opens the door at number fourteen. I'm afraid, she says, that Mr. Heggarty is busy. Dad tells her he just walked all the way from the middle of Dublin with his small son, that he left wife and three children waiting for him at the bus place, and if Mr. Heggarty is that busy then we'll wait for him on the doorstep.

The woman is back in a minute to say Mr. Heggarty has a little time to spare and would you come this way. Mr. Heggarty is sitting at a desk near a glowing fire. He says, What can I do for you? Dad stands before the desk and says, I have just returned from America with wife and four children. We have nothing. I fought with a Flying Column during the Troubles and I'm hoping you can help me now in the time of need.

Mr. Heggarty takes Dad's name and turns the pages of a big book on his desk. He shakes his head, No, no record of your service here.

Dad makes a long speech. He tells Mr. Heggarty how he fought, where, when, how he had to be smuggled out of Ireland because of the price on his head, how he was raising his sons to love Ireland.

Mr. Heggarty says he's sorry but he can't be handing out money to every man who wanders in claiming he did his bit. Dad says to me, Remember this, Francis. This is the new Ireland. Little men in little chairs with little bits of paper. This is the Ireland men died for.

Mr. Heggarty says he'll look into Dad's claim and he'll be sure to let him know what turns up. He'll let us have money to take the bus back into the city. Dad looks at the coins in Mr. Heggarty's hand and says, You could add to that and make the price of a pint.

Oh, it's the drink you want, is it?

One pint is hardly drink.

You'd walk the miles back and make the boy walk because you want a pint, wouldn't you?

Walking never killed anyone.

I want you to leave this house, says Mr. Heggarty, or I'll call a guard, and you can be sure you'll never hear from me again. We're not handing out money to support the Guinness family.

Night falls along the streets of Dublin. Children laugh and play under streetlights, mothers call from doorways, smells of cooking come at us all the way, through windows we see people around tables, eating. I'm tired and hungry and I want Dad to carry me but I know there's no use asking him now the way his face is tight and set. I let him hold my hand and I run to keep up with him till we reach the bus place where Mam is waiting with my brothers.

They're all asleep on the bench, my mother and three brothers. When Dad tells Mam there's no money she shakes her head and sobs, Oh, Jesus, what are we going to do? A man in a blue uniform comes over and asks her, What's up, missus? Dad tells him we're stranded there at the bus station, we have no money and no place to stay and the children are hungry. The man says he's going off duty now, he'll take us to the police barracks where he has to report anyway, and they'll see what can be done.

The man in uniform tells us we can call him guard. That's what you call policeman in Ireland. He asks us what you call policemen in America and Malachy says, cop. The guard pats him on the head and tells him he's a clever little Yankee.

At the police barracks the sergeant tells us we can spend the night. He's sorry but all he can offer is the floor. It's Thursday and the cells are filled with men who drank their dole money and wouldn't leave the pubs.

The guards give us hot sweet tea and thick slices of bread slathered with butter and jam and we're so happy we run around the barracks, playing. The guards say we're a great bunch of little Yanks and they'd like to take us home but I say, No, Malachy says, No, the twins say, No, No, and all the guards laugh. Men in cells reach out and pat our heads, they smell like Dad when he comes home singing about Kevin Barry and Roddy McCorley going to die. The men say, Jasus, will ye listen to them. They sound like bloody fillum stars. Did yez fall outa the sky or what? Women in cells at the other end tell Malachy he's gorgeous and the twins are dotes. One woman talks to me. C'mere, love, would you like a sweet? I nod, and she says, All right, put your hand out. She takes something sticky from her mouth and puts it on my hand. There you are now, she says, a nice bit of butterscotch. Put that in your mouth. I don't want to put it in my mouth because it's sticky and wet from her mouth but I don't know what you're supposed to do when a woman in a cell offers you sticky butterscotch and I'm about to put it in my mouth when a guard comes, takes the butterscotch and throws it back at the woman. You drunken hoor, he says, leave the child alone, and all the women laugh.

The sergeant gives my mother a blanket and she sleeps stretched out on a bench. The rest of us lie on the floor. Dad sits with his back to the wall, his eyes open under the peak of his cap, and he smokes when the guards give him cigarettes. The guard who threw the butterscotch at the woman says he's from Ballymena in the north and he talks with Dad about people they know there and in other places like Cushendall and Toome. The guard says he'll have a pension some day and he'll live on the shores of Lough Neagh and fish his days away. Eels, he says, eels galore. Jasus, I love a fried eel. I ask Dad, Is this Cuchulain? and the guard laughs till his face turns red. Ah, Mother o' God, did yez hear this? The lad wants to know if I'm Cuchulain. A little Yank and he knows all about Cuchulain.

Dad says, No, he's not Cuchulain but he's a fine man who will live on the shores of Lough Neagh and fish his days away.

*   *   *

Dad is shaking me. Up, Francis, up. It is noisy in the barracks. A boy mopping the floor is singing,

> *Anyone can see why I wanted your kiss,*
> *It had to be and the reason is this,*
> *Could it be true, someone like you*
> *Could love me, love me?*

I tell him that's my mother's song and he's to stop singing it but he just puffs on his cigarette and walks away and I wonder why people have to sing other people's songs. Men and women coming out of the cells are yawning and grunting. The woman who offered me the butterscotch stops and says, I had a drop taken, child. I'm sorry I made a fool of you, but the guard from Ballymena tells her, Move on, you oul' hoor, before I lock you up again.

Oh, lock me up, she says. In, out. What does it matter, you blue-arsed bastard.

Mam is sitting up on the bench, the blanket wrapped around her. A woman with gray hair brings her a mug of tea and tells her, Sure, I'm the sergeant's wife and he said you might need help. Would you like a nice soft-boiled egg, missus?

Mam shakes her head, no.

Ah, now, missus, surely you should have a nice egg in your condition.

But Mam shakes her head and I wonder how she can say no to a soft-boiled egg when there's nothing in the world like it.

All right, ma'am, says the sergeant's wife, a bit of toast, then, and something for the children and your poor husband.

She goes back to another room and soon there's tea and bread. Dad drinks his tea but gives us his bread and Mam says, Will you eat your bread, for God's sake. You won't be much use to us falling down with the hunger. He shakes his head and asks the sergeant's wife is there any chance of a

53

cigarette. She brings him the cigarette and tells Mam the guards in the barracks have taken up a collection to pay our train fares to Limerick. There will be a motor car to pick up our trunk and leave us at Kingsbridge Railway Station and, You'll be in Limerick in three or four hours.

Mam puts up her arms and hugs the sergeant's wife. God bless you and your husband and all the guards, Mam says. I don't know what we'd do without you. God knows 'tis a lovely thing to be back among our own.

'Tis the least we could do, says the sergeant's wife. These are lovely children you have and I'm from Cork meself and I know what 'tis to be in Dublin without two pennies to rub together.

Dad sits at the other end of the bench, smoking his cigarette, drinking his tea. He stays that way till the motor car comes to take us through the streets of Dublin. Dad asks the driver if he'd mind going by way of the G.P.O. and the driver says, Is it a stamp you want or what? No, says Dad. I hear they put up a new statue of Cuchulain to honor the men who died in 1916 and I'd like to show it to my son here who has a great admiration for Cuchulain.

The driver says he has no notion of who this Cuchulain was but he wouldn't mind stopping one bit. He might come in himself and see what the commotion is all about for he hasn't been in the G.P.O. since he was a boy and the English nearly wrecked it with their big guns firing up from the Liffey River. He says you'll see the bullet holes all over the front and they should be left there to remind the Irish of English perfidy. I ask the man what's perfidy and he says ask your father and I would but we're stopping outside a big building with columns and that's the G.P.O.

Mam stays in the motor car while we follow the driver into the G.P.O. There he is, he says, there's your man Cuchulain.

And I feel tears coming because I'm looking at him at last, Cuchulain, there on his pedestal in the G.P.O. He's golden and he has long hair, his head is hanging and there's a big bird perched on his shoulder.

The driver says, Now what in God's name is this all about? What's this fellow doin' with the long hair and the bird on his shoulder? And will you kindly tell me, mister, what this has to do with the men of 1916?

Dad says, Cuchulain fought to the end like the men of Easter Week. His enemies were afraid to go near him till they were sure he was dead and when the bird landed on him and drank his blood they knew.

Well, says the driver, 'tis a sad day for the men of Ireland when they need a bird to tell them a man is dead. I think we better go now or we'll be missing that train to Limerick.

The sergeant's wife said she'd send a telegram to Grandma to meet us in Limerick and there she was on the platform, Grandma, with white hair, sour eyes, a black shawl, and no smile for my mother or any of us, even my brother, Malachy, who had the big smile and the sweet white teeth. Mam pointed to Dad. This is Malachy, she said, and Grandma nodded and looked away. She called two boys who were hanging around the railway station and paid them to carry the trunk. The boys had shaved heads, snotty noses, and no shoes and we followed them through the streets of Limerick. I asked Mam why they had no hair and she said their heads were shaved so that the lice would have no place to hide. Malachy said, What's a lice? and Mam said, Not lice. One of them is a louse. Grandma said, Will ye stop it! What kind o' talk is this? The boys whistled and laughed and trotted along as if they had shoes and Grandma told them, Stop that laughin' or 'tis droppin' an' breakin' that trunk ye'll be. They stopped the whistling and laughing and we followed them into a park with a tall pillar and a statue in the middle and grass so green it dazzled you.

Dad carried the twins, Mam carried a bag in one hand

and held Malachy's hand with the other. When she stopped every few minutes to catch her breath, Grandma said, Are you still smokin' them fags? Them fags will be the death of you. There's enough consumption in Limerick without people smokin' fags on top of it an' 'tis a rich man's foolishness.

Along the path through the park there were hundreds of flowers of different colors that excited the twins. They pointed and made squeaky noises and we laughed, everyone except Grandma, who pulled her shawl over her head. Dad stopped and put the twins down so that they could be closer to the flowers. He said, Flowers, and they ran back and forth, pointing, trying to say Flowers. One of the boys with the trunk said, God, are they Americans? and Mam said, They are. They were born in New York. All the boys were born in New York. The boy said to the other boy, God, they're Americans. They put the trunk down and stared at us and we stared back at them till Grandma said, Are ye goin' to stand here all day lookin' at flowers an' gawkin' at each other? And we all moved on again, out of the park, down a narrow lane and into another lane to Grandma's house.

There is a row of small houses on each side of the lane and Grandma lives in one of the small houses. Her kitchen has a shiny polished black iron range with a fire glowing in the grate. There is a table along the wall under the window and a press opposite with cups and saucers and vases. This press is always locked and she keeps the key in her purse because you're not supposed to use anything in there unless someone dies or returns from foreign parts or there's a visit by a priest.

There is a picture on the wall by the range of a man with long brown hair and sad eyes. He is pointing to his chest where there is a big heart with flames coming out of it. Mam tells us, That's the Sacred Heart of Jesus, and I want to know why the man's heart is on fire and why doesn't He throw water on it? Grandma says, Don't these children know anything about their religion? and Mam tells her it's different in America. Grandma says the Sacred Heart is everywhere and there's no excuse for that kind of ignorance.

Under the picture of the man with the burning heart there is a shelf with a red glass holding a flickering candle and next to it a small statue. Mam tells us, That's the Baby Jesus, the Infant of Prague, and if ye ever need anything pray to Him.

Malachy says, Mam, could I tell Him I'm hungry, and Mam puts her finger to her lips.

Grandma grumbles around the kitchen making tea and telling Mam to cut the loaf of bread and don't make the cuts too thick. Mam sits by the table with her breath coming hard and says she'll cut the bread in a minute. Dad takes the knife and starts slicing the bread and you can see Grandma doesn't like that. She frowns at him but says nothing even though he makes thick slices.

There aren't enough chairs for everyone so I sit on the stairs with my brothers to have bread and tea. Dad and Mam sit at the table and Grandma sits under the Sacred Heart with her mug of tea. She says, I don't know under God what I'm goin' to do with ye. There is no room in this house. There isn't room for even one of ye.

Malachy says, Ye, ye, and starts to giggle and I say, Ye, ye, and the twins say, Ye, ye, and we're laughing so hard we can hardly eat our bread.

Grandma glares at us. What are ye laughin' at? There's nothin' to laugh at in this house. Ye better behave yeerselves before I go over to ye.

She won't stop saying Ye, and now Malachy is helpless with laughter, spewing out his bread and tea, his face turning red.

Dad says, Malachy and the rest of you, stop it. But Malachy can't, he goes on laughing till Dad says, Come over here. He rolls up Malachy's sleeve and raises his hand to slap his arm.

Are you going to behave yourself?

Malachy's eyes fill with tears and he nods, I will, because Dad never raised his hand like that before. Dad says, Be a good boy and go sit with your brothers, and he pulls down the sleeve and pats Malachy on the head.

That night Mam's sister, Aunt Aggie, came home from her job in the clothing factory. She was big like the MacNamara sisters, and she had flaming red hair. She wheeled a large bicycle into the little room behind the kitchen and came out to her supper. She was living in Grandma's because she had a fight with her husband, Pa Keating, who told her, when he had drink taken, You're a great fat cow, go home to your mother. That's what Grandma told Mam and that's why there was no room for us in Grandma's house. She had herself, Aunt Aggie, and her son Pat, who was my uncle and who was out selling newspapers.

Aunt Aggie complained when Grandma told her Mam would have to sleep with her that night. Grandma said, Oh, will you shut your gob. 'Tis only for one night an' that won't kill you an' if you don't like it you can go back to your husband where you belong anyway instead of runnin' home to me. Jesus, Mary an' Holy St. Joseph, look at this house— you an' Pat an' Angela and her clatther of Americans. Will I have any peace in the latter end of my life?

She spread coats and rags on the floor of the little back room and we slept there with the bicycle. Dad stayed on a chair in the kitchen, took us to the lavatory in the backyard when we needed it, and in the night hushed the twins when they cried from the cold.

In the morning, Aunt Aggie came for her bicycle telling us, Will ye mind yeerselves, will ye? Will ye get out of my way?

When she left, Malachy kept saying, Will ye mind yeer-selves, will ye? Will ye get out of the way, will ye? and I could hear Dad laughing out in the kitchen till Grandma came down the stairs and he had to tell Malachy be quiet.

That day Grandma and Mam went out and found a furnished room on Windmill Street where Aunt Aggie had a flat with her husband, Pa Keating. Grandma paid the rent, ten shillings for two weeks. She gave Mam money for food, loaned us a kettle, a pot, a frying pan, knives and spoons, jam jars to be used for mugs, a blanket and a pillow. She said that was all she could afford anymore, that Dad would have to get up off his arse, get a job, go on the dole, go for the charity at the St. Vincent de Paul Society or go on the relief.

The room had a fireplace where we could boil water for our tea or an egg in case we ever came into money. We had a table and three chairs and a bed, which Mam said was the biggest she had ever seen. We were glad of the bed that night, worn out after nights on floors in Dublin and in Grandma's. It didn't matter that there were six of us in the bed, we were together, away from grandmothers and guards, Malachy could say ye ye ye and we could laugh as much as we liked.

Dad and Mam lay at the head of the bed, Malachy and I at the bottom, the twins wherever they could find comfort. Malachy made us laugh again. Ye, ye, ye, he said, and oy oy oy, and then fell asleep. Mam made the little hink hink snore sound that told us she was sleeping. In the moonlight I could look up the length of the bed and see Dad still awake and when Oliver cried in his sleep Dad reached for him and held him. Whisht, he said. Whisht.

Then Eugene sat up, screaming, tearing at himself. Ah, ah, Mommy, Mommy. Dad sat up. What? What's up, son? Eugene went on crying and when Dad leaped from the bed and turned on the gaslight we saw the fleas, leaping, jumping, fastened to our flesh. We slapped at them and slapped but they hopped from body to body, hopping, biting. We tore at the bites till they bled. We jumped from the bed, the twins crying, Mam moaning, Oh, Jesus, will we have no rest! Dad poured water and salt into a jam jar and dabbed at our bites. The salt burned but he said we'd feel better soon.

Mam sat by the fireplace with the twins on her lap. Dad pulled on his trousers and dragged the mattress off the bed and out to the street. He filled the kettle and the pot with water, stood the mattress against the wall, pounded it with a shoe, told me to keep pouring water on the ground to drown the fleas dropping there. The Limerick moon was so bright I could see bits of it shimmering in the water and I wanted to scoop up moon bits but how could I with the fleas leaping on my legs. Dad kept pounding with the shoe and I had to run back through the house to the backyard tap for more water in the kettle and the pot. Mam said, Look at you. Your shoes are drenched and you'll catch your death and your father will surely get the pneumonia without a shoe to his foot.

A man on a bicycle stopped and wanted to know why Dad was beating that mattress. Mother o' God, he said, I never heard such a cure for fleas. Do you know that if a man could jump like a flea one lep would take him halfway to the moon? The thing to do is this, when you go back inside with that mattress stick it on the bed upside down and that will confuse the little buggers. They won't know where they are and they'll be biting the mattress or each other, which is the best cure of all. After they bite the human being they have the frenzy, you know, for there are other fleas around them that also bit the human being and the smell of the blood is too much for them and they go out of their minds. They're a right bloody torment an' I should know for didn't I grow up in Limerick, down in the Irishtown, an' the fleas there were so plentiful an' forward they'd sit on the toe of your boot an' discuss Ireland's woeful history with you. It is said there were no fleas in ancient Ireland, that they were brought in be the English to drive us out of our wits entirely, an' I wouldn't put it past the English. An' isn't it a very curious thing that St. Patrick drove the snakes out of Ireland an' the English brought in the fleas. For centuries Ireland was a lovely peaceful place, snakes gone, not a flea to be found. You could stroll the four green fields of Ireland without fear of snakes an' have a good night's sleep with no fleas to bother you. Them snakes were doin' no harm, they wouldn't bother you unless you cornered them an' they lived off other creatures that move under bushes an' such places, whereas the flea sucks the blood from you mornin' noon an' night for that's his nature an' he can't help himself. I hear for a fact that places that have snakes galore have no fleas. Arizona, for instance. You're forever hearing about the snakes of Arizona but when did you ever hear of fleas in Arizona? Good luck to you. I have to be careful standin' here for if one of them gets on my clothes I might as well invite his whole family home. They multiply faster than Hindus.

Dad said, You wouldn't by any chance have a cigarette, would you?

A cigarette? Oh, sure, of course. Here you are. Aren't I nearly destroyed from the fags myself. The oul' hacking cough, you know. So powerful it nearly knocks me off the bicycle. I can feel that cough stirring in me solar plexus an' workin' its way up through me entrails till the next thing it takes off the top o' me head.

He struck a match on a box, lit a cigarette for himself and held out the match for Dad. Of course, he said, you're bound to have the cough when you live in Limerick because this is the capital city of the weak chest and the weak chest leads to the consumption. If all the people that has consumption in Limerick were to die this would be a ghost town, though I don't have consumption meself. No, this cough was a present from the Germans. He paused, puffed on his cigarette, and struggled with a cough. Bejesus, excuse the language, but the fags'll get me in the end. Well, I'll leave you now to the mattress an' remember what I told you, confuse the little buggers.

He wobbled away on his bicycle, the cigarette dangling

from his mouth, the cough racking his body. Dad said, Limerickmen talk too much. Come on, we'll put this mattress back and see if there's any sleep in this night.

Mam sat by the fireplace with the twins asleep on her lap, and Malachy lay curled up on the floor by her feet. She said, Who was that you were talking to? It sounded very like Pa Keating, Aggie's husband. I could tell by the cough. He got that cough in France in the war when he swallowed the gas.

We slept the rest of that night, and in the morning we saw where the fleas had feasted, our flesh pink with flea welts and bright with the blood of our scratches.

Mam made tea and fried bread, and once more Dad dabbed at our bites with the salty water. He hauled the mattress outside again to the backyard. On a cold day like this the fleas would surely freeze to death and we'd all have a good night's sleep.

A few days later when we're settled into the room Dad is shaking me out of my dreams. Up, Francis, up. Put on your clothes and run over for your aunt Aggie. Your mother needs her. Hurry.

Mam is moaning in the bed, her face pure white. Dad has Malachy and the twins out of the bed and sitting on the floor by the dead fire. I run across the street and knock on Aunt Aggie's door till Uncle Pat Keating comes coughing and grumbling, What's up? What's up?

My mother is moaning in the bed. I think she's sick.

Now Aunt Aggie comes grumbling. Ye are nothing but trouble since ye came from America.

Leave him alone, Aggie, he's only a child that's doing what he's told.

She tells Uncle Pa go back to bed, that he has to go to work in the morning not like some from the North that she won't mention. He says, No, no, I'm coming. There's something wrong with Angela.

Dad tells me sit over there with my brothers. I don't know what's up with Mam because everyone is whispering and I can barely hear Aunt Aggie telling Uncle Pa the child is lost run for the ambulance and Uncle Pa is out the door, Aunt Aggie telling Mam you can say what you like about Limerick but the ambulance is fast. She doesn't talk to my father, never looks at him.

Malachy says, Dad, is Mammy sick?

Och, she'll be all right, son. She has to see the doctor.

I wonder what child is lost because we're all here, one two three four of us, not a lost child anywhere and why can't they tell me what's wrong with my mother. Uncle Pa comes back and the ambulance is right behind him. A man comes in with a stretcher and after they carry Mam away there are blood spots on the floor by the bed. Malachy bit his tongue and there was blood and the dog on the street had blood and he died. I want to ask Dad to tell me if Mam will be gone forever like my sister Margaret but he's going with Mam and there's no use asking Aunt Aggie anything for fear she'd bite your head off. She wipes away the blood spots and tells us get back into bed and stay there till Dad comes home.

It's the middle of the night and the four of us are warm in the bed and we fall asleep till Dad comes home and tells us Mam is nice and comfortable in the hospital and she'll be home in no time.

Later, Dad goes to the Labour Exchange for the dole. There is no hope of a laboring man with a North of Ireland accent getting a job in Limerick.

When he returns, he tells Mam we'll be getting nineteen shillings a week. She says that's just enough for all of us to starve on. Nineteen shillings for six of us? That's less than four dollars in American money and how are we supposed to live on that? What are we to do when we have to pay rent in a fortnight? If the rent for this room is five shillings a week we'll have fourteen shillings for food and clothes and coal to boil the water for the tea.

Dad shakes his head, sips his tea from a jam jar, stares out the window and whistles "The Boys of Wexford." Malachy and Oliver clap their hands and dance around the room and Dad doesn't know whether to whistle or smile because you can't do both and he can't help himself. He has to stop and smile and pat Oliver's head and then go back to the whistling. Mam smiles, too, but it's a very quick smile and when she looks into the ashes you can see the worry where the corners of her mouth turn down.

Next day she tells Dad to mind the twins and takes Malachy and me with her to the St. Vincent de Paul Society. We stand in a queue with women wearing black shawls. They ask our names and smile when we talk. They say, Lord above, would you listen to the little Yankees, and they wonder why Mam in her American coat would be looking for charity since there's hardly enough for the poor people of Limerick without Yanks coming over and taking the bread out of their mouths.

Mam tells them a cousin gave her that coat in Brooklyn, that her husband has no work, that she has other children at home, twin boys. The women sniff and pull their shawls about them, they have their own troubles. Mam tells them she had to leave America because she couldn't stand it after her baby girl died. The women sniff again but now it's because Mam is crying. Some say they lost little ones, too, and there's nothing worse in the world, you could live as long as Methuselem's wife but you never get over it. No man can ever know what it is to be a mother that has lost a child, not if the man lived longer than two Methuselems.

They all have a good cry till a red-haired woman passes a little box around. The women pick something from the box between their fingers and stuff it up their noses. A young woman sneezes and the red-haired woman laughs. Ah, sure, Biddy, you're not able for that snuff. Come here, little Yankee boys, have a pinch. She plants the brown stuff in our nostrils and we sneeze so hard the women stop crying

64

and laugh till they have to wipe their eyes with their shawls. Mam tells us, That's good for ye, 'twill clear yeer heads.

The young woman, Biddy, tells Mam we're two lovely boys. She points at Malachy. That little fella with the goldy ringlet, isn't he gorgeous? He could be a film star with Shirley Temple. And Malachy smiles and warms up the queue.

The woman with the snuff says to Mam, Missus, I don't want to be forward but I think you should be sitting down for we heard about your loss.

Another woman worries, Ah, no, they don't like that.

Who don't like what?

Ah, sure, Nora Molloy, the Society don't like us sittin' on the steps. They want us to be standin' respectful against the wall.

They can kiss my arse, says Nora, the red-haired woman. Sit down there, missus, on that step an' I'll sit next to you an' if there's one word out of the St. Vincent de Paul Society I'll take the face off 'em, so I will. Do you smoke, missus?

I do, says Mam, but I don't have them.

Nora takes a cigarette from a pocket in her apron, breaks it, and offers half to Mam.

The worried woman says, They don't like that either. They say every fag you smoke is taking food from the mouth of your child. Mr. Quinlivan inside is dead against it. He says if you have money for the fags you have money for food.

Quinlivan can kiss my arse, too, the grinny oul' bastard. Is he going to begrudge us a puff of a fag, the only comfort we have in the world?

A door opens at the end of the hall and a man appears. Are any of ye waiting for children's boots?

Women raise their hands, I am. I am.

Well, the boots are all gone. Ye'll have to come back next month.

But my Mikey needs boots for school.

They're all gone, I told you.

But 'tis freezin' abroad, Mr. Quinlivan.

The boots are all gone. Nothing I can do. What's this? Who's smoking?

Nora waves her cigarette. I am, she says, and enjoying it down to the last ash.

Every puff you take, he starts.

I know, she says, I'm taking food out of the mouths of my children.

You're insolent, woman. You'll get no charity here.

Is that a fact? Well, Mr. Quinlivan, if I don't get it here I know where I will.

What are you talking about?

I'll go to the Quakers. They'll give me the charity.

Mr. Quinlivan steps toward Nora and points a finger. Do you know what we have here? We have a souper in our midst. We had the soupers in the Famine. The Protestants went round telling good Catholics that if they gave up their faith and turned Protestant they'd get more soup than their bellies could hold and, God help us, some Catholics took the soup, and were ever after known as soupers and lost their immortal souls doomed to the deepest part of hell. And you, woman, if you go to the Quakers you'll lose your immortal soul and the souls of your children.

Then, Mr. Quinlivan, you'll have to save us, won't you?

He stares at her and she stares back at him. His eyes wander to the other women. One puts her hand to her mouth to smother a laugh.

What are you tittering about? he barks.

Oh, nothing, Mr. Quinlivan. Honest to God.

I'm telling ye once more, no boots. And he slams the door behind him.

One by one the women are called into the room. When Nora comes out she's smiling and waving a piece of paper. Boots, she says. Three pairs I'm gettin' for my children. Threaten the men in there with the Quakers and they'll give you the drawers off their arses.

When Mam is called she brings Malachy and me in with her. We stand before a table where three men are sitting asking questions. Mr. Quinlivan starts to say something but the man in the middle says, Enough out of you, Quinlivan. If we left it up to you we'd have the poor people of Limerick jumping into the arms of the Protestants.

He turns to Mam, he wants to know where she got that fine red coat. She tells him what she told the women outside and when she comes to the death of Margaret she shakes and sobs. She tells the men she's very sorry for crying like that but it was only a few months ago and she's not over it yet, not even knowing where her baby was buried if she was buried at all, not knowing even if she was baptized itself because she was so weak from having the four boys she didn't have the energy to be going to the church for the baptism and it's a heart scald to think Margaret might be in Limbo forever with no hope of her ever seeing the rest of us whether we're in heaven, hell, or Purgatory itself.

Mr. Quinlivan brings her his chair. Ah, now, missus. Ah, now. Sit down, will you. Ah, now.

The other men look at the table, the ceiling. The man in the middle says he's giving Mam a docket to get a week's groceries at McGrath's shop on Parnell Street. There will be tea, sugar, flour, milk, butter and a separate docket for a bag of coal from Sutton's coal yard on the Dock Road.

The third man says, Of course you won't be getting this every week, missus. We will be visiting your house to see if there's a real need. We have to do that, missus, so we can review your claim.

Mam wipes her face on the back of her sleeve and takes the docket. She tells the men, God bless you for your kindness. They nod and look at the table, the ceiling, the walls and tell her send in the next woman.

The women outside tell Mam, When you go to McGrath's, keep an eye on the oul' bitch for she'll cheat you on the weight. She'll put stuff on a paper on the scale with the paper hanging down on her side behind the counter where she thinks you can't see it. She'll pull on that paper so that you're lucky if you get half of what you're supposed to get. And she has pictures of the Virgin Mary and the Sacred Heart of Jesus all over the shop, and she's forever on her knees abroad in St. Joseph's chapel clackin' her rosary beads an' breathing like a virgin martyr, the oul' bitch.

Nora says, I'll go with you, missus. I'm on to the same Mrs. McGrath and I'll know if she's cheating you.

She leads the way to the shop in Parnell Street. The woman behind the counter is pleasant to Mam in her American coat till Mam shows the St. Vincent de Paul docket. The woman says, I don't know what you're doing here at this hour of the day. I never serve the charity cases before six in the evening. But this is your first time and I'll make an exception.

She says to Nora, Do you have a docket, too?

No. I'm a friend helping this poor family with their first docket from the St. Vincent de Paul.

The woman lays a sheet of newspaper on the scale and pours on flour from a large bag. When she finishes pouring, she says, There's a pound of flour.

I don't think so, says Nora. That's a very small pound of flour.

The woman flushes and glares, Are you accusin' me?

Ah, no, Mrs. McGrath, says Nora. I think there was a little accident there the way your hip was pressed against that paper and you didn't even know the paper was pulled down a bit. Oh, God, no. A woman like you that's forever on her knees before the Virgin Mary is an inspiration to us all and is that your money I see on the floor there?

Mrs. McGrath steps back quickly and the needle on the scale jumps and quivers. What money? she says, till she looks at Nora, and knows. Nora smiles. Must be a trick of the shadows, she says, and smiles at the scale. There was a mistake right enough for that shows barely half a pound of flour.

That scale gives me more trouble, says Mrs. McGrath.

I'm sure it does, says Nora.

But my conscience is clear before God, says Mrs. McGrath.

I'm sure it is, says Nora, and you're admired by one and all at the St. Vincent de Paul Society and the Legion of Mary.

I try to be a good Catholic.

Try? God knows 'tis little trying you'd have for you're well known for having a kind heart and I was wondering if you could spare a couple of sweets for the little boys here.

Well, now, I'm not a millionaire, but here . . .

God bless you, Mrs. McGrath, and I know it's asking a lot but could you possibly lend me a couple of cigarettes?

Well, now, they're not on the docket. I'm not here to supply luxuries.

If you could see your way, missus, I'd be sure to mention your kindness to the St. Vincent de Paul.

All right, all right, says Mrs. McGrath. Here. One time for the cigarettes and one time only.

God bless you, says Nora, and I'm sorry you had so much trouble with that scale.

On the way home we stopped in the People's Park and sat on a bench while Malachy and I sucked on our sweets and Mam and Nora smoked their cigarettes. The smoking brought on Nora's cough and she told Mam the fags would kill her in the end, that there was a touch of consumption in her family and no one lived to a ripe old age, though who would want to in Limerick, a place where you could look around and the first thing you noticed was a scarcity of gray hairs, all the gray hairs either in the graveyard or across the Atlantic working on railroads or sauntering around in police uniforms.

You're lucky, missus, that you saw a bit of the world. Oh, God, I'd give anything to see New York, people dancing up and down Broadway without a care. No, I had to go and fall for a boozer with the charm, Peter Molloy, a champion pint drinker that had me up the pole and up the aisle when I was barely seventeen. I was ignorant, missus. We grew up ignorant in Limerick, so we did, knowing feck all about anything and signs on, we're mothers before we're women. And there's nothing here but rain and oul' biddies saying the rosary. I'd give me teeth to get out, go to America or even England itself. The champion pint drinker is always on the dole and sometimes he even drinks that and drives me so demented I wind up in the lunatic asylum.

She drew on her cigarette and gagged, coughing till her body rocked back and forth, and in between the coughs she whimpered, Jesus, Jesus. When the cough died away she said she had to go home and take her medicine. She said, I'll see you next week, missus, at the St. Vincent de Paul. If you're stuck for anything send a message to me at Vize's Field. Ask anyone for the wife of Peter Molloy, champion pint drinker.

Eugene is sleeping under a coat on the bed. Dad sits by the fireplace with Oliver on his lap. I wonder why Dad is telling Oliver a Cuchulain story. He knows the Cuchulain stories are mine, but when I look at Oliver I don't mind. His cheeks are bright red, he's staring into the dead fire, and you can see he has no interest in Cuchulain. Mam puts her hand on his forehead. I think he has a fever, she says. I wish I had an onion and I'd boil it in milk and pepper. That's good for the fever. But even if I had what would I boil the milk on? We need coal for that fire.

She gives Dad the docket for the coal down the Dock Road. He takes me with him but it's dark and all the coal yards are closed.

What are we going to do now, Dad?

I don't know, son.

Ahead of us women in shawls and small children are picking up coal along the road.

There, Dad, there's coal.

Och, no, son. We won't pick coal off the road. We're not beggars.

He tells Mam the coal yards are closed and we'll have to drink milk and eat bread tonight, but when I tell her about the women on the road she passes Eugene to him.

If you're too grand to pick coal off the road I'll put on my coat and go down the Dock Road.

She gets a bag and takes Malachy and me with her. Beyond the Dock Road there is something wide and dark with lights glinting in it. Mam says that's the River Shannon. She says that's what she missed most of all in America, the River Shannon. The Hudson was lovely but the Shannon sings. I can't hear the song but my mother does and that makes her happy. The other women are gone from the Dock Road and we search for the bits of coal that drop from lorries. Mam tells us gather anything that burns, coal, wood, cardboard, paper. She says, There are them that burn the horse droppings but we're not gone that low yet. When her bag is nearly full she says, Now we have to find an onion for Oliver. Malachy says he'll find one but she tells him, No, you don't find onions on the road, you get them in shops.

The minute he sees a shop he cries out, There's a shop, and runs in.

Oonyen, he says. Oonyen for Oliver.

Mam runs into the shop and tells the women behind the counter, I'm sorry. The woman says, Lord, he's a dote. Is he an American or what?

Mam says he is. The woman smiles and shows two teeth, one on each side of her upper gum. A dote, she says, and look at them gorgeous goldy curls. And what is it he wants now? A sweet?

Ah, no, says Mam. An onion.

The woman laughs, An onion? I never heard a child wanting an onion before. Is that what they like in America?

Mam says, I just mentioned I wanted to get an onion

71

for my other child that's sick. Boil the onion in milk, you know.

True for you, missus. You can't beat the onion boiled in milk. And look, little boy, here's a sweet for yourself and one for the other little boy, the brother, I suppose.

Mam says, Ah, sure, you shouldn't. Say thank you, boys.

The woman says, Here's a nice onion for the sick child, missus.

Mam says, Oh, I can't buy the onion now, missus. I don't have a penny on me.

I'm giving you the onion, missus. Let it never be said a child went sick in Limerick for want of an onion. And don't forget to sprinkle in a little pepper. Do you have pepper, missus?

Ah, no, I don't but I should be getting it any day now.

Well, here, missus. Pepper and a little salt. Do the child all the good in the world.

Mam says, God bless you, ma'am, and her eyes are watery.

Dad is walking back and forth with Oliver in his arms and Eugene is playing on the floor with a pot and a spoon. Dad says, Did you get the onion?

I did, says Mam, and more. I got coal and the way of lighting it.

I knew you would. I said a prayer to St. Jude. He's my favorite saint, patron of desperate cases.

I got the coal. I got the onion, no help from St. Jude.

Dad says, You shouldn't be picking up coal off the road like a common beggar. It isn't right. Bad example for the boys.

Then you should have sent St. Jude down the Dock Road.

Malachy says, I'm hungry, and I'm hungry, too, but Mam says, Ye'll wait till Oliver has his onion boiled in milk.

She gets the fire going, cuts the onion in half, drops it in the boiling milk with a little butter and sprinkles the milk with pepper. She takes Oliver on her lap and tries to feed him but he turns away and looks into the fire.

Ah, come on, love, she says. Good for you. Make you big and strong.

He tightens his mouth against the spoon. She puts the pot down, rocks him till he's asleep, lays him on the bed and tells the rest of us be quiet or she'll demolish us. She slices the other half of the onion and fries it in butter with slices of bread. She lets us sit on the floor around the fire where we eat the fried bread and sip at the scalding sweet tea in jam jars. She says, That fire is good and bright so we can turn off that gaslight till we get money for the meter.

The fire makes the room warm and with the flames dancing in the coal you can see faces and mountains and valleys and animals leaping. Eugene falls asleep on the floor and Dad lifts him to the bed beside Oliver. Mam puts the boiled onion pot up on the mantelpiece for fear a mouse or rat might be at it. She says she's tired out from the day, the Vincent de Paul Society, Mrs. McGrath's shop, the search for coal down the Dock Road, the worry over Oliver not wanting the boiled onion, and if he's like this tomorrow she's taking him to the doctor, and now she's going to bed.

Soon we're all in bed and if there's the odd flea I don't mind because it's warm in the bed with the six of us and I love the glow of the fire the way it dances on the walls and ceiling and makes the room go red and black, red and black, till it dims to white and black and all you can hear is a little cry from Oliver turning in my mother's arms.

In the morning Dad is lighting the fire, making tea, cutting the bread. He's already dressed and he's telling Mam hurry up and get dressed. He says to me, Francis, your little brother Oliver is sick and we're taking him to the hospital. You are to be a good boy and take care of your two brothers. We'll be back soon.

Mam says, When we're out go easy with that sugar. We're not millionaires.

When Mam picks up Oliver and wraps him in a coat Eugene stands on the bed. I want Ollie, he says. Ollie play.

Ollie will be back soon, she says, and you can play with him. Now you can play with Malachy and Frank.

Ollie, Ollie, I want Ollie.

He follows Oliver with his eyes and when they're gone he sits on the bed looking out the window. Malachy says, Genie, Genie, we have bread, we have tea. Sugar on your bread, Genie. He shakes his head and pushes away the bread Malachy is offering. He crawls to the place where Oliver slept with Mam, puts his head down and stares out the window.

Grandma is at the door. I heard your father and mother were running down Henry Street with the child in their arms. Now where are they gone to?

Oliver is sick, I said. He wouldn't eat the boiled onion in milk.

What are you blatherin' about?

Wouldn't eat the boiled onion and got sick.

And who's minding ye?

I am.

And what's up with the child in the bed? What's his name?

That's Eugene. He misses Oliver. They're twins.

I know they're twins. That child looks starved. Have ye any porridge here?

What's porridge? says Malachy.

Jesus, Mary and Holy St. Joseph! What's porridge! Porridge is porridge. That's what porridge is. Ye are the most ignorant bunch o' Yanks I ever seen. Come on, put on yeer clothes and we'll go across the street to your aunt Aggie. She's there with the husband, Pa Keating, and she'll give ye some porridge.

She picks up Eugene, wraps him in her shawl and we cross the street to Aunt Aggie's. She's living with Uncle Pa again because he said she wasn't a fat cow after all.

Do you have any porridge? Grandma says to Aunt Aggie.

Porridge? Am I supposed to be feeding porridge to a crowd of Yanks?

Pity about you, says Grandma. It won't kill you to give them a little porridge.

And I suppose they'll be wanting sugar and milk on top of everything or they might be banging on my door looking for an egg if you don't mind. I don't know why we have to pay for Angela's mistakes.

Jesus, says Grandma, 'tis a good thing you didn't own that stable in Bethlehem or the Holy Family would still be wanderin' the world crumblin' with the hunger.

Grandma pushes her way past Aunt Aggie, puts Eugene on a chair near the fire and makes the porridge. A man comes in from another room. He has black curly hair and his skin is black and I like his eyes because they're very blue and ready to smile. He's Aunt Aggie's husband, the man who stopped the night we were attacking the fleas and told us all about fleas and snakes, the man with the cough he got from swallowing gas in the war.

Malachy says, Why are you all black? and Uncle Pa Keating laughs and coughs so hard he has to ease himself with a cigarette. Oh, the little Yanks, he says. They're not a bit shy. I'm black because I work at the Limerick Gas Works shoveling coal and coke into the furnaces. Gassed in France and back to Limerick to work in the gas works. When you grow up you'll laugh.

Malachy and I have to leave the table so the big people can sit and have tea. They have their tea but Uncle Pa Keating, who is my uncle because he's married to my aunt Aggie, picks up Eugene and takes him on his lap. He says, This is a sad little fella, and makes funny faces and silly sounds. Malachy and I laugh but Eugene only reaches up to touch the blackness of Pa Keating's skin, and then when Pa pretends to bite his little hand, Eugene laughs and everyone in the room laughs. Malachy goes to Eugene and tries to make him laugh even more but Eugene turns away and hides his face in Pa Keating's shirt.

I think he likes me, says Pa, and that's when Aunt Aggie puts down her teacup and starts to bawl, Waah, waah, waah, big teardrops tumbling down her fat red face.

Aw, Jesus, says Grandma, there she is again. What's up with you this time?

And Aunt Aggie blubbers, To see Pa there with a child on his lap an' me with no hope of having my own.

Grandma barks at her, Stop talkin' like that in front of the children. Have you no shame? When God is good and ready He'll send you your family.

Aunt Aggie sobs, Angela with five born an' one just gone an' her so useless she couldn't scrub a floor an' me with none an' I can scrub an' clean with the best and make any class of a stew or a fry.

Pa Keating laughs, I think I'll keep this little fella.

Malachy runs to him. No, no, no. That's my brother, that's Eugene. And I say, No, no, no, that's our brother.

Aunt Aggie pats the tears on her cheeks. She says, I don't want nothing of Angela's. I don't want nothing that's half Limerick and half North of Ireland, so I don't, so ye can take him home. I'll have me own someday if I have to do a hundred novenas to the Virgin Mary and her mother, St. Ann, or if I have to crawl from here to Lourdes on me two bended knees.

Grandma says, That's enough. Ye have had yeer porridge and 'tis time to go home and see if yeer father and mother are back from the hospital.

She puts on her shawl and goes to pick up Eugene but he clutches so hard at Pa Keating's shirt she has to pull him away though he keeps looking back at Pa till we're out the door.

*   *   *

We followed Grandma back to our room. She put Eugene in the bed and gave him a drink of water. She told him to be a good boy and go to sleep for his little brother, Oliver, would be home soon and they'd be playing again there on the floor.

But he kept looking out the window.

She told Malachy and me we could sit on the floor and play but to be quiet because she was going to say her prayers. Malachy went to the bed and sat by Eugene and I sat on a chair at the table making out words on the newspaper that was our tablecloth. All you could hear in the room was Malachy whispering to make Eugene happy and Grandma mumbling to the click of her rosary beads. It was so quiet I put my head on the table and fell asleep.

Dad is touching my shoulder. Come on, Francis, you have to take care of your little brothers.

Mam is slumped on the edge of the bed, making small crying sounds like a bird. Grandma is pulling on her shawl. She says, I'll go down to Thompson the undertaker about the coffin and the carriage. The St. Vincent de Paul Society will surely pay for that, God knows.

She goes out the door. Dad stands facing the wall over the fire, beating on his thighs with his fists, sighing, Och, och, och.

Dad frightens me with his och, och, och, and Mam frightens me with her small bird sounds and I don't know what to do though I wonder if anyone will light the fire in the grate so that we can have tea and bread because it's a long time since we had the porridge. If Dad would move away from the fireplace I could light the fire myself. All you need is paper, a few bits of coal or turf, and a match. He won't move so I try to go around his legs while he's beating on his thighs but he notices me and wants to know why I'm trying to light the fire. I tell him we're all hungry and he

77

lets out a crazy laugh. Hungry? he says. Och, Francis, your wee brother Oliver is dead. Your wee sister is dead and your wee brother is dead.

He picks me up and hugs me so hard I cry out. Then Malachy cries, my mother cries, Dad cries, I cry, but Eugene stays quiet. Then Dad sniffles, We'll have a feast. Come on, Francis.

He tells my mother we'll be back in awhile but she has Malachy and Eugene on her lap in the bed and she doesn't look up. He carries me through the streets of Limerick and we go from shop to shop with him asking for food or anything they can give to a family that has two children dead in a year, one in America, one in Limerick, and in danger of losing three more for the want of food and drink. Most shopkeepers shake their heads. Sorry for your troubles but you could go to the St. Vincent de Paul Society or get the public assistance.

Dad says he's glad to see the spirit of Christ alive in Limerick and they tell him they don't need the likes of him with his northern accent to be telling them about Christ and he should be ashamed of himself dragging a child around like that like a common beggar, a tinker, a knacker.

A few shopkeepers give bread, potatoes, tins of beans and Dad says, We'll go home now and you boys can eat something, but we meet Uncle Pa Keating and he tells Dad he's very sorry for his troubles and would Dad like to have a pint in this pub here?

There are men sitting in this pub with great glasses of black stuff before them. Uncle Pa Keating and Dad have the black stuff, too. They lift their glasses carefully and slowly drink. There is creamy white stuff on their lips, which they lick with little sighs. Uncle Pa gets me a bottle of lemonade and Dad gives me a piece of bread and I don't feel hungry anymore. Still, I wonder how long we'll sit here with Malachy and Eugene hungry at home, hours from the porridge, which Eugene didn't eat anyway.

Dad and Uncle Pa drink their glass of black stuff and have

another. Uncle Pa says, Frankie, this is the pint. This is the staff of life. This is the best thing for nursing mothers and for those who are long weaned.

He laughs and Dad smiles and I laugh because I think that's what you're supposed to do when Uncle Pa says something. He doesn't laugh when he tells the other men about Oliver dying. The other men tip their hats to Dad. Sorry for your troubles, mister, and surely you'll have a pint.

Dad says yes to the pints and soon he's singing Roddy McCorley and Kevin Barry and song after song I never heard before and crying over his lovely little girl, Margaret, that died in America and his little boy, Oliver, dead beyond in the City Home Hospital. It frightens me the way he yells and cries and sings and I wish I could be at home with my three brothers, no, my two brothers, and my mother.

The man behind the bar says to Dad, I think now, mister, you've had enough. We're sorry for your troubles but you have to take that child home to his mother that must be heartbroken by the fire.

Dad says, One, one more pint, just one, eh? and the man says no. Dad shakes his fist. I did me bit for Ireland, and when the man comes out and takes Dad's arm, Dad tries to push him away.

Uncle Pa says, Come on now, Malachy, stop the blaguarding. You have to go home to Angela. You have a funeral tomorrow and the lovely children waiting for you.

But Dad struggles till a few men push him out into the darkness. Uncle Pa stumbles out with the bag of food. Come on, he says. We'll go back to your room.

Dad wants to go to another place for a pint but Uncle Pa says he has no more money. Dad says he'll tell everyone his sorrows and they'll give him pints. Uncle Pa says that's a disgraceful thing to do and Dad cries on his shoulder. You're a good friend, he tells Uncle Pa. He cries again till Uncle Pa pats him on the back. It's terrible, terrible, says Uncle Pa, but you'll get over this in time.

Dad straightens up and looks at him. Never, he says. Never.

Next day we rode to the hospital in a carriage with a horse. They put Oliver in a white box that came with us in the carriage and we took him to the graveyard. They put the white box into a hole in the ground and covered it with earth. My mother and Aunt Aggie cried, Grandma looked angry, Dad, Uncle Pa Keating, and Uncle Pat Sheehan looked sad but did not cry and I thought that if you're a man you can cry only when you have the black stuff that is called the pint.

I did not like the jackdaws that perched on trees and gravestones and I did not want to leave Oliver with them. I threw a rock at a jackdaw that waddled over toward Oliver's grave. Dad said I shouldn't throw rocks at jackdaws, they might be somebody's soul. I didn't know what a soul was but I didn't ask him because I didn't care. Oliver was dead and I hated jackdaws. I'd be a man someday and I'd come back with a bag of rocks and I'd leave the graveyard littered with dead jackdaws.

The morning after Oliver's burial Dad went to the Labour Exchange to sign and collect the week's dole, nineteen shillings and sixpence. He said he'd be home by noon, that he'd get coal and make a fire, that we'd have rashers and eggs and tea in honor of Oliver, that we might even have a sweet or two.

He wasn't home by noon, or one, or two, and we boiled and ate the few potatoes the shopkeepers had given the day before. He wasn't home anytime before the sun went down that day in May. There was no sign of him till we heard him, long after the pubs closed, rolling along Windmill Street, singing,

When all around a vigil keep,
The West's asleep, the West's asleep—
Alas, and well may Erin weep
When Connacht lies in slumber deep.
There lake and plain smile fair and free,
'Mid rocks their guardian chivalry.
Sing, Oh, let man learn liberty
From crashing wind and lashing sea.

He stumbled into the room, hanging on to the wall. A snot oozed from his nose and he wiped it away with the back of his hand. He tried to speak. Zeeze children should be in bed. Lishen to me. Shildren go to bed.

Mam faced him. These children are hungry. Where's the dole money? We'll get fish and chips so they'll have something in their bellies when they go to sleep.

She tried to stick her hands into his pockets but he pushed her away. Have respheck, he said. Reshpeck in front of shildren.

She struggled to get at his pockets. Where's the money? The children are hungry. You mad oul' bastard, did you drink all the money again? Just what you did in Brooklyn.

He blubbered, Och, poor Angela. And poor wee Margaret and poor wee Oliver.

He staggered to me and hugged me and I smelled the drink I used to smell in America. My face was wet from his tears and his spit and his snot and I was hungry and I didn't know what to say when he cried all over my head.

Then he let me go and hugged Malachy, still going on about the wee sister and the wee brother cold in the ground, and how we all have to pray and be good, how we have to be obedient and do what our mother tells us. He said we have our troubles but it's time for Malachy and me to start school because there's nothing like an education, it will stand to you in the end, and you have to get ready to do your bit for Ireland.

*   *   *

Mam says she can't spend another minute in that room on Windmill Street. She can't sleep with the memory of Oliver in that room, Oliver in the bed, Oliver playing on the floor, Oliver sitting on Dad's lap by the fire. She says it's not good for Eugene to be in that place, that a twin will suffer more over the loss of his brother than even a mother can understand. There's a room going on Hartstonge Street with two beds instead of the one we have here for the six of us, no, the five of us. We're getting that room and to make sure she's going to the Labour Exchange on Thursday to stand in the queue to take the dole money the minute it's handed to Dad. He says she can't do that, he'd be disgraced with the other men. The Labour Exchange is a place for men not for women taking the money from under their noses. She says, Pity about you. If you didn't squander the money in the pubs I wouldn't have to follow you the way I did in Brooklyn.

He tells her he'll be shamed forever. She says she doesn't care. She wants that room on Hartstonge Street, a nice warm comfortable room with a lavatory down the hall like the one in Brooklyn, a room without fleas and the dampness that kills. She wants that room because it's on the same street as Leamy's National School and Malachy and I can come home at the dinner hour, which is noon, for a cup of tea and a cut of fried bread.

On Thursday Mam follows Dad to the Labour Exchange. She marches in behind him and when the man pushes the money toward Dad she takes it. The other men on the dole nudge each other and grin and Dad is disgraced because a woman is never supposed to interfere with a man's dole money. He might want to put sixpence on a horse or have a pint and if all the women start acting like Mam the horses will stop running and Guinness will go broke. But she has the money now and we move to Hartstonge Street. Then she carries Eugene in her arms and we go up the street to Leamy's National School. The headmaster, Mr. Scallan, says we are to return on Monday with a composition book, a pencil, and a pen with a good nib on it. We are not to come to school with ringworm or lice and our noses are to be blown at all times, not on the floor, that spreads the consumption, or on our sleeves, but in a handkerchief or a clean rag. He asks us if we are good boys and when we say we are, he says, Good Lord, what's this? Are they Yanks or what?

Mam tells him about Margaret and Oliver and he says, Lord above, Lord above, there's great suffering in the world. Anyway, we'll put the little fellow, Malachy, in the infants' class and his brother in first class. They're in the same room with one master. Monday morning, then, nine o'clock prompt.

The boys in Leamy's want to know why we talk like that. Are ye Yanks or what? And when we tell them we came from America they want to know, Are ye gangsters or cowboys?

A big boy sticks his face up to mine. I'm asking ye a question, he says. Are ye gangsters or cowboys?

I tell him I don't know and when he pokes his finger into my chest Malachy says, I'm a gangster, Frank's a cowboy. The big boy says, Your little brother is smart and you're a stupid Yank.

The boys around him are excited. Fight, they yell, fight, and he pushes me so hard I fall. I want to cry but the blackness comes over me the way it did with Freddie Leibowitz and I rush at him, kicking and punching. I knock him down and try to grab his hair to bang his head on the ground but there's a sharp sting across the backs of my legs and I'm pulled away from him.

Mr. Benson, the master, has me by the ear and he's whacking me across the legs. You little hooligan, he says. Is that the kind of behavior you brought from America? Well, by God, you'll behave yourself before I'm done with you.

He tells me hold out one hand and then the other and hits me with his stick once on each hand. Go home now, he says, and tell your mother what a bad boy you were. You're a bad Yank. Say after me, I'm a bad boy.

I'm a bad boy.

Now say, I'm a bad Yank.

I'm a bad Yank.

Malachy says, He's not a bad boy. It's that big boy. He said we were cowboys and gangsters.

Is that what you did, Heffernan?

I was only jokin', sir.

No more joking, Heffernan. It's not their fault that they're Yanks.

'Tisn't, sir.

And you, Heffernan, should get down on your two knees every night and thank God you're not a Yank for if you were, Heffernan, you'd be the greatest gangster on two sides of the Atlantic. Al Capone would be coming to you for lessons. You're not to be bothering these two Yanks anymore, Heffernan.

I won't, sir.

And if you do, Heffernan, I'll hang your pelt on the wall. Now go home, all of ye.

There are seven masters in Leamy's National School and they all have leather straps, canes, blackthorn sticks. They hit you with the sticks on the shoulders, the back, the legs, and, especially, the hands. If they hit you on the hands it's called a slap. They hit you if you're late, if you have a leaky nib on your pen, if you laugh, if you talk, and if you don't know things.

They hit you if you don't know why God made the world, if you don't know the patron saint of Limerick, if you can't recite the Apostles' Creed, if you can't add nineteen to forty-seven, if you can't subtract nineteen from forty-seven, if you don't know the chief towns and products of the thirty-two counties of Ireland, if you can't find Bulgaria on the wall map of the world that's blotted with spit, snot, and blobs of ink thrown by angry pupils expelled forever.

They hit you if you can't say your name in Irish, if you can't say the Hail Mary in Irish, if you can't ask for the lavatory pass in Irish.

It helps to listen to the big boys ahead of you. They can tell you about the master you have now, what he likes and what he hates.

One master will hit you if you don't know that Eamon de Valera is the greatest man that ever lived. Another master will hit you if you don't know that Michael Collins was the greatest man that ever lived.

Mr. Benson hates America and you have to remember to hate America or he'll hit you.

Mr. O'Dea hates England and you have to remember to hate England or he'll hit you.

If you ever say anything good about Oliver Cromwell they'll all hit you.

Even if they slap you six times on each hand with the ash plant or the blackthorn with the knobs you must not cry. You'll be a sissy. There are boys who might jeer at you and mock you on the street but even they have to be careful because the day will come when the master hits and slaps them and they have to keep the tears behind their eyes or be disgraced forever. Some boys say it is better to cry because that pleases the masters. If you don't cry the masters hate you because you've made them look weak before the class and they promise themselves the next time they have you up they'll draw tears or blood or both.

Big boys in fifth class tell us Mr. O'Dea likes to get you in front of the class so that he can stand behind you, pinch your sideburns, which are called cossicks, pull up on them. Up, up, he says, till you're on tiptoe and the tears are filling your eyes. You don't want the boys in the class to see you cry but pulling on the cossicks makes the tears come whether you like it or not and the master likes that. Mr. O'Dea is the one master who can always bring the tears and the shame.

It is better not to cry because you have to stick with the boys in the school and you never want to give the masters any satisfaction.

If the master hits you there's no use complaining to your father or mother. They always say, You deserve it. Don't be a baby.

I know Oliver is dead and Malachy knows Oliver is dead but Eugene is too small to know anything. When he wakes in the morning he says, Ollie, Ollie, and toddles around the room looking under the beds or he climbs up on the bed by the window and points to children on the street, especially children with fair hair like him and Oliver. Ollie, Ollie, he says, and Mam picks him up, sobs, hugs him. He struggles to get down because he doesn't want to be picked up and hugged. He wants to find Oliver.

Dad and Mam tell him Oliver is in heaven playing with angels and we'll all see him again someday but he doesn't understand because he's only two and doesn't have the words and that's the worst thing in the whole world.

Malachy and I play with him. We try to make him laugh. We make funny faces. We put pots on our heads and pretend to let them fall off. We run across the room and pretend to fall down. We take him to the People's Park to see the lovely flowers, play with dogs, roll in the grass.

He sees small children with fair hair like Oliver. He doesn't say Ollie anymore. He only points.

Dad says Eugene is lucky to have brothers like Malachy and me because we help him forget and soon, with God's help, he'll have no memory of Oliver at all.

*   *   *

He died anyway.

Six months after Oliver went, we woke on a mean November morning and there was Eugene, cold in the bed beside us. Dr. Troy came and said that child died of pneumonia and why wasn't he in the hospital long ago? Dad said he didn't know and Mam said she didn't know and Dr. Troy said that's why children die. People don't know. He said if Malachy or I showed the slightest sign of a cough or the faintest rattle in the throat we were to be brought to him no matter what time of day or night. We were to be kept dry at all times because there seemed to be a bit of a weakness in the chest in this family. He told Mam he was very sorry for her troubles and he'd give her a prescription for something to ease the pain of the days to come. He said God was asking too much, too damn much.

Grandma came over to our room with Aunt Aggie. She washed Eugene, and Aunt Aggie went to a shop for a little white gown and a set of rosary beads. They dressed him in a white gown and laid him on the bed by the window where he used to look out for Oliver. They placed his hands on his chest, one hand on top of the other, bound in the little white rosary beads. Grandma brushed the hair back from his eyes and forehead and she said, Doesn't he have lovely soft silky hair? Mam went to the bed and pulled a blanket over his legs to keep him warm. Grandma and Aunt Aggie looked at each other and said nothing. Dad stood at the end of the bed beating his fists against his thighs, talking to Eugene, telling him, Och, it was the River Shannon that harmed you, the dampness from that river that came and took you and Oliver. Grandma said, Will you stop that? You're making the whole house nervous. She took Dr. Troy's prescription and told me run over to O'Connor the chemist for the pills, that there would be no charge due to the kindness of Dr. Troy. Dad said he'd come with me, that we'd go to the Jesuit church and say a prayer for Margaret and Oliver and Eugene, all happy in heaven. The chemist gave us the pills, we stopped to say the prayers, and when we returned to the room, Grandma gave Dad money to bring a few bottles of stout from the pub. Mam said, No, no, but Grandma said, He doesn't have the pills to ease him, God help us, and a bottle of stout will be some small comfort. Then she told him he'd have to go to the undertaker tomorrow to bring the coffin back in a carriage. She told me to go with my father and make sure he didn't stay in the pub all night and drink all the money. Dad said, Och, Frankie shouldn't be in pubs, and she said, Then don't stay there. He put on his cap and we went to South's pub and he told me at the door I could go home now, that he'd be home after one pint. I said, No, and he said, Don't be disobedient. Go home to your poor mother. I said, No, and he said I was a bad boy and God would be displeased. I said I wasn't going home without him and he said, Och, what is the world coming to? He had one quick pint of porter in the pub and we went home with the bottles of stout. Pa Keating was in our room with a small bottle of whiskey and bottles of stout and Uncle Pat Sheehan brought two bottles of stout for himself. Uncle Pat sat on the floor with his arms around his bottles and he kept saying, They're mine, they're mine, for fear they'd be taken from him. People who were dropped on their heads always worry someone will steal their stout. Grandma said, All right, Pat, drink your stout yourself. No one will bother you. She and Aunt Aggie sat on the bed by Eugene. Pa Keating sat at the kitchen table drinking his stout and offering everyone a sip of his whiskey. Mam took her pills and sat by the fire with Malachy on her lap. She kept saying Malachy had hair like Eugene and Aunt Aggie said no he did not till Grandma drove her elbow into Aunt Aggie's chest and told her shut up. Dad stood against the wall drinking his stout between the fireplace and the bed with Eugene. Pa Keating told stories and the big people laughed even though they didn't want to laugh or they weren't supposed to laugh in the presence of a dead child. He said when he was in the

English army in France the Germans sent gas over which made him so sick they had to take him to the hospital. They kept him in the hospital a while and then sent him back to the trenches. English soldiers were sent home but they didn't give a fiddler's fart about the Irish soldiers, whether they lived or died. Instead of dying Pa made a vast fortune. He said he solved one of the great problems of trench warfare. In the trenches it was so wet and muddy they had no way of boiling the water for the tea. He said to himself, Jasus, I have all this gas in my system and 'tis a great pity to waste it. So he shoved a pipe up his arse, lit a match to it, and there in a second he had a fine flame ready to boil water in any billycan. Tommies came running from trenches all around when they heard the news and they gave him any amount of money if he'd let them boil water. He made so much money he was able to bribe the generals to let him out of the army and off he went to Paris where he had a fine time drinking wine with artists and models. He had such a high time of it he spent all his money and when he came back to Limerick the only job he could get was in the gas works shoveling coal into the furnaces. He said there was so much gas in his system now he could supply light to a small town for a year. Aunt Aggie sniffed and said that was not a proper story to be telling in the presence of a dead child and Grandma said it was better to have a story like that than to be sitting around with the long face. Uncle Pat Sheehan, sitting on the floor with his stout, said he was going to sing a song. More power to you, said Pa Keating, and Uncle Pat sang "The Road to Rasheen." He kept saying, Rasheen, Rasheen, mavourneen mean, and the song made no sense because his father dropped him on his head long ago and every time he sang that song he had different words. Grandma said that was a fine song and Pa Keating said Caruso better look over his shoulder. Dad went over to the bed in the corner where he slept with Mam. He sat on the edge, put his bottle on the floor, covered his face with his hands and cried. He said, Frank, Frank, come here, and I had to go to him so that he could hug me the way Mam was hugging Malachy. Grandma said, We better go now and sleep a bit before the funeral tomorrow. They each knelt by the bed and said a prayer and kissed Eugene's forehead. Dad put me down, stood up and nodded to them as they left. When they were gone he lifted each of the stout bottles to his mouth and drained it. He ran his finger inside the whiskey bottle and licked it. He turned down the flame in the paraffin oil lamp on the table and said it was time for Malachy and me to be in bed. We'd have to sleep with him and Mam that night as little Eugene would be needing the bed for himself. It was dark in the room now except for the sliver of streetlight that fell on Eugene's lovely soft silky hair.

Dad lights the fire in the morning, makes the tea, toasts the bread in the fire. He brings Mam's toast and tea but she waves it away and turns to the wall. He brings Malachy and me to Eugene to kneel and say a prayer. He says the prayers of one child like us are worth more in heaven than the prayers of ten cardinals and forty bishops. He shows us how to bless ourselves, In the name of the Father, and of the Son, and of the Holy Ghost. Amen, and he says, Dear God, this is what you want, isn't it? You want my son, Eugene. You took his brother, Oliver, You took his sister, Margaret. I'm not supposed to question that, am I? Dear God above, I don't know why children have to die but that is Your will. You told the river to kill and the Shannon killed. Could You at last be merciful? Could You leave us the children we have? That is all we ask. Amen.

He helps Malachy and me wash our heads and feet so that we'll be clean for Eugene's funeral. We have to be very quiet even when he hurts us cleaning our ears with the corner of the towel we brought from America. We have to be quiet because Eugene is there with his eyes closed and we don't want him to be waking up and looking out the window for Oliver.

Grandma comes and tells Mam she has to get up. There are children dead, she says, but there are children alive and they need their mother. She brings Mam a little tea in a mug to wash down the pills that ease the pain. Dad tells Grandma it's Thursday and he has to go to the Labour Exchange for the dole and then down to the undertaker to bring the mourning carriage and the coffin. Grandma tells him to take me with him but he says it's better for me to stay with Malachy so that I can pray for my little brother dead in the bed. Grandma says, Is it coddin' me you are? Pray for a little child that's barely two and already playing with his little brother in heaven? You'll take your son with you and he'll remind you this is no day for the pubs. She looks at him and he looks at her and he puts on his cap.

At the Labour Exchange we stand at the end of the queue till a man comes from behind the counter and tells Dad he's very sorry for his troubles and he should go ahead of everyone else on this sorrowful day. Men touch their caps and say they're sorry for his troubles and some pat my head and give me pennies, twenty-four pennies, two shillings. Dad tells me I'm rich now and I should buy myself a sweet while he goes into this place for a minute. I know this place is a pub and I know he wants to get the black stuff that is called a pint but I don't say anything because I want to go to the shop next door for a piece of toffee. I chew my toffee till it melts and leaves my mouth all sweet and sticky. Dad is still in the pub and I wonder if I should get another piece of toffee as long as he's in there with the pint. I'm about to give the money to the woman in the shop when my hand is slapped down and there's Aunt Aggie, raging. Is this what you do, she says, on the day of your brother's funeral? Gorgin' yourself on sweets. And where's that father of yours?

He's, he's, in the pub.

Of course he's in the pub. You out here stuffin' yourself

with sweets and him in there gettin' himself into a staggerin' condition the day your poor little brother goes to the grave-yard. She tells the shop woman, Just like his father, the same odd manner, the same oul' northern jaw.

She tells me get into that pub and tell my father to stop the drinking and get the coffin and the carriage. She will not set foot inside the pub for the drink is the curse of this poor godforsaken country.

Dad is sitting at the back of the pub with a man who has a dirty face and hair growing out of his nose. They're not talking but staring straight ahead and their black pints are resting on a small white coffin on the seat between them. I know that's Eugene's coffin because Oliver had one like it and I want to cry when I see the black pints on top of it. I'm sorry now I ever ate that toffee and I wish I could take it out of my stomach and give it back to the woman in the shop because it's not right to be eating toffee when Eugene is dead in the bed and I'm frightened by the two black pints on his white coffin. The man with Dad is saying, No, mister, you can't leave a child's coffin in a carriage no more. I did that once, went in for a pint and they robbed that little coffin out of the bloody carriage. Can you credit that? It was empty, thank God, but there you are. Desperate times we live in, desperate. The man with Dad lifts his pint and takes a long swallow and when he puts his glass down there's a hollow sound in the coffin. Dad nods at me. We'll be going in a minute, son, but when he goes to put his glass on the coffin after the long swallow I push it away.

That's Eugene's coffin. I'll tell Mam you put your glass on Eugene's coffin.

Now, son. Now, son.

Dad, that's Eugene's coffin.

The other man says, Will we have another pint, mister?

Dad says to me, Wait outside another few minutes, Francis.

No.

Don't be a bad boy.

No.

The other man says, By Jesus, if that was my son I'd kick his arse from here to the County Kerry. He have no right to be talkin' to his father in that manner on a sorrowful day. If a man can't have a pint the day of a funeral what's the use of livin' at all, at all.

Dad says, All right. We'll go.

They finish their pints and wipe the wet brown stains off the coffin with their sleeves. The man climbs up to the driver's seat of the carriage and Dad and I ride inside. He has the coffin on his lap and he presses it against his chest. At home our room is filled with big people, Mam, Grandma, Aunt Aggie, her husband, Pa Keating, Uncle Pat Sheehan, Uncle Tom Sheehan, who is Mam's oldest brother and who never came near us before because he hates people from the North of Ireland. Uncle Tom has his wife, Jane, with him. She's from Galway and people say she has the look of a Spaniard and that's why no one in the family talks to her.

The man takes the coffin from Dad and when he brings it into the room Mam moans, Oh, no, oh, God, no. The man tells Grandma he'll be back in awhile to take us to the graveyard. Grandma tells him he'd better not come back to this house in a drunken state because this child that's going to the graveyard suffered greatly and deserves a bit of dignity and she won't put up with a driver that's drunk and ready to fall out of the high seat.

The man says, Missus, I drove dozens o' children to the graveyard an' never once fell out of any seat, high or low.

The men are drinking stout from bottles again and the women are sipping sherry from jam jars. Uncle Pat Sheehan tells everyone, This is my stout, this is my stout, and Grandma says, 'Tis all right, Pat. No one will take your stout. Then he says he wants to sing "The Road to Rasheen" till Pa Keating says, No, Pat, you can't sing on the day of a funeral. You can sing the night before. But Uncle Pat keeps saying, This is my stout and I want to sing "The Road to Rasheen," and everyone knows he talks like that because he was dropped on his head. He starts to sing his song but stops when Grandma takes the lid off the coffin and Mam sobs, Oh, Jesus, oh, Jesus, will it ever stop? Will I be left with one child?

Mam is sitting on a chair at the head of the bed. She's stroking Eugene's hair and face and hands. She tells him that of all the children in the world he was the sweetest and the most delicate and loving. She tells him 'tis a terrible thing to lose him but isn't he in heaven now with his brother and his sister and isn't that a comfort to us, knowing Oliver is no longer lonesome for his twin. Still, she puts her head down next to Eugene and cries so hard all the women in the room cry with her. She cries till Pa Keating tells her we have to go before the darkness falls, that we can't be in graveyards in the dark.

Grandma whispers to Aunt Aggie, Who'll put the child in the coffin? and Aunt Aggie whispers, I won't. That's the job for the mother.

Uncle Pat hears them. I'll put the child in the coffin, he says. He limps to the bed and places his arms around Mam's shoulders. She looks up at him and her face is drenched. He says, I'll put the child in the coffin, Angela.

Oh, Pat, she says. Pat.

I can do it, he says. Sure he's only a small child an' I never lifted a small child before in my life. I never had a small child in me arms. I won't drop him, Angela. I won't. Honest to God, I won't.

I know you won't, Pat. I know you won't.

I'll lift him an' I won't be singin' "The Road to Rasheen."

I know you won't, Pat, Mam says.

Pat pulls down the blanket Mam put there to keep Eugene warm. Eugene's feet are white and bright with little blue veins. Pat bends over, picks up Eugene and holds him against his chest. He kisses Eugene's forehead and then everyone in the room kisses Eugene. He places Eugene in the coffin and steps back. We are all gathered around looking at Eugene for the last time.

Uncle Pat says, See, I didn't drop him, and she touches his face.

Aunt Aggie goes to the pub for the driver. He puts the lid on the coffin and screws it down. He says, Who's comin' in the carriage? and takes the coffin to the carriage. There's room only for Mam and Dad, Malachy and me. Grandma says, Ye go ahead to the graveyard and we'll wait here.

I don't know why we can't keep Eugene. I don't know why they have to send him away with that man who puts his pint on the white coffin. I don't know why they had to send Margaret away and Oliver. It is a bad thing to put my sister and my brothers in a box and I wish I could say something to someone.

The horse clop-clopped through the streets of Limerick. Malachy said, Are we going to see Oliver? and Dad said, No, Oliver is in heaven and don't ask me what heaven is because I don't know.

Mam said, Heaven is a place where Oliver and Eugene and Margaret are happy and warm and we'll see them there some day.

Malachy said, The horse did his doodoo on the street and there was a smell, and Mam and Dad had to smile.

At the graveyard the driver climbs down and opens the door of the carriage. Gimme that coffin, he says, an' I'll carry it up to the grave. He yanks at the coffin and stumbles. Mam says, You're not carrying my child in the condition you're in. She turns to Dad. You carry him, she says.

Do what you like, says the driver. Do what you bloody well like, and he climbs up to his seat.

It's getting dark now and the coffin seems whiter than ever in Dad's arms. Mam takes our hands and we follow Dad through the graves. The jackdaws are quiet in the trees because their day is nearly over and they have to rest so that they can get up early in the morning and feed their babies.

Two men with shovels are waiting by a small open grave. One man says, Ye are very late. Good thing this is a small job or we'd be gone. He climbs into the grave. Hand it to me, he says, and Dad hands him the coffin.

The man sprinkles some straw and grass on the coffin and as he climbs out the other man shovels in the earth. Mam lets out a long cry, Oh, Jesus, Jesus, and a jackdaw croaks in a tree. I wish I had a rock to hit that jackdaw. When the men finish shoveling in the earth they wipe their foreheads and wait. One says, Ah, well, now, there's usually a little something for the thirst that's in it.

Dad says, Oh, yes, yes, and gives them money. They say, Sorry for your troubles, and they leave.

We make our way back to the carriage at the graveyard gate but the carriage is gone. Dad looks around in the darkness and comes back shaking his head. Mam says, That driver is nothing but a dirty old drunkard, God forgive me.

It's a long walk from the graveyard to our room. Mam tells Dad, These children need some nourishment and you have money left from the dole this morning. If you're thinking of going to the pubs tonight you can forget it. We're taking them to Naughton's and they can have fish and chips and lemonade for 'tisn't every day they bury a brother.

The fish and chips are delicious with vinegar and salt and the lemonade is tart in our throats.

When we get home the room is empty. There are empty stout bottles on the table and the fire is out. Dad lights the paraffin oil lamp and you can see the hollow left in the pillow by Eugene's head. You expect to hear him and see him toddling across the room, climbing up on the bed to look out the window for Oliver.

Dad tells Mam he's going out for a walk. She says no. She knows what he's up to, that he can't wait to spend his last few shillings in the pubs. All right, he says. He lights the fire and Mam makes tea and soon we're in bed.

Malachy and I are back in the bed where Eugene died. I hope he's not cold in that white coffin in the graveyard though I know he's not there anymore because angels come to the graveyard and open the coffin and he's far from the Shannon dampness that kills, up in the sky in heaven with Oliver and Margaret where they have plenty of fish and chips and toffee and no aunts to bother you, where all the fathers bring home the money from the Labour Exchange and you don't have to be running around to pubs to find them.

III

Mam says she can't spend another minute in that room on Hartstonge Street. She sees Eugene morning, noon and night. She sees him climbing the bed to look out at the street for Oliver and sometimes she sees Oliver outside and Eugene inside, the two of them chatting away. She's happy they're chatting like that but she doesn't want to be seeing and hearing them the rest of her life. It's a shame to move when we're so near Leamy's National School but if she doesn't move soon she'll go out of her mind and wind up in the lunatic asylum.

We move to Roden Lane on top of a place called Barrack Hill. There are six houses on one side of the lane, one on the opposite side. The houses are called two up, two down, two rooms on top, two on the bottom. Our house is at the end of the lane, the last of the six. Next to our door is a small shed, a lavatory, and next to that a stable.

Mam goes to the St. Vincent de Paul Society to see if there's any chance of getting furniture. The man says he'll give us a docket for a table, two chairs, and two beds. He says we'll have to go to a secondhand furniture shop down in the Irishtown and haul the furniture home ourselves. Mam says we can use the pram she had for the twins and when she says that she cries. She wipes her eyes on her sleeves and asks the man if the beds we're getting are secondhand. He says of course they are, and she says she's very worried about sleeping in beds someone might have died in, especially if they had the consumption. The man says, I'm very sorry, but beggars can't be choosers.

It takes us all day to haul the furniture on the pram from one end of Limerick to the other. There are four wheels on the pram but one is bockety, it wants to go in a different direction. We have two beds, one sideboard with a mirror, a table and two chairs. We're happy with the house. We can walk from room to room and up and down the stairs. You feel very rich when you can go up and down the stairs all day as much as you please. Dad lights the fire and Mam makes the tea. He sits at the table on one chair, she sits on the other and Malachy and I sit on the trunk we brought from America. While we're drinking our tea an old man passes our door with a bucket in his hand. He empties the bucket into the lavatory and flushes and there's a powerful stink in our kitchen. Mam goes to the door and says, Why are you emptying your bucket in our lavatory? He raises his cap to her. Your lavatory, missus? Ah, no. You're making a bit of a mistake there, ha, ha. This is not your lavatory. Sure, isn't this the lavatory for the whole lane. You'll see passing your door here the buckets of eleven families and I can tell you it gets very powerful here in the warm weather, very powerful altogether. 'Tis December now, thank God, with a chill in the air and Christmas around the corner and the lavatory isn't that bad, but the day will come when you'll be calling for a gas mask. So, good night to you, missus, and I hope you'll be happy in your house.

Mam says, Wait a minute, sir. Could you tell me who cleans this lavatory?

Cleans? Ah, Jasus, that's a good one. Cleans, she says. Is it joking you are? These houses were built in the time of Queen Victoria herself and if this lavatory was ever cleaned it must have been done by someone in the middle of the night when no one was lookin'.

And he shuffles up the lane laughing away to himself.

Mam comes back to her chair and her tea. We can't stay here, she says. That lavatory will kill us with all diseases.

Dad says, We can't move again. Where will we get a

house for six shillings a week? We'll keep the lavatory clean ourselves. We'll boil buckets of water and throw them in there.

Oh, will we? says Mam, and where will we get the coal or turf or blocks to be boiling water?

Dad says nothing. He finishes his tea and looks for a nail to hang our one picture. The man in the picture has a thin face. He wears a yellow skullcap and a black robe with a cross on his chest. Dad says he was a Pope, Leo the Thirteenth, a great friend of the workingman. He brought this picture all the way from America where he found it thrown out by someone who had no time for the workingman. Mam says he's talking a lot of bloody nonsense and he says she shouldn't say bloody in front of the children. Dad finds a nail but wonders how he's going to get it into the wall without a hammer. Mam says he could go borrow one from the people next door but he says you don't go around borrowing from people you don't know. He leans the picture against the wall and drives the nail with the bottom of a jam jar. The jam jar breaks and cuts his hand and a blob of blood falls on the Pope's head. He wraps his hand in the dish rag and tells Mam, Quick, quick, wipe the blood off the Pope before it dries. She tries to wipe the blood away with her sleeve but it's wool and spreads the blood till the whole side of the Pope's face is smeared. Dad says, Lord above, Angela, you've destroyed the Pope entirely, and she says, Arrah, stop your whining, we'll get some paint and go over his face some day, and Dad says, He's the only Pope that was ever a friend to the workingman and what are we to say if someone from the St. Vincent de Paul Society comes in and sees blood all over him? Mam says, I don't know. It's your blood and 'tis a sad thing when a man can't even drive a nail straight. It just goes to show how useless you are. You'd be better off digging fields and anyway I don't care. I have pain in my back and I'm going to bed.

Och, what am I going to do? Dad says.

Take down the Pope and hide him in the coal hole under the stairs where he won't be seen and he'll be out of harm's way.

I can't, says Dad. It would be bad luck. Coal hole is no place for a Pope. When the Pope is up, he's up.

Suit yourself, says Mam.

I will, says Dad.

This is our first Christmas in Limerick and the girls are out in the lane, skipping rope and singing,

> Christmas is coming
> And the goose is getting fat,
> Please put a penny
> In the old man's hat.
> If you haven't a penny
> A ha'penny will do
> And if you haven't a ha'penny
> God bless you.

Boys tease the girls and call out,

> May your mother have an accident
> Abroad in the loo.

Mam says she'd like to have a nice Christmas dinner but what can you do when the Labour Exchange reduces the dole to sixteen shillings after Oliver and Eugene died? You pay the rent of six shillings, you have ten shillings left, and what use is that to four people?

Dad can't get any work. He gets up early on weekdays, lights the fire, boils water for the tea and his shaving mug. He puts on a shirt and attaches a collar with studs. He puts on his tie and his cap and goes to the Labour Exchange to sign for the dole. He will never leave the house without collar and tie. A man without collar and tie is a man with no respect for himself. You never know when the clerk at the Labour Exchange might tell you there's a job going at Rank's Flour Mills or the Limerick Cement Company, and even if it's a laboring job what will they think if you appear without collar and tie?

Bosses and foremen always show him respect and say they're ready to hire him, but when he opens his mouth and they hear the North of Ireland accent, they take a Limerickman instead. That's what he tells Mam by the fire and when she says, Why don't you dress like a proper workingman? he says he'll never give an inch, never let them know, and when she says, Why can't you try to talk like a Limerickman? he says he'll never sink that low and the greatest sorrow of his life is that his sons are now afflicted with the Limerick accent. She says, Sorry for your troubles and I hope that's all you'll ever have, and he says that some day, with God's help, we'll get out of Limerick and far from the Shannon that kills.

I ask Dad what afflicted means and he says, Sickness, son, and things that don't fit.

When he's not looking for work Dad goes for long walks, miles into the country. He asks farmers if they need any help, that he grew up on a farm and can do anything. If they hire him he goes to work right away with his cap on and his collar and tie. He works so hard and long the farmers have to tell him to stop. They wonder how a man can work through a long hot day with no thought of food or drink. Dad smiles. He never brings home the money he earns on farms. That money seems to be different from the dole, which is supposed to be brought home. He takes the farm money to the pub and drinks it. If he's not home when the Angelus rings at six o'clock Mam knows he had a day of work. She hopes he might think of his family and pass the pub even once, but he never does. She hopes he might bring home something from the farm, potatoes, cabbage, turnips, carrots, but he'll never bring home anything because he'd never stoop so low as to ask a farmer for anything. Mam says 'tis all right for her to be begging at the St. Vincent de Paul Society for a docket for food but he can't stick a few spuds in his pocket. He says it's different for a man. You have to keep the dignity. Wear your collar and tie, keep up the appearance, and never ask for anything. Mam says, I hope it keeps fine for you.

When the farm money is gone he rolls home singing and crying over Ireland and his dead children, mostly about Ireland. If he sings Roddy McCorley, it means he had only the price of a pint or two. If he sings Kevin Barry, it means he had a good day, that he is now falling down drunk and ready to get us out of bed, line us up and make us promise to die for Ireland, unless Mam tells him leave us alone or she'll brain him with the poker.

You wouldn't do that, Angela.

I would and more. You better stop the nonsense and go to bed.

Bed, bed, bed. What's the use of going to bed? If I go to bed I'll only have to get up again and I can't sleep in a place where there's a river sending poison to us in mist and fog.

He goes to bed, pounds the wall with his fist, sings a woeful song, falls asleep. He's up at daylight because no one should sleep beyond the dawn. He wakes Malachy and me and we're tired from being kept up the night before with his talking and singing. We complain and say we're sick, we're tired, but he pulls back the overcoats that cover us and forces us out on the floor. It's December and it's freezing and we can see our breath. We pee into the bucket by the bedroom door and run down stairs for the warmth of the fire Dad has already started. We wash our faces and hands in a basin that sits under the water tap by the door. The pipe that leads to the tap has to be held to the wall by a piece of twine looped around a nail. Everything around the tap is damp, the floor, the wall, the chair the basin sits on. The water from the tap is icy and our fingers turn numb. Dad says this is good for us, it will make men of us. He throws the icy water on his face and neck and chest to show there's nothing to fear. We hold our hands to the fire for the heat that's in it but we can't stay there long because we have to drink our tea and eat our bread and go to school. Dad makes us say grace before meals and grace after meals and he tells us be good boys at school because God is watching every move and the slightest disobedience will send us straight to hell where we'll never have to worry about the cold again.

And he smiles.

Two weeks before Christmas Malachy and I come home from school in a heavy rain and when we push in the door we find the kitchen empty. The table and chairs and trunk are gone and the fire is dead in the grate. The Pope is still there and that means we haven't moved again. Dad would never move without the Pope. The kitchen floor is wet, little pools of water all around, and the walls are twinkling with the damp. There's a noise upstairs and when we go up we find Dad and Mam and the missing furniture. It's nice and warm there with a fire blazing in the grate, Mam sitting in the bed, and Dad reading *The Irish Press* and smoking a cigarette by the fire. Mam tells us there was a terrible flood, that the rain came down the lane and poured in under our door. They tried to stop it with rags but they only turned sopping wet and let the rain in. People emptying their buckets made it worse and there was a sickening stink in the kitchen. She thinks we should stay upstairs as long as there is rain. We'll be warm through the winter months and then we can go downstairs in the springtime if there is any sign of a dryness in the walls or the floor. Dad says it's like going away on our holidays to a warm foreign place like Italy. That's what we'll call the upstairs from now on, Italy. Malachy says the Pope is still on the wall downstairs and he's going to be all cold and couldn't we bring him up? but Mam says, No, he's going to stay where he is because I don't want him on the wall glaring at me in the bed. Isn't it enough that we dragged him all the way from Brooklyn to Belfast to Dublin to Limerick? All I want now is a little peace, ease and comfort.

Mam takes Malachy and me to the St. Vincent de Paul Society to stand in the queue and see if there's any chance of getting something for the Christmas dinner—a goose or a ham, but the man says everyone in Limerick is desperate this Christmas. He gives her a docket for groceries at McGrath's shop and another one for the butcher.

No goose, says the butcher, no ham. No fancy items when you bring the docket from the St. Vincent de Paul. What you can have now, missus, is black pudding and tripe or a sheep's head or a nice pig's head. No harm in a pig's head, missus, plenty of meat and children love it, slice that cheek, slather it with mustard and you're in heaven, though I suppose they wouldn't have the likes of that in America where they're mad for the steak and all classes of poultry, flying, walking or swimming itself.

He tells Mam, no, she can't have boiled bacon or sausages and if she has any sense she'll take the pig's head before they're all gone the way the poor people of Limerick are clamoring for them.

Mam says the pig's head isn't right for Christmas and he says 'tis more than the Holy Family had in that cold stable in Bethlehem long ago. You wouldn't find them complaining if someone offered them a nice fat pig's head.

No, they wouldn't complain, says Mam, but they'd never eat the pig's head. They were Jewish.

And what does that have to do with it? A pig's head is a pig's head.

And a Jew is a Jew and 'tis against their religion and I don't blame them.

The butcher says, Are you a bit of an expert, missus, on the Jews and the pig.

I am not, says Mam, but there was a Jewish woman, Mrs.

Leibowitz, in New York, and I don't know what we would have done without her.

The butcher takes the pig's head off a shelf and when Malachy says, Ooh, look at the dead dog, the butcher and Mam burst out laughing. He wraps the head in newspaper, hands it to Mam and says, Happy Christmas. Then he wraps up some sausages and tells her, Take these sausages for your breakfast on Christmas Day. Mam says, Oh, I can't afford sausages, and he says, Am I asking you for money? Am I? Take these sausages. They might help make up for the lack of a goose or a ham.

Sure, you don't have to do that, says Mam.

I know that, missus. If I had to do it, I wouldn't.

Mam says she has a pain in her back, that I'll have to carry the pig's head. I hold it against my chest but it's damp and when the newspaper begins to fall away everyone can see the head. Mam says, I'm ashamed of me life that the world should know we're having pig's head for Christmas. Boys from Leamy's National School see me and they point and laugh. Aw, Gawd, look at Frankie McCourt an' his pig's snout. Is that what the Yanks ate for Christmas dinner, Frankie?

One calls to another, Hey, Christy, do you know how to ate a pig's head?

No, I don't, Paddy.

Grab him by the ears an' chew the face offa him.

And Christy says, Hey, Paddy, do you know the only part of the pig the McCourts don't ate?

No, I don't, Christy.

The only part they don't ate is the oink.

After a few streets the newspaper is gone altogether and everyone can see the pig's head. His nose is flat against my chest and pointing up at my chin and I feel sorry for him because he's dead and the world is laughing at him. My sister and two brothers are dead, too, but if anyone laughed at them I'd hit them with a rock.

I wish Dad would come and help us because Mam has to stop every few steps and lean against a wall. She's holding her back and telling us she'll never be able to climb Barrack Hill. Even if Dad came he wouldn't be much use because he never carries anything, parcels, bags, packages. If you carry such things you lose your dignity. That's what he says. He carried the twins when they were tired and he carried the Pope, but that was not the same as carrying ordinary things like a pig's head. He tells Malachy and me that when you grow up you have to wear a collar and tie and never let people see you carry things.

He's upstairs sitting by the fire, smoking a cigarette, reading *The Irish Press*, which he loves because it's de Valera's paper and he thinks de Valera is the greatest man in the world. He looks at me and the pig's head and tells Mam it's a disgraceful thing to let a boy carry an object like that through the streets of Limerick. She takes off her coat and eases herself into the bed and tells him that next Christmas he can go out and find the dinner. She's worn out and gasping for a cup of tea so would he drop his grand airs, boil the water for the tea and fry some bread before his two small sons starve to death.

On Christmas morning he lights the fire early so that we can have sausages and bread and tea. Mam sends me to Grandma to see if we can borrow a pot for the pig's head. Grandma says, What are ye having for yeer dinner? Pig's head! Jesus, Mary an' Joseph, that's goin' beyond the beyonds. Couldn't your father get out and find a ham or a goose at least? What kind of man is he at all, at all?

Mam puts the head in the pot, just covered with water, and while the pig is boiling away Dad takes Malachy and me to Mass at the Redemptorist church. It's warm in the church and sweet with flowers and incense and candles. He takes us to see the Baby Jesus in the crib. He's a big fat baby with fair curls like Malachy. Dad tells us that's Jesus' mother there, Mary, in the blue dress, and his father, St. Joseph, the old man with the beard. He says they're sad because they know Jesus will grow up and be killed so that we can all go to heaven. I ask why the Baby Jesus has to die and Dad says you can't ask questions like that. Malachy says, Why? and Dad tells him be quiet.

Mam is in a terrible state at home. There isn't enough coal to cook the dinner, the water isn't boiling anymore and she says she's demented with worry. We'll have to go down the Dock Road again to see if there's any coal or turf lying around from the lorries. Surely we'll find something on the road this day of all days. Even the poorest of the poor don't go out on Christmas Day picking coal off the road. There's no use asking Dad to go because he will never stoop that low and even if he did he won't carry things through the streets. It's a rule he has. Mam can't go because of the pain in her back.

She says, You'll have to go, Frank, and take Malachy with you.

It's a long way to the Dock Road but we don't mind because our bellies are filled with sausages and bread and it's not raining. We carry a canvas bag Mam borrowed from Mrs. Hannon next door and Mam is right, there is no one on the Dock Road. The poor are all at home having pig's head or maybe a goose and we have the Dock Road to ourselves. We find bits of coal and turf stuck in cracks on the road and in the walls of the coal yards. We find bits of paper and cardboard that will be useful in starting the fire again. We're wandering around trying to fill the bag when Pa Keating comes along. He must have washed himself for Christmas because he's not as black as he was when Eugene died. He wants to know what we're doing with that bag and when Malachy tells him he says, Jesus, Mary and Holy St.Joseph! Christmas Day and ye don't have a fire for yeer pig's head. That's a bloody disgrace.

He takes us to South's pub, which is not supposed to be open, but he's a regular customer and there's a back door for men who want their pint to celebrate the birthday of the Baby Jesus above in the crib. He orders his pint and lemonade for us and asks the man if there's any chance of getting a few lumps of coal. The man says he's been serving drink for twenty-seven years and nobody ever asked him for coal before. Pa says it would be a favor and the man says if Pa asked for the moon he'd fly up and bring it back. The man leads us to the coal hole under the stairs and tells us take what we can carry. It's real coal and not bits from the Dock Road and if we can't carry it we can drag it along the ground.

It takes us a long time to go from South's pub to Barrack Hill because of a hole in the bag. I pull the bag and it's Malachy's job to pick up the lumps that fall through the hole and put them back again. Then it starts to rain and we can't stand in a doorway till it passes because we have that coal and it's leaving a black trail along the pavement and Malachy is turning black from picking up the lumps, pushing them into the bag and wiping the rain from his face with his wet black hands. I tell him he's black, he tells me I'm black, and a woman in a shop tells us get away from that door, 'tis Christmas Day and she doesn't want to be looking at Africa.

We have to keep dragging the bag or we'll never have our Christmas dinner. It will take ages to get a fire going and ages more to get our dinner because the water has to be boiling when Mam puts in the head of cabbage and the potatoes to keep the pig company in the pot. We drag the bag up O'Connell Avenue and we see people in their houses sitting around tables with all kinds of decorations and bright lights. At one house they push up the window and the children point and laugh and call to us, Look at the Zulus. Where are yeer spears?

Malachy makes faces at them and wants to throw coal at them but I tell him if he throws coal there's less for the pig and we'll never get our dinner.

The downstairs in our house is a lake again from the rain pouring under the door but it doesn't matter because we're drenched anyway and we can wade through the water. Dad comes down and drags the bag upstairs to Italy. He says we're good boys for getting so much coal, that the Dock Road must have been covered with it. When Mam sees us she starts to laugh, and then she cries. She's laughing because we're so black and crying because we're sopping wet. She tells us take off all our clothes and she washes the coal off our hands and faces. She tells Dad the pig's head can wait a while so that we can have a jam jar of hot tea.

It's raining outside and there's a lake downstairs in our kitchen but up here in Italy the fire is going again and the room is so dry and warm that, after our tea, Malachy and I doze off in the bed and we don't wake till Dad tells us the dinner is ready. Our clothes are still wet, so Malachy sits on the trunk at the table wrapped in Mam's red American over-coat and I'm wrapped in an old coat that Mam's father left behind when he went to Australia.

There are delicious smells in the room, cabbage, potatoes, and the pig's head, but when Dad lifts the head from the pot to a plate Malachy says, Oh, the poor pig. I don't want to eat the poor pig.

Mam says, If you were hungry you'd eat it. Now stop the nonsense and eat your dinner.

Dad says, Wait a minute. He takes slices from the two cheeks, places them on our plates and smears them with mustard. He takes the plate that holds the pig's head and puts it on the floor under the table. Now, he says to Malachy, that's ham, and Malachy eats it because he's not looking at what it came from and it isn't pig's head anymore. The cabbage is soft and hot and there are plenty of potatoes with butter and salt. Mam peels our potatoes but Dad eats his skin and all. He says all the nourishment of a potato is in the skin and Mam says it's a good thing he's not eating eggs, he'd be chewing the shells and all.

He says he would, and it's a disgrace that the Irish throw out millions of potato skins every day and that's why thousands are dying of consumption and surely there's nourishment in the shell of an egg since waste is the eighth deadly sin. If he had his way, and Mam says, Never mind your way. Eat your dinner.

He eats half a potato with its skin on and puts the other half back in the pot. He eats a small slice of the pig's cheek and a leaf of cabbage and leaves the rest on his plate for Malachy and me. He makes more tea and we have that with bread and jam so that no one can say we didn't have a sweet on Christmas Day.

It's dark now and still raining outside and the coal is glowing in the grate where Mam and Dad sit and smoke their cigarettes. There's nothing to do when your clothes are wet but get back into bed where it's cozy and your father can tell you a story about how Cuchulain became a Catholic and you fall asleep and dream about the pig standing in the crib at the Redemptorist church crying because he and the Baby Jesus and Cuchulain all have to grow up and die.

The angel that brought Margaret and the twins comes again and brings us another brother, Michael. Dad says he found Michael on the seventh step of the stairs to Italy. He says that's what you have to watch for when you ask for a new baby, the Angel on the Seventh Step.

Malachy wants to know how you can get a new brother from the Angel on the Seventh Step if you don't have any stairs in your house and Dad tells him that asking too many questions is an affliction.

Malachy wants to know what an affliction is.

Affliction. I'd like to know what that word means. Affliction, but Dad says, Och, child, the world is an affliction and everything in it, puts on his cap and goes to the Bedford Row Hospital to see Mam and Michael. She's in the hospital with the pain in her back and she has the baby with her to make sure he was healthy when he was left on the seventh step. I don't understand this because I'm sure angels would never leave a sick baby on the seventh step. There's no use asking Dad or Mam about this. They say, You're getting as bad as your brother for asking questions. Go play.

I know that big people don't like questions from children. They can ask all the questions they like, How's school? Are you a good boy? Did you say your prayers? but if you ask them did they say their prayers you might be hit on the head.

Dad brings Mam home with the new baby and she has to stay in bed for a few days with the pain in her back. She says this baby is the spitting image of our sister who died, with his wavy black hair, his lovely blue eyes, and the gorgeous eyebrows. That's what Mam says.

I want to know if the baby will be spitting. I also want to know which is the seventh step because there are nine steps on the stairs and I'd like to know if you count from the bottom or the top. Dad doesn't mind answering this question. Angels come down from above, he says, and not up from kitchens like ours which are lakes from October till April.

So I find the seventh step by counting from the top.

The baby Michael has a cold. His head is stuffed and he can barely breathe. Mam worries because it's Sunday and the Dispensary for the poor is closed. If you go to the doctor's house and the maid sees you're from the lower classes she tells you go to the Dispensary where you belong. If you tell her the child is dying in your arms she'll say the doctor is in the country riding his horse.

Mam cries because the baby is struggling to get air through his mouth. She tries to clear his nostrils with a bit of rolled-up paper but she's afraid to push it too far up. Dad says, There's no need for that. You're not supposed to be pushing things inside a child's head. It looks like he's going to kiss the baby. Instead, he has his mouth on the little nose and he's sucking

sucking the bad stuff out of Michael's head. He spits it into the fire, Michael gives out a loud cry and you can see him drawing the air into his head and kicking his legs and laughing. Mam looks at Dad as if he just came down from heaven and Dad says, That's what we did in Antrim long before there were doctors riding their horses.

Michael entitles us to a few extra shillings on the dole but Mam says it isn't enough and now she has to go to the St. Vincent de Paul Society for food. One night there is a knock on the door and Mam sends me down to see who it is. There are two men from the St. Vincent de Paul and they want to see my mother and father. I tell them my parents are upstairs in Italy and they say, What?

Upstairs where 'tis dry. I'll tell them.

They want to know what that little shed is beside our front door. I tell them it's the lavatory. They want to know why it isn't in the back of the house and I tell them it's the lavatory for the whole lane and it's a good thing it's not in the back of our house or we'd have people traipsing through our kitchen with buckets that would make you sick.

They say, Are you sure there's one lavatory for the whole lane?

I am.

They say, Mother of God.

Mam calls down from Italy. Who's down there?

The men.

What men?

From the St. Vincent de Paul.

They're careful the way they step into the lake in the kitchen and they make tsk tsk and tut tut noises and they tell one another. Isn't this a disgrace? till they get upstairs to Italy. They tell Mam and Dad they're sorry to disturb them but the Society has to be sure they're helping deserving cases. Mam offers them a cup of tea but they look around and say,

No, thank you. They want to know why we're living upstairs. They want to know about the lavatory. They ask questions because big people can ask all the questions they like and write in notebooks, especially when they're wearing collars and ties and suits. They ask how old Michael is, how much Dad gets at the Labour Exchange, when did he last have a job, why doesn't he have a job now and what class of an accent is that he has?

Dad tells them the lavatory could kill us with every class of disease, that the kitchen floods in the winter and we have to move upstairs to stay dry. He says the River Shannon is responsible for all the dampness in the world and killing us one by one.

Malachy tells them we're living in Italy and they smile.

Mam asks if there's any chance of getting boots for Malachy and me and they say she'll have to come down to Ozanam House and apply. She says she hasn't been feeling well since the baby came and she wouldn't be able to stand long in a queue, but they say everyone has to be treated the same, even a woman down in the Irishtown that had triplets and, thank you, we'll make our report to the Society.

When they're leaving Malachy wants to show them where the angel left Michael on the seventh step but Dad tells him, Not now, not now. Malachy cries and one of the men gives him a piece of toffee from his pocket and I wish I had something to cry about so that I'd get a piece, too.

I have to go downstairs again and show the men where to step to keep their feet dry. They keep shaking their heads and saying, God Almighty and Mother of God, this is desperate. That's not Italy they have upstairs, that's Calcutta.

Dad is telling Mam up in Italy she should never beg like that.

What do you mean, beg?

Don't you have any pride, begging for boots like that?

And what would you do, Mr. Grand Manner? Would you let them go barefoot?

I'd rather fix the shoes they have.

The shoes they have are falling to pieces.

I can fix them, he says.

You can't fix anything. You're useless, she says.

He comes home the next day with an old bicycle tire. He sends me to Mr. Hannon next door for the loan of a last and a hammer. He takes Mam's sharp knife and he hacks at the tire till he has pieces to fit on the soles and heels of our shoes. Mam tells him he's going to destroy the shoes altogether but he pounds away with the hammer, driving the nails through the rubber pieces and into the shoes. Mam says, God above, if you left the shoes alone they'd last till Easter, at least, and we might get the boots from the St. Vincent de Paul. But he won't stop till the soles and heels are covered with squares of rubber tire which stick out on each side of the shoe and flop before and behind. He makes us put on the shoes and tells us our feet will be good and warm but we don't want to wear them anymore because the tire pieces are so lumpy we stumble when we walk around Italy. He sends me back to Mr. Hannon with the last and hammer and Mrs. Hannon says, God above, what's up with your shoes? She laughs and Mr. Hannon shakes his head and I feel ashamed. I don't want to go to school next day and I pretend to be sick but Dad gets us up and gives us our fried bread and tea and tells us we should be grateful we have any shoes at all, that there are boys in Leamy's National School who go to school barefoot on bitter days. On our way to school Leamy's boys laugh at us because the tire pieces are so thick they add a few inches to our height and the boys say, How's the air up there? There are six or seven barefoot boys in my class and they don't say anything and I wonder if it's better to have shoes with rubber tires that make you trip and stumble or to go barefoot. If you have no shoes at all you'll have all the barefoot boys on your side. If you have rubber tires on your shoes you're all alone with your brother and you have to fight your own battles. I sit on a bench in the schoolyard shed and take off my shoes and stockings but when I go into the class the master wants to know where my shoes are. He knows I'm not one of the barefoot boys and he makes me go back to the yard, bring in the shoes and put them on. Then he says to the class, There is sneering here. There is jeering at the misfortunes of others. Is there anyone in this class that thinks he's perfect? Raise your hands.

There are no hands.

Is there anyone in this class that comes from a rich family with money galore to spend on shoes? Raise your hands.

There are no hands.

He says, There are boys here who have to mend their shoes whatever way they can. There are boys in this class with no shoes at all. It's not their fault and it's no shame. Our Lord had no shoes. He died shoeless. Do you see Him hanging on the cross sporting shoes? Do you, boys?

No, sir.

What is it you don't see Our Lord doing?

Hanging on the cross and sporting shoes, sir.

Now if I hear of one boy in this class jeering and sneering at McCourt or his brother over their shoes the stick will come out. What will come out, boys?

The stick, sir.

The stick will sting, boys. The ash plant will whistle through the air, it will land on the backside of the boy that jeers, the boy that sneers. Where will it land, boys?

On the boy that jeers, sir.

And?

The boy that sneers, sir.

The boys bother us no more and we wear our shoes with the rubber tires the few weeks to Easter when the St. Vincent de Paul Society gives us the gift of boots.

*   *   *

If I have to get up in the middle of the night to pee in the bucket I go to the top of the stairs and look down to see if the angel might be on the seventh step. Sometimes I'm sure there's a light there and if everyone's asleep I sit on the step in case the angel might be bringing another baby or just coming for a visit. I ask Mam if the angel just brings the babies and then forgets about them. She says, Of course not. The angel never forgets the babies and comes back to make sure the baby is happy.

I could ask the angel all kinds of questions and I'm sure he'd answer, unless it's a girl angel. But I'm sure a girl angel would answer questions, too. I never heard anyone say they didn't.

I sit on the seventh step a long time and I'm sure the angel is there. I tell him all the things you can't tell your mother or father for fear of being hit on the head or told go out and play. I tell him all about school and how I'm afraid of the master and his stick when he roars at us in Irish and I still don't know what he's talking about because I came from America and the other boys were learning Irish a year before me.

I stay on the seventh step till it gets too cold or Dad gets up and tells me go back to bed. He's the one who told me the angel comes to the seventh step in the first place and you'd think he'd know why I'm sitting there. I told him one night that I was waiting for the angel, and he said, Och, now, Francis, you're a bit of a dreamer.

I get back into bed but I can hear him whisper to my mother. The poor wee lad was sitting on the stairs talking away to an angel.

He laughs and my mother laughs and I think, Isn't it curious the way big people laugh over the angel who brought them a new child.

Before Easter we move back downstairs to Ireland. Easter is better than Christmas because the air is warmer, the walls are not dripping with the damp, and the kitchen isn't a lake anymore, and if we're up early we might catch the sun slanting for a minute through the kitchen window.

In fine weather men sit outside smoking their cigarettes if they have them, looking at the world and watching us play. Women stand with their arms folded, chatting. They don't sit because all they do is stay at home, take care of the children, clean the house and cook a bit and the men need the chairs. The men sit because they're worn out from walking to the Labour Exchange every morning to sign for the dole, discussing the world's problems and wondering what to do with the rest of the day. Some stop at the bookie to study the form and place a shilling or two on a sure thing. Some spend hours in the Carnegie Library reading English and Irish newspapers. A man on the dole needs to keep up with things because all the other men on the dole are experts on what's going on in the world. A man on the dole must be ready in case another man on the dole brings up Hitler or Mussolini or the terrible state of the Chinese millions. A man on the dole goes home after a day with the bookie or the newspaper and his wife will not begrudge him a few minutes with the ease and peace of his cigarette and his tea and time to sit in his chair and think of the world.

Easter is better than Christmas because Dad takes us to the Redemptorist church where all the priests wear white and sing. They're happy because Our Lord is in heaven. I ask Dad if the baby in the crib is dead and he says, No, He was thirty-three when He died and there He is, hanging on the cross. I don't understand how He grew up so fast that He's hanging there with a hat made of thorns and blood every-where, dripping from His head, His hands, His feet, and a big hole near His belly.

Dad says I'll understand when I grow up. He tells me that all the time now and I want to be big like him so that I can understand everything. It must be lovely to wake up in the morning and understand everything. I wish I could be like all the big people in the church, standing and kneeling and praying and understanding everything.

At the Mass people go up to the altar and the priest puts something into their mouths. They come back to their seats with their heads down, their mouths moving. Malachy says he's hungry and he wants some, too. Dad says, Shush, that's Holy Communion, the body and blood of Our Lord.

But, Dad.

Shush, it's a mystery.

There's no use asking more questions. If you ask a question they tell you it's a mystery, you'll understand when you grow up, be a good boy, ask your mother, ask your father, for the love o' Jesus leave me alone, go out and play.

Dad gets his first job in Limerick at the cement factory and Mam is happy. She won't have to stand in the queue at the St. Vincent de Paul Society asking for clothes and boots for Malachy and me. She says it's not begging, it's charity, but Dad says it's begging and shameful. Mam says she can now pay off the few pounds she owes at Kathleen O'Connell's shop and she can pay back what she owes her own mother. She hates to be under obligation to anyone, especially her own mother.

The cement factory is miles outside Limerick and that means Dad has to be out of the house by six in the morning. He doesn't mind because he's used to the long walks. The night before Mam makes him a flask of tea, a sandwich, a hard-boiled egg. She feels sorry for him the way he has to walk three miles out and three miles back. A bicycle would be handy but you'd have to be working a year for the price of it.

Friday is payday and Mam is out of the bed early, cleaning the house and singing.

Anyone can see why I wanted your kiss,
It had to be and the reason is this . . .

There isn't much to clean in the house. She sweeps the kitchen floor and the floor of Italy upstairs. She washes the four jam jars we use for mugs. She says if Dad's job lasts we'll get proper cups and maybe saucers and some day, with the help of God and His Blessed Mother, we'll have sheets on the bed and if we save a long time a blanket or two instead of those old coats which people must have left behind during the Great Famine. She boils water and washes the rags that keep Michael from shitting all over the pram and the house itself. Oh, she says, we'll have a lovely tea when your Pop brings home the wages tonight.

Pop. She's in a good mood.

Sirens and whistles go off all over the city when the men finish work at half-past five. Malachy and I are excited because we know that when your father works and brings home the wages you get the Friday Penny. We know this from other boys whose fathers work and we know that after your tea you can go to Kathleen O'Connell's shop and buy sweets. If your mother is in a good mood she might even give you tuppence to go to the Lyric Cinema the next day to see a film with James Cagney.

The men who work in factories and shops in the city are coming into the lanes to have their supper, wash themselves and go to the pub. The women go to the films at the Coliseum or the Lyric Cinema. They buy sweets and Wild Woodbine cigarettes and if their husbands are working a long time they treat themselves to boxes of Black Magic chocolates. They love the romance films and they have a great time crying their eyes out when there's an unhappy ending or a handsome lover goes away to be shot by Hindus and other non-Catholics.

We have to wait a long time for Dad to walk the miles from the cement factory. We can't have our tea till he's home and that's very hard because you smell the cooking of other families in the lane. Mam says it's a good thing payday is Friday when you can't eat meat because the smell of bacon or sausages in other houses would drive her out of her mind. We can still have bread and cheese and a nice jam jar of tea with lashings of milk and sugar and what more do you want?

The women are gone to the cinemas, the men are in the pubs, and still Dad isn't home. Mam says it's a long way to the cement factory even if he's a fast walker. She says that but her eyes are watery and she's not singing anymore. She's sitting by the fire smoking a Wild Woodbine she got on credit from Kathleen O'Connell. The fag is the only luxury she has and she'll never forget Kathleen for her goodness. She doesn't know how long she can keep the water boiling in this kettle. There's no use making the tea till Dad gets home because it will be stewed, coddled, boiled and unfit to drink. Malachy says he's hungry and she gives him a piece of bread and cheese to keep him going. She says, This job could be the saving of us. 'Tis hard enough for him to get a job with his northern accent and if he loses this one I don't know what we're going to do.

The darkness is in the lane and we have to light a candle. She has to give us our tea and bread and cheese because we're so hungry we can't wait another minute. She sits at the table, eats a bit of bread and cheese, smokes her Wild Woodbine. She goes to the door to see if Dad is coming down the lane and she talks about the paydays when we searched for him all over Brooklyn. She says, Some day we'll all go back to America and we'll have a nice warm place to live and a lavatory down the hall like the one in Classon Avenue and not this filthy thing outside our door.

The women are coming home from the cinemas, laughing, and the men, singing, from the pubs. Mam says there's no use waiting up any longer. If Dad stays in the pubs till closing time there will be nothing left from his wages and we might as well go to bed. She lies in her bed with Michael in her arms. It's quiet in the lane and I can hear her crying even though she pulls an old coat over her face and I can hear in the distance, my father.

I know it's my father because he's the only one in Limerick who sings that song from the North, Roddy McCorley goes to die on the bridge of Toome today. He comes round the corner at the top of the lane and starts Kevin Barry. He sings a verse, stops, holds on to a wall, cries over Kevin Barry. People stick their heads out windows and doors and tell him, For Jasus' sake, put a sock in it. Some of us have to get up in the morning for work. Go home and sing your feckin' patriotic songs.

He stands in the middle of the lane and tells the world to step outside, he's ready to fight, ready to fight and die for Ireland, which is more than he can say for the men of Limerick, who are known the length and breadth of the world for collaborating with the perfidious Saxons.

He's pushing in our door and singing,

> And if, when all a vigil keep,
> The West's asleep, the West's asleep!
> Alas! and well my Erin weep,
> That Connacht lies in slumber deep,
> But hark! a voice like thunder spake
> 'The West's awake! the West's awake!
> Sing, Oh, hurrah, let England quake,
> We'll watch till death for Erin's sake!'

He calls from the bottom of the stairs, Angela, Angela, is there a drop of tea in this house?

She doesn't answer and he calls again, Francis, Malachy, come down here, boys. I have the Friday Penny for you.

I want to go down and get the Friday Penny but Mam is sobbing with the coat over her mouth and Malachy says, I don't want his old Friday Penny. He can keep it.

Dad is stumbling up the stairs, making a speech about how

we all have to die for Ireland. He lights a match and touches it to the candle by Mam's bed. He holds the candle over his head and marches around the room, singing,

See who comes over the red-blossomed heather,
Their green banners kissing the pure mountain air,
Heads erect, eyes to front, stepping proudly together,
Sure freedom sits throned on each proud spirit there.

Michael wakes and lets out a loud cry, the Hannons are banging on the wall next door, Mam is telling Dad he's a disgrace and why doesn't he get out of the house altogether.

He stands in the middle of the floor with the candle over his head. He pulls a penny from his pocket and waves it to Malachy and me. Your Friday Penny, boys, he says. I want you to jump out of that bed and line up here like two soldiers and promise to die for Ireland and I'll give the two of you the Friday Penny.

Malachy sits up in the bed. I don't want it, he says.

And I tell him I don't want it, either.

Dad stands for a minute, swaying, and puts the penny back in his pocket. He turns toward Mam and she says, You're not sleeping in this bed tonight. He makes his way downstairs with the candle, sleeps on a chair, misses work in the morning, loses the job at the cement factory, and we're back on the dole again.

IV

The master says it's time to prepare for First Confession and First Communion, to know and remember all the questions and answers in the catechism, to become good Catholics, to know the difference between right and wrong, to die for the Faith if called on.

The master says it's a glorious thing to die for the Faith and Dad says it's a glorious thing to die for Ireland and I wonder if there's anyone in the world who would like us to live. My brothers are dead and my sister is dead and I wonder if they died for Ireland or the Faith. Dad says they were too young to die for anything. Mam says it was disease and starvation and him never having a job. Dad says, Och, Angela, puts on his cap and goes for a long walk.

The master says we're each to bring threepence for the First Communion catechism with the green cover. The catechism has all the questions and answers we have to know by heart before we can receive First Communion. Older boys in the fifth class have the thick Confirmation catechism with the red cover and that costs sixpence. I'd love to be big and important and parade around with the red Confirmation catechism but I don't think I'll live that long the way I'm expected to die for this or that. I want to ask why there are so many big people who haven't died for Ireland or the Faith but I know if you ask a question like that you get you the thump on the head or you're told go out and play.

It's very handy to have Mikey Molloy living around the corner from me. He's eleven, he has fits and behind his back we call him Molloy the Fit. People in the lane say the fit is an affliction and now I know what affliction means. Mikey knows everything because he has visions in his fits and he reads books. He's the expert in the lane on Girls' Bodies and Dirty Things in General and he promises, I'll tell you everything, Frankie, when you're eleven like me and you're not so thick and ignorant.

It's a good thing he says Frankie so I'll know he's talking to me because he has crossed eyes and you never know who he's looking at. If he's talking to Malachy and I think he's talking to me he might go into a rage and have a fit that will carry him off. He says it's a gift to have crossed eyes because you're like a god looking two ways at once and if you had crossed eyes in the ancient Roman times you had no problem getting a good job. If you look at pictures of Roman emperors you'll see there's always a great hint of crossed eyes. When he's not having the fit he sits on the ground at the top of the lane reading the books his father brings home from the Carnegie Library. His mother says books books books, he's ruining his eyes with the reading, he needs an operation to straighten them but who'll pay for it. She tells him if he keeps on straining his eyes they'll float together till he has one eye in the middle of his head. Ever after his father calls him Cyclops, who is in a Greek story.

Nora Molloy knows my mother from the queues at the St. Vincent de Paul Society. She tells Mam that Mikey has more sense than twelve men drinking pints in a pub. He knows the names of all the Popes from St. Peter to Pius the Eleventh. He's only eleven but he's a man, oh, a man indeed. Many a week he saves the family from pure starvation. He borrows a handcart from Aidan Farrell and knocks on doors all over Limerick to see if there are people who want coal or turf delivered, and down the Dock Road he'll go to haul back great bags a hundredweight or more. He'll run messages for old people who can't walk and if they don't have a penny to give him a prayer will do.

If he earns a little money he hands it over to his mother, who loves her Mikey. He is her world, her heart's blood, her pulse, and if anything ever happened to him they might as well stick her in the lunatic asylum and throw away the key.

Mikey's father, Peter, is a great champion. He wins bets in the pubs by drinking more pints than anyone. All he has to do is go out to the jakes, stick his finger down his throat and bring it all up so that he can start another round. Peter is such a champion he can stand in the jakes and throw up without using his finger. He's such a champion they could chop off his fingers and he'd carry on regardless. He wins all that money but doesn't bring it home. Sometimes he's like my father and drinks the dole itself and that's why Nora Molloy is often carted off to the lunatic asylum demented with worry over her hungry famishing family. She knows as long as you're in the asylum you're safe from the world and its torments, there's nothing you can do, you're protected, and what's the use of worrying. It's well known that all the lunatics in the asylum have to be dragged in but she's the only one that has to be dragged out, back to her five children and the champion of all pint drinkers.

You can tell when Nora Molloy is ready for the asylum when you see her children running around white with flour from poll to toe. That happens when Peter drinks the dole money and leaves her desperate and she knows the men will come to take her away. You know she's inside frantic with the baking. She wants to make sure the children won't starve while she's gone and she roams Limerick begging for flour. She goes to priests, nuns, Protestants, Quakers. She goes to Rank's Flour Mills and begs for the sweepings from the floor. She bakes day and night. Peter begs her to stop but she screams, This is what comes of drinking the dole. He tells her the bread will only go stale. There's no use talking to her. Bake bake bake. If she had the money she'd bake all the flour in Limerick and regions beyond. If the men didn't come from the lunatic asylum to take her away she'd bake till she fell to the floor.

The children stuff themselves with so much bread people in the lane say they're looking like loaves. Still the bread goes stale and Mikey is so bothered by the waste he talks to a rich woman with a cookbook and she tells him make bread pudding. He boils the hard bread in water and sour milk and throws in a cup of sugar and his brother loves it even if that's all they have the fortnight their mother is in the lunatic asylum.

My father says, Do they take her away because she's gone mad baking bread or does she go mad baking bread because they're taking her away?

Nora comes home calm as if she had been at the seaside. She always says, Where's Mikey? Is he alive? She worries over Mikey because he's not a proper Catholic and if he had a fit and died who knows where he might wind up in the next life. He's not a proper Catholic because he could never receive his First Communion for fear of getting anything on his tongue that might cause a fit and choke him. The master tried over and over with bits of the *Limerick Leader* but Mikey kept spitting them out till the master got into a state and sent him to the priest, who wrote to the bishop, who said, Don't bother me, handle it yourself. The master sent a note home saying Mikey was to practice receiving Communion with his father or mother but even they couldn't get him to swallow a piece of the *Limerick Leader* in the shape of a wafer. They even tried a piece of bread shaped like the wafer with bread and jam and it was no use. The priest tells Mrs. Molloy not to worry. God moves in mysterious ways His wonders to perform and surely He has a special purpose for Mikey, fits and all. She says, Isn't it remarkable he can swally all kinds of sweets and buns but if he has to swally the body of Our Lord he goes into a fit? Isn't that remarkable? She worries Mikey might have the fit and die and go to hell if he has any class of a sin on his soul though everyone knows he's an angel out of heaven. Mikey tells her God is not going to afflict you with the fit and then boot you into hell on top of it. What kind of a God would do a thing like that?

Are you sure, Mikey?

I am. I read it in a book.

He sits under the lamppost at the top of the lane and laughs over his First Communion day, which was all a cod. He couldn't swallow the wafer but did that stop his mother from parading him around Limerick in his little black suit for The Collection? She said to Mikey, Well, I'm not lying so I'm not. I'm only saying to the neighbors, Here's Mikey in his First Communion suit. That's all I'm saying, mind you. Here's Mikey. If they think you swallied your First Communion who am I to contradict them and disappoint them? Mikey's father said, Don't worry, Cyclops. You have loads of time. Jesus didn't become a proper Catholic till he took the bread and wine at the Last Supper and He was thirty-three years of age. Nora Molloy said, Will you stop calling him Cyclops? He has two eyes in his head and he's not a Greek. But Mikey's father, champion of all pint drinkers, is like my uncle Pa Keating, he doesn't give a fiddler's fart what the world says and that's the way I'd like to be myself.

Mikey tells me the best thing about First Communion is The Collection. Your mother has to get you a new suit somehow so she can show you off to the neighbors and relations and they give you sweets and money and you can go to the Lyric Cinema to see Charlie Chaplin.

What about James Cagney?

Never mind James Cagney. Lots of blather. Charlie Chaplin is your only man. But you have to be with your mother on The Collection. The grown-up people of Limerick are not going to be handing out money to every little Tom Dick and Mick with a First Communion suit that doesn't have his mother with him.

Mikey got over five shillings on his First Communion day and ate so many sweets and buns he threw up in the Lyric

Cinema and Frank Goggin, the ticket man, kicked him out. He says he didn't care because he had money left over and went to the Savoy Cinema the same day for a pirate film and ate Cadbury chocolate and drank lemonade till his stomach stuck out a mile. He can't wait for Confirmation day because you're older, there's another collection and that brings more money than First Communion. He'll go to the cinema the rest of his life, sit next to girls from lanes and do dirty things like an expert. He loves his mother but he'll never get married for fear he might have a wife in and out of the lunatic asylum. What's the use of getting married when you can sit in cinemas and do dirty things with girls from lanes who don't care what they do because they already did it with their brothers. If you don't get married you won't have any children at home bawling for tea and bread and gasping with the fit and looking in every direction with their eyes. When he's older he'll go to the pub like his father, drink pints galore, stick the finger down the throat to bring it all up, drink more pints, win the bets and bring the money home to his mother to keep her from going demented. He says he's not a proper Catholic which means he's doomed so he can do anything he bloody well likes.

He says, I'll tell you more when you grow up, Frankie. You're too young now and you don't know your arse from your elbow.

The master, Mr. Benson, is very old. He roars and spits all over us every day. The boys in the front row hope he has no diseases for it's the spit that carries all the diseases and he might be spreading consumption right and left. He tells us we have to know the catechism backwards, forwards and sideways. We have to know the Ten Commandments, the Seven Virtues, Divine and Moral, the Seven Sacraments, the Seven Deadly Sins. We have to know by heart all the prayers, the Hail Mary, the Our Father, the Confiteor, the Apostles'

Creed, the Act of Contrition, the Litany of the Blessed Virgin Mary. We have to know them in Irish and English and if we forget an Irish word and use English he goes into a rage and goes at us with the stick. If he had his way we'd be learning our religion in Latin, the language of the saints who communed intimately with God and His Holy Mother, the language of the early Christians, who huddled in the catacombs and went forth to die on rack and sword, who expired in the foaming jaws of the ravenous lion. Irish is fine for patriots, English for traitors and informers, but it's the Latin that gains us entrance to heaven itself. It's the Latin the martyrs prayed in when the barbarians pulled out their nails and cut their skin off inch by inch. He tells us we're a disgrace to Ireland and her long sad history, that we'd be better off in Africa praying to bush or tree. He tells us we're hopeless, the worst class he ever had for First Communion but as sure as God made little apples he'll make Catholics of us, he'll beat the idler out of us and the Sanctifying Grace into us.

Brendan Quigley raises his hand. We call him Question Quigley because he's always asking questions. He can't help himself. Sir, he says, what's Sanctifying Grace?

The master rolls his eyes to heaven. He's going to kill Quigley. Instead he barks at him, Never mind what's Sanctifying Grace, Quigley. That's none of your business. You're here to learn the catechism and do what you're told. You're not here to be asking questions. There are too many people wandering the world asking questions and that's what has us in the state we're in and if I find any boy in this class asking questions I won't be responsible for what happens. Do you hear me, Quigley?

I do.

I do what?

I do, sir.

He goes on with his speech, There are boys in this class who will never know the Sanctifying Grace. And why? Because of the greed. I have heard them abroad in the schoolyard talking about First Communion day, the happiest day of your life. Are they talking about receiving the body and blood of Our Lord? Oh, no. Those greedy little blaguards are talking about the money they'll get, The Collection. They'll go from house to house in their little suits like beggars for The Collection. And will they take any of that money and send it to the little black babies in Africa? Will they think of those little pagans doomed forever for lack of baptism and knowledge of the True Faith? Little black babies denied knowledge of the Mystical Body of Christ? Limbo is packed with little black babies flying around and crying for their mothers because they'll never be admitted to the ineffable presence of Our Lord and the glorious company of saints, martyrs, virgins. Oh, no. It's off to the cinemas, our First Communion boys run to wallow in the filth spewed across the world by the devil's henchmen in Hollywood. Isn't that right, McCourt?

'Tis, sir.

Question Quigley raises his hand again. There are looks around the room and we wonder if it's suicide he's after.

What's henchmen, sir?

The master's face goes white, then red. His mouth tightens and opens and spit flies everywhere. He walks to Question and drags him from his seat. He snorts and stutters and his spit flies around the room. He flogs Question across the shoulders, the bottom, the legs. He grabs him by the collar and drags him to the front of the room.

Look at this specimen, he roars.

Question is shaking and crying. I'm sorry, sir.

The master mocks him. I'm sorry, sir. What are you sorry for?

I'm sorry I asked the question. I'll never ask a question again, sir.

The day you do, Quigley, will be the day you wish God would take you to His bosom. What will you wish, Quigley?

That God will take me to His bosom, sir.

Go back to your seat, you omadhaun, you poltroon, you thing from the far dark corner of a bog.

He sits down with the stick before him on the desk. He tells Question to stop the whimpering and be a man. If he hears a single boy in this class asking foolish questions or talking about The Collection again he'll flog that boy till the blood spurts.

What will I do, boys?

Flog the boy, sir.

Till?

Till the blood spurts, sir.

Now, Clohessy, what is the Sixth Commandment?

Thou shalt not commit adultery.

Thou shalt not commit adultery what?

Thou shalt not commit adultery, sir.

And what is adultery, Clohessy?

Impure thoughts, impure words, impure deeds, sir.

Good, Clohessy. You're a good boy. You may be slow and forgetful in the sir department and you may not have a shoe to your foot but you're powerful with the Sixth Commandment and that will keep you pure.

Paddy Clohessy has no shoe to his foot, his mother shaves his head to keep the lice away, his eyes are red, his nose always snotty. The sores on his kneecaps never heal because he picks at the scabs and puts them in his mouth. His clothes are rags he has to share with his six brothers and a sister and when he comes to school with a bloody nose or a black eye you know he had a fight over the clothes that morning. He hates school. He's seven going on eight, the biggest and oldest boy in the class, and he can't wait to grow up and be fourteen so that he can run away and pass for seventeen and join the English army and go to India where it's nice and warm and he'll live in a tent with a dark girl with the red dot on her forehead and he'll be lying there eating figs, that's what they eat in India, figs, and she'll cook the curry day and night and plonk on a ukelele and when he has enough money he'll send for the whole family and they'll all live in the tent especially his poor father who's at home coughing up great gobs of blood because of the consumption. When my mother sees Paddy on the street she says, Wisha, look at that poor child. He's a skeleton with rags and if they were making a film about the famine he'd surely be put in the middle of it.

I think Paddy likes me because of the raisin and I feel a bit guilty because I wasn't that generous in the first place. The master, Mr. Benson, said the government was going to give us the free lunch so we wouldn't have to be going home in the freezing weather. He led us down to a cold room in the dungeons of Leamy's School where the charwoman, Nellie Ahearn, was handing out the half pint of milk and the raisin bun. The milk was frozen in the bottles and we had to melt it between our thighs. The boys joked and said the bottles would freeze our things off and the master roared, Any more of that talk and I'll warm the bottles on the backs of yeer heads. We all searched our raisin buns for a raisin but Nellie said they must have forgotten to put them in and she'd inquire from the man who delivered. We searched again every day till at last I found a raisin in my bun and held it up. The boys started grousing and said they wanted a raisin and Nellie said it wasn't her fault. She'd ask the man again. Now the boys were begging me for the raisin and offering me everything, a slug of their milk, a pencil, a comic book. Toby Mackey said I could have his sister and Mr. Benson heard him and took him out to the hallway and knocked him around till he howled. I wanted the raisin for myself but I saw Paddy Clohessy standing in the corner with no shoes and the room was freezing and he was shivering like a dog that had been kicked and I always felt sad over kicked dogs so I walked over and gave Paddy the raisin because I didn't know what else to do and all the boys yelled that I was a fool and a feckin' eejit and I'd regret the day and after I handed the raisin to Paddy I longed for it but it was too late now because he pushed it right into his mouth and gulped it and looked at me and said nothing and I said in my head what kind of an eejit are you to be giving away your raisin.

Mr. Benson gave me a look and said nothing and Nellie Ahearn said, You're a great oul' Yankee, Frankie.

The priest will come soon to examine us on the catechism and everything else. The master himself has to show us how to receive Holy Communion. He tells us gather round him. He fills his hat with the *Limerick Leader* torn into little bits. He gives Paddy Clohessy the hat, kneels on the floor, tells Paddy to take one bit of paper and place it on his tongue. He shows us how to stick out the tongue, receive the bit of paper, hold it a moment, draw in the tongue, fold your hands in prayer, look toward heaven, close your eyes in adoration, wait for the paper to melt in your mouth, swallow it, and thank God for the gift, the Sanctifying Grace wafting in on the odor of sanctity. When he sticks out his tongue we have to hold in the laugh because we never saw a big purple tongue before. He opens his eyes to catch the boys who are giggling but he can't say anything because he still has God on his tongue and it's a holy moment. He gets off his knees and tells us kneel around the classroom for the Holy Communion practice. He goes around the room placing bits of paper on our tongues and mumbling in Latin. Some boys giggle and he roars at them that if the giggling doesn't stop it's not Holy Communion they'll be getting but the Last Rites and what is that sacrament called, McCourt?

Extreme Unction, sir.

That's right, McCourt. Not bad for a Yank from the sinful shores of Amerikay.

He tells us we have to be careful to stick out our tongues

134

far enough so that the Communion wafer won't fall to the floor. He says, That's the worst thing that can happen to a priest. If the wafer slides off your tongue that poor priest has to get down on his two knees, pick it up with his own tongue and lick the floor around it in case it bounced from one spot to another. The priest could get a splinter that would make his tongue swell to the size of a turnip and that's enough to choke you and kill you entirely.

He tells us that next to a relic of the True Cross the Communion wafer is the holiest thing in the world and our First Communion is the holiest moment in our lives. Talking about First Communion makes the master all excited. He paces back and forth, waves his stick, tells us we must never forget that the moment the Holy Communion is placed on our tongues we become members of that most glorious congregation, the One, Holy, Roman, Catholic and Apostolic Church, that for two thousand years men, women and children have died for the Faith, that the Irish have nothing to be ashamed of in the martyr department. Haven't we provided martyrs galore? Haven't we bared our necks to the Protestant ax? Haven't we mounted the scaffold, singing, as if embarking on a picnic, haven't we, boys?

We have, sir.

What have we done, boys?

Bared our necks to the Protestant ax, sir.

And?

Mounted the scaffold singing, sir.

As if?

Embarking on a picnic, sir.

He says that, perhaps, in this class there is a future priest or a martyr for the Faith, though he doubts it very much for we are the laziest gang of ignoramuses it has ever been his misfortune to teach.

But it takes all kinds, he says, and surely God had some purpose when He sent the likes of ye to infest this earth. Surely God had a purpose when among us He sent Clohessy with no shoes, Quigley with his damnable questions and McCourt heavy with sin from America. And remember this, boys, God did not send His only begotten Son to hang on the cross so that ye can go around on yeer First Communion day with the paws clutching for The Collection. Our Lord died so that ye might be redeemed. It is enough to receive the gift of Faith. Are ye listening to me?

We are, sir.

And what's enough?

The gift of Faith, sir.

Good. Go home.

At night three of us sit under the light pole at the top of the lane reading, Mikey, Malachy and I. The Molloys are like us with their father drinking the dole money or the wages and leaving no money for candles or paraffin oil for the lamp. Mikey reads books and the rest of us read comic books. His father, Peter, brings books from the Carnegie Library so that he'll have something to do when he's not drinking pints or when he's looking after the family anytime Mrs. Molloy is in the lunatic asylum. He lets Mikey read any book he likes and now Mikey is reading this book about Cuchulain and talking as if he knows everything about him. I want to tell him I knew all about Cuchulain when I was three going on four, that I saw Cuchulain in Dublin, that Cuchulain thinks nothing of dropping into my dreams. I want to tell him stop talking about Cuchulain, he's mine, he was mine years ago when I was young, but I can't because Mikey reads us a story I never heard of before, a dirty story about Cuchulain which I can never tell my father or mother, the story of how Emer became Cuchulain's wife.

Cuchulain was getting to be an old man of twenty-one. He was lonely and wanted to get married, which made him weak, says Mikey, and got him killed in the end. All the women in Ireland were mad about Cuchulain and they wanted to marry him. He said that would be grand, he wouldn't mind marrying all the women of Ireland. If he could fight all the men of Ireland why couldn't he marry all the women? But the King, Conor MacNessa, said, That's all very well for you, Cu, but the men of Ireland don't want to be lonely in the far reaches of the night. The King decided there would have to be a contest to see who would marry Cuchulain and it would be a pissing contest. All the women of Ireland assembled on the plains of Muirthemne to see who could piss the longest and it was Emer. She was the champion woman pisser of Ireland and married Cuchulain and that's why to this day she is called Great Bladdered Emer.

Mikey and Malachy laugh over this story though I don't think Malachy understands it. He's young and far from his First Communion and he's only laughing over the piss word. Then Mikey tells me I've committed a sin by listening to a story that has that word in it and when I go to my First Confession I'll have to tell the priest. Malachy says, That's right. Piss is a bad word and you have to tell the priest because 'tis a sin word.

I don't know what to do. How can I go to the priest and tell him this terrible thing in my First Confession? All the boys know what sins they're going to tell so that they'll get the First Communion and make The Collection and go to see James Cagney and eat sweets and cakes at the Lyric Cinema. The master helped us with our sins and everyone has the same sins. I hit my brother. I told a lie. I stole a penny from my mother's purse. I disobeyed my parents, I ate a sausage on Friday.

But now I have a sin no one else has and the priest is going to be shocked and drag me out of the confession box into the aisle and out into the street where everyone will know I listened to a story about Cuchulain's wife being the champion woman pisser in all Ireland. I'll never be able to make my First Communion and mothers will hold their small children up and point at me and say, Look at him. He's like Mikey Molloy, never made his First Communion, wandering around in a state of sin, never made The Collection, never saw James Cagney.

I'm sorry I ever heard of First Communion and The Collection. I'm sick and I don't want any tea or bread or anything. Mam tells Dad it's a strange thing when a child won't have his bread and tea and Dad says, Och, he's just nervous over the First Communion. I want to go over to him and sit on his lap and tell him what Mikey Molloy did to me but I'm too big to be sitting on laps and if I did Malachy would go out in the lane and tell everyone I was a big baby. I'd like to tell my troubles to the Angel on the Seventh Step but he's busy bringing babies to mothers all over the world. Still, I'll ask Dad.

Dad, does the Angel on the Seventh Step have other jobs besides bringing babies?

He does.

Would the Angel on the Seventh Step tell you what to do if you didn't know what to do?

Och, he would, son, he would. That's the job of an angel, even the one on the seventh step.

Dad goes for a long walk, Mam takes Michael and goes to see Grandma, Malachy plays in the lane, and I have the house to myself so that I can sit on the seventh step and talk to the angel. I know he's there because the seventh step feels warmer than the other steps and there's a light in my head. I tell him my troubles and I hear a voice. Fear not, says the voice.

He's talking backward and I tell him I don't know what he's talking about.

Do not fear, says the voice. Tell the priest your sin and you'll be forgiven.

Next morning I'm up early and drinking tea with Dad and telling him about the Angel on the Seventh Step. He places his hand on my forehead to see if I'm feeling all right.

He asks if I'm sure I had a light in my head and heard a voice and what did the voice say?

I tell him the voice said Fear not and that means Do not fear.

Dad tells me the angel is right, I shouldn't be afraid, and I tell him what Mikey Molloy did to me. I tell him all about Great Bladdered Emer and I even use the piss word because the angel said, Fear not. Dad puts down his jam jar of tea and pats the back of my hand. Och, och, och, he says, and I wonder if he's going demented like Mrs. Molloy, in and out of the lunatic asylum, but he says, Is that what you were worried about last night?

I tell him it is and he says it's not a sin and I don't have to tell the priest.

But the Angel on the Seventh Step said I should.

All right. Tell the priest if you like but the Angel on the Seventh Step said that only because you didn't tell me first. Isn't it better to be able to tell your father your troubles rather than an angel who is a light and a voice in your head?

'Tis, Dad.

The day before First Communion the master leads us to St. Joseph's Church for First Confession. We march in pairs and if we so much as move a lip on the streets of Limerick he'll kill us on the spot and send us to hell bloated with sin. That doesn't stop the bragging about the big sins. Willie Harold is whispering about his big sin, that he looked at his sister's naked body. Paddy Hartigan says he stole ten shillings from his aunt's purse and made himself sick with ice cream and chips. Question Quigley says he ran away from home and spent half the night in a ditch with four goats. I try to tell them about Cuchulain and Emer but the master catches me talking and gives me a thump on the head.

We kneel in the pews by the confession box and I wonder if my Emer sin is as bad as looking at your sister's naked body because I know now that some things in the world are worse than others. Thats why they have different sins, the sacrilege, the mortal sin, the venial sin. Then the masters and grown-up people in general talk about the unforgivable sin, which is a great mystery. No one knows what it is and you wonder how you can know if you've committed it if you don't know what it is. If I tell a priest about Great Bladdered Emer and the pissing contest he might say that's the unforgivable sin and kick me out of the confession box and I'll be disgraced all over Limerick and doomed to hell tormented forever by devils who have nothing else to do but stab me with hot pitchforks till I'm worn out.

I try to listen to Willie's confession when he goes in but all I can hear is a hissing from the priest and when Willie comes out he's crying.

It's my turn. The confession box is dark and there's a big crucifix hanging over my head. I can hear a boy mumbling his confession on the other side. I wonder if there's any use trying to talk to the Angel on the Seventh Step. I know he's not supposed to be hanging around confession boxes but I feel the light in my head and the voice is telling me, Fear not.

The panel slides back before my face and the priest says, Yes, my child?

Bless me, Father, for I have sinned. This is my First Confession.

Yes, my child, and what sins have you committed?

I told a lie. I hit my brother. I took a penny from my mother's purse. I said a curse.

Yes, my child. Anything else?

I, I listened to a story about Cuchulain and Emer.

Surely that's not a sin, my child. After all we are assured by certain writers that Cuchulain turned Catholic in his last moments as did his King, Conor MacNessa.

'Tis about Emer, Father, and how she married him.

How was that, my child?

She won him in a pissing contest.

There is heavy breathing. The priest has his hand over his mouth and he's making choking sounds and talking to himself, Mother o' God.

Who, who told you that story, my child?

Mikey Molloy, Father.

And where did he hear it?

He read it in a book, Father.

Ah, a book. Books can be dangerous for children, my child. Turn your mind from those silly stories and think of the lives of the saints. Think of St. Joseph, the Little Flower, the sweet and gentle St. Francis of Assisi, who loved the birds of the air and the beasts of the field. Will you do that, my child?

I will, Father.

Are there any other sins, my child?

No, Father.

For your penance say three Hail Marys, three Our Fathers, and say a special prayer for me.

I will. Father, was that the worst sin?

What do you mean?

Am I the worst of all the boys, Father?

No, my child, you have a long way to go. Now say an Act of Contrition and remember Our Lord watches you every minute. God bless you, my child.

First Communion day is the happiest day of your life because of The Collection and James Cagney at the Lyric Cinema. The night before I was so excited I couldn't sleep till dawn. I'd still be sleeping if my grandmother hadn't come banging at the door.

Get up! Get up! Get that child outa the bed. Happiest day of his life an' him snorin' above in the bed.

I ran to the kitchen. Take off that shirt, she said. I took off the shirt and she pushed me into a tin tub of icy cold water. My mother scrubbed me, my grandmother scrubbed me. I was raw, I was red.

They dried me. They dressed me in my black velvet First Communion suit with the white frilly shirt, the short pants, the white stockings, the black patent leather shoes. Around my arm they tied a white satin bow and on my lapel they pinned the Sacred Heart of Jesus, a picture of the Sacred Heart, with blood dripping from it, flames erupting all around it and on top a nasty-looking crown of thorns.

Come here till I comb your hair, said Grandma. Look at that mop, it won't lie down. You didn't get that hair from my side of the family. That's that North of Ireland hair you got from your father. That's the kind of hair you see on Presbyterians. If your mother had married a proper decent Limerickman you wouldn't have this standing up, North of Ireland, Presbyterian hair.

She spat twice on my head.

Grandma, will you please stop spitting on my head.

If you have anything to say, shut up. A little spit won't kill you. Come on, we'll be late for the Mass.

We ran to the church. My mother panted along behind with Michael in her arms. We arrived at the church just in time to see the last of the boys leaving the altar rail where the priest stood with the chalice and the host, glaring at me. Then he placed on my tongue the wafer, the body and blood of Jesus. At last, at last.

It's on my tongue. I draw it back.

It stuck.

I had God glued to the roof of my mouth. I could hear the master's voice, Don't let that host touch your teeth for if you bite God in two you'll roast in hell for eternity.

I tried to get God down with my tongue but the priest hissed at me, Stop that clucking and get back to your seat.

God was good. He melted and I swallowed Him and now, at last, I was a member of the True Church, an official sinner.

When the Mass ended there they were at the door of the

church, my mother with Michael in her arms, my grand-mother. They each hugged me to their bosoms. They each told me it was the happiest day of my life. They each cried all over my head and after my grandmother's contribution that morning my head was a swamp.

Mam, can I go now and make The Collection?

She said, After you have a little breakfast.

No, said Grandma. You're not making no collection till you've had a proper First Communion breakfast at my house. Come on.

We followed her. She banged pots and rattled pans and complained that the whole world expected her to be at their beck and call. I ate the egg, I ate the sausage, and when I reached for more sugar for my tea she slapped my hand away.

Go aisy with that sugar. Is it a millionaire you think I am? An American? Is it bedecked in glitterin' jewelry you think I am? Smothered in fancy furs?

The food churned in my stomach. I gagged. I ran to her backyard and threw it all up. Out she came.

Look at what he did. Thrun up his First Communion breakfast. Thrun up the body and blood of Jesus. I have God in me backyard. What am I goin' to do? I'll take him to the Jesuits for they know the sins of the Pope himself.

She dragged me through the streets of Limerick. She told the neighbors and passing strangers about God in her back-yard. She pushed me into the confession box.

In the name of the Father, the Son, the Holy Ghost. Bless me, Father, for I have sinned. It's a day since my last confession.

A day? And what sins have you committed in a day, my child?

I overslept. I nearly missed my First Communion. My grandmother said I have standing up, North of Ireland, Pres-byterian hair. I threw up my First Communion breakfast. Now Grandma says she has God in her backyard and what should she do.

The priest is like the First Confession priest. He has the heavy breathing and the choking sounds.

Ah . . . ah . . . tell your grandmother to wash God away with a little water and for your penance say one Hail Mary and one Our Father. Say a prayer for me and God bless you, my child.

Grandma and Mam were waiting close to the confession box. Grandma said, Were you telling jokes to that priest in the confession box? If 'tis a thing I ever find out you were telling jokes to Jesuits I'll tear the bloody kidneys outa you. Now what did he say about God in me backyard?

He said wash Him away with a little water, Grandma.

Holy water or ordinary water?

He didn't say, Grandma.

Well, go back and ask him.

But, Grandma . . .

She pushed me back into the confessional.

Bless me, Father, for I have sinned, it's a minute since my last confession.

A minute! Are you the boy that was just here?

I am, Father.

What is it now?

My grandma says, Holy water or ordinary water?

Ordinary water, and tell your grandmother not to be bothering me again.

I told her, Ordinary water, Grandma, and he said don't be bothering him again.

Don't be bothering him again. That bloody ignorant bog-trotter.

I asked Mam, Can I go now and make The Collection? I want to see James Cagney.

Grandma said, You can forget about The Collection and James Cagney because you're not a proper Catholic the way you left God on the ground. Come on, go home.

Mam said, Wait a minute. That's my son. That's my son on his First Communion day. He's going to see James Cagney.

144

No he's not.

Yes he is.

Grandma said, Take him then to James Cagney and see if that will save his Presbyterian North of Ireland American soul. Go ahead.

She pulled her shawl around her and walked away.

Mam said, God, it's getting very late for The Collection and you'll never see James Cagney. We'll go to the Lyric Cinema and see if they'll let you in anyway in your First Communion suit.

We met Mikey Molloy on Barrington Street. He asked if I was going to the Lyric and I said I was trying. Trying? he said. You don't have money?

I was ashamed to say no but I had to and he said, That's all right. I'll get you in. I'll create a diversion.

What's a diversion?

I have the money to go and when I get in I'll pretend to have the fit and the ticket man will be out of his mind and you can slip in when I let out the big scream. I'll be watching the door and when I see you in I'll have a miraculous recovery. That's a diversion. That's what I do to get my brothers in all the time.

Mam said, Oh, I don't know about that, Mikey. Wouldn't that be a sin and surely you wouldn't want Frank to commit a sin on his First Communion day.

Mikey said if there was a sin it would be on his soul and he wasn't a proper Catholic anyway so it didn't matter. He let out his scream and I slipped in and sat next to Question Quigley and the ticket man, Frank Goggin, was so worried over Mikey he never noticed. It was a thrilling film but sad in the end because James Cagney was a public enemy and when they shot him they wrapped him in bandages and threw him in the door, shocking his poor old Irish mother, and that was the end of my First Communion day.

V

Grandma won't talk to Mam anymore because of what I did with God in her backyard. Mam doesn't talk to her sister, Aunt Aggie, or her brother Uncle Tom. Dad doesn't talk to anyone in Mam's family and they don't talk to him because he's from the North and he has the odd manner. No one talks to Uncle Tom's wife, Jane, because she's from Galway and she has the look of a Spaniard. Everyone talks to Mam's brother Uncle Pat, because he was dropped on his head, he's simple, and he sells newspapers. Everyone calls him The Abbot or Ab Sheehan and no one knows why. Everyone talks to Uncle Pa Keating because he was gassed in the war and married Aunt Aggie and if they didn't talk to him he wouldn't give a fiddler's fart anyway and that's why the men in South's pub call him a gas man.

That's the way I'd like to be in the world, a gas man, not giving a fiddler's fart, and that's what I tell the Angel on the Seventh Step till I remember you're not supposed to say fart in the presence of an angel.

Uncle Tom and Galway Jane have children but we're not supposed to talk to them because our parents are not talking. They have a son and daughter, Gerry and Peggy, and Mam will yell at us for talking to them but we don't know how not to talk to our cousins.

People in families in the lanes of Limerick have their ways of not talking to each other and it takes years of practice. There are people who don't talk to each other because their fathers were on opposite sides in the Civil War in 1922. If a man goes off and joins the English army his family might as well move to another part of Limerick where there are families with men in the English army. If anyone in your family was the least way friendly to the English in the last eight hundred years it will be brought up and thrown in your face and you might as well move to Dublin where no one cares. There are families that are ashamed of themselves because their forefathers gave up their religion for the sake of a bowl of Protestant soup during the Famine and those families are known ever after as soupers. It's a terrible thing to be a souper because you're doomed forever to the souper part of hell. It's even worse to be an informer. The master at school said that everytime the Irish were about to demolish the English in a fair fight a filthy informer betrayed them. A man who's discovered to be an informer deserves to be hanged or, even worse, to have no one talk to him for if no one talks to you you're better off hanging at the end of a rope.

In every lane there's always someone not talking to someone or everyone not talking to someone or someone not talking to everyone. You can always tell when people are not talking by the way they pass each other. The women hoist their noses, tighten their mouths and turn their faces away. If the woman is wearing a shawl she takes a corner and flings it over her shoulder as if to say, One word or look from you, you ma-faced bitch, and I'll tear the countenance from the front of your head.

It's bad when Grandma won't talk to us because we can't run to her when we need to borrow sugar or tea or milk. There's no use going to Aunt Aggie. She'll only bite your head off. Go home, she'll say, and tell your father to get off his northern arse and get a job like the decent men of Limerick.

They say she's always angry because she has red hair or she has red hair because she's always angry.

Mam is friendly with Bridey Hannon, who lives next door with her mother and father. Mam and Bridey talk all the time. When my father goes for his long walk Bridey comes in and she and Mam sit by the fire drinking tea and smoking cigarettes. If Mam has nothing in the house Bridey brings tea, sugar and milk. Sometimes they use the same tea leaves over and over and Mam says the tea is stewed, coddled and boiled.

Mam and Bridey sit so close to the fire their shins turn red and purple and blue. They talk for hours and they whisper and laugh over secret things. We're not supposed to hear the secret things so we're told go out and play. I often sit on the seventh step listening and they have no notion I'm there. It might be lashing rain out but Mam says, Rain or no, out you go, and she'll tell us, If you see your father coming, run in and tell me. Mam says to Bridey, Did you ever hear that poem that someone must have made up about me and him?

What poem, Angela?

'Tis called "The Man from the North." I got this poem from Minnie MacAdorey in America.

I never heard that poem. Say it for me.

Mam says the poem but she laughs all through it and I don't know why,

> He came from the North so his words were few
> But his voice was kind and his heart was true.
> And I knew by his eyes that no guile had he,
> So I married my man from the North Country.
>
> Oh, Garryowen may be more gay
> Than this quiet man from beside Lough Neagh
> And I know that the sun shines softly down
> On the river that runs through my native town.
>
> But there's not—and I say it with joy and with pride
> A better man in all Munster wide
> And Limerick town has no happier hearth
> Than mine has been with my man from the North.

> I wish that in Limerick they only knew
> The kind kind neighbors I came unto.
> Small hate or scorn would there ever be
> Between the South and the North Country.

She always repeats the third verse and laughs so hard she's crying and I don't know why. She goes into hysterics when she says,

> And Limerick town has no happier hearth
> Than mine has been with my man from the North.

If he comes back early and sees Bridey in the kitchen the man from the North says, Gossip, gossip, gossip, and stands there with his cap on till she leaves.

Bridey's mother and other people in our lane and lanes beyond will come to the door to ask Dad if he'll write a letter to the government or a relation in a distant place. He sits at the table with his pen and bottle of ink and when the people tell him what to write he says, Och, no, that's not what you want to say, and he writes what he feels like writing. The people tell him that's what they wanted to say in the first place, that he has a lovely way with the English language and a fine fist for the writing. They offer him sixpence for his trouble but he waves it away and they hand it to Mam because he's too grand to be taking sixpence. When the people leave he takes the sixpence and sends me to Kathleen O'Connell's shop for cigarettes.

Grandma sleeps in a big bed upstairs with a picture of the Sacred Heart of Jesus over her head and a statue of the Sacred Heart on the mantelpiece. She wants to switch from gaslight to electric light someday so that she'll have a little red light under the statue forever. Her devotion to the Sacred Heart is known up and down the lane and in lanes beyond.

Uncle Pat sleeps in a small bed in a corner of the same room where Grandma can make sure he comes in at a proper hour and kneels by the bed to say his prayers. He might have been dropped on his head, he may not know how to read and write, he may drink one pint too many, but there's no excuse for not saying his prayers before he goes to sleep.

Uncle Pat tells Grandma he met a man who is looking for a place to stay that will let him wash himself morning and night and give him two meals a day, dinner and tea. His name is Bill Galvin and he has a good job down at the lime kiln. He's covered all the time with white lime dust but surely that's better than coal dust.

Grandma will have to give up her bed and move into the small room. She'll take the Sacred Heart picture and leave the statue to watch over the two men. Besides, she has no place for a statue in her little room.

Bill Galvin comes after work to see the place. He's small, all white, and he snuffles like a dog. He asks Grandma if she'd mind taking down that statue because he's a Protestant and he wouldn't be able to sleep. Grandma barks at Uncle Pat for not telling her he was dragging a Protestant into the house. Jesus, she says, there will be gossip up and down the lane and beyond.

Uncle Pat says he didn't know Bill Galvin was a Protestant. You could never tell by looking at him especially the way he's covered with lime. He looks like an ordinary Catholic and you'd never imagine a Protestant would be shoveling lime.

Bill Galvin says his poor wife that just died was a Catholic and she had the walls covered with pictures of the Sacred Heart and the Virgin Mary showing their hearts. He's not against the Sacred Heart himself, it's just that seeing the statue will remind him of his poor wife and give him the heartache.

Grandma says, Ah, God help us, why didn't you tell me that in the first place? Sure I can put the statue on the windowsill in my room and your heart won't be tormented at the sight of it.

Every morning Grandma cooks Bill's dinner and takes it to him at the lime kiln. Mam wonders why he can't take it with him in the morning and Grandma says, Do you expect me to get up at dawn and boil cabbage and pig's toes for his lordship to take in his dinner can?

Mam tells her, In another week school will be over and if you give Frank sixpence a week he'll surely be glad to take Bill Galvin his dinner.

I don't want to go to Grandma's every day. I don't want to take Bill Galvin his dinner all the way down the Dock Road, but Mam says that's sixpence we could use and if I don't do it I'm going nowhere else.

You're staying in the house, she says. You're not playing with your pals.

Grandma warns me to take the dinner can directly and not be meandering, looking this way and that, kicking canisters and ruining the toes of my shoes. This dinner is hot and that's the way Bill Galvin wants it.

There's a lovely smell from the dinner can, boiled bacon and cabbage and two big floury white potatoes. Surely he won't notice if I try half a potato. He won't complain to Grandma because he hardly ever talks outside of a snuffle or two.

It's better if I eat the other half potato so that he won't be asking why he got a half. I might as well try the bacon and cabbage too and if I eat the other potato he'll surely think she didn't send one at all.

The second potato melts in my mouth and I'll have to try another bit of cabbage, another morsel of bacon. There isn't much left now and he'll be very suspicious so I might as well finish off the rest.

What am I going to do now? Grandma will destroy me, Mam will keep me in for a year. Bill Galvin will bury me in lime. I'll tell him I was attacked by a dog on the Dock

151

Road and he ate the whole dinner and I'm lucky I escaped without being eaten myself.

Oh, is that so? says Bill Galvin. And what's that bit of cabbage hanging on your gansey? Did the dog lick you wit his cabbagey gob? Go home and tell your grandmother you ate me whole dinner and I'm falling down with the hunger here in this lime kiln.

She'll kill me.

Tell her don't kill you till she sends me some class of a dinner and if you don't go to her now and get me a dinner I'll kill you and throw your body into the lime there and there won't be much left for your mother to moan over.

Grandma says, What are you doin' back with that can? He could bring that back by himself.

He wants more dinner.

What do you mean more dinner? Jesus above, is it a hole he has in his leg?

He's falling down with the hunger below in the lime kiln.

Is it coddin' me you are?

He says send him any class of a dinner.

I will not. I sent him his dinner.

He didn't get it.

He didn't? Why not?

I ate it.

What?

I was hungry and I tasted it and I couldn't stop.

Jesus, Mary and holy St. Joseph.

She gives me a clout on the head that brings tears to my eyes. She screams at me like a banshee and jumps around the kitchen and threatens to drag me to the priest, the bishop, the Pope himself if he lived around the corner. She cuts bread and waves the knife at me and makes sandwiches of brawn and cold potatoes.

Take these sandwiches to Bill Galvin and if you even look cross-eyed at them I'll skin your hide.

Of course she runs to Mam and they agree the only way

I can make up for my terrible sin is to deliver Bill Galvin's dinner for a fortnight without pay. I'm to bring back the can every day and that means I have to sit watching him stuff the food into his gob and he's not one that would ever ask you if you had a mouth in your head.

Every day I take the can back Grandma makes me kneel to the statue of the Sacred Heart and tell Him I'm sorry and all this over Bill Galvin, a Protestant.

Mam says, I'm a martyr for the fags and so is your father.

There may be a lack of tea or bread in the house but Mam and Dad always manage to get the fags, the Wild Woodbines. They have to have the Woodbines in the morning and any-time they drink tea. They tell us every day we should never smoke, it's bad for your lungs, it's bad for your chest, it stunts your growth, and they sit by the fire puffing away. Mam says, If 'tis a thing I ever see you with a fag in your gob I'll break your face. They tell us the cigarettes rot your teeth and you can see they're not lying. The teeth turn brown and black in their heads and fall out one by one. Dad says he has holes in his teeth big enough for a sparrow to raise a family. He has a few left but he gets them pulled at the clinic and applies for a false set. When he comes home with the new teeth he shows his big new white smile that makes him look like an American and whenever he tells us a ghost story by the fire he pushes the lower teeth up beyond his lip to his nose and frightens the life out of us. Mam's teeth are so bad she has to go to Barrington's Hospital to have them all pulled at the same time and when she comes home she's holding at her mouth a rag bright with blood. She has to sit up all night by the fire because you can't lie down when your gums are pumping blood or you'll choke in your sleep. She says she'll give up smoking entirely when this bleeding stops but she needs one puff of a fag this minute for the comfort that's in it. She tells Malachy go to Kathleen O'Connell's shop and ask her would she ever let her have five Woodbines till Dad collects the dole on Thursday. If anyone can get the fags out of Kathleen, Malachy can. Mam says he has the charm, and she tells me, There's no use sending you with your long puss and your father's odd manner.

When the bleeding stops and Mam's gums heal she goes to the clinic for her false teeth. She says she'll give up the smoking when her new teeth are in but she never does. The new teeth rub on her gums and make them sore and the smoke of the Woodbines eases them. She and Dad sit by the fire when we have one and smoke their cigarettes and when they talk their teeth clack. They try to stop the clacking by moving their jaws back and forth but that only makes it worse and they curse the dentists and the people above in Dublin who made the teeth and while they curse they clack. Dad claims these teeth were made for rich people in Dublin and didn't fit so they were passed on to the poor of Limerick who don't care because you don't have much to chew when you're poor anyway and you're grateful you have any class of a tooth in your head. If they talk too long their gums get sore and the teeth have to come out. Then they sit talking by the fire with their faces collapsed. Every night they leave the teeth in the kitchen in jam jars filled with water. Malachy wants to know why and Dad tells him it cleans them. Mam says, No, you can't have teeth in your head while you're sleeping for they'll slip and choke you to death entirely.

The teeth are the cause of Malachy going to Barrington's Hospital and me having an operation. Malachy whispers to me in the middle of the night, Do you want to go downstairs and see if we can wear the teeth?

The teeth are so big we have trouble getting them into our mouths but Malachy won't give up. He forces Dad's upper teeth into his mouth and can't get them out again. His lips are drawn back and the teeth make a big grin. He looks like a monster in a film and it makes me laugh but he pulls at them and grunts, Uck, uck, and tears come to his eyes. The more he goes Uck, uck, the harder I laugh till Dad calls from upstairs, What are you boys doing? Malachy runs from me, up the stairs, and now I hear Dad and Mam laughing till they see he can choke on the teeth. They both stick their fingers in to pull out the teeth but Malachy gets frightened and makes desperate uck uck sounds. Mam says, We'll have to take him to the hospital, and Dad says he'll take him. He makes me go in case the doctor has questions because I'm older than Malachy and that means I must have started all the trouble. Dad rushes through the streets with Malachy in his arms and I try to keep up. I feel sorry for Malachy up there on Dad's shoulder, looking back at me, tears on his cheeks and Dad's teeth bulging in his mouth. The doctor at Barrington's Hospital says, No bother. He pours oil into Malachy's mouth and has the teeth out in a minute. Then he looks at me and says to Dad, Why is that child standing there with his mouth hanging open?

Dad says, That's a habit he has, standing with his mouth open.

The doctor says, Come here to me. He looks up my nose, in my ears, down my throat, and feels my neck.

The tonsils, he says. The adenoids. They have to come out. The sooner the better or he'll look like an idiot when he grows up with that gob wide as a boot.

Next day Malachy gets a big piece of toffee as a reward for sticking in teeth he can't get out and I have to go to the hospital to have an operation that will close my mouth.

On a Saturday morning Mam finishes her tea and says, You're going to dance.

Dance? Why?

You're seven years old, you made your First Communion, and now 'tis time for the dancing. I'm taking you down to Catherine Street to Mrs. O'Connor's Irish dancing classes. You'll go there every Saturday morning and that'll keep you off the streets. That'll keep you from wandering around Limerick with hooligans.

She tells me wash my face not forgetting ears and neck, comb my hair, blow my nose, take the look off my face, what look? never mind, just take it off, put on my stockings and my First Communion shoes which, she says, are destroyed because I can't pass a canister or a rock without kicking it. She's worn out standing in the queue at the St.Vincent de Paul Society begging for boots for me and Malachy so that we can wear out the toes with the kicking. Your father says it's never too early to learn the songs and dances of your ancestors.

What's ancestors?

Never mind, she says, you're going to dance.

I wonder how I can die for Ireland if I have to sing and dance for Ireland, too. I wonder why they never say, You can eat sweets and stay home from school and go swimming for Ireland.

Mam says, Don't get smart or I'll warm your ear.

Cyril Benson dances. He has medals hanging from his shoulders to his kneecaps. He wins contests all over Ireland and he looks lovely in his saffron kilt. He's a credit to his mother and he gets his name in the paper all the time and you can be sure he brings home the odd few pounds. You don't see him roaming the streets kicking everything in sight till the toes hang out of his boots, oh, no, he's a good boy, dancing for his poor mother.

Mam wets an old towel and scrubs my face till it stings, she wraps the towel around her finger and sticks it in my ears and claims there's enough wax there to grow potatoes, she wets my hair to make it lie down, she tells me shut up and stop the whinging, that these dancing lessons will cost her sixpence every Saturday, which I could have earned bringing Bill Galvin his dinner and God knows she can barely afford it. I try to tell her, Ah, Mam, sure you don't have to send me to dancing school when you could be smoking a nice Woodbine and having a cup of tea, but she says, Oh, aren't you clever. You're going to dance if I have to give up the fags forever.

If my pals see my mother dragging me through the streets to an Irish dancing class I'll be disgraced entirely. They think it's all right to dance and pretend you're Fred Astaire because you can jump all over the screen with Ginger Rogers. There is no Ginger Rogers in Irish dancing and you can't jump all over. You stand straight up and down and keep your arms against yourself and kick your legs up and around and never smile. My uncle Pa Keating said Irish dancers look like they have steel rods up their arses, but I can't say that to Mam, she'd kill me.

There's a gramophone in Mrs. O'Connor's playing an Irish jig or a reel and boys and girls are dancing around kicking their legs out and keeping their hands to their sides. Mrs. O'Connor is a great fat woman and when she stops the record to show the steps all the fat from her chin to her ankles jiggles and I wonder how she can teach the dancing. She comes over to my mother and says, So, this is little Frankie? I think we have the makings of a dancer here. Boys and girls, do we have the makings of a dancer here?

We do, Mrs. O'Connor.

Mam says, I have the sixpence, Mrs. O'Connor.

Ah, yes, Mrs. McCourt, hold on a minute.

She waddles to a table and brings back the head of a black boy with kinky hair, big eyes, huge red lips and an open mouth. She tells me put the sixpence in the mouth and take my hand out before the black boy bites me. All the boys and girls watch and they have little smiles. I drop in the sixpence and pull my hand back before the mouth snaps shut. Everyone laughs and I know they wanted to see my hand caught in the mouth. Mrs. O'Connor gasps and laughs and says to my mother, Isn't that a howl, now? Mam says it's a howl. She tells me behave myself and come home dancing.

I don't want to stay in this place where Mrs. O'Connor

can't take the sixpence herself instead of letting me nearly lose my hand in the black boy's mouth. I don't want to stay in this place where you have to stand in line with boys and girls, straighten your back, hands by your sides, look ahead, don't look down, move your feet, move your feet, look at Cyril, look at Cyril, and there goes Cyril, all dressed up in his saffron kilt and the medals jingling, medals for this and medals for that and the girls love Cyril and Mrs. O'Connor loves Cyril for didn't he bring her fame and didn't she teach him every step he knows, oh, dance, Cyril, dance, oh, Jesus, he floats around the room, he's an angel out of heaven and stop the frowning, Frankie McCourt, or you'll have a puss on you like a pound of tripe, dance, Frankie, dance, pick up your feet for the love o' Jesus, onetwothreefourfivesixseven onetwothree and a onetwothree, Maura, will you help that Frankie McCourt before he ties his two feet around his poll entirely, help him, Maura.

Maura is a big girl about ten. She dances up to me with her white teeth and her dancer's dress with all the gold and yellow and green figures that are supposed to come from olden times and she says, Give me your hand, little boy, and she wheels me around the room till I'm dizzy and making a pure eejit of myself and blushing and foolish till I want to cry but I'm saved when the record stops and the gramophone goes hoosh hoosh.

Mrs. O'Connor says, Oh, thank you, Maura, and next week, Cyril, you can show Frankie a few of the steps that made you famous. Next week, boys and girls, and don't forget the sixpence for the little black boy.

Boys and girls leave together. I make my own way down the stairs and out the door hoping my pals won't see me with boys who wear kilts and girls with white teeth and fancy dresses from olden times.

Mam is having tea with Bridey Hannon, her friend from next door. Mam says, What did you learn? and makes me dance around the kitchen, onetwothreefourfivesixseven onetwothree and a onetwothree. She has a good laugh with Bridey. That's not too bad for your first time. In a month you'll be like a regular Cyril Benson.

I don't want to be Cyril Benson. I want to be Fred Astaire.

They turn hysterical, laughing and squirting tea out of their mouths, Jesus love him, says Bridey. Doesn't he have a great notion of himself. Fred Astaire how are you.

Mam says Fred Astaire went to his lessons every Saturday and didn't go around kicking the toes out of his boots and if I wanted to be like him I'd have to go to Mrs. O'Connor's every week.

The fourth Saturday morning Billy Campbell knocks at our door. Mrs. McCourt, can Frankie come out and play? Mam tells him, No, Billy. Frankie is going to his dancing lesson.

He waits for me at the bottom of Barrack Hill. He wants to know why I'm dancing, that everyone knows dancing is a sissy thing and I'll wind up like Cyril Benson wearing a kilt and medals and dancing all over with girls. He says next thing I'll be sitting in the kitchen knitting socks. He says dancing will destroy me and I won't be fit to play any kind of football, soccer, rugby or Gaelic football itself because the dancing teaches you to run like a sissy and everyone will laugh.

I tell him I'm finished with the dancing, that I have sixpence in my pocket for Mrs. O'Connor that's supposed to go into the black boy's mouth, that I'm going to the Lyric Cinema instead. Sixpence will get the two of us in with tuppence left over for two squares of Cleeves' toffee, and we have a great time looking at *Riders of the Purple Sage*.

Dad is sitting by the fire with Mam and they want to know what steps I learned today and what they're called. I already did "The Siege of Ennis" and "The Walls of Limerick," which are real dances. Now I have to make up names and dances. Mam says she never heard of a dance called "The Siege of Dingle" but if that's what I learned go ahead, dance it, and I dance around the kitchen with my hands down by my sides making my own music, diddley eye di eye di eye diddley eye do you do you, Dad and Mam clapping in time with my feet. Dad says, Och, that's a fine dance and you'll be a powerful Irish dancer and a credit to the men who died for their country. Mam says, That wasn't much for a sixpence.

Next week it's a George Raft film and the week after that a cowboy film with George O'Brien. Then it's James Cagney and I can't take Billy because I want to get a bar of chocolate to go with my Cleeves' toffee and I'm having a great time till there's a terrible pain in my jaw and it's a tooth out of my gum stuck in my toffee and the pain is killing me. Still, I can't waste the toffee so I pull out the tooth and put it in my pocket and chew the toffee on the other side of my mouth blood and all. There's pain on one side and delicious toffee on the other and I remember what my uncle Pa Keating would say, There are times when you wouldn't know whether to shit or go blind.

I have to go home now and worry because you can't go through the world short a tooth without your mother knowing. Mothers know everything and she's always looking into our mouths to see if there's any class of disease. She's there by the fire and Dad is there and they're asking me the same old questions, the dance and the name of the dance. I tell them I learned "The Walls of Cork" and I dance around the kitchen trying to hum a made-up tune and dying with the pain of my tooth. Mam says, "Walls o' Cork," my eye, there's no such dance, and Dad says, Come over here. Stand there before me. Tell us the truth, Did you go to your dancing classes today?

I can't tell a lie anymore because my gum is killing me and there's blood in my mouth. Besides, I know they know everything and that's what they're telling me now. Some snake of a boy from the dancing school saw me going to the Lyric Cinema and told and Mrs. O'Connor sent a note to say she hadn't seen me in ages and was I all right because I had great promise and could follow in the footsteps of the great Cyril Benson.

Dad doesn't care about my tooth or anything. He says I'm going to confession and drags me over to the Redemptorist church because it's Saturday and confessions go on all day. He tells me I'm a bad boy, he's ashamed of me that I went to the pictures instead of learning Ireland's national dances, the jig, the reel, the dances that men and women fought and died for down those sad centuries. He says there's many a young man that was hanged and now moldering in a line pit that would be glad to rise up and dance the Irish dance.

The priest is old and I have to yell my sins at him and he tells me I'm a hooligan for going to the pictures instead of my dancing lessons although he thinks himself that dancing is a dangerous thing almost as bad as the films, that it stirs up thoughts sinful in themselves, but even if dancing is an abomination I sinned by taking my mother's sixpence and lying and there's a hot place in hell for the likes of me, say a decade of the rosary and ask God's forgiveness for you're dancing at the gates of hell itself, child.

I'm seven, eight, nine going on ten and still Dad has no work. He drinks his tea in the morning, signs for the dole at the Labour Exchange, reads the papers at the Carnegie Library, goes for his long walks far into the country. If he gets a job at the Limerick Cement Company or Rank's Flour Mills he loses it in the third week. He loses it because he goes to the pubs on the third Friday of the job, drinks all his wages and misses the half day of work on Saturday morning.

Mam says, Why can't he be like the other men from the lanes of Limerick? They're home before the Angelus rings at six o'clock, they hand over their wages, change their shirts, have their tea, get a few shillings from the wife and they're off to the pub for a pint or two.

Mam tells Bridey Hannon that Dad can't be like that and

won't be like that. She says he's a right bloody fool the way he goes to pubs and stands pints to other men while his own children are home with their bellies stuck to their backbones for the want of a decent dinner. He'll brag to the world he did his bit for Ireland when it was neither popular nor profitable, that he'll gladly die for Ireland when the call comes, that he regrets he has only one life to give for his poor misfortunate country and if anyone disagrees they're invited to step outside and settle this for once and for all.

Oh, no, says Mam, they won't disagree and they won't step outside, that bunch of tinkers and knackers and begrudgers that hang around the pubs. They tell him he's a grand man, even if he's from the North, and 'twould be an honor to accept a pint from such a patriot.

Mam tells Bridey, I don't know under God what I'm going to do. The dole is nineteen shillings and sixpence a week, the rent is six and six, and that leaves thirteen shillings to feed and clothe five people and keep us warm in the winter.

Bridey drags on her Woodbine, drinks her tea and declares that God is good. Mam says she's sure God is good for someone somewhere but He hasn't been seen lately in the lanes of Limerick.

Bridey laughs. Oh, Angela, you could go to hell for that, and Mam says, Aren't I there already, Bridey?

And they laugh and drink their tea and smoke their Woodbines and tell one another the fag is the only comfort they have.

'Tis.

Question Quigley tells me I have to go to the Redemptorist church on Friday and join the boys' division of the Arch Confraternity. You have to join. You can't say no. All the boys in the lanes and back streets that have fathers on the dole or working in laboring jobs have to join.

Question says, Your father is a foreigner from the North and he don't matter but you still have to join.

Everyone knows Limerick is the holiest city in Ireland because it has the Arch Confraternity of the Holy Family, the biggest sodality in the world. Any city can have a Confraternity, only Limerick has the Arch.

Our Confraternity fills the Redemptorist church five nights a week, three for the men, one for the women, one for the boys. There is Benediction and hymn singing in English, Irish and Latin and best of all the big powerful sermon Redemptorist priests are famous for. It's the sermon that saves millions of Chinese and other heathens from winding up in hell with the Protestants.

The Question says you have to join the Confraternity so that your mother can tell the St. Vincent de Paul Society and they'll know you're a good Catholic. He says his father is a loyal member and that's how he got a good pensionable job cleaning lavatories at the railway station and when he grows up himself he'll get a good job too unless he runs away and joins the Royal Canadian Mounted Police so that he can sing "I'll Be Calling You Ooo Ooo Ooo," like Nelson Eddy singing to Jeanette MacDonald expiring with consumption there on the sofa. If he brings me to the Confraternity the man in the office will write his name in a big book and some day he might be promoted to prefect of a section, which is all he wants in life next to wearing the Mountie uniform.

The prefect is head of a section which is thirty boys from the same lanes and streets. Every section has the name of a saint whose picture is painted on a shield stuck on top of a pole by the prefect's seat. The prefect and his assistant take the attendance and keep an eye on us so that they can give us a thump on the head in case we laugh during Benediction or commit any other sacrileges. If you miss one night the man in the office wants to know why, wants to know if you're slipping away from the Confraternity or he might say to the other man in the office, I think our little friend here has taken the soup. That's the worst thing you can say to any Catholic in Limerick or Ireland itself because of what happened in the Great Famine. If you're absent twice the man in the office sends you a yellow summons to appear and explain yourself and if you're absent three times he sends The Posse, which is five or six big boys from your section who search the streets to make sure you're not out enjoying yourself when you should be on your knees at the Confraternity praying for the Chinese and other lost souls. The Posse will go to your house and tell your mother your immortal soul is in danger. Some mothers worry but others will say, Get away from my door or I'll come out and give every one o' ye a good fong in the hole of yeer arse. These are not good Confraternity mothers and the director will say we should pray for them that they'll see the error of their ways.

The worst thing of all is a visit from the director of the Confraternity himself, Father Gorey. He'll stand at the top of the lane and roar in the voice that converted the Chinese millions, Where is the house of Frank McCourt? He roars even though he has your address in his pocket and knows very well where you live. He roars because he wants the world to know you're slipping away from the Confraternity and putting your immortal soul in danger. The mothers are terrified and the fathers will whisper, I'm not here, I'm not here, and they'll make sure you go to the Confraternity from this on out so they won't be disgraced and shamed entirely with the neighbors muttering behind their hands.

The Question takes me to the section St. Finbar's, and the prefect tells me sit over there and shut up. His name is Declan Collopy, he's fourteen and he has lumps on his forehead that look like horns. He has thick ginger eyebrows that meet in the middle and hang over his eyes and his arms hang down to his kneecaps. He tells me he's making this the best section in the Confraternity and if I'm ever absent he'll break my arse and send the bits to my mother. There's no excuse for absence because there was a boy in another section that was dying and still they brought him in on a stretcher. He says, If you're ever absent it better be a death, not a death in the family but your own death. Do you hear me?

I do, Declan.

Boys in my section tell me that prefects get rewards if there is perfect attendance. Declan wants to get out of school as soon as he can and get a job selling linoleum at Cannock's big shop on Patrick Street. His uncle, Foncey, sold linoleum there for years and made enough money to start his own shop in Dublin, where he has his three sons selling linoleum. Father Gorey, the director, can easily get Declan the reward of a job at Cannock's if he's a good prefect and has perfect attendance in his section and that's why Declan will destroy us if we're absent. He tells us, No one will stand between me and the linoleum.

Declan likes Question Quigley and lets him miss an occasional Friday night because the Question said, Declan, when I grow up and get married I'm going to cover my house in linoleum and I'll buy it all from you.

Other boys in the section try this trick with Declan but he says, Bugger off, ye'll be lucky enough to have a pot to piss in never mind yards of linoleum.

Dad says when he was my age in Toome he served Mass for years and it's time for me to be an altar boy. Mam says, What's the use? The child doesn't have proper clothes for school never mind the altar. Dad says the altar boy robes will cover the clothes and she says we don't have the money for robes and the wash they need every week.

He says God will provide and makes me kneel on the kitchen floor. He takes the part of the priest for he has the whole Mass in his head and I have to know the responses. He says, *Introibo ad altare Dei*, and I have to say, *Ad Deum qui laetificat juventutem meam.*

Every evening after tea I kneel for the Latin and he won't let me move till I'm perfect. Mam says he could at least let me sit but he says Latin is sacred and it is to be learned and recited on the knees. You won't find the Pope sitting around drinking tea while he speaks the Latin.

The Latin is hard and my knees are sore and scabby and I'd like to be out in the lane playing though still I'd like to be an altar boy helping the priest vest in the sacristy, up there on the altar all decked out in my red and white robes like my pal Jimmy Clark, answering the priest in Latin, moving the big book from one side of the tabernacle to the other, pouring water and wine into the chalice, pouring water over the priest's hands, ringing the bell at Consecration, kneeling, bowing, swinging the censer at Benediction, sitting off to the side with the palms of my hands on my knees all serious while he gives his sermon, everyone in St. Joseph's looking at me and admiring my ways.

In a fortnight I have the Mass in my head and it's time to go to St. Joseph's to see the sacristan, Stephen Carey, who is in charge of altar boys. Dad polishes my boots. Mam darns my socks and throws an extra coal on the fire to heat up the iron to press my shirt. She boils water to scrub my head, neck, hands and knees and any inch of skin that shows. She scrubs till my skin burns and tells Dad she wouldn't give it to the world to say her son went on the altar dirty. She wishes I didn't have scabby knees from running around kicking canisters and falling down pretending I was the greatest footballer in the world. She wishes we had a drop of hair oil in the house but water and spit will keep my hair from sticking up like black straw in a mattress. She warns me speak up when I go to St. Joseph's and don't be mumbling in English or Latin. She says, 'Tis a great pity you grew out of your First Communion suit but you have nothing to be ashamed of, you come from good blood, McCourts, Sheehans, or my mother's family the Guilfoyles that owned acre after acre in County Limerick before the English took it away and gave it to footpads from London.

Dad holds my hand going through the streets and people look at us because of the way we're saying Latin back and forth. He knocks at the sacristy door and tells Stephen Carey, This is my son, Frank, who knows the Latin and is ready to be an altar boy.

Stephen Carey looks at him, then me. He says, We don't have room for him, and closes the door.

Dad is still holding my hand and squeezes till it hurts and I want to cry out. He says nothing on the way home. He takes off his cap, sits by the fire and lights a Woodbine. Mam is smoking, too. Well, she says, is he going to be an altar boy?

There's no room for him.

Oh. She puffs on her Woodbine. I'll tell you what it is, she says. 'Tis class distinction. They don't want boys from lanes on the altar. They don't want the ones with scabby knees and hair sticking up. Oh, no, they want the nice boys with hair oil and new shoes that have fathers with suits and ties and steady jobs. That's what it is and 'tis hard to hold on to the Faith with the snobbery that's in it.

Och, aye.

Oh, och aye my arse. That's all you ever say. You could go to the priest and tell him you have a son that has a head stuffed with Latin and why can't he be an altar boy and what is he going to do with all that Latin?

Och, he might grow up to be a priest.

I ask him if I can go out and play. Yes, he says, go out and play.

Mam says, You might as well.

VI

Mr. O'Neill is the master in the fourth class at school. We call him Dotty because he's small like a dot. He teaches in the one classroom with a platform so that he can stand above us and threaten us with his ash plant and peel his apple for all to see. The first day of school in September he writes on the blackboard three words which are to stay there the rest of the year, Euclid, geometry, idiot. He says if he catches any boy interfering with these words that boy will go through the rest of his life with one hand. He says anyone who doesn't understand the theorems of Euclid is an idiot. Now, repeat after me, Anyone who doesn't understand the theorems of Euclid is an idiot. Of course we all know what an idiot is because that's what the masters keep telling us we are.

Brendan Quigley raises his hand. Sir, what's a theorem and what's a Euclid?

We expect Dotty to lash at Brendan the way all the masters do when you ask them a question but he looks at Brendan with a little smile. Ah, now, here's a boy with not one but two questions. What is your name, boy?

Brendan Quigley, sir.

This is a boy who will go far. Where will he go, boys?

Far, sir.

Indeed and he will. The boy who wants to know something about the grace, elegance and beauty of Euclid can go nowhere but up. In what direction and no other can this boy go, boys?

Up, sir.

Without Euclid, boys, mathematics would be a poor doddering thing. Without Euclid we wouldn't be able to go from here to there. Without Euclid the bicycle would have no wheel. Without Euclid St. Joseph could not have been a carpenter for carpentry is geometry and geometry is carpentry. Without Euclid this very school could never have been built.

Paddy Clohessy mutters behind me, Feckin' Euclid.

Dotty barks at him. You, boy, what is your name?

Clohessy, sir.

Ah, the boy flies on one wing. What is your Christian name?

Paddy.

Paddy what?

Paddy, sir.

And what, Paddy, were you saying to McCourt?

I said we should get down on our two knees and thank God for Euclid.

I'm sure you did, Clohessy. I see the lie festering in your teeth. What do I see, boys?

The lie, sir.

And what is the lie doing, boys?

Festering, sir.

Where, boys, where?

In his teeth, sir.

Euclid, boys, was a Greek. What, Clohessy, is a Greek?

Some class of a foreigner, sir.

Clohessy, you are a half-wit. Now, Brendan, surely you know what a Greek is?

Yes, sir. Euclid was a Greek.

Dotty gives him the little smile. He tells Clohessy he should model himself on Quigley, who knows what a Greek is. He draws two lines side by side and tells us these are parallel lines and the magical and mysterious thing is that they never meet, not if they were to be extended to infinity, not if they were extended to God's shoulders and that, boys, is a long way though there is a German Jew who is upsetting the whole world with his ideas on parallel lines.

We listen to Dotty and wonder what all this has to do with the state of the world with the Germans marching everywhere and bombing everything that stands. We can't ask him ourselves but we can get Brendan Quigley to do it. Anyone can see Brendan is the master's pet and that means he can ask any question he likes. After school we tell Brendan he has to ask the question tomorrow, What use is Euclid and all those lines that go on forever when the Germans are bombing everything? Brendan says he doesn't want to be the master's pet, he didn't ask for it, and he doesn't want to ask the question. He's afraid if he asks that question Dotty will attack him. We tell him if he doesn't ask the question we'll attack him.

Next day Brendan raises his hand. Dotty gives him the little smile. Sir, what use is Euclid and all the lines when the Germans are bombing everything that stands?

The little smile is gone. Ah, Brendan. Ah, Quigley. Oh, boys, oh, boys.

He lays his stick on the desk and stands on the platform with his eyes closed. What use is Euclid? he says. Use? Without Euclid the Messerschmitt could never have taken to the sky. Without Euclid the Spitfire could not dart from cloud to cloud. Euclid brings us grace and beauty and elegance. What does he bring us, boys?

Grace, sir.

And?

Beauty, sir.

And?

Elegance, sir.

Euclid is complete in himself and divine in application. Do you understand that, boys?

We do, sir.

I doubt it, boys, I doubt it. To love Euclid is to be alone in this world.

He opens his eyes and sighs and you can see the eyes are a little watery.

Paddy Clohessy is leaving the school that day and he's stopped by Mr. O'Dea, who teaches the fifth class. Mr. O'Dea says, You, what's your name?

Clohessy, sir.

What class are you in?

Fourth class, sir.

Now tell me, Clohessy, is that master of yours talking to you about Euclid?

He is, sir.

And what is he saying?

He's saying he's a Greek.

Of course he is, you diddering omadhaun. What else is he saying?

He's saying there would be no school without Euclid.

Ah. Now is he drawing anything on the board?

He's drawing lines side by side that will never meet even if they land on God's shoulders.

Mother o' God.

No, sir. God's shoulders.

I know, you idiot. Go home.

The next day there's a great noise at our classroom door and Mr. O'Dea is yelling, Come out, O'Neill, you chancer, you poltroon. We can hear everything he's saying because of the broken glass over the door.

The new headmaster, Mr. O'Halloran, is saying, Now, now, Mr. O'Dea. Control yourself. No quarreling in front of our pupils.

Well, then, Mr. O'Halloran, tell him stop teaching the geometry. The geometry is for the fifth form and not the fourth. The geometry is mine. Tell him to teach the long division and leave Euclid to me. Long division will stretch his intellect such as it is, God help us. I don't want the minds of these boys destroyed by that chancer up there on the platform, him handing out apple skins and causing diarrhea right and left. Tell him Euclid is mine, Mr. O'Halloran, or I'll put a stop to his gallop.

Mr. O'Halloran tells Mr. O'Dea to return to his classroom and asks Mr. O'Neill to step into the hall. Mr. O'Halloran says, Now, Mr. O'Neill, I have asked you before to stay away from Euclid.

You have, Mr. O'Halloran, but you might as well ask me to stop eating my daily apple.

I'll have to insist, Mr. O'Neill. No more Euclid.

Mr. O'Neill comes back to the room and his eyes are watery again. He says little has changed since the time of the Greeks for the barbarians are within the gates and their names are legion. What has changed since the time of the Greeks, boys?

It is torture to watch Mr. O'Neill peel the apple every day, to see the length of it, red or green, and if you're up near him to catch the freshness of it in your nose. If you're the good boy for that day and you answer the questions he gives it to you and lets you eat it there at your desk so that you can eat it in peace with no one to bother you the way they would if you took it into the yard. Then they'd torment you, Gimme a piece, gimme a piece, and you'd be lucky to have an inch left for yourself.

There are days when the questions are too hard and he torments us by dropping the apple peel into the wastebasket. Then he borrows a boy from another class to take the wastebasket down to the furnace to burn papers and apple peel or he'll leave it for the charwoman, Nellie Ahearn, to take it all away in her big canvas sack. We'd like to ask Nellie to keep the peel for us before the rats get it but she's weary from cleaning the whole school by herself and she snaps at us, I have other things to be doin' with me life besides watchin' a scabby bunch rootin' around for the skin of an apple. Go 'way.

He peels the apple slowly. He looks around the room with the little smile. He teases us, Do you think, boys, I should give this to the pigeons on the windowsill? We say, No, sir, pigeons don't eat apples. Paddy Clohessy calls out, 'Twill give them the runs, sir, and we'll have it on our heads abroad in the yard.

Clohessy, you are an omadhaun. Do you know what an omadhaun is?

I don't, sir.

It's the Irish, Clohessy, your native tongue, Clohessy. An omadhaun is a fool, Clohessy. You are an omadhaun. What is he, boys?

An omadhaun, sir.

Clohessy says, That's what Mr. O'Dea called me, sir, a diddering omadhaun.

He pauses in his peeling to ask us questions about everything in the world and the boy with the best answers wins. Hands up, he says, who is the President of the United States of America?

Every hand in the class goes up and we're all disgusted when he asks a question that any omadhaun would know. We call out, Roosevelt.

Then he says, You, Mulcahy, who stood at the foot of the cross when Our Lord was crucified?

Mulcahy is slow. The Twelve Apostles, sir.

Mulcahy, what is the Irish word for fool?

Omadhaun, sir.

And what are you, Mulcahy?

An omadhaun, sir.

Fintan Slattery raises his hand. I know who stood at the foot of the cross, sir.

Of course Fintan knows who stood at the foot of the cross. Why wouldn't he? He's always running off to Mass with his mother, who is known for her holiness. She's so holy her husband ran off to Canada to cut down trees, glad to be gone and never to be heard from again. She and Fintan say the rosary every night on their knees in the kitchen and read all kinds of religious magazines: *The Little Messenger of the Sacred Heart, The Lantern, The Far East*, as well as every little book printed by the Catholic Truth Society. They go to Mass and Communion rain or shine and every Saturday they confess to the Jesuits who are known for their interest in intelligent sins not the usual sins you hear from people in lanes who are known for getting drunk and sometimes eating meat on Fridays before it goes bad and cursing on top of it. Fintan and his mother live on Catherine Street and Mrs. Slattery's neighbors call her Mrs. Offer-It-Up because no matter what happens, a broken leg, a spilled cup of tea, a disappeared husband, she says, Well, now, I'll offer that up and I'll have no end of Indulgences to get me into heaven. Fintan is just as bad. If you push him in the schoolyard or call him names he'll smile and tell you he'll pray for you and he'll offer it up for his soul and yours. The boys in Leamy's don't want Fintan praying for them and they threaten to give him a good fong in the arse if they catch him praying for them. He says he wants to be a saint when he grows up, which is ridiculous because you can't be a saint till you're dead. He says our grandchildren will be praying to his picture. One big boy says, My grandchildren will piss on your picture, and Fintan just smiles. His sister ran away to England when she was seventeen and everyone knows he wears her blouse at home and curls his hair with hot iron tongs every Saturday night so that he'll look gorgeous at Mass on Sunday. If he meets you going to Mass he'll say, Isn't my hair gorgeous, Frankie? He loves that word, gorgeous, and no other boy will ever use it.

Of course he knows who stood at the foot of the cross. He probably knows what they were wearing and what they had for breakfast and now he's telling Dotty O'Neill it was the three Marys.

Dotty says, Come up here, Fintan, and take your reward.

He takes his time going to the platform and we can't believe our eyes when he takes out a pocketknife to cut the apple peel into little bits so that he can eat them one by one and not be stuffing the whole thing into his mouth like the rest of us when we win. He raises his hand, Sir, I'd like to give some of my apple away.

The apple, Fintan? No, indeed. You do not have the apple, Fintan. You have the peel, the mere skin. You have not nor will you ever achieve heights so dizzy you'll be feasting on the apple itself. Not my apple, Fintan. Now did I hear you say you want to give away your reward?

You did, sir. I'd like to give three pieces, to Quigley, Clohessy and McCourt.

Why, Fintan?

They're my friends, sir.

The boys around the room are sneering and nudging each other and I feel ashamed because they'll say I curl my hair and I'll be tormented in the schoolyard and why does he think I'm his friend? If they say I wear my sister's blouse there's no use telling them I don't have a sister because they'll say, You'd wear it if you had a sister. There's no use saying anything in the schoolyard because there's always someone with an answer and there's nothing you can do but punch them in the nose and if you were to punch everyone who has an answer you'd be punching morning noon and night.

Quigley takes the bit of peel from Fintan. Thanks, Fintan.

The whole class is looking at Clohessy because he's the biggest and the toughest and if he says thanks I'll say thanks. He says, Thanks very much, Fintan, and blushes and I say, Thanks very much, Fintan, and I try to stop myself from blushing but I can't and all the boys sneer again and I'd like to hit them.

After school the boys call to Fintan, Hoi, Fintan, are you goin' home to curl your gorgeous hair? Fintan smiles and climbs the steps of the schoolyard. A big boy from seventh class says to Paddy Clohessy, I suppose you'd be curlin' your hair too if you wasn't a baldy with a shaved head.

Paddy says, Shurrup, and the boy says, Oh, an' who's goin' to make me? Paddy tries a punch but the big boy hits his nose and knocks him down and there's blood. I try to hit the big boy but he grabs me by the throat and bangs my head against the wall till I see lights and black dots. Paddy walks away holding his nose and crying and the big boy pushes me after him. Fintan is outside on the street and he says, Oh, Francis, Francis, oh, Patrick, Patrick, what's up? Why are you crying, Patrick? and Paddy says, I'm hungry. I can't fight nobody because I'm starving with the hunger an' fallin' down an' I'm ashamed of meself.

Fintan says, Come with me, Patrick. My mother will give us something, and Paddy says, Ah, no, me nose is bleedin'.

Don't worry. She'll put something on your nose or a key on the back of your neck. Francis, you must come, too. You always look hungry.

Ah, no, Fintan.

Ah, do, Francis.

All right, Fintan.

Fintan's flat is like a chapel. There are two pictures, the Sacred Heart of Jesus and the Immaculate Heart of Mary. Jesus is showing His heart with the crown of thorns, the fire, the blood. His head is tilted to the left to show His great sorrow. The Virgin Mary is showing her heart and it would be a pleasant heart if it didn't have that crown of thorns. Her head is tilted to the right to show her sorrow because she knows her Son will come to a sad end.

There's a picture on another wall of a man with a brown robe and birds sitting all over him. Fintan says, Do you know who that is, Francis? No? That's your patron, St. Francis of Assisi, and do you know what today is?

The fourth of October.

That's right and it's his feast day and special for you because you can ask St. Francis for anything and he'll surely give it to you. That's why I wanted you to come here today. Sit down, Patrick, sit down, Francis.

Mrs. Slattery comes in with her rosary beads in her hand. She's happy to meet Fintan's new friends and would we like a cheese sandwich? And look at your poor nose, Patrick. She touches his nose with the cross on her rosary beads and says a little prayer. She tells us these rosary beads were blessed by the Pope himself and would stop the flow of a river if requested never mind Patrick's poor nose.

Fintan says he won't have a sandwich because he's fasting and praying for the boy who hit Paddy and me. Mrs. Slattery gives him a kiss on the head and tells him he's a saint out of heaven and asks if we'd like mustard on our sandwiches and I tell her I never heard of mustard on cheese and I'd love it. Paddy says, I dunno. I never had a sangwidge in me life, and we all laugh and I wonder how you could live ten years like Paddy and never have a sandwich. Paddy laughs, too, and you can see his teeth are white and black and green.

We eat the sandwich and drink tea and Paddy wants to know where the lavatory is. Fintan takes him through the bedroom to the backyard and when they come back Paddy says, I have to go home. Me mother'll kill me. I'll wait for you outside, Frankie.

Now I have to go to the lavatory and Fintan leads me to the backyard. He says, I have to go, too, and when I unbutton my fly I can't pee because he's looking at me and he says, You were fooling. You don't have to go at all. I like to look at you, Francis. That's all. I wouldn't want to commit any class of a sin with our Confirmation coming next year.

Paddy and I leave together. I'm bursting and run behind a garage to pee. Paddy is waiting for me and as we walk along Hartstonge Street he says, That was a powerful sangwidge, Frankie, an' him an' his mother is very holy but I wouldn't want to go to Fintan's flat anymore because he's very odd, isn't he, Frankie?

He is, Paddy.

The way he looks at it when you take it out, that's odd, isn't it, Frankie?

'Tis, Paddy.

A few days later Paddy whispers, Fintan Slattery said we could come to his flat at lunchtime. His mother won't be there and she leaves his lunch for him. He might give us some too and he has lovely milk. Will we go?

Fintan sits two rows from us. He knows what Paddy is saying to me and he moves his eyebrows up and down as if to say, Will you come? I whisper yes to Paddy and he nods to Fintan and the master barks at us to stop waggling our eyebrows and our lips or the ash plant will sing across our backsides.

Boys in the schoolyard see the three of us walk out and they pass remarks. Oh, Gawd, look at Fintan and his ingles. Paddy says, Fintan, what's an ingle? and Fintan says it's just a boy from olden times who sits in a corner, that's all. He tells us sit at the table in his kitchen and we can read his comic books if we like, Film Fun, the Beano, the Dandy, or the religious magazines or his mother's romance magazines, the Miracle and the Oracle, which always have stories about factory girls who are poor but beautiful in love with sons of earls and vice versa and the factory girl ends up throwing herself into the Thames with the hopelessness only to be rescued by a passing carpenter who is poor but honest and will love the factory girl for her own humble self though it turns out the passing carpenter is really the son of a duke, which is much higher than an earl, so that now the poor factory girl is a duchess and can look down her nose at the earl who spurned her because she's happy tending her roses on her twelve-thousand-acre estate in Shropshire and being kind to her poor old mother, who refuses to leave her humble little cottage for all the money in the world.

Paddy says, I don't want to read nothing, it's all a cod, all them stories. Fintan removes the cloth covering his sandwich and glass of milk. The milk looks creamy and cool and

delicious and the sandwich bread is almost as white. Paddy
says, Is that a ham sangwidge? and Fintan says, 'Tis. Paddy
says, That's a lovely looking sangwidge and is there mustard
on it? Fintan nods and slices the sandwich in two. Mustard seeps
out. He licks it off his fingers and takes a nice mouthful
of milk. He cuts the sandwich again into quarters, eighths,
sixteenths, takes *The Little Messenger of the Sacred Heart* from
the pile of magazines and reads while he eats his sandwich
bits and drinks his milk and Paddy and I look at him and I
know Paddy is wondering what we're doing here at all, at
all, because that's what I'm wondering myself hoping Fintan
will pass over the plate to us but he doesn't, he finishes the
milk, leaves bits of sandwich on the plate, covers it with the
cloth and wipes his lips in his dainty way, lowers his head,
blesses himself and says grace after meals and, God, we'll be
late for school, and blesses himself again on the way out with
holy water from the little china font hanging by the door
with the little image of the Virgin Mary showing her heart
and pointing at it with two fingers as if we couldn't make it
out for ourselves.

It's too late for Paddy and me to run and get the bun and
milk from Nellie Ahearn and I don't know how I'm going
to last from now till I can run home after school and get a
piece of bread. Paddy stops at the school gate. He says, I
can't go in there starving with the hunger. I'd fall asleep and
Dotty'd kill me.

Fintan is anxious. Come on, come on, we'll be late. Come
on, Francis, hurry up.

I'm not going in, Fintan. You had your lunch. We had
nothing.

Paddy explodes. You're a feckin' chancer, Fintan. That's
what you are an' a feckin' begrudger too with your feckin'
sangwidge an' your feckin' Sacred Heart of Jesus on the wall
an' your feckin' holy water. You can kiss my arse, Fintan.

Oh, Patrick.

Oh, Patrick my feckin' arse, Fintan. Come on, Frankie.

Fintan runs into school and Paddy and I make our way to an orchard in Ballinacurra. We climb a wall and a fierce dog comes at us till Paddy talks to him and tells him he's a good dog and we're hungry and go home to your mother. The dog licks Paddy's face and trots away waving his tail and Paddy is delighted with himself. We stuff apples into our shirts till we can barely get back over the wall to run into a long field and sit under a hedge eating the apples till we can't swallow another bit and we stick our faces into a stream for the lovely cool water. Then we run to opposite ends of a ditch to shit and wipe ourselves with grass and thick leaves. Paddy is squatting and saying, There's nothing in the world like a good feed of apples, a drink of water and a good shit, better than any sangwidge of cheese and mustard and Dotty O'Neill can shove his apple up his arse.

There are three cows in a field with their heads over a stone wall and they say moo to us. Paddy says, Bejasus, 'tis milkin' time, and he's over the wall, stretched on his back under a cow with her big udder hanging into his face. He pulls on a teat and squirts milk into his mouth. He stops squirting and says, Come on, Frankie, fresh milk. 'Tis lovely. Get that other cow, they're all ready for the milkin'.

I get under the cow and pull on a teat but she kicks and moves and I'm sure she's going to kill me. Paddy comes over and shows me how to do it, pull hard and straight and the milk comes out in a powerful stream. The two of us lie under the one cow and we're having a great time filling ourselves with milk when there's a roar and there's a man with a stick charging across the field. We're over the wall in a minute and he can't follow us because of his rubber boots. He stands at the wall and shakes his stick and shouts that if he ever catches us we'll have the length of his boot up our arses and we laugh because we're out of harm's way and I'm wondering why anyone should be hungry in a world full of milk and apples.

It's all right for Paddy to say Dotty can shove the apple

up his arse but I don't want to rob orchards and milk cows forever and I'll always try to win Dotty's apple peel so that I can go home and tell Dad how I answered the hard questions.

We're walking back through Ballinacurra. There's rain and lightning and we run but it's hard for me with the sole of my shoe flapping and threatening to trip me. Paddy can run all he wants in his long bare feet and you hear them slapping on the pavement. My shoes and stockings are soaked and they make their own sound, squish, squish. Paddy notices that and we make a song from our two sounds, slap slap, squish, squish, slap squish, squish slap. We laugh so hard over our song we have to hold on to one another. The rain gets heavier and we know we can't stand under a tree or we'll be fried entirely so we stand by a door which is opened in a minute by a big fat maid in a little white hat and a black dress with a little white apron who tells us get away from this door we're a disgrace. We run from the door and Paddy calls back, Mullingar heifer, beef to the heels, and he laughs till he chokes and has to lean against a wall with the weakness. There's no sense in standing in from the rain anymore, we're soaked to the skin, so we take our time down O'Connell Avenue. Paddy says he learned that Mullingar heifer thing from his uncle Peter, the one that was in India in the English army and they have a photo of him standing with a group of soldiers with their helmets and guns and bandoliers around their chests and there are dark men in uniform who are Indians and loyal to the King. Uncle Peter had a great time for himself in a place called Kashmir, which is lovelier than Killarney that they're always bragging about and singing. Paddy goes on again about running away and winding up in India in a silken tent with the girl with the red dot and the curry and the figs and he's making me hungry even if I'm stuffed with apples and milk.

The rain is clearing and there are birds honking over our heads. Paddy says they're ducks or geese or something on their way to Africa where it's nice and warm. The birds have more sense than the Irish. They come to the Shannon for their holidays and then they go back to the warm places, maybe even India. He says he'll write me a letter when he's over there and I can come to India and have my own girl with a red dot.

What's that dot for, Paddy?

It shows they're high class, the quality.

But, Paddy, would the quality in India talk to you if they knew you were from a lane in Limerick and had no shoes?

Course they would, but the English quality wouldn't. The English quality wouldn't give you the steam of their piss.

Steam of their piss? God, Paddy, did you think of that yourself?

Naw, naw, that's what my father says below in the bed when he's coughin' up the gobs and blamin' the English for everything.

And I think, Steam of their piss. I'll keep that for myself. I'll go around Limerick saying it, Steam of their piss, Steam of their piss, and when I go to America some day I'll be the only one who knows it.

Question Quigley is wobbling toward us on a big woman's bicycle and calls to me, Hoi, Frankie McCourt, you're going to be killed. Dotty O'Neill sent a note to your house and said you didn't come back to school after lunch, that you went on the mooch with Paddy Clohessy. Your mother is going to kill you. Your father is out looking for you and he's going to kill you, too.

Oh, God, I feel cold and empty and I wish I could be in India where it's nice and warm and there's no school and my father could never find me to kill me. Paddy tells the Question, He didn't go on the mooch and I didn't either. Fintan Slattery starved us to death and we were too late for the bun and the milk. Then Paddy says to me, Don't mind 'em, Frankie, 'tis all a cod. They're always sendin' notes to our house and we wipe our arses with them.

My mother and father would never wipe their arses with a note from the master and I'm afraid now to go home. The Question rides off on the bicycle, laughing, and I don't know why because he once ran away from home and slept in a ditch with four goats and that's worse than mooching from school half a day anytime.

I could turn up the Barrack Road now and go home and tell my parents I'm sorry I went on the mooch and I did it because of the hunger but Paddy says, Come on, we'll go down the Dock Road and throw rocks in the Shannon.

We throw rocks in the river and we swing on the iron chains along the bank. It's getting dark and I don't know where I'm going to sleep. I might have to stay there by the Shannon or find a door or I might have to go back out the country and find a ditch like Brendan Quigley with four goats. Paddy says I can go home with him, I can sleep on the floor and I'll dry out.

Paddy lives in one of the tall houses on Arthur's Quay looking at the river. Everyone in Limerick knows these houses are old and might fall down at any minute. Mam often says, I don't want any of ye going down to Arthur's Quay and if I find ye there I'll break yeer faces. The people down there are wild and ye could get robbed and killed.

It's raining again and small children are playing in the hallway and up the stairs. Paddy says, Mind yourself, because some of the steps are missing and there is shit on the ones that are still there. He says that's because there's only one privy and it's in the backyard and children don't get down the stairs in time to put their little arses on the bowl, God help us.

There's a woman with a shawl sitting on the fourth flight smoking a cigarette. She says, Is that you, Paddy?

'Tis, Mammy.

I'm fagged out, Paddy. Them steps is killin' me. Did you have your tea?

I didn't.

Well, I don't know if there's any bread left. Go up an' see.

Paddy's family live in one big room with a high ceiling and a small fireplace. There are two tall windows and you can see out to the Shannon. His father is in a bed in the corner, groaning and spitting into a bucket. Paddy's brothers and sisters are on mattresses on the floor, sleeping, talking, looking at the ceiling. There's a baby with no clothes crawling over to Paddy's father's bucket and Paddy pulls him away. His mother comes in, gasping, from the stairs. Jesus, I'm dead, she says.

She finds some bread and makes weak tea for Paddy and me. I don't know what I'm supposed to do. They don't say anything. They don't say what are you doing here or go home or anything till Mr. Clohessy says, Who's that? and Paddy tells him, 'Tis Frankie McCourt.

Mr. Clohessy says, McCourt? What class of a name is that?

My father is from the North, Mr. Clohessy.

And what's your mother's name?

Angela, Mr. Clohessy.

Ah, Jaysus, 'twouldn't be Angela Sheehan, would it?

'Twould, Mr. Clohessy.

Ah, Jaysus, he says, and he has a coughing fit which brings up all kinds of stuff from his insides and has him hanging over the bucket. When the cough passes he falls back on the pillow. Ah, Frankie, I knew your mother well. Danced with her, Mother o' Christ, I'm dying inside, danced with her I did below in the Wembley Hall and a champion dancer she was too.

He hangs over the bucket again. He gasps for air and reaches his arms out to get it. He suffers but he won't stop talking.

Champion dancer she was, Frankie. Not skinny mind you but a feather in my arms and there was many a sorry man when she left Limerick. Can you dance, Frankie?

Ah, no, Mr. Clohessy.

Paddy says, He can, Dada. He had the lessons from Mrs. O'Connor and Cyril Benson.

Well, dance, Frankie. Round the house an' mind the dresser, Frankie. Lift the foot, lad.

I can't, Mr. Clohessy. I'm no good.

No good? Angela's Sheehan's son? Dance, Frankie, or I'll get outa this bed an' wheel you round the house.

My shoe is broken, Mr. Clohessy.

Frankie, Frankie, you're bringin' the cough on me. Will you dance for the love o' Jesus so I can remember me youth with your mother in the Wembley Hall. Take off the feckin' shoe, Frankie, an' dance.

I have to make up dances and tunes to go with them the way I did a long time ago when I was young. I dance around the room with one shoe because I forgot to take it off. I try to make up words, Oh, The Walls of Limerick are falling down, falling down, falling down, The Walls of Limerick falling down and the River Shannon kills us.

Mr. Clohessy is laughing in the bed. Oh, Jaysus, I never heard likes o' that on land or sea. That's a great leg for the dancing you have there, Frankie. Oh, Jaysus. He coughs and brings up ropes of green and yellow stuff. It makes me sick to look at it and I wonder if I should go home from all this sickness and this bucket and let my parents kill me if they want to.

Paddy lies down on a mattress by the window and I lie beside him. I keep my clothes on like everybody else and I even forget to take off my other shoe, which is wet and squishy and stinks. Paddy falls asleep right away and I look at his mother sitting by the bit of a fire smoking another cigarette. Paddy's father groans and coughs and spits into the bucket. He says, Feckin' blood, and she says, You'll have to go into the sanatorium sooner or later.

I will not. The day they put you in there is the end of you.

You could be givin' the consumption to the children. I

could get the guards to take you away you're that much of a danger to the children.

If they were to get it they'd have it be now.

The fire dies and Mrs. Clohessy climbs over him into the bed. In a minute she's snoring even if he's still coughing and laughing about the days of his youth when he danced with Angela Sheehan light as a feather in the Wembley Hall.

It's cold in the room and I'm shivering in my wet clothes. Paddy is shivering too but he's asleep and he doesn't know he's cold. I don't know if I should stay here or get up and go home but who wants to be wandering the streets when a guard might ask you what you're doing out. It's my first time away from my family and I know I'd rather be in my own house with the smelly lavatory and stable next door. It's bad when our kitchen is a lake and we have to go up to Italy but it's worse in the Clohessys' when you have to go down four flights to the lavatory and slip on shit all the way down. I'd be better off with four goats in a ditch.

I drift in and out of sleep but I have to wake up for good when Mrs. Clohessy goes around pulling at her family to get them up. They all went to bed with their clothes on so they don't have to get dressed and there's no fighting. They grumble and run out the door to get downstairs to the back-yard lavatory. I have to go too and I run down with Paddy but his sister Peggy is on the bowl and we have to piss against a wall. She says, I'll tell Ma what ye did, and Paddy says, Shurrup or I'll push you down into that feckin' lavatory. She jumps off the lavatory, pulls her drawers up and runs up the stairs crying, I'll tell, I'll tell, and when we get back to the room Mrs. Clohessy gives Paddy a belt on the head for what he did to his poor little sister. Paddy says nothing because Mrs. Clohessy is spooning porridge into mugs and jam jars and one bowl and telling us to eat up and go to school. She sits at the table eating her porridge. Her hair is gray black and dirty. It dangles in the bowl and picks up bits of porridge and drops of milk. The children slurp the porridge and complain they didn't get enough, they're starving with the hunger. They have snotty noses and sore eyes and scabby knees. Mr. Clohessy coughs and squirms on the bed and brings up the great gobs of blood and I run out of the room and puke on the stairs where there's a step missing and there's a shower of porridge and bits of apple to the floor below where people go back and forth to the lavatory in the yard. Paddy comes down and says, Sure that's all right. Everywan gets sick an' shits on them stairs an' the whole feckin' place is falling down anyway.

I don't know what I'm supposed to do now. If I go back to school I'll be killed and why should I go back to school or go home to get killed when I can go out the road and live on milk and apples the rest of my life till I go to America. Paddy says, Come on. School is all a cod anyway an' the masters is all madmen.

There's a knock at the Clohessys' door and it's Mam holding my little brother, Michael, by the hand, and Guard Dennehy, who is in charge of school attendance. Mam sees me and says, What are you doing with one shoe on? and Guard Dennehy says, Ah, now, missus, I think a more important question would be, What are you doing with one shoe off, ha, ha.

Michael runs to me. Mammy was crying. Mammy was crying for you, Frankie.

She says, Where were you all night?

I was here.

You had me demented. Your father walked every street in Limerick looking for you.

Mr. Clohessy says, Who's at the door?

It's my mother, Mr. Clohessy.

God above, is that Angela?

'Tis, Mr. Clohessy.

He struggles up on his elbows. Well, for the love of God, will you come in, Angela. Don't you know me?

Mam looks puzzled. It's dark in the room and she tries to

make out who is in the bed. He says, 'Tis me, Dennis Clohessy, Angela.

Ah, no.

'Tis, Angela.

Ah, no.

I know, Angela. I'm changed. The cough is killin' me. But I remember the nights at the Wembley Hall. Aw, Jaysus, you were a great dancer. Nights at the Wembley Hall, Angela, and the fish and chips after. Oh, boys, oh, boys, Angela.

My mother has tears running down her face. She says, You were a great dancer yourself, Dennis Clohessy.

We could have won competitions, Angela. Fred and Ginger would have been lookin' over their shoulders but you had to run off to America. Aw, Jaysus.

He has another coughing fit and we have to stand and watch him hang over the bucket again and bring up the bad stuff from his insides. Guard Dennehy says, I think, missus, we found the by an' I'll be going. He says to me, If you ever go on the mooch again, by, we'll have you in the jail above. Are you listenin' to me, by?

I am, Guard.

Don't be tormentin' your mother, by. That's wan thing the guards won't put up with, the tormentin' of mothers.

I won't, Guard. I won't torment her.

He leaves and Mam goes to the bed to take Mr. Clohessy's hand. His face is caved in all around his eyes and his hair is shiny black with the sweat running from the top of his head. His children stand around the bed looking at him and looking at Mam. Mrs. Clohessy sits by the fire rattling the poker in the grate and pushing the baby away from the fire. She says, 'Tis his own bloody fault for not goin' into hospital, so 'tis.

Mr. Clohessy gasps, I'd be all right if I could live in a dry place. Angela, is America a dry place?

'Tis, Dennis.

The doctor told me go to Arizona. A funny man that

doctor. Arizona how are you. I don't have the money to go around the corner for a pint.

Mam says, You'll be all right, Dennis. I'll light a candle for you.

Save your money, Angela. My dancin' days are done.

I have to go now, Dennis. My son has to go to school.

Before you go, Angela, will you do one thing for me?

I will, Dennis, if 'tis in my power.

Would you ever give us a verse of that song you sang the night before you went to America?

That's a hard song, Dennis. I wouldn't have the wind for it.

Ah, come on, Angela. I never hear a song anymore. There isn't a song in this house. The wife there doesn't have a note in her head an' no step in her foot.

Mam says, All right. I'll try.

> *Oh, the nights of the Kerry dancing, Oh, the ring of the piper's*
> *tune,*
> *Oh, for one of those hours of gladness, gone, alas, like our*
> *youth too soon.*
> *When the boys began to gather in the glen of a Summer night,*
> *And the Kerry piper's tuning made us long with wild delight.*

She stops and presses her hand to her chest, Oh, God, my wind is gone. Help me, Frank, with the song, and I sing along,

> *Oh, to think of it, Oh, to dream of it, fills my heart with*
> *tears.*
> *Oh, the nights of the Kerry dancing, Oh, the ring of the piper's*
> *tune*
> *Oh, for one of those hours of gladness, gone, alas, like our*
> *youth too soon.*

Mr. Clohessy tries to sing with us, gone, alas, like our youth too soon, but it brings on the cough. He shakes his head and cries, I wouldn't doubt you, Angela. It takes me back. God bless you.

God bless you, too, Dennis, and thanks, Mrs. Clohessy, for having Frankie here off the streets.

'Twas no trouble, Mrs. McCourt. He's quiet enough.

Quiet enough, says Mr. Clohessy, but he's not the dancer his mother was.

Mam says, 'Tis hard to dance with one shoe, Dennis.

I know, Angela, but you'd wonder why he didn't take it off. Is he a bit strange?

Ah, sometimes he has the odd manner like his father.

Oh, yes. The father is from the North, Angela, and that would account for it. They'd think nothing of dancing with one shoe in the North.

We walk up Patrick Street and O'Connell Street, Paddy Clohessy and Mam and Michael and myself, and Mam sobs all the way. Michael says, Don't cry, Mammy. Frankie won't run away.

She lifts him up and hugs him. Oh, no, Michael, 'tisn't Frankie I'm crying about. 'Tis Dennis Clohessy and the dancing nights at the Wembley Hall and the fish and chips after.

She comes into the school with us. Mr. O'Neill looks cross and tells us sit down he'll be with us in a minute. He talks a long time at the door with my mother and when she leaves he walks between the seats and pats Paddy Clohessy on the head.

I'm very sorry for the Clohessys and all their troubles but I think they saved me from getting into trouble with my mother.

VII

There are Thursdays when Dad gets his dole money at the Labour Exchange and a man might say, Will we go for a pint, Malachy? and Dad will say, One, only one, and the man will say, Oh, God, yes, one, and before the night is over all the money is gone and Dad comes home singing and getting us out of bed to line up and promise to die for Ireland when the call comes. He even gets Michael up and he's only three but there he is singing and promising to die for Ireland at the first opportunity. That's what Dad calls it, the first opportunity. I'm nine and Malachy is eight and we know all the songs. We sing all the verses of Kevin Barry and Roddy McCorley, "The West's Asleep," "O'Donnell Abu," "The Boys of Wexford." We sing and promise to die because you never know when Dad might have a penny or two left over from the drinking and if he gives it to us we can run to Kathleen O'Connell's next day for toffee. Some nights he says Michael is the best singer of all and he gives him the penny. Malachy and I wonder what's the use of being eight and nine and knowing all the songs and ready to die when Michael gets the penny so that he can go to the shop next day and stuff his gob with toffee galore. No one can ask him to die for Ireland at the age of three, not even Padraig Pearse, who was shot by the English in Dublin in 1916 and expected the whole world to die with him. Besides, Mikey Molloy's father said anyone who wants to die for Ireland is a donkey's arse. Men have been dying for Ireland since the beginning of time and look at the state of the country.

It's bad enough that Dad loses jobs in the third week but now he drinks all the dole money once a month. Mam gets desperate and in the morning she has the bitter face and she won't talk to him. He has his tea and leaves the house early for the long walk into the country. When he returns in the evening she still won't talk to him and she won't make his tea. If the fire is dead for the want of coal or turf and there's no way of boiling water for the tea, he says, Och, aye, and drinks water out of a jam jar and smacks his lips the way he would with a pint of porter. He says good water is all a man needs and Mam makes a snorting sound. When she's not talking to him the house is heavy and cold and we know we're not supposed to talk to him either for fear she'll give us the bitter look. We know Dad has done the bad thing and we know you can make anyone suffer by not talking to him. Even little Michael knows that when Dad does the bad thing you don't talk to him from Friday to Monday and when he tries to lift you to his lap you run to Mam.

I'm nine years old and I have a pal, Mickey Spellacy, whose relations are dropping one by one of the galloping consumption. I envy Mickey because every time someone dies in his family he gets a week off from school and his mother stitches a black diamond patch on his sleeve so that he can wander from lane to lane and street to street and people will know he has the grief and pat his head and give him money and sweets for his sorrow.

But this summer Mickey is worried. His sister, Brenda, is wasting away with the consumption and it's only August and if she dies before September he won't get his week off from school because you can't get a week off from school when there's no school. He comes to Billy Campbell and me to ask if we'll go around the corner to St. Joseph's Church and pray for Brenda to hang on till September.

What's in it for us, Mickey, if we go around the corner praying?

Well, if Brenda hangs on and I get me week off ye can come to the wake and have ham and cheese and cake and sherry and lemonade and everything and ye can listen to the songs and stories all night.

Who could say no to that? There's nothing like a wake for having a good time. We trot around to the church where they have statues of St. Joseph himself as well as the Sacred Heart of Jesus, the Virgin Mary and St. Thérèse of Lisieux, the Little Flower. I pray to the Little Flower because she died of the consumption herself and she'd understand.

One of our prayers must have been powerful because Brenda stays alive and doesn't die till the second day of school. We tell Mickey we're sorry for his troubles but he's delighted with his week off and he gets the black diamond patch which will bring the money and sweets.

My mouth is watering at the thought of the feast at Brenda's wake. Billy knocks on the door and there's Mickey's aunt. Well?

We came to say a prayer for Brenda and Mickey said we could come to the wake.

She yells, Mickey!

What?

Come here. Did you tell this gang they could come to your sister's wake?

No.

But, Mickey, you promised . . .

She slams the door in our faces. We don't know what to do till Billy Campbell says, We'll go back to St. Joseph's and pray that from now on everyone in Mickey Spellacy's family will die in the middle of the summer and he'll never get a day off from school for the rest of his life.

One of our prayers is surely powerful because next summer Mickey himself is carried off by the galloping consumption and he doesn't get a day off from school and that will surely teach him a lesson.

> *Proddy Woddy ring the bell,*
> *Not for heaven but for hell.*

On Sunday mornings in Limerick I watch them go to church, the Protestants, and I feel sorry for them, especially the girls, who are so lovely, they have such beautiful white teeth. I feel sorry for the beautiful Protestant girls, they're doomed. That's what the priests tell us. Outside the Catholic Church there is no salvation. Outside the Catholic Church there is nothing but doom. And I want to save them. Protestant girl, come with me to the True Church. You'll be saved and you won't have the doom. After Mass on Sunday I go with my friend Billy Campbell to watch them play croquet on the lovely lawn beside their church on Barrington Street. Croquet is a Protestant game. They hit the ball with the mallet, pock and pock again, and laugh. I wonder how they can laugh or don't they even know they're doomed? I feel sorry for them and I say, Billy, what's the use of playing croquet when you're doomed?

He says, Frankie, what's the use of not playing croquet when you're doomed?

Grandma says to Mam, Your brother Pat, bad leg an' all, was selling papers all over Limerick by the time he was eight and that Frank of yours is big and ugly enough to work.

But he's only nine and still in school.

School. 'Tis school that has him the way he is talkin' back an' goin' around with the sour puss an' the odd manner like his father. He could get out an' help poor Pat of a Friday night when the *Limerick Leader* is a ton weight. He could run up the long garden paths of the quality an' save Pat's poor legs an' earn a few pennies into the bargain.

He has to go to the Confraternity on Friday nights.

Never mind the Confraternity. There's nothin' in the catechism about confraternities.

I meet Uncle Pat at the *Limerick Leader* on Friday evening at five. The man handing out the papers says my arms are that skinny I'd be lucky to carry two stamps but Uncle Pat sticks eight papers under each arm. He tells me, I'll kill you if you drop 'em for 'tis raining abroad, pelting out of the heavens. He tells me hug the walls going up O'Connell Street to keep the papers dry. I'm to run in where there's a delivery, climb the outside steps, in the door, up the stairs, yell Paper, get the money they owe him for the week, down the stairs, give him the money and on to the next stop. Customers give him tips for his troubles and he keeps them for himself.

We make our way up O'Connell Avenue, out Ballinacurra, in by the South Circular Road, down Henry Street and back to the office for more papers. Uncle Pat wears a cap and a thing like a cowboy poncho to keep his papers dry but he complains his feet are killing him and we stop in a pub for a pint for his poor feet. Uncle Pa Keating is there all black and having a pint and he says to Uncle Pat, Ab, are you going to let that boy stand there with his face hanging out for the want of a lemonade?

Uncle Pat says, Wha? and Uncle Pa Keating gets impatient. Christ, he's dragging your feckin' papers all over Limerick and you can't—Oh, never mind. Timmy, give the child a lemonade. Frankie, don't you have a raincoat at home?

No, Uncle Pa.

You're not supposed to be out in this weather. You're drenched entirely. Who sent you out in this muck?

Grandma said I had to help Uncle Pat because of his bad leg.

Course she did, the oul' bitch, but don't tell them I said that.

Uncle Pat is struggling off the seat and gathering up his papers. Come on, 'tis gettin' dark.

He hobbles along the streets calling, Anna Lie Sweets Lie, which doesn't sound a bit like *Limerick Leader* and it doesn't matter because everyone knows this is Ab Sheehan that was dropped on his head. Here, Ab, give us a *Leader*, how's your poor leg, keep the change an' get yourself a fag for 'tis an awful feckin' night to be out sellin' the feckin' papers.

Tanks, says Ab, my uncle. Tanks, tanks, tanks, and it's hard to keep up with him on the streets bad as his leg is. He says, How many *Leaders* have you under your oxter?

One, Uncle Pat.

Take that *Leader* in to Mr. Timoney. He owes me for a fortnight now. Get that money an' there's a tip. He's a good man for the tip an' don't be shovin' it in your pocket like your cousin Gerry. Shoved it in his pocket, the little bugger.

I bang on the door with the knocker and there's a great howl from a dog so big he makes the door shake. A man's voice says, Macushla, quit the bloody racket or I'll give you a good fong in the arse for yourself. The racket stops, the door opens and the man is there, white hair, thick glasses, white sweater, a stick in his hand. He says, Who is it? Who do we have?

The paper, Mr. Timoney.

We don't have Ab Sheehan here, do we?

I'm his nephew, sir.

Is it Gerry Sheehan we have here?

No, sir. I'm Frank McCourt.

Another nephew? Does he make them? Is there a little nephew factory in the backyard? Here's the money for the fortnight and give me the paper or keep it. What's the use? I can't read anymore and Mrs. Minihan that's supposed to read to me didn't come. Legless with the sherry, that's what she is. What's your name?

Frank, sir.

Can you read?

I can, sir.

Do you want to earn a sixpence?

I do, sir.

Come here tomorrow. Your name is Francis, isn't it?

Frank, sir.

Your name is Francis. There was never a St. Frank. That's a name for gangsters and politicians. Come here tomorrow at eleven and read to me.

I will, sir.

Are you sure you can read?

I am, sir.

You can call me Mr. Timoney.

I will, Mr. Timoney.

Uncle Pat is mumbling at the gate, rubbing his leg. Where's me money an' you're not supposed to be chattin' with the customers an' me here with the leg destroyed be the rain. He has to stop at the pub at Punch's Cross to have a pint for the destroyed leg. After the pint he says he can't walk another inch and we get on a bus. The conductor says, Fares, please, fares, but Uncle Pat says, Go 'way an' don't be botherin' me, can't you see the state o' me leg?

Oh, all right, Ab, all right.

The bus stops at the O'Connell Monument and Uncle Pat goes to the Monument Fish and Chip Café where the smells are so delicious my stomach beats with the hunger. He gets a shilling's worth of fish and chips and my mouth is watering but when we get to Grandma's door he gives me a threepenny bit, tells me meet him again next Friday and go home now to my mother.

The dog Macushla is lying outside Mr. Timoney's door and when I open the little garden gate to go up the path she rushes at me and knocks me back out on the pavement and she'd eat my face if Mr. Timoney didn't come out and flail at her with his stick and yell, Come in out of it, ye hoor, ye overgrown man-eatin' bitch. Didn't you have your breakfast, you hoor? Are you all right, Francis, Come in. That

197

dog is a right Hindu, so she is, and that's where I found her
mother wandering around Bangalore. If ever you're getting
a dog, Francis, make sure it's a Buddhist. Good-natured dogs,
the Buddhists. Never, never get a Mahommedan. They'll eat
you sleeping. Never a Catholic dog. They'll eat you every
day including Fridays. Sit down and read to me.

The *Limerick Leader*, Mr. Timoney?

No, not the bloody *Limerick Leader*. I wouldn't wipe the
hole of my arse with the *Limerick Leader*. There's a book over
there on the table, *Gulliver's Travels*. That's not what I want
you to read. Look in the back for another thing. *A Modest
Proposal*. Read that to me. It begins, It is a melancholy object
to those who walk . . . Do you have that? I have the whole
bloody thing in my head but I still want you to read to me.

He stops me after two or three pages. You're a good
reader. And what do you think of that, Francis, that a young
healthy child well nursed is at a year old a most delicious,
nourishing, and wholesome food, whether stewed, roasted,
baked, or boiled, eh? Macushla would love a dinner of a nice
plump Irish infant, wouldn't you, you oul' hoor?

He gives me sixpence, and tells me return next Saturday.

Mam is delighted I earned sixpence for reading to Mr.
Timoney and what was it he wanted read, the *Limerick Leader*?
I tell her I had to read *A Modest Proposal* from the back of
Gulliver's Travels and she says, That's all right, 'tis only a
children's book. You'd expect him to want something strange
for he's a little off in the head after years in the sun in the
English army in India and they say he was married to one
of them Indian women and she was accidentally shot by a
soldier during some class of a disturbance. That's the kind of
thing that would drive you to children's books. She knows
this Mrs. Minihan who lives next door to Mr. Timoney and
used to clean house but couldn't stand it anymore the way
he laughed at the Catholic Church and said one man's sin
was another man's romp. Mrs. Minihan didn't mind the odd
drop of sherry of a Saturday morning but then he tried to

turn her into a Buddhist, which he said he was himself and the Irish would be much better off in general if they sat under a tree and watched the Ten Commandments and the Seven Deadly Sins float down the Shannon and far out to sea.

The next Friday Declan Collopy from the Confraternity sees me on the street delivering the papers with my uncle Pat Sheehan. Hoi, Frankie McCourt, what are you doin' with Ab Sheehan?

He's my uncle.

You're supposed to be at the Confraternity.

I'm working, Declan.

You're not supposed to be working. You're not even ten and you're destroyin' the perfect attendance in our section. If you're not there next Friday I'll give you a good thump in the gob, do you hear me?

Uncle Pat says, Go 'way, go 'way, or I'll walk on you.

Ah, shut up, Mr. Stupid that was dropped on your head. He pushes Uncle Pat on the shoulder and knocks him back against the wall. I drop the papers and run at him but he steps aside and punches me on the back of the neck and my forehead is rammed into the wall and it puts me in such a rage I can't see him anymore. I go at him with arms and legs and if I could tear his face off with my teeth I would but he has long arms like a gorilla and he just keeps pushing me away so that I can't touch him. He says, You mad feckin' eejit. I'll destroy you in the Confraternity, and he runs away.

Uncle Pat says, You shouldn't be fightin' like that an' you dropped all me papers an' some o' them is wet an' how am I supposed to sell wet papers, and I wanted to jump on him too and hit him for talking about papers after I stood up to Declan Collopy.

At the end of the night he gives me three chips from his bag and sixpence instead of threepence. He complains it's too much money and it's all my mother's fault for going on to Grandma about the low pay.

Mam is delighted I'm getting sixpence on Fridays from Uncle Pat and sixpence on Saturdays from Mr. Timoney. A shilling a week makes a big difference and she gives me tuppence to see the Dead End Kids at the Lyric after I'm finished the reading.

Next morning Mr. Timoney says, Wait till we get to *Gulliver*, Francis. You'll know Jonathan Swift is the greatest Irish writer that ever lived, no, the greatest man to put pen to parchment. A giant of a man, Francis. He laughs all through *A Modest Proposal* and you'd wonder what he's laughing at when it's all about cooking Irish babies. He says, You'll laugh when you grow up, Francis.

You're not supposed to talk back to grown-ups but Mr. Timoney is different and he doesn't mind when I say, Mr. Timoney, big people are always telling us that. Oh, you'll laugh when you grow up. You'll understand when you grow up. Everything will come when you grow up.

He lets out such a roar of a laugh I think he's going to collapse. Oh, Mother o' God, Francis. You're a treasure. What's up with you? Do you have a bee up your arse? Tell me what's up.

Nothing, Mr. Timoney.

I think you have the long puss, Francis, and I wish I could see it. Go over to the mirror on the wall, Snow White, and tell me if you have the long puss. Never mind. Just tell me what's up.

Declan Collopy was at me last night and I got into a fight.

He makes me tell him about the Confraternity and Declan and my uncle Pat Sheehan, who was dropped on his head, and then he tells me he knows my uncle Pa Keating, who was gassed in the war and works in the gas works. He says, Pa Keating is a jewel of a man. And I'll tell you what I'll do, Francis. I'll talk to Pa Keating and we'll go to the craw-thumpers at the Confraternity. I'm a Buddhist myself and I don't hold with fighting but I haven't lost it. They're not going to interfere with my little reader, oh, by Jesus, no.

Mr. Timoney is an old man but he talks like a friend and I can say what I feel. Dad would never talk to me like Mr. Timoney. He'd say, Och, aye, and go for a long walk.

Uncle Pat Sheehan tells Grandma he doesn't want me to help with the papers anymore, he can get another boy much cheaper and he thinks I should be giving him some of my Saturday morning sixpence anyway since I'd never have the reading job without him.

A woman next door to Mr. Timoney tells me I'm wasting my time knocking on the door, Macushla bit the postman, the milkman and a passing nun on the same day and Mr. Timoney couldn't stop laughing though he cried when the dog was taken away to be put down. You can bite postmen and milkmen all you like but the case of the passing nun goes all the way to the bishop and he takes steps especially if the owner of the dog is a known Buddhist and a danger to good Catholics around him. Mr. Timoney was told this and cried and laughed so hard the doctor came and said he was gone beyond recall so they carted him off to the City Home, where they keep old people who are helpless or demented.

That's the end of my Saturday sixpence but I'll read to Mr. Timoney money or no money. I wait down the street till the woman next door goes in, I climb in Mr. Timoney's window for *Gulliver's Travels* and walk miles to the City Home so that he won't miss his reading. The man at the gate says, What? You want to come in an' read to an oul' man? Is it coddin' me you are? Get outa here before I call the guards.

Could I leave the book for someone else to read to Mr. Timoney?

Leave it. Leave it for Jaysus sake an' don't be botherin' me. I'll send it up to him.

And he laughs.

Mam says, What's up with you? Why are you moping? And I tell her how Uncle Pat doesn't want me anymore and how they put Mr. Timoney in the City Home for laughing just because Macushla bit the postman, the milkman and a passing nun. She laughs too and I'm sure the world is gone mad. Then she says, Ah, I'm sorry and it's a pity you lost two jobs. You might as well start going to the Confraternity again to keep The Posse away and, worse, the director, Father Gorey.

Declan tells me sit in front of him and if there's any bla-guarding he'll break my feckin' neck for he'll be watching me as long as he's prefect and no little shit like me is going to keep him from a life in linoleum.

Mam says she has trouble climbing the stairs and she's moving her bed to the kitchen. She laughs, I'll come back up to Sorrento when the walls are damp and the rain runs under the door. School is over and she can stay in bed in the kitchen as long as she likes because she doesn't have to get up for us. Dad lights the fire, makes the tea, cuts the bread, makes sure we wash our faces and tells us go out and play. He lets us stay in bed if we like but you never want to stay in bed when there's no school. We're ready to run out and play in the lane the minute we wake.

Then one day in July he says we can't go downstairs. We have to stay up here and play.

Why, Dad?

Never mind. Play here with Malachy and Michael and you can go down later when I tell you.

He stands at the door in case we might get a notion to wander down the stairs. We push our blanket up in the air with our feet and pretend we're in a tent, Robin Hood and his Merry Men. We hunt fleas and squash them between our thumbnails.

Then there's a baby's cry and Malachy says, Dad, did Mam get a new baby?

Och, aye, son.

I'm older so I tell Malachy the bed is in the kitchen so that the angel can fly down and leave the baby on the seventh step but Malachy doesn't understand because he's only eight going on nine and I'll be ten next month.

Mam is in the bed with the new baby. He has a big fat face and he's red all over. There's a woman in the kitchen in a nurse's uniform and we know she's there to wash new babies who are always dirty from the long journey with the angel. We want to tickle the baby but she says, No, no, ye can look at him but don't lay a finger.

Don't lay a finger. That's the way nurses talk.

We sit at the table with our tea and bread looking at our new brother but he won't even open his eyes to look back at us so we go out and play.

In a few days Mam is out of the bed holding the baby on her lap by the fire. His eyes are open and when we tickle him he makes a gurgling sound, his belly shakes and that makes us laugh. Dad tickles him and sings a Scottish song,

> *Oh, oh, stop your ticklin', Jock,*
> *Stop your ticklin', Jock.*
> *Stop your ticklin',*
> *Ickle ickle icklin*
> *Stop your ticklin', Jock.*

Dad has a job so Bridey Hannon is able to visit Mam and the baby any time she likes and for once Mam doesn't tell us go out and play so they can talk about secret things. They sit by the fire smoking and talking about names. Mam says she likes the names Kevin and Sean but Bridey says, Ah, no, there's too many of them in Limerick. Jesus, Angela, if you stuck your head out the door and called, Kevin or Sean, come in for your tea, you'd have half o'Limerick running to your door.

Bridey says if she had a son which please God she will some day she'll call him Ronald because she's mad about

Ronald Colman that you see in the Coliseum Cinema. Or Errol, now that's another lovely name, Errol Flynn.

Mam says, Will you go way outa that, Bridey. I'd never be able to stick my head out the door and say, Errol, Errol, come in for your tea. Sure the poor child would be a laughingstock.

Ronald, says Bridey, Ronald. He's gorgeous.

No, says Mam, it has to be Irish. Isn't that what we fought for all these years? What's the use of fighting the English for centuries if we're going to call our children Ronald?

Jesus, Angela, you're starting to talk like himself with his Irish this and his English that.

Still an' all, Bridey, he's right.

Suddenly Bridey is gasping, Jesus, Angela, there's something wrong with that child.

Mam is out of the chair, hugging the child, moaning. Oh, Jesus, Bridey, he's choking.

Bridey says, I'll run for my mother, and she's back in a minute with Mrs. Hannon. Castor oil, says Mrs. Hannon. Do you have it? Any oil. Cod liver oil? That'll do.

She pours the oil into the baby's mouth, turns him over, presses on his back, turns him back over, sticks a spoon down his throat and brings up a white ball. That's it now, she says. The milk. It collects and gets hard in their little throats so you have to ease it with any class of an oil.

Mam is crying, Jesus, I nearly lost him. Oh, I'd die so I would.

She's clutching the baby and crying and trying to thank Mrs. Hannon.

Yerra, don't mention it, missus. Take the child and get back into that bed for the two o'ye had a great shock.

While Bridey and Mrs. Hannon are helping Mam to the bed I notice spots of blood on her chair. Is my mother bleeding to death? Is it all right to say, Look, there's blood on Mam's chair? No, you can't say anything because they always have secrets. I know if you say anything the grown-up people will tell you, Never mind, you're always gawking, none of your business, go out and play.

I have to keep it inside or I can talk to the angel. Mrs. Hannon and Bridey leave and I sit on the seventh step. I try to tell the angel Mam is bleeding to death. I want him to tell me, Fear not, but the step is cold and there's no light, no voice. I'm sure he's gone forever and I wonder if that happens when you go from nine to ten.

Mam doesn't bleed to death. She's out of the bed next day getting the baby ready for baptism, telling Bridey she could never forgive herself if the baby died and went to Limbo, a place for unbaptized babies, where it may be nice and warm but, still, dark forever and no hope of escape even on the Judgment Day.

Grandma is there to help and she says, That's right, no hope in heaven for the infant that's not baptized.

Bridey says it would be a hard God that would do the likes of that.

He has to be hard, says Grandma, otherwise you'd have all kinds of babies clamorin' to get into heaven, Protestants an' everything, an'why should they get in after what they did to us for eight hundred years?

The babies didn't do it, says Bridey. They're too small.

They would if they got the chance, says Grandma. They're trained for it.

They dress the baby in the Limerick lace dress we were all baptized in. Mam says we can all go to St. Joseph's and we're excited because there will be lemonade and buns after.

Malachy says, Mam, what's the baby's name?

Alphonsus Joseph.

The words fly out of my mouth, That's a stupid name. It's not even Irish.

Grandma glares at me with her old red eyes. She says, That fella needs a good clitther on the gob. Mam slaps me across the face and sends me flying across the kitchen. My heart is pounding and I want to cry but I can't because my father isn't there and I'm the man of the family. Mam says, You go upstairs with your big mouth and don't move from that room.

I stop at the seventh step but it's still cold, no light, no voice.

The house is quiet with everyone gone to the chapel. I sit and wait upstairs, knocking the fleas off my arms and legs, wishing I had Dad here, thinking of my little brother and his foreign name, Alphonsus, an affliction of a name.

In awhile there are voices downstairs and there is talk of tea, sherry, lemonade, buns, and isn't that child the loveliest little fella in the world, little Alphie, foreign name but still an' all still an' all not a sound outa him the whole time he's that good-natured God bless him sure he'll live forever with the sweetness that's in him the little dote spittin' image of his mother his father his grandma his little brothers dead an' gone.

Mam calls from the bottom of the stairs, Frank, come down and have lemonade and a bun.

I don't want it. You can keep it.

I said come down this minute for if I have to climb these stairs I'll warm your behind and you'll rue the day.

Rue? What's rue?

Never mind what's rue. Come down here at once.

Her voice is sharp and rue sounds dangerous. I'll go down.

In the kitchen Grandma says, Look at the long puss on him. You'd think he'd be happy for his little brother except that a boy that's going from nine to ten is always a right pain in the arse an' I know for didn't I have two of 'em.

The lemonade and bun are delicious and Alphie the new baby is chirping away enjoying his baptism day too innocent to know his name is an affliction.

Grandpa in the North sends a telegram money order for five pounds for the baby Alphie. Mam wants to cash it but she can't go far from the bed. Dad says he'll cash it at the post office. She tells Malachy and me to go with him. He cashes it and tells us, All right, boys, go home and tell your mother I'll be home in a few minutes.

Malachy says, Dad, you're not to go to the pub. Mam said you're to bring home the money. You're not to drink the pint.

Now, now, son. Go home to your mother.

Dad, give us the money. That money is for the baby.

Now, Francis, don't be a bad boy. Do what your father tells you.

He walks away from us and into South's pub.

Mam is sitting by the fireplace with Alphie in her arms. She shakes her head. He went to the pub, didn't he?

He did.

I want ye to go back down to that pub and read him out of it. I want ye to stand in the middle of the pub and tell every man your father is drinking the money for the baby. Ye are to tell the world there isn't a scrap of food in this house, not a lump of coal to start the fire, not a drop of milk for the baby's bottle.

We walk through the streets and Malachy practices his speech at the top of his voice, Dad, Dad, that five pounds is for the new baby. That's not for the drink. The child is above in the bed bawling and roaring for his milk and you're drinking the pint.

He's gone from South's pub. Malachy still wants to stand and make his speech but I tell him we have to hurry and look in other pubs before Dad drinks the whole five pounds. We can't find him in other pubs either. He knows Mam would come for him or send us and there are so many pubs at this end of Limerick and beyond we could be looking for a month. We have to tell Mam there's no sign of him and she tells us we're pure useless. Oh, Jesus, I wish I had my strength and I'd search every pub in Limerick. I'd tear the mouth out of his head, so I would. Go on, go back down and try all the pubs around the railway station and try Naughton's fish and chip shop.

I have to go by myself because Malachy has the runs and can't stray far from the bucket. I search all the pubs on Parnell Street and around. I look into the snugs where the women drink and in all the men's lavatories. I'm hungry but I'm afraid to go home till I find my father. He's not in Naughton's fish and chip shop but there's a drunken man asleep at a table in the corner and his fish and chips are on the floor in their *Limerick Leader* wrapping and if I don't get them the cat will so I shove them under my jersey and I'm out the door and up the street to sit on the steps at the railway station eat my fish and chips watch the drunken soldiers pass by with the girls that giggle thank the drunken man in my mind for drowning the fish and chips in vinegar and smothering them in salt and then remember that if I die tonight I'm in a state of sin for stealing and I could go straight to hell stuffed with fish and chips but it's Saturday and if the priests are still in the confession boxes I can clear my soul after my feed.

The Dominican church is just up Glentworth Street.

Bless me, Father, for I have sinned, it's a fortnight since my last confession. I tell him the usual sins and then, I stole fish and chips from a drunken man.

Why, my child?

I was hungry, Father.

And why were you hungry?

There was nothing in my belly, Father.

He says nothing and even though it's dark I know he's shaking his head. My dear child, why can't you go home and ask your mother for something?

Because she sent me out looking for my father in the pubs, Father, and I couldn't find him and she hasn't a scrap in the house because he's drinking the five pounds Grandpa sent from the North for the new baby and she's raging by the fire because I can't find my father.

I wonder if this priest is asleep because he's very quiet till he says, My child, I sit here. I hear the sins of the poor. I assign the penance. I bestow absolution. I should be on my knees washing their feet. Do you understand me, my child?

I tell him I do but I don't.

Go home, child. Pray for me.

No penance, Father?

No, my child.

I stole the fish and chips. I'm doomed.

You're forgiven. Go. Pray for me.

He blesses me in Latin, talks to himself in English and I wonder what I did to him.

I wish I could find my father so I could say to Mam, Here he is and he has three pounds left in his pocket. I'm not hungry now so I can go up one side of O'Connell Street and down the other and search pubs on the side streets and there he is in Gleeson's, how could I miss him with his singing,

> 'Tis alone my concern if the grandest surprise
> Would be shining at me out of somebody's eyes.
> 'Tis my private affair what my feelings would be
> While the Green Glens of Antrim were welcoming me.

My heart is banging away in my chest and I don't know what to do because I know I'm raging inside like my mother by the fire and all I can think of doing is running in and giving him a good kick in the leg and running out again but I don't because we have the mornings by the fire when he tells me about Cuchulain and de Valera and Roosevelt and if he's there drunk and buying pints with the baby's money he has that look in his eyes Eugene had when he searched for Oliver and I might as well go home and tell my mother a lie that I never saw him couldn't find him.

She's in the bed with the baby. Malachy and Michael are up in Italy asleep. I know I don't have to tell Mam anything, that soon when the pubs close he'll be home singing and offering us a penny to die for Ireland and it will be different now because it's bad enough to drink the dole or the wages but a man that drinks the money for a new baby is gone beyond the beyonds as my mother would say.

VIII

I'm ten years old and ready to go to St. Joseph's Church for my Confirmation. In school the master, Mr. O'Dea, prepares us. We have to know all about Sanctifying Grace, a pearl of great price, bought for us by Jesus in His dying. Mr. O'Dea's eyes roll in his head when he tells us that with Confirmation we will become part of Divinity. We will have the Gifts of the Holy Ghost: Wisdom, Understanding, Counsel, Fortitude, Knowledge, Piety, the Fear of the Lord. Priests and masters tell us Confirmation means you're a true soldier of the Church and that entitles you to die and be a martyr in case we're invaded by Protestants or Mahommedans or any other class of a heathen. More dying. I want to tell them I won't be able to die for the Faith because I'm already booked to die for Ireland.

Mikey Molloy says, Is it jokin' you are? That thing about dying for the Faith is all a cod. 'Tis only a saying they made up to frighten you. Ireland too. No one dies for anything anymore. All the dying is done. I wouldn't die for Ireland or the Faith. I might die for my mother but that's all.

Mikey knows everything. He's going on fourteen. He gets the fits. He has visions.

The grown-ups tell us it's a glorious thing to die for the Faith, only we're not ready for that yet because Confirmation day is like First Communion day, you make the rounds of lanes and back streets and you get cakes and sweets and money, The Collection.

That's where poor Peter Dooley comes in. We call him Quasimodo because he has a hump on his back like the one on the hunchback of Notre Dame, whose real name we know is Charles Laughton.

Quasimodo has nine sisters and it is said his mother never wanted him but that was what the angel brought her and it's a sin to question what's sent. Quasimodo is old, he's fifteen. His red hair sticks up in all directions. He has green eyes and one rolls around in his head so much he's constantly tapping his temple to keep it where it's supposed to be. His right leg is short and twisted and when he walks he does a little twirly dance and you never know when he'll fall. That's when you're surprised. He curses his leg, he curses the world, but he curses in a lovely English accent which he got from the radio, the BBC. Before he leaves his house he always sticks his head out the door and tells the lane, Here's me head, me arse is coming. When he was twelve Quasimodo decided that with the way he looked and the way the world looked at him the best thing would be to prepare for a job where he could be heard and not seen and what better than sitting behind a microphone at the BBC in London reading the news?

But you can't get to London without money and that's why he hobbles up to us that Friday, the day before Confirmation. He has an idea for Billy and me. He knows the next day we'll be getting Confirmation money and if we promise to pay him a shilling each he'll let us climb up the rainspout behind his house this very night to look in the window and see his sisters' naked bodies when they take their weekly wash. I sign right away. Billy says, I have my own sister. Why should I pay to see your naked sisters?

Quasimodo says that looking at your own sister's naked body is the worst sin of all and he's not sure if there's a priest in the world can forgive you, that you might have to go to the bishop, who everyone knows is a holy terror.

Billy signs.

Friday night we climb the wall of Quasimodo's backyard. It's a lovely night with the June moon floating high over

Limerick and you can feel a warm breeze off the Shannon River. Quasimodo is about to let Billy up the spout and who comes clambering over the wall but Mikey Molloy the Fit himself hissing at Quasimodo, Here's a shilling, Quasimodo. Let me up the spout. Mikey is fourteen now, bigger than any of us and strong from his job delivering coal. He's black from the coal like Uncle Pa Keating and all you can see are the whites of his eyes and the white froth on his lower lip, which means he could have the fit anytime.

Quasimodo says, Wait, Mikey. They're first. Wait, my arse, says Mikey, and he's away up the spout. Billy complains but Quasimodo shakes his head, I can't help it. He comes every week with the shilling. I have to let him up the spout or he'll beat me up and tell my mother and the next thing she locks me in the coal hole all day with the rats. The Fit is up hanging on to the spout with one hand. The other hand is in his pocket moving, moving and when the spout itself starts to move and creak Quasimodo hisses, Molloy, there's to be no whankin' up the spout. He hops around the yard cackling. His BBC accent is gone and he's pure Limerick. Jaysus, Molloy, come down off that spout or I'll tell me mother. Mikey's hand goes faster in his pocket, so fast the spout gives a lurch and collapses and Mikey is rolling on the ground yelping, I'm dead. I'm destroyed. Oh, God. You can see the froth on his lips and the blood that comes from biting his tongue.

Quasimodo's mother comes screaming through the door, What in the name of Jesus! and the kitchen light fills the yard. The sisters are squawking from the window above. Billy tries to escape and she drags him off the wall. She tells him run to O'Connor the chemist around the corner to ring up an ambulance or a doctor or something for Mikey. She screams at us to get into the kitchen. She kicks Quasimodo into the hall. He's on his hands and knees and she drags him to the coal hole under the stairs and locks him in. Stay there till you come to your senses.

He's crying and calling to her in a pure Limerick accent. Ah, Mamma, Mamma, let me out. The rats is here. I only want to go to the BBC, Mamma. Aw, Jasus, Mamma, Jasus. I'll never let anyone up the spout again. I'll send money from London, Mamma. Mamma!

Mikey is still on his back, jerking and twisting around the yard. The ambulance takes him off to the hospital with a broken shoulder and his tongue in ribbons.

Our mothers are there in no time. Mrs. Dooley says, I'm disgraced, so I am, disgraced. My daughters can't wash theirselves of a Friday night without the whole world gawking in the window and them boys there are in a state of sin and should be taken to the priest for confession before their Confirmation tomorrow.

But Mam says, I don't know about the rest of the world but I saved a whole year for Frank's Confirmation suit and I'm not going to the priest to have him tell me my son is not fit for Confirmation so that I'll have to wait another year when he grows out of this suit and all because he climbed a spout for an innocent gawk at the scrawny arse of Mona Dooley.

She drags me home by the ear and makes me kneel before the Pope. Swear, she says, swear to that Pope that you didn't look at Mona Dooley in her pelt.

I swear.

If you're lying you won't be in a state of grace for Confirmation tomorrow and that's the worst kind of sacrilege.

I swear.

Only the bishop himself could forgive a sacrilege like that.

I swear.

All right. Go to bed and from this day out stay far away from that misfortunate Quasimodo Dooley.

We are all confirmed the next day. The bishop asks me a catechism question, What is the Fourth Commandment? and I tell him, Honor thy father and thy mother. He pats my cheek and that makes me a soldier of the True Church. I kneel in the pew and think of Quasimodo locked in the coal hole under the stairs and I wonder, Should I give him the shilling anyway for his career at the BBC?

But I forget all about Quasimodo because my nose starts bleeding and I feel dizzy. Confirmation boys and girls are outside St. Joseph's with their parents and there is hugging and kissing in the bright sun and I don't care. My father is working and I don't care. My mother kisses me and I don't care. The boys talk about The Collection and I don't care. My nose won't stop and Mam is worried I'll ruin my suit. She runs into the church to see if Stephen Carey, the sacristan, would spare her a rag and he gives her some kind of canvas cloth that makes my nose sore. She says, Do you want to make your collection? and I tell her I don't care. Malachy says, Do, do, Frankie, and he's sad because I promised I'd take him to the Lyric Cinema to see the film and stuff ourselves with sweets. I want to lie down. I could lie down there on the steps of St. Joseph's and sleep forever. Mam says, Grandma is making a nice breakfast, and the mention of food makes me so sick I run to the edge of the pavement to throw up and the whole world is looking at me and I don't care. Mam says she'd better take me home and put me to bed and my pals look surprised that anyone can go to bed when there's a collection to be made.

She helps me take off my Confirmation suit and puts me to bed. She wets a rag and places it under my neck and after awhile the bleeding stops. She brings tea but the look of it makes me sick and I have to throw up in the bucket. Mrs. Hannon comes in from next door and I can hear her say that's a very sick child and he should have a doctor. Mam says it's Saturday, the Dispensary is closed and where would you get a doctor?

Dad comes home from his job at Rank's Flour Mills and tells Mam I'm going through a stage, growing pains.

Grandma comes up and says the same thing. She says when boys go from the one number year, which is nine, to the two number year, which is ten, they're changing and prone to the nosebleed. She says I might have too much blood in me anyway and a good cleaning out wouldn't do me one bit of harm.

The day passes and I'm in and out of sleep. Malachy and Michael come into the bed at night and I can hear Malachy say, Frankie is very hot. Michael says, He's bleeding on my leg. Mam puts the wet rag on my nose and a key on my neck but it won't stop the bleeding. On Sunday morning there's blood on my chest and all around me. Mam tells Dad I'm bleeding through my bottom and he says I might have a case of the runs, which is common with the growing pains.

Dr. Troy is our doctor but he's away on holiday and the man that comes to see me on Monday has a smell of whiskey on him. He examines me and tells my mother I have a bad cold and keep me in bed. Days pass and I sleep and bleed. Mam makes tea and beef tea and I don't want it. She even brings ice cream and the look of it makes me sick. Mrs. Hannon comes in again and says that doctor doesn't know what he's talking about, see if Dr. Troy is back.

Mam comes with Dr. Troy. He feels my forehead, rolls up my eyelids, turns me over to see my back, picks me up and runs to his motor car. Mam runs after him and he tells her I have typhoid fever. Mam cries, Oh, God, oh, God, am I to lose the whole family? Will it ever end? She gets into the car, holds me in her lap and moans all the way to the Fever Hospital at the City Home.

The bed has cool white sheets. The nurses have clean white uniforms and the nun, Sister Rita, is all in white. Dr. Humphrey and Dr. Campbell have white coats and things hanging from their necks which they stick against my chest and all over. I sleep and sleep but I'm awake when they bring in jars of bright red stuff that hang from tall poles above my bed and they stick tubes into my ankles and the back of my right hand. Sister Rita says, You're getting blood, Francis. Soldier's blood from the Sarsfield Barracks.

Mam is sitting by the bed and the nurse is saying, You know, missus, this is very unusual. No one is ever allowed into the Fever Hospital for fear they'd catch something but they made an exception for you with his crisis coming. If he gets over this he'll surely recover.

I fall asleep. Mam is gone when I wake but there's movement in the room and it's the priest, Father Gorey, from the Confraternity saying Mass at a table in the corner. I drift off again and now they're waking me and pulling down the bedclothes. Father Gorey is touching me with oil and praying in Latin. I know it's Extreme Unction and that means I'm going to die and I don't care. They wake me again to receive Communion. I don't want it, I'm afraid I might get sick. I keep the wafer on my tongue and fall asleep and when I wake up again it's gone.

It's dark and Dr. Campbell is sitting by my bed. He's holding my wrist and looking at his watch. He has red hair and glasses and he always smiles when he talks to me. He sits now and hums and looks out the window. His eyes close and he snores a little. He tilts over on the chair and farts and smiles to himself and I know now I'm going to get better because a doctor would never fart in the presence of a dying boy.

Sister Rita's white habit is bright in the sun that comes in the window. She's holding my wrist, looking at her watch, smiling. Oh, she says, we're awake, are we? Well, Francis, I think we've come through the worst. Our prayers are answered and all the prayers of those hundreds of little boys at the Confraternity. Can you imagine that? Hundreds of boys saying the rosary for you and offering up their communion.

My ankles and the back of my hand are throbbing from the tubes bringing in the blood and I don't care about boys praying for me. I can hear the swish of Sister Rita's habit and the click of her rosary beads when she leaves the room. I fall asleep and when I wake it's dark and Dad is sitting by the bed with his hand on mine.

Son, are you awake?

I try to talk but I'm dry, nothing will come out and I point to my mouth. He holds a glass of water to my lips and it's sweet and cool. He presses my hand and says I'm a great old soldier and why wouldn't I? Don't I have the soldier's blood in me?

The tubes are not in me anymore and the glass jars are gone.

Sister Rita comes in and tells Dad he has to go. I don't want him to go because he looks sad. He's like Paddy Clohessy the day I gave him the raisin. When he looks sad it's the worst thing in the world and I start crying. Now what's this? says Sister Rita. Crying with all that soldier blood in you? There's a big surprise for you tomorrow, Francis. You'll never guess. Well, I'll tell you, we're bringing you a nice biscuit with your tea in the morning. Isn't that a treat? And your father will be back in a day or two, won't you, Mr. McCourt?

Dad nods and puts his hand on mine again. He looks at me, steps away, stops, comes back, kisses me on the forehead for the first time in my life and I'm so happy I feel like floating out of the bed.

The other two beds in my room are empty. The nurse says I'm the only typhoid patient and I'm a miracle for getting over the crisis.

The room next to me is empty till one morning a girl's voice says, Yoo hoo, who's there?

I'm not sure if she's talking to me or someone in the room beyond.

Yoo hoo, boy with the typhoid, are you awake?

I am.

Are you better?

I am.

Well, why are you here?

218

I don't know. I'm still in the bed. They stick needles in me and give me medicine.

What do you look like?

I wonder, What kind of a question is that? I don't know what to tell her.

Yoo hoo, are you there, typhoid boy?

I am.

What's your name?

Frank.

That's a good name. My name is Patricia Madigan. How old are you?

Ten.

Oh. She sounds disappointed.

But I'll be eleven in August, next month.

Well, that's better than ten. I'll be fourteen in September. Do you want to know why I'm in the Fever Hospital?

I do.

I have diphtheria and something else.

What's something else?

They don't know. They think I have a disease from foreign parts because my father used to be in Africa. I nearly died. Are you going to tell me what you look like?

I have black hair.

You and millions.

I have brown eyes with bits of green that's called hazel.

You and thousands.

I have stitches on the back of my right hand and my two feet where they put in the soldier's blood.

Oh, God, did they?

They did.

You won't be able to stop marching and saluting.

There's a swish of habit and click of beads and then Sister Rita's voice Now, now, what's this? There's to be no talking between two rooms especially when it's a boy and a girl. Do you hear me, Patricia?

I do, Sister.

Do you hear me, Francis?

I do, Sister.

You could be giving thanks for your two remarkable recoveries. You could be saying the rosary. You could be reading *The Little Messenger of the Sacred Heart* that's beside your beds. Don't let me come back and find you talking.

She comes into my room and wags her finger at me. Especially you, Francis, after thousands of boys prayed for you at the Confraternity. Give thanks, Francis, give thanks.

She leaves and there's silence for awhile. Then Patricia whispers, Give thanks, Francis, give thanks, and say your rosary, Francis, and I laugh so hard a nurse runs in to see if I'm all right. She's a very stern nurse from the County Kerry and she frightens me. What's this, Francis? Laughing? What is there to laugh about? Are you and that Madigan girl talking? I'll report you to Sister Rita. There's to be no laughing for you could be doing serious damage to your internal apparatus.

She plods out and Patricia whispers again in a heavy Kerry accent, No laughing, Francis, you could be doin' serious damage to your internal apparatus. Say your rosary, Francis, and pray for your internal apparatus.

Mam visits me on Thursdays. I'd like to see my father, too, but I'm out of danger, crisis time is over, and I'm allowed only one visitor. Besides, she says, he's back at work at Rank's Flour Mills and please God this job will last a while with the war on and the English desperate for flour. She brings me a chocolate bar and that proves Dad is working. She could never afford it on the dole. He sends me notes. He tells me my brothers are all praying for me, that I should be a good boy, obey the doctors, the nuns, the nurses, and don't forget to say my prayers. He's sure St. Jude pulled me through the crisis because he's the patron saint of desperate cases and I was indeed a desperate case.

Patricia says she has two books by her bed. One is a poetry book and that's the one she loves. The other is a short history of England and do I want it? She gives it to Seamus, the man who mops the floors every day, and he brings it to me. He says, I'm not supposed to be bringing anything from a dipteria room to a typhoid room with all the germs flying around and hiding between the pages and if you ever catch dipteria on top of the typhoid they'll know and I'll lose my good job and be out on the street singing patriotic songs with a tin cup in my hand, which I could easily do because there isn't a song ever written about Ireland's sufferings I don't know and a few songs about the joy of whiskey too.

Oh, yes, he knows Roddy McCorley. He'll sing it for me right enough but he's barely into the first verse when the Kerry nurse rushes in. What's this, Seamus? Singing? Of all the people in this hospital you should know the rules against singing. I have a good mind to report you to Sister Rita.

Ah, God, don't do that, nurse.

Very well, Seamus. I'll let it go this one time. You know the singing could lead to a relapse in these patients.

When she leaves he whispers he'll teach me a few songs because singing is good for passing the time when you're by yourself in a typhoid room. He says Patricia is a lovely girl the way she often gives him sweets from the parcel her mother sends every fortnight. He stops mopping the floor and calls to Patricia in the next room, I was telling Frankie you're a lovely girl, Patricia, and she says, You're a lovely man, Seamus. He smiles because he's an old man of forty and he never had children but the ones he can talk to here in the Fever Hospital. He says, Here's the book, Frankie. Isn't it a great pity you have to be reading all about England after all they did to us, that there isn't a history of Ireland to be had in this hospital.

The book tells me all about King Alfred and William the Conqueror and all the kings and queens down to Edward, who had to wait forever for his mother, Victoria, to die before he could be king. The book has the first bit of Shakespeare I ever read.

> *I do believe, induced by potent circumstances*
> *That thou art mine enemy.*

The history writer says this is what Catherine, who is a wife of Henry the Eighth, says to Cardinal Wolsey, who is trying to have her head cut off. I don't know what it means and I don't care because it's Shakespeare and it's like having jewels in my mouth when I say the words. If I had a whole book of Shakespeare they could keep me in the hospital for a year.

Patricia says she doesn't know what induced means or potent circumstances and she doesn't care about Shakespeare, she has her poetry book and she reads to me from beyond the wall a poem about an owl and a pussycat that went to sea in a green boat with honey and money and it makes no sense and when I say that Patricia gets huffy and says that's the last poem she'll ever read to me. She says I'm always reciting the lines from Shakespeare and they make no sense either. Seamus stops mopping again and tells us we shouldn't be fighting over poetry because we'll have enough to fight about when we grow up and get married. Patricia says she's sorry and I'm sorry too so she reads me part of another poem which I have to remember so I can say it back to her early in the morning or late at night when there are no nuns or nurses about,

> *The wind was a torrent of darkness among the gusty trees,*
> *The moon was a ghostly galleon tossed upon cloudy seas,*
> *The road was a ribbon of moonlight over the purple moor,*
> *And the highwayman came riding*
>   *Riding riding*
> *The highwayman came riding, up to the old inn-door.*
> *He'd a French cocked-hat on his forehead, a bunch of lace at*
>   *his chin,*
> *A coat of the claret velvet, and breeches of brown doe-skin,*
> *They fitted with never a wrinkle, his boots were up to the thigh.*

And he rode with a jewelled twinkle,
  His pistol butts a-twinkle,
His rapier hilt a-twinkle, under the jewelled sky.

Every day I can't wait for the doctors and nurses to leave me alone so I can learn a new verse from Patricia and find out what's happening to the highwayman and the landlord's red-lipped daughter. I love the poem because it's exciting and almost as good as my two lines of Shakespeare. The redcoats are after the highwayman because they know he told her, I'll come to thee by moonlight, though hell should bar the way.

I'd love to do that myself, come by moonlight for Patricia in the next room not giving a fiddler's fart though hell should bar the way. She's ready to read the last few verses when in comes the nurse from Kerry shouting at her, shouting at me, I told ye there was to be no talking between rooms. Dipthteria is never allowed to talk to typhoid and visa versa. I warned ye. And she calls out, Seamus, take this one. Take the by. Sister Rita said one more word out of him and upstairs with him. We gave ye a warning to stop the blathering but ye wouldn't. Take the by, Seamus, take him.

Ah, now, nurse, sure isn't he harmless. 'Tis only a bit o' poetry.

Take that by, Seamus, take him at once.

He bends over me and whispers, Ah, God, I'm sorry, Frankie. Here's your English history book. He slips the book under my shirt and lifts me from the bed. He whispers that I'm a feather. I try to see Patricia when we pass through her room but all I can make out is a blur of dark head on a pillow.

Sister Rita stops us in the hall to tell me I'm a great disappointment to her, that she expected me to be a good boy after what God had done for me, after all the prayers said by hundreds of boys at the Confraternity, after all the care from the nuns and nurses of the Fever Hospital, after the way they let my mother and father in to see me, a thing rarely allowed, and this is how I repaid them lying in the bed reciting silly poetry back and forth with Patricia Madigan knowing very well there was a ban on all talk between typhoid and diphtheria. She says I'll have plenty of time to reflect on my sins in the big ward upstairs and I should beg God's forgiveness for my disobedience reciting a pagan English poem about a thief on a horse and a maiden with red lips who commits a terrible sin when I could have been praying or reading the life of a saint. She made it her business to read that poem so she did and I'd be well advised to tell the priest in confession.

The Kerry nurse follows us upstairs gasping and holding on to the banister. She tells me I better not get the notion she'll be running up to this part of the world every time I have a little pain or a twinge.

There are twenty beds in the ward, all white, all empty. The nurse tells Seamus put me at the far end of the ward against the wall to make sure I don't talk to anyone who might be passing the door, which is very unlikely since there isn't another soul on this whole floor. She tells Seamus this was the fever ward during the Great Famine long ago and only God knows how many died here brought in too late for anything but a wash before they were buried and there are stories of cries and moans in the far reaches of the night. She says 'twould break your heart to think of what the English did to us, that if they didn't put the blight on the potato they didn't do much to take it off. No pity. No feeling at all for the people that died in this very ward, children suffering and dying here while the English feasted on roast beef and guzzled the best of wine in their big houses, little children with their mouths all green from trying to eat the grass in the fields beyond, God bless us and save us and guard us from future famines.

Seamus says 'twas a terrible thing indeed and he wouldn't want to be walking these halls in the dark with all the little green mouths gaping at him. The nurse takes my temperature, 'Tis up a bit, have a good sleep for yourself now that you're away from the chatter with Patricia Madigan below who will never know a gray hair.

She shakes her head at Seamus and he gives her a sad shake back.

Nurses and nuns never think you know what they're talking about. If you're ten going on eleven you're supposed to be simple like my uncle Pat Sheehan who was dropped on his head. You can't ask questions. You can't show you understand what the nurse said about Patricia Madigan, that she's going to die, and you can't show you want to cry over this girl who taught you a lovely poem which the nun says is bad.

The nurse tells Seamus she has to go and he's to sweep the lint from under my bed and mop up a bit around the ward. Seamus tells me she's a right oul' bitch for running to Sister Rita and complaining about the poem going between the two rooms, that you can't catch a disease from a poem unless it's love ha ha and that's not bloody likely when you're what? ten going on eleven? He never heard the likes of it, a little fella shifted upstairs for saying a poem and he has a good mind to go to the *Limerick Leader* and tell them print the whole thing except he has this job and he'd lose it if ever Sister Rita found out. Anyway, Frankie, you'll be outa here one of these fine days and you can read all the poetry you want though I don't know about Patricia below, I don't know about Patricia, God help us.

He knows about Patricia in two days because she got out of the bed to go to the lavatory when she was supposed to use a bedpan and collapsed and died in the lavatory. Seamus is mopping the floor and there are tears on his cheeks and he's saying, 'Tis a dirty rotten thing to die in a lavatory when you're lovely in yourself. She told me she was sorry she had you reciting that poem and getting you shifted from the room, Frankie. She said 'twas all her fault.

It wasn't, Seamus.

I know and didn't I tell her that.

Patricia is gone and I'll never know what happened to the highwayman and Bess, the landlord's daughter. I ask Seamus but he doesn't know any poetry at all especially English poetry. He knew an Irish poem once but it was about fairies and had no sign of a highwayman in it. Still he'll ask the men in his local pub where there's always someone reciting something and he'll bring it back to me. Won't I be busy meanwhile reading my short history of England and finding out all about their perfidy. That's what Seamus says, perfidy, and I don't know what it means and he doesn't know what it means but if it's something the English do it must be terrible.

He comes three times a week to mop the floor and the nurse is there every morning to take my temperature and pulse. The doctor listens to my chest with the thing hanging from his neck. They all say, And how's our little soldier today? A girl with a blue dress brings meals three times a day and never talks to me. Seamus says she's not right in the head so don't say a word to her.

The July days are long and I fear the dark. There are only two ceiling lights in the ward and they're switched off when the tea tray is taken away and the nurse gives me pills. The nurse tells me go to sleep but I can't because I see people in the nineteen beds in the ward all dying and green around their mouths where they tried to eat grass and moaning for soup Protestant soup any soup and I cover my face with the pillow hoping they won't come and stand around the bed clawing at me and howling for bits of the chocolate bar my mother brought last week.

No, she didn't bring it. She had to send it in because I can't have any more visitors. Sister Rita tells me a visit to the Fever Hospital is a privilege and after my bad behavior with Patricia Madigan and that poem I can't have the privilege anymore. She says I'll be going home in a few weeks and my job is to concentrate on getting better and learn to walk again after being in bed for six weeks and I can get out of bed tomorrow after breakfast. I don't know why she says I have to learn how to walk when I've been walking since I was a baby but when the nurse stands me by the side of the bed I fall to the floor and the nurse laughs, See, you're a baby again.

I practice walking from bed to bed back and forth back and forth. I don't want to be a baby. I don't want to be in this empty ward with no Patricia and no highwayman and no red-lipped landlord's daughter. I don't want the ghosts of children with green mouths pointing bony fingers at me and clamoring for bits of my chocolate bar.

Seamus says a man in his pub knew all the verses of the highwayman poem and it has a very sad end. Would I like him to say it because he never learned how to read and he had to carry the poem in his head? He stands in the middle of the ward leaning on his mop and recites,

> *Tlot-tlot, in the frosty silence! Tlot-tlot in the echoing night!*
> *Nearer he came and nearer! Her face was like a light!*
> *Her eyes grew wide for a moment, she drew one last deep breath,*
> *Then her finger moved in the moonlight,*
> > *Her musket shattered the moonlight,*
> *Shattered her breast in the moonlight and warned him—with*
> > *her death.*

He hears the shot and escapes but when he learns at dawn how Bess died he goes into a rage and returns for revenge only to be shot down by the redcoats.

> *Blood-red were his spurs in the golden noon; wine-red was his*
> > *velvet coat,*
> *When they shot him down on the highway,*
> > *Down like a dog on the highway,*
> *And he lay in his blood on the highway, with a bunch of lace*
> > *at his throat.*

Seamus wipes his sleeve across his face and sniffles. He says, There was no call at all to shift you up here away from Patricia when you didn't even know what happened to the highwayman and Bess. 'Tis a very sad story and when I said it to my wife she wouldn't stop crying the whole night till we went to bed. She said there was no call for them redcoats to shoot that highwayman, they are responsible for half the troubles of the world and they never had any pity on the Irish, either. Now if you want to know any more poems, Frankie, tell me and I'll get them from the pub and bring 'em back in my head.

The girl with the blue dress who's not right in the head suddenly says one day, Would you like a book for to read? and she brings me *The Amazing Quest of Mr. Ernest Bliss* by E. Phillips Oppenheim, which is all about an Englishman who is fed up and doesn't know what to do with himself every day even though he's so rich he can't count his money. His manservant brings him the morning paper the tea the egg the toast and marmalade and he says, Take it away, life is empty. He can't read his paper, he can't eat his egg, and he pines away. His doctor tells him go and live among the poor in the East End of London and he'll learn to love life, which he does and falls in love with a girl who is poor but honest and very intelligent and they get married and move into his house in the West End which is the rich part because it's easier to help the poor and not be fed up when you're nice and comfortable.

Seamus likes me to tell him what I'm reading. He says that story about Mr. Ernest Bliss is a made-up story because no one in his right mind would have to go to a doctor over having too much money and not eating his egg though you never know. It might be like that in England. You'd never find the likes of that in Ireland. If you didn't eat your egg here you'd be carted off to the lunatic asylum or reported to the bishop.

I can't wait to go home and tell Malachy about this man

who won't eat his egg. Malachy will fall down on the floor laughing because such a thing could never happen. He'll say I'm making it up but when I tell him this story is about an Englishman he'll understand.

I can't tell the girl in the blue dress that this story was silly because she might have a fit. She says if you're finished with that book I'll bring you another one because there's a whole box of books left behind by patients from the old days. She brings me a book called *Tom Brown's School-Days*, which is hard to read, and no end of books by P.G. Wodehouse, who makes me laugh over Ukridge and Bertie Wooster and Jeeves and all the Mulliners. Bertie Wooster is rich but he eats his egg every morning for fear of what Jeeves might say. I wish I could talk to the girl in the blue dress or anyone about the books but I'm afraid the Kerry nurse or Sister Rita might find out and they'd move me to a bigger ward upstairs with fifty empty beds and Famine ghosts galore with green mouths and bony fingers pointing. At night I lie in bed thinking about Tom Brown and his adventures at Rugby School and all the characters in P.G. Wodehouse. I can dream about the red-lipped landlord's daughter and the highwayman, and the nurses and nuns can do nothing about it. It's lovely to know the world can't interfere with the inside of your head.

It's August and I'm eleven. I've been in this hospital for two months and I wonder if they'll let me out for Christmas. The Kerry nurse tells me I should get down on my two knees and thank God I'm alive at all at all and not be complaining.

I'm not complaining, nurse, I'm only wondering if I'll be home for Christmas.

She won't answer me. She tells me behave myself or she'll send Sister Rita up to me and then I'll behave myself.

Mam comes to the hospital on my birthday and sends up a package with two chocolate bars and a note with names of people in the lane telling me get better and come home and you're a great soldier, Frankie. The nurse lets me talk to her through the window and it's hard because the windows are high and I have to stand on Seamus's shoulders. I tell Mam I want to go home but she says I'm a bit too weak and surely I'll be out in no time. Seamus says, 'Tis a grand thing to be eleven because any day now you'll be a man shaving and all and ready to get out and get a job and drink your pint good as any man.

After fourteen weeks Sister Rita tells me I can go home and aren't I a lucky boy that the day will be the feast of St. Francis of Assisi. She tells me I was a very good patient, except for that little problem with the poem and Patricia Madigan, God rest her, and I'm invited to come back and have a big Christmas dinner in the hospital. Mam comes for me and with my weak legs it takes us a long time to walk to the bus at Union Cross. She says, Take your time. After three and a half months we can spare an hour.

People are at their doors on Barrack Road and Roden Lane telling me it's grand to see me back, that I'm a great soldier, a credit to my father and mother. Malachy and Michael run up to me in the lane and say, God, you're walking very slow. Can't you run anymore?

It's a bright day and I'm happy till I see Dad sitting in the kitchen with Alphie on his lap and there's an empty feeling in my heart because I know he's out of work again. All along I was sure he had a job, Mam told me he did, and I thought there would be no shortage of food and shoes. He smiles at me and tells Alphie, Och, there's your big brother home from the hospital.

Mam tells him what the doctor said, that I'm to have plenty of nourishing food and rest. The doctor said beef would be the right thing for building me up again. Dad nods. Mam makes beef tea from a cube and Malachy and Mike watch me drink it. They say they'd like some too but Mam says go away, ye didn't have the typhoid. She says the doctor wants me to go to bed early. She tried to get rid of the fleas but they're worse than ever with the warm weather we're having. Besides, she says, they won't get much out of you all bones and little skin.

I lie in bed and think of the hospital where the white sheets were changed every day and there wasn't a sign of a flea. There was a lavatory where you could sit and read your book till someone asked if you were dead. There was a bath where you could sit in hot water as long as you liked and say,

> *I do believe,*
> *Induced by potent circumstances*
> *That thou art mine enemy,*

And saying that helps me fall asleep.

When Malachy and Michael get up for school in the morning Mam tells me I can stay in bed. Malachy is in fifth class now with Mr. O'Dea and he likes to tell everyone he's learning the big red catechism for Confirmation and Mr. O'Dea is telling them all about state of grace and Euclid and how the English tormented the Irish for eight hundred long years.

I don't want to stay in bed anymore. The October days are lovely and I want to sit outside looking up the lane at the way the sun slants along the wall opposite our house. Mikey Moloney brings me P.G. Wodehouse books his father gets from the library and I have great days with Ukridge and Bertie Wooster and all the Mulliners. Dad lets me read his favorite book, John Mitchel's *Jail Journal*, which is all about a great Irish rebel the English condemned to exile in Van Diemen's land in Australia. The English tell John Mitchel he's free to come and go as he pleases all over Van Diemen's land if he gives his word of honor as a gentleman he won't try to escape. He gives his word till a ship comes to help him escape and he goes to the office of the English magistrate and says, I'm escaping, jumps on his horse and winds up in

New York. Dad says he doesn't mind if I read silly English books by P.G. Wodehouse as long as I don't forget the men who did their bit and gave their lives for Ireland.

I can't stay at home forever and Mam takes me back to Leamy's School in November. The new headmaster, Mr. O'Halloran, says he's sorry, I've missed over two months of school and I have to be put back in fifth class. Mam says surely I'm ready for sixth class. After all, she says, he's missed only a few weeks. Mr. O'Halloran says he's sorry, take the boy next door to Mr. O'Dea.

We walk along the hallway and I tell Mam I don't want to be in fifth class. Malachy is in that class and I don't want to be in a class with my brother who is a year younger. I made my Confirmation last year. He didn't. I'm older. I'm not bigger anymore because of the typhoid but I'm older.

Mam says, It won't kill you.

She doesn't care and I'm put into that class with Malachy and I know all his friends are there sneering at me because I was put back. Mr. O'Dea makes me sit in the front and tells me get that sour look off my puss or I'll feel the end of his ash plant.

Then a miracle happens and it's all because of St. Francis of Assisi, my favorite saint, and Our Lord Himself. I find a penny in the street that first day back at school and I want to run to Kathleen O'Connell's for a big square of Cleeves' toffee but I can't run because my legs are still weak from the typhoid and sometimes I have to hold on to a wall. I'm desperate for the Cleeves' toffee but I'm also desperate to get out of fifth class.

I know I have to go to the statue of St. Francis of Assisi. He's the only one who will listen but he's at the other end of Limerick and it takes me an hour to walk there, sitting on steps, holding on to walls. It's a penny to light a candle and I wonder if I should just light the candle and keep the penny. No, St. Francis would know. He loves the bird in the air and the fish in the stream but he's not a fool. I light the candle, I kneel at his statue and beg him to get me out of fifth class where I'm stuck with my brother, who is probably going around the lane now bragging that his big brother was kept back. St. Francis doesn't say a word but I know he's listening and I know he'll get me out of that class. It's the least he could do after all my trouble coming to his statue, sitting on steps, holding on to walls, when I could have gone to St. Joseph's Church and lit a candle to the Little Flower or the Sacred Heart of Jesus Himself. What's the use of being named after him if he's going to desert me in my hour of need?

I have to sit in Mr. O'Dea's class listening to the catechism and all the other stuff he taught last year. I'd like to raise my hand and give the answers but he says, Be quiet, let your brother answer. He gives them tests in arithmetic and makes me sit there and correct them. He dictates to them in Irish and makes me correct what they've written. Then he gives me special compositions to write and makes me read them to the class because of all I learned from him last year. He tells the class, Frank McCourt is going to show you how well he learned to write in this class last year. He's going to write a composition on Our Lord, aren't you, McCourt? He's going to tell us what it would be like if Our Lord had grown up in Limerick which has the Arch Confraternity of the Holy Family and is the holiest city in Ireland. We know that if Our Lord had grown up in Limerick He would never have been crucified because the people of Limerick were always good Catholics and not given to crucifixion. So, McCourt, you are to go home and write that composition and bring it in tomorrow.

Dad says Mr. O'Dea has a great imagination but didn't Our Lord suffer enough on the cross without sticking Him in Limerick on top of it with the damp from the River Shannon. He puts on his cap and goes for a long walk and I have to think about Our Lord by myself and wonder what I'm going to write tomorrow.

The next day Mr. O'Dea says, All right, McCourt, read your composition to the class.

The name of my composition is—

The title, McCourt, the title.

The title of my composition is, "Jesus and the Weather."

What?

"Jesus and the Weather."

All right, read it.

This is my composition. I don't think Jesus Who is Our Lord would have liked the weather in Limerick because it's always raining and the Shannon keeps the whole city damp. My father says the Shannon is a killer river because it killed my two brothers. When you look at pictures of Jesus He's always wandering around ancient Israel in a sheet. It never rains there and you never hear of anyone coughing or getting consumption or anything like that and no one has a job there because all they do is stand around and eat manna and shake their fists and go to crucifixions.

Anytime Jesus got hungry all He had to do was walk up the road to a fig tree or an orange tree and have His fill. If He wanted a pint He could wave His hand over a big glass and there was the pint. Or He could visit Mary Magdalene and her sister, Martha, and they'd give Him His dinner no questions asked and He'd get his feet washed and dried with Mary Magdalene's hair while Martha washed the dishes, which I don't think is fair. Why should she have to wash the dishes while her sister sits out there chatting away with Our Lord? It's a good thing Jesus decided to be born Jewish in that warm place because if he was born in Limerick he'd catch the consumption and be dead in a month and there wouldn't be any Catholic Church and there wouldn't be any Communion or Confirmation and we wouldn't have to learn the catechism and write compositions about Him. The End.

Mr. O'Dea is quiet and gives me a strange look and I'm worried because when he's quiet like that it means someone is going to suffer. He says, McCourt, who wrote that composition?

I did, sir.

Did your father write that composition?

He didn't, sir.

Come here, McCourt.

I follow him out the door, along the hall to the headmaster's room. Mr. O'Dea shows him my composition and Mr. O'Halloran gives me the strange look, too. Did you write this composition?

I did, sir.

I'm taken out of the fifth class and put into Mr. O'Halloran's sixth class with all the boys I know, Paddy Clohessy, Fintan Slattery, The Question Quigley, and when school is over that day I have to go back down to the statue of St. Francis of Assisi to thank him even if my legs are still weak from the typhoid and I have to sit on steps and hold on to walls and I wonder was it something good I said in that composition or something bad.

Mr. Thomas L. O'Halloran teaches three classes in one room, sixth, seventh, eighth. He has a head like President Roosevelt and he wears gold glasses. He wears suits, navy blue or gray, and there's a gold watch chain that hangs across his belly from pocket to pocket in his waistcoat. We call him Hoppy because he has a short leg and hops when he walks. He knows what we call him and he says, Yes, I'm Hoppy and I'll hop on you. He carries a long stick, a pointer, and if you don't pay attention or give a stupid answer he gives you three slaps on each hand or whacks you across the backs of your legs. He makes you learn everything by heart, everything, and that makes him the hardest master in the school. He loves America and makes us know all the American states in alphabetical order. He makes charts of Irish grammar, Irish history and algebra at home, hangs them on an easel and we have to chant our way through the cases, conjugations and declensions of Irish, famous names and battles, proportions, ratios, equations. We have to know all the important dates in Irish history. He tells us what is important and why. No master ever told us why before. If you asked why you'd be hit on the head. Hoppy doesn't call us idiots and if you ask a question he doesn't go into a rage. He's the only master who stops and says, Do ye understand what I'm talking about? Do ye want to ask a question?

It's a shock to everyone when he says, the Battle of Kinsale in sixteen nought one was the saddest moment in Irish history, a close battle with cruelty and atrocities on both sides.

Cruelty on both sides? The Irish side? How could that be? All the other masters told us the Irish always fought nobly, they always fought the fair fight. He recites and makes us remember,

> They went forth to battle, but they always fell,
> Their eyes were fixed above the sullen shields.
> Nobly they fought and bravely, but not well,
> And sank heart-wounded by a subtle spell.

If they lost it was because of traitors and informers. But I want to know about these Irish atrocities.

Sir, did the Irish commit atrocities at the Battle of Kinsale?

They did, indeed. It is recorded that they killed prisoners but they were no better nor worse than the English.

Mr. O'Halloran can't lie. He's the headmaster. All these years we were told the Irish were always noble and they made brave speeches before the English hanged them. Now Hoppy O'Halloran is saying the Irish did bad things. Next thing he'll be saying the English did good things. He says, You have to study and learn so that you can make up your own mind about history and everything else but you can't make up an empty mind. Stock your mind, stock your mind. It is your house of treasure and no one in the world can interfere with it. If you won the Irish Sweepstakes and bought a house that needed furniture would you fill it with bits and pieces of rubbish? Your mind is your house and if you fill it with rubbish from the cinemas it will rot in your head. You might be poor, your shoes might be broken, but your mind is a palace.

He calls us one by one to the front of the room and looks at our shoes. He wants to know why they're broken or why we have no shoes at all. He tells us this is a disgrace and he's going to have a raffle to raise money so that we can have strong warm boots for the winter. He gives us books of tickets and we swarm all over Limerick for Leamy's School boot fund, first prize five pounds, five prizes of a pound each. Eleven boys with no boots get new boots. Malachy and I don't get any because we have shoes on our feet even if the soles are worn away and we wonder why we ran all over Limerick selling tickets so that other boys could get boots. Fintan Slattery says we gain plenary Indulgences for works of charity and Paddy Clohessy says, Fintan, would you ever go and have a good shit for yourself.

I know when Dad does the bad thing. I know when he drinks the dole money and Mam is desperate and has to beg at the St. Vincent de Paul Society and ask for credit at Kathleen O'Connell's shop but I don't want to back away from him and run to Mam. How can I do that when I'm up with him early every morning with the whole world asleep? He lights the fire and makes the tea and sings to himself or reads the paper to me in a whisper that won't wake up the rest of the family. Mikey Molloy stole Cuchulain, the Angel on the Seventh Step is gone someplace else, but my father in the morning is still mine. He gets the *Irish Press* early and tells me about the world, Hitler, Mussolini, Franco. He says this war is none of our business because the English are up to their tricks again. He tells me about the great Roosevelt in Washington and the great de Valera in Dublin. In the morning we have the world to ourselves and he never tells me I should die for Ireland. He tells me about the old days in Ireland when the English wouldn't let the Catholics have schools because they wanted to keep the people ignorant, that the Catholic children met in hedge schools in the depths of the country and learned English, Irish, Latin and Greek. The people loved learning. They loved stories and poetry even if none of this was any good for getting a job. Men, women and children would gather in ditches to hear those great masters and everyone wondered at how much a man could carry in his head. The masters risked their lives going from ditch to ditch and hedge to hedge because if the English caught them teaching they might be transported to foreign parts or worse. He tells me school is easy now, you don't have to sit in a ditch learning your sums or the glorious history of Ireland. I should be good in school and some day I'll go back to America and get an inside job where I'll be sitting at a desk with two fountain pens in my pocket, one red and one blue, making decisions. I'll be in out of the rain and I'll have a suit and shoes and a warm place to live and what more could a man want? He says you can do anything in America, it's the land of opportunity. You can be a fisherman in Maine or a farmer in California. America is not like Limerick, a gray place with a river that kills.

When you have your father to yourself by the fire in the morning you don't need Cuchulain or the Angel on the Seventh Step or anything.

At night he helps us with our exercises. Mam says they call it homework in America but here it's exercises, the sums, the English, the Irish, the history. He can't help us with Irish because he's from the North and lacking in the native tongue. Malachy offers to teach him all the Irish words he knows but Dad says it's too late, you can't teach an old dog a new bark. Before bed we sit around the fire and if we say, Dad, tell us a story, he makes up one about someone in the lane and the story will take us all over the world, up in the air, under the sea and back to the lane. Everyone in the story is a different color and everything is upside down and backward. Motor cars and planes go under water and submarines fly through the air. Sharks sit in trees and giant salmon sport with kangaroos on the moon. Polar bears wrestle with elephants in Australia and penguins teach Zulus how to play bagpipes. After the story he takes us upstairs and kneels with us while we say our prayers. We say the Our Father, three Hail Marys, God bless the Pope. God bless Mam, God bless our dead sister and brothers, God bless Ireland, God bless de Valera, and God bless anyone who gives Dad a job. He says, Go to sleep, boys, because holy God is watching you and He always knows if you're not good.

I think my father is like the Holy Trinity with three people in him, the one in the morning with the paper, the one at night with the stories and the prayers, and then the one who does the bad thing and comes home with the smell of whiskey and wants us to die for Ireland.

I feel sad over the bad thing but I can't back away from him because the one in the morning is my real father and if I were in America I could say, I love you, Dad, the way they do in the films, but you can't say that in Limerick for fear you might be laughed at. You're allowed to say you love God and babies and horses that win but anything else is a softness in the head.

Day and night we're tormented in that kitchen with people emptying their buckets. Mam says it's not the River Shannon that will kill us but the stink from that lavatory outside our door. It's bad enough in the winter when everything flows over and seeps under our door but worse in the warm weather when there are flies and bluebottles and rats.

There is a stable next to the lavatory where they keep the big horse from Gabbett's coal yard. His name is Finn the Horse and we all love him but the stable man from the coal yard doesn't take proper care of the stable and the stink travels to our house. The stink from the lavatory and the stable attracts rats and we have to chase them with our new dog, Lucky. He loves to corner the rats and then we smash them to bits with rocks or sticks or stab them with the hay fork in the stable. The horse himself is frightened by the rats and we have to be careful when he rears up. He knows we're not rats because we bring him apples when we rob an orchard out the country.

Sometimes the rats escape and run into our house and into the coal hole under the stairs where it's pitch dark and you can't see them. Even when we bring in a candle we can't find them because they dig holes everywhere and we don't know where to look. If we have a fire we can boil water and pour it slowly in from the kettle spout and that will drive them out of the hole between our legs and out the door again unless Lucky is there to catch them in his teeth and shake the life out of them. We expect him to eat the rats but he'll leave them in the lane with their guts hanging out and run to my father for a piece of bread dipped in tea. People in the lane say that's a peculiar way for a dog to behave but then what would you expect from a dog of the McCourts.

The minute there's a sign of a rat or a mention of one Mam is out the door and up the lane. She'd rather walk the streets of Limerick forever than stay one minute in a house that has a rat in it and she can never rest because she knows that with the stable and the lavatory there's always a rat nearby with his family waiting for their dinner.

We fight the rats and we fight the stink from that lavatory. We'd like to keep our door open in the warm weather but you can't when people are trotting down the lane to empty their brimming buckets. Some families are worse than others and Dad hates all of them even though Mam tells him it's not their fault if the builders a hundred years ago put up houses with no lavatories but this one outside our door. Dad says the people should empty their buckets in the middle of the night when we are asleep so that we won't be disturbed by the stink.

The flies are nearly as bad as the rats. On warm days they swarm to the stable and when a bucket is emptied they swarm to the lavatory. If Mam cooks anything they swarm into the kitchen and Dad says it's disgusting to think the fly sitting there on the sugar bowl was on the toilet bowl, or what's left of it, a minute ago. If you have an open sore they find it and torment you. By day you have the flies, by night you have the fleas. Mam says there's one good thing about fleas, they're clean, but flies are filthy, you never know where they came from and they carry diseases galore.

We can chase the rats and kill them. We can slap at the flies and the fleas and kill them but there's nothing we can do about the neighbors and their buckets. If we're out in the lane playing and we see someone with a bucket we call to our own house, Bucket coming, close the door, close the door, and whoever is inside runs to the door. In warm weather we run to close the door all day because we know which families have the worst buckets. There are families whose fathers have jobs and if they get into the habit of cooking with curry we know their buckets will stink to the heavens and make us sick. Now with the war on and men sending money from England more and more families are cooking with curry and our house is filled with the stink day and night. We know the families with the curry, we know the ones with the cabbage. Mam is sick all the time, Dad takes longer and longer walks into the country, and we play outside as much as we can and far from the lavatory. Dad doesn't complain about the River Shannon anymore. He knows now the lavatory is worse and he takes me with him to the Town Hall to complain. The man there says, Mister, all I can tell you is you can move. Dad says we can't afford to move and the man says there's nothing he can do. Dad says, This is not India. This is a Christian country. The lane needs more lavatories. The man says, Do you expect

Limerick to start building lavatories in houses that are falling down anyway, that will be demolished after the war? Dad says that lavatory could kill us all. The man says we live in dangerous times.

Mam says it's hard enough keeping a fire going to cook the Christmas dinner but if I'm going to Christmas dinner at the hospital I'll have to wash myself from top to bottom. She wouldn't give it to Sister Rita to say I was neglected or ripe for another disease. She boils a pot of water early in the morning before Mass and nearly scalds the scalp off me. She scours my ears and scrubs my skin so hard it tingles. She can afford tuppence for the bus out to the hospital but I'll have to walk back and that will be good for me because I'll be stuffed with food and now she has to get the fire going again for the pig's head and cabbage and floury white potatoes which she got once again through the kindness of the St. Vincent de Paul Society and she's determined this will be the last time we celebrate the birth of Our Lord with pig's head. Next year we'll have a goose or a nice ham and why wouldn't we, isn't Limerick famous the world over for the ham?

Sister Rita says, Now would you look at this, our little soldier looking so healthy. No meat on the bones but still. Now tell me, did you go to Mass this morning?

I did, Sister.

And did you receive?

I did, Sister.

She takes me into an empty ward and tells me sit there on that chair it won't be long now till I get my dinner. She leaves and I wonder if I'll be eating with nuns and nurses or will I be in a ward with children having their Christmas dinner. In awhile my dinner is brought in by the girl in the blue dress who brought me the books. She places the tray on the side of a bed and I pull up a chair. She frowns at me and screws up her face. You, she says, that's your dinner an' I'm not bringin' you any books.

The dinner is delicious, turkey, mashed potatoes, peas, jelly and custard, and a pot of tea. The jelly and custard dish looks delicious and I can't resist it so I'll have it first there's no one there to notice but when I'm eating it the girl in the blue dress comes in with bread and says, What are you doin'?

Nothing.

Yes, you are. You're atin' the sweet before the dinner, and she runs out calling, Sister Rita, Sister Rita, come in quick, and the nun rushes in, Francis, are you all right?

I am, Sister.

He's not all right, Sister. He do be atin' his jelly an custard before his dinner. That's a sin, Sister.

Ah, now, dear, you run along and I'll talk to Francis about that.

Do, Sister, talk to him or all the childer in the hospital will be atin' their sweet before their dinner an' then where will we be?

Indeed, indeed, where will we be? Run along now.

The girl leaves and Sister Rita smiles at me. God love her, she doesn't miss a thing even in her confusion. We have to be patient with her, Francis, the way she's touched.

She leaves and it's quiet in that empty ward and when I'm finished I don't know what to do because you're not supposed to do anything till they tell you. Hospitals and schools always tell you what to do. I wait a long time till the girl in the blue dress comes in for the tray. Are you finished? she says.

I am.

Well, that's all you're gettin' an' now you can go home.

Surely girls who are not right in the head can't tell you go home and I wonder if I should wait for Sister Rita. A nurse in the hallway tells me Sister Rita is having her dinner and is not to be bothered.

It's a long walk from Union Cross to Barrack Hill and when I get home my family are up in Italy and well into their pig's head and cabbage and floury white potatoes. I tell them about my Christmas dinner. Mam wants to know if I had it with the nurses and nuns and she gets a bit angry when I tell her I ate alone in a ward and that's no way to treat a child. She tells me sit down and have some pig's head and I force it into my mouth and I'm so stuffed I have to lie on the bed with my belly sticking out a mile.

It's early in the morning and there's a motor car outside our door, the first one we've ever seen in the lane. There are men in suits looking in the door of the stable of Finn the Horse and there must be something wrong because you never see men with suits in the lane.

It's Finn the Horse. He's lying on the floor of the stable looking up the lane and there's white stuff like milk around his mouth. The stable man who takes care of Finn the Horse says he found him like that this morning and it's strange because he's always up and ready for his feed. The men are shaking their heads. My brother Michael says to one of the men, Mister, what's up with Finn?

Sick horse, son. Go home.

The stable man who takes care of Finn has the whiskey smell on him. He says to Michael, That horse is a goner. We have to shoot him.

Michael pulls at my hand. Frank, they're not to shoot him. Tell them. You're big.

The stable man says, Go home, boy. Go home.

Michael attacks him, kicks him, scrawbs the back of his hand, and the man sends Michael flying. Hould that brother of yours, he tells me, hould him.

One of the other men takes something yellow and brown from a bag, goes to Finn, puts it to his head and there's a sharp crack. Finn shivers. Michael screams at the man and attacks him too but the man says, The horse was sick, son. He's better off.

The men in suits drive away and the stable man says he has to wait for the lorry to take Finn away, he can't leave him alone or the rats will be at him. He wants to know if we'd keep an eye on the horse with our dog Lucky while he goes to the pub, he's blue mouldy for a pint.

No rat has a chance to get near Finn the Horse the way Michael is there with a stick small as he is. The man comes back smelling of porter and then there's the big lorry to take the horse away, a big lorry with three men and two great planks that slope from the back of the lorry to Finn's head. The three men and the stable man tie ropes around Finn and pull him up the planks and the people in the lane yell at the men because of the nails and broken wood in the planks that catch at Finn and tear out bits of his hide and streak the planks with bright pink horse blood.

Ye are destroyin' that horse.

Can't ye have respect for the dead?

Go easy with that poor horse.

The stable man says, For the love o'Jaysus what are ye squawkin' about? 'Tis only a dead horse, and Michael runs at him again with his head down and his small fists flying till the stable man gives him a shove that sends him on his back and Mam goes at the stable man in such a rage he runs up the planks and over Finn's body to escape. He comes back drunk in the evening to sleep it off and after he leaves there's a smoldering in the hay and the stable burns down the rats running up the lane with every boy and dog chasing them till they escape into the streets of respectable people.

IX

Mam says, Alphie is enough. I'm worn out. That's the end of it. No more children.

Dad says, The good Catholic woman must perform her wifely duties and submit to her husband or face eternal damnation.

Mam says, As long as there are no more children eternal damnation sounds attractive enough to me.

What is Dad to do? There's a war on. English agents are recruiting Irishmen to work in their munitions factories, the pay is good, there are no jobs in Ireland, and if the wife turns her back to you there's no shortage of women in England where the able men are off fighting Hitler and Mussolini and you can do anything you like as long as you remember you're Irish and lower class and don't try to rise above your station.

Families up and down the lane are getting telegram money orders from their fathers in England. They rush to the post office to cash the money orders so they can shop and show the world their good fortune on Saturday night and Sunday morning. The boys get their hair cut on Saturdays, the women curl their hair with iron tongs hot from the fire. They're very grand now the way they pay sixpence or even a shilling for seats at the Savoy Cinema where you'll meet a better class of people than the lower classes who fill the tuppenny seats in the gods at the Lyric Cinema and are never done shouting at the screen, the kind of people if you don't mind who are liable to cheer on the Africans when they throw spears at Tarzan or the Indians when they're scalping the United States Cavalry. The new rich people go home after Mass on Sundays all airs and stuff themselves with meat and potatoes, sweets and cakes galore, and they think nothing of drinking their tea from delicate little cups which stand in saucers to catch the tea that overflows and when they lift the cups they stick out their little fingers to show how refined they are. Some stop going to fish and chip shops altogether because you see nothing in those places but drunken soldiers and night girls and men that drank their dole and their wives screeching at them to come home. The brave new rich will be seen at the Savoy Restaurant or the Stella drinking tea, eating little buns, patting their lips with serviettes if you don't mind, coming home on the bus and complaining the service is not what it used to be. They have electricity now so they can see things they never saw before and when darkness falls they turn on the new wireless to hear how the war is going. They thank God for Hitler because if he hadn't marched all over Europe the men of Ireland would still be at home scratching their arses on the queue at the Labour Exchange.

Some families sing,

> Yip aye aidy aye ay aye oh
> Yip aye aidy aye ay,
> We don't care about England or France,
> All we want is the German advance.

If there's a chill in the air they'll turn on the electric fire for the comfort that's in it and sit in their kitchens listening to the news declaring how sorry they are for the English women and children dying under the German bombs but look what England did to us for eight hundred years.

The families with fathers in England are able to lord it over the families that don't. At dinnertime and teatime the new rich mothers stand at their doors and call to their children, Mikey, Kathleen, Paddy, come in for yeer dinner.

Come in for the lovely leg o'lamb and the gorgeous green peas and the floury white potatoes.

Sean, Josie, Peggy, come in for yeer tea, come in at wanst for the fresh bread and butter and the gorgeous blue duck egg what no one else in the lane have.

Brendan, Annie, Patsy, come in for the fried black puddin', the sizzlin' sausages and the lovely trifle soaked in the best of Spanish sherry.

At times like this Mam tells us to stay inside. We have nothing but bread and tea and she doesn't want the tormenting neighbors to see us with our tongues hanging out, suffering over the lovely smells floating up and down the lane. She says 'tis easy to see they're not used to having anything the way they brag about everything. 'Tis a real low-class mind that will call out the door and tell the world what they're having for the supper. She says 'tis their way of getting a rise out of us because Dad is a foreigner from the North and he won't have anything to do with any of them. Dad says all that food comes from English money and no luck will come to those who took it but what could you expect from Limerick anyway, people who profit from Hitler's war, people who will work and fight for the English. He says he'll never go over there and help England win a war. Mam says, No, you'll stay here where there's no work and hardly a lump of coal to boil water for the tea. No, you'll stay here and drink the dole when the humor is on you. You'll watch your sons going around with broken shoes and their arses hanging out of their trousers. Every house in the lane has electricity and we're lucky if we have a candle. God above, if I had the fare I'd be off to England myself for I'm sure they need women in the factories.

Dad says a factory is no place for a woman.

Mam says, Sitting on your arse by the fire is no place for a man.

I say to him, Why can't you go to England, Dad, so we can have electricity and a wireless and Mam can stand at

the door and tell the world what we're having at dinnertime?

He says, Don't you want to have your father here at home
with you?

I do but you can come back at the end of the war and
we can all go to America.

He sighs, Och, aye, och, aye. All right he'll go to England
after Christmas because America is in the war now and the
cause must be just. He'd never go if the Americans hadn't
gone in. He tells me I'll have to be the man of the house,
and he signs up with an agent to work in a factory in Coventry which, everyone says, is the most bombed city in England. The agent says, There's plenty of work for willing men.
You can work overtime till you drop and if you save it up,
mate, you'll be Rockefeller at the end of the war.

We're up early to see Dad off at the railway station. Kathleen O'Connell at the shop knows Dad is off to England and
money will be flowing back so she's happy to let Mam have
credit for tea, milk, sugar, bread, butter and an egg.

An egg.

Mam says, This egg is for your father. He needs the nourishment for the long journey before him.

It's a hard-boiled egg and Dad peels off the shell. He slices
the egg five ways and gives each of us a bit to put on our
bread. Mam says, Don't be such a fool. Dad says, What
would a man be doing with a whole egg to himself? Mam
has tears on her eyelashes. She pulls her chair over to the
fireplace. We all eat our bread and egg and watch her cry
till she says, What are ye gawkin' at? and turns away to look
into the ashes. Her bread and egg are still on the table and
I wonder if she has any plans for them. They look delicious
and I'm still hungry but Dad gets up and brings them to her
with the tea. She shakes her head but he presses them on
her and she eats and drinks, snuffling and crying. He sits
opposite her a while, silent, till she looks up at the clock and
says, 'Tis time to go. He puts on his cap and picks up his

bag. Mam wraps Alphie in an old blanket and we set off through the streets of Limerick.

There are other families in the streets. The going-away fathers walk ahead, the mothers carry babies or push prams. A mother with a pram will say to other mothers, God above, missus, you must be fagged out carrying that child. Sure, why don't you stick him into the pram here and rest your poor arms.

Prams might be packed with four or five babies squalling away because the prams are old and the wheels bockety and the babies are rocked till they get sick and throw up their goody.

The men call to each other. Grand day, Mick. Lovely day for the journey, Joe. 'Tis, indeed, Mick. Arrah, we might as well have a pint before we go, Joe. We might as well, Mick. Might as well be drunk as the way we are, Joe.

They laugh and the women behind them are teary-eyed and red-nosed.

In the pubs around the railway station the men are packed in drinking the money the agents gave them for travel food. They're having the last pint, the last drop of whiskey on Irish soil, For God knows it might be the last we'll ever have, Mick, the way the Jerries are bombing the bejesus outa England and not a minute too soon after what they did to us and isn't it a tragic thing entirely the way we have to go over there and save the arse of the ancient foe.

The women stay outside the pubs talking. Mam tells Mrs. Meehan, The first telegram money order I get I'll be in the shop buying a big breakfast so that we can all have our own egg of a Sunday morning.

I look at my brother Malachy. Did you hear that? Our own egg of a Sunday morning. Oh, God, I already had plans for my egg. Tap it around the top, gently crack the shell, lift with a spoon, a dab of butter down into the yolk, salt, take my time, a dip of the spoon, scoop, more salt, more butter, into the mouth, oh, God above, if heaven has a taste it must be an egg with butter and salt, and after the egg is there anything in the world lovelier than fresh warm bread and a mug of sweet golden tea?

Some men are already too drunk to walk and the English agents are paying sober men to drag them out of the pubs and throw them on a great horse-drawn float to be hauled to the station and dumped into the train. The agents are desperate to get everyone out of the pubs. Come on, men. Miss this train and you'll miss a good job. Come on, men, we have the Guinness in England. We have the Jameson. Now, men, please, men. You're drinking your food money and you'll get no more.

The men tell the agents to kiss their Irish arses, that the agents are lucky they're alive, lucky they're not hanging from the nearest lamppost after what they did to Ireland. And the men sing,

> *On Mountjoy one Monday morning*
> *High upon the gallows tree,*
> *Kevin Barry gave his young life*
> *For the cause of liberty*

The train wails in the station and the agents beg the women to get their men out of the pubs and the men stumble out singing and crying and hugging their wives and children and promising to send so much money Limerick will be turned into another New York. The men climb the station steps and the women and children call after them,

Kevin, love, mind yourself and don't be wearing damp shirts.

Dry your socks, Michael, or the bunions will destroy you entirely.

Paddy, go easy on the drink, are you listenin', Paddy?

Dad, Dad, don't go, Dad.

Tommy, don't forget to send the money. The children are skin and bones.

Peter, don't forget to be takin' the medicine for your weak chest, God help us.

Larry, mind them bloody bombs.

Christy, don't be talkin' to them Englishwomen. They're full of diseases.

Jackie, come back. Sure we'll manage somehow. Don't go, Jack-e-e, Jack-e-e, oh, Jesus, don't go.

Dad pats our heads. He tells us remember our religious duties but, above all, obey our mother. He stands before her. She has the baby Alphie in her arms. She says, Mind yourself. He drops the bag and puts his arms around her. They stay that way a moment till the baby yelps between them. He nods, picks up his bag, climbs the steps to the station, turns to wave and he's gone.

Back at home Mam says, I don't care I know it sounds extravagant but I'm going to light the fire and make more tea for it isn't every day your father goes to England.

We sit around the fire and drink our tea and cry because we have no father, till Mam says, Don't cry, don't cry. Now that your father is gone to England surely our troubles will be over.

Surely.

Mam and Bridey Hannon sit by the fire upstairs in Italy smoking Woodbines, drinking tea, and I sit on the stairs listening. We have a father in England so that we can get all we want from Kathleen O'Connell's shop and pay when he starts sending the money in a fortnight. Mam tells Bridey she can't wait to get out of this bloody lane to a place with a decent lavatory that we don't have to share with half the world. We'll all have new boots and coats to keep off the rain so we won't be coming home from school famished. We'll have eggs and rashers on Sunday for breakfast and ham and cabbage and potatoes for dinner. We'll have electric light and why shouldn't we? Weren't Frank and Malachy born to it in America where everyone has it?

All we have to do now is wait for two weeks till the telegram boy knocks at the door. Dad will have to settle into his job in England, buy work clothes and get a place to stay, so the first money order won't be big, three pounds or three pounds ten, but soon we'll be like other families in the lane, five pounds a week, paying off debts, buying new clothes, putting something in the savings against the time we'll pack up and move to England entirely and save there to go to America. Mam herself could get a job in an English factory making bombs or something and God knows we wouldn't know ourselves with the money pouring in. She wouldn't be happy if we grew up with English accents but better an English accent than an empty belly.

Bridey says it doesn't matter what class of an accent an Irishman has for he'll never forget what the English did to us for eight hundred long years.

We know what Saturdays are in the lane. We know some families like the Downeses across from us get their telegram early because Mr. Downes is a steady man who knows how to have a pint or two on a Friday and go home to his bed. We know men like him run to the post office the minute they're paid so their families won't know a minute of waiting or worry. Men like Mr. Downes send their sons RAF wings to wear on their coats. That's what we want and that's what we told Dad before he left, Don't forget the RAF badges, Dad.

We see the telegram boys on their bicycles swing into the lane. They're happy telegram boys because the tips they get in the lanes are bigger than anything they get in the grand streets and avenues where rich people will begrudge you the steam of their piss.

The families that get the early telegrams have that contented look. They'll have all day Saturday to enjoy the money. They'll shop, they'll eat, they'll have all day to think about what they'll do that night and that's almost as good as the thing itself because Saturday night when you have a few shillings in your pocket is the most delicious night of the week.

There are families don't get the telegram every week and you know them by the anxious look. Mrs. Meagher has waited at her door every Saturday for two months. My mother says she'd be ashamed of her life to wait at the door like that. All the children play in the lane and keep an eye out for the telegram boy. Hoi, telegram boy, do you have anything for Meagher? and when he says no they say, Are you sure? and he'll say, Course I'm sure. I know what I have in my feckin' pouch.

Everyone knows the telegram boys stop coming when the Angelus rings at six and darkness brings desperation to the women and children.

Telegram boy, will you look in your pouch again? Please. Aw, God.

I did. I have nothing for ye.

Aw, God, please look. Our name is Meagher. Will you look?

I know bloody well yeer name is Meagher and I looked.

The children claw at him up on his bicycle and he kicks at them, Jesus, will ye get away from me.

Once the Angelus rings at six in the evening the day is over. The ones with the telegrams are having their supper with the electric light blazing away and the ones that didn't get the telegrams have to light candles and see if Kathleen O'Connell might let them have tea and bread till this time next week when surely with the help of God and His Blessed Mother the telegram will come.

Mr. Meehan at the top of the lane went to England with Dad and when the telegram boy stops at Meehan's we know we'll be next. Mam has her coat ready to go to the post office but she won't leave the chair by the fire in Italy till she has the telegram in her hand. The telegram boy rides down the lane and swings over to Downeses'. He hands them their telegram, takes the tip and turns his bicycle around

254

to head back up the lane. Malachy calls, Telegram boy, do you have something for McCourt? Ours is coming today. The telegram boy shakes his head and rides away.

Mam puffs on her Woodbine. Well, we have all day though I'd like to do a bit of shopping early before the best hams are gone at Barry the butcher. She can't leave the fire and we can't leave the lane for fear the telegram boy might come and find no one at home. Then we'd have to wait till Monday to cash the money order and that would destroy the weekend entirely. We'd have to watch the Meehans and everyone else parading around in their new clothes and staggering home with eggs and potatoes and sausages for Sunday and sailing off to the films on Saturday night. No, we can't move an inch till that telegram boy comes. Mam says don't be too worried between noon and two because so many telegram boys go for their dinner and there will surely be a big rush between two and the Angelus. We don't have a thing to worry about till six. We stop every telegram boy. We tell them our name is McCourt, that this is our first telegram, it should be three pounds or more, they might have forgotten to put our name on it or our address, is he sure? is he sure? One boy tells us he'll inquire at the post office. He says he knows what 'tis like to wait for the telegram because his own father is a drunken oul' shit over in England that never sent a penny. Mam hears him inside and tells us you should never talk about your father like that. The same telegram boy comes back just before the Angelus at six and tells us he asked Mrs. O'Connell at the post office if they had anything for McCourt all day and they didn't. Mam turns toward the dead ashes in the fire and sucks at the last bit of goodness in the Woodbine butt caught between the brown thumb and the burnt middle finger. Michael who is only five and won't understand anything till he's eleven like me wants to know if we're having fish and chips tonight because he's hungry. Mam says, Next week, love, and he goes back out to play in the lane.

You don't know what to do with yourself when the first telegram doesn't come. You can't stay out in the lane playing with your brothers all night because everyone else is gone in and you'd be ashamed to stay out in the lane to be tormented with smells of sausages and rashers and fried bread. You don't want to look at electric light coming through the windows after dark and you don't want to hear the news from the BBC or Radio Eireann from other people's wirelesses. Mrs. Meagher and her children are gone in and there's only the dim light of a candle from their kitchen. They're ashamed too. They stay inside on Saturday nights and they don't even go to Mass on Sunday mornings. Bridey Hannon told Mam that Mrs. Meagher is in a constant state of shame over the rags they wear and so desperate she goes down to the Dispensary for the public assistance. Mam says that's the worst thing that could happen to any family. It's worse than going on the dole, it's worse than going to the St. Vincent de Paul Society, it's worse than begging on the streets with the tinkers and the knackers. It's the last thing you'd do to keep yourself out of the poor house and the children from the orphanage.

There's a sore at the top of my nose between my eyebrows, gray and red and itching. Grandma says, Don't touch that sore and don't put water near it or it'll spread. If you broke your arm she'd say don't touch that with water it'll spread. The sore spreads into my eyes anyway and now they're red and yellow from the stuff that oozes and makes them stick in the morning. They stick so hard I have to force my eyelids open with my fingers and Mam has to scrub off that yellow stuff with a damp rag and boric powder. The eyelashes fall off and every bit of dust in Limerick blows into my eyes on windy days. Grandma tells me I have naked eyes and she says it's my own fault, all that eye trouble comes from sitting up there at the top of the lane under the light pole in all kinds of weather with my nose stuck in books and the same thing will happen to Malachy if he doesn't give over with the reading. You can see little Michael is getting just as bad sticking his nose in books when he should be out playing like a healthy child. Books, books, books, says Grandma, ye will ruin yeer eyes entirely.

She's having tea with Mam and I hear her whisper, The thing to do is give him St. Anthony's spit.

What's that? says Mam.

Your fasting spit in the morning. Go to him before he wakes and spit on his eyes for the spit of a fasting mother has powerful cures in it.

But I'm always awake before Mam. I force my eyes open long before she stirs. I can hear her coming across the floor and when she stands over me for the spit I open my eyes. God, she says, your eyes are open.

I think they're getting better.

That's good, and she goes back to bed.

The eyes don't heal and she takes me to the Dispensary where the poor people see doctors and get their medicines. It's the place to apply for public assistance when a father is dead or disappeared and there's no dole money, no wages.

There are benches along the walls by the doctors' offices. The benches are always packed with people talking about their ailments. Old men and women sit and groan and babies scream and mothers say hush, love, hush. There's a high platform in the middle of the Dispensary with a counter circling it chest-high. When you want anything you stand in a queue before that platform to see Mr. Coffey or Mr. Kane. The women in the queue are like the women at the St. Vincent de Paul Society. They wear shawls and they're respectful to Mr. Coffey and Mr. Kane because if they're not they might be told go away and come back next week when it's this minute you need the public assistance or a docket to see the doctor. Mr. Coffee and Mr. Kane love to have a good laugh with the women. They'll decide if you're desperate enough for the public assistance or if you're sick enough to see a doctor. You have to tell them in front of everyone what's wrong with you and they often have a good laugh with that. They'll say, And what is it you want, Mrs. O'Shea? A docket for the doctor, is it? And what is your trouble, Mrs. O'Shea? A pain, is it? A touch of the wind, maybe. Or maybe too much cabbage. Oh, the cabbage will do it right enough. They laugh and Mrs. O'Shea laughs and all the women laugh and say Mr. Coffee and Mr. Kane are funny men, they'd give Laurel and Hardy a run for their money.

Mr. Coffee says, Now, woman, what's your name?

Angela McCourt, sir.

And what's up with you?

'Tis my son, sir. He has two bad eyes.

Oh, by God, he does, woman. They're desperate-looking eyes altogether. They look like two rising suns. The Japs could use him on their flag, ha ha ha. Did he pour acid on his face or what?

'Tis some class of infection, sir. He had the typhoid last year and then this came.

All right, all right, we don't need the life story. Here's your docket to Dr. Troy.

Two long benches are filled with patients for Dr. Troy. Mam sits next to a woman who has a big sore on her nose that won't go away. I tried everything, missus, every known cure on God's lovely earth. I'm eighty-three years of age and I'd like to go to my grave healthy. Is it too much to ask that I meet my Redeemer with a healthy nose? And what's up with yourself, missus?

My son. The eyes.

Ah, God bless us and save us, look at them eyes. They're the sorest two eyes I ever seen in me life. I never seen that color red before.

'Tis an infection, missus.

Sure there's a cure for that. You need the caul.

258

What's that now?

Babies are born with this thing on their heads, a class of a hood, rare and magical. Get a caul and put that on his head any day that has a three in it, make him hold his breath for three minutes even if you have to clap your hand over his face, sprinkle him with holy water three times head to toenail and his two eyes will shine in the dawn.

And where would I get a caul?

Don't all the midwives have cauls, missus. What's a mid-wife without a caul? It cures all classes of disease and keeps off more.

Mam says she'll talk to Nurse O'Halloran and see if she has a spare caul.

Dr. Troy looks at my eyes. Into the hospital with this boy at once. Take him to the eye ward at the City Home. Here's the docket to get him in.

What does he have, Doctor?

The worst case of conjunctivitis I've ever seen in my life and something else in there I can't make out. He needs the eye man.

How long will he be in, Doctor?

Only God knows that. I should have seen this child weeks ago.

There are twenty beds in the ward and there are men and boys with bandages around their heads, black patches on their eyes, thick glasses. Some walk around tapping at beds with sticks. A man cries all the time that he'll never see again, he's too young, his children are babies, he'll never see them again. Jesus Christ, oh, Jesus Christ, and the nuns are shocked at the way he takes the name of the Lord in vain. Stop that, Maurice, stop the blasphemy. You have your health. You're alive. We all have our problems. Offer it up and think of the sufferings of Our Lord on the cross, the crown of thorns, the nails in His poor hands and feet, the wound in His side. Maurice says, Oh, Jesus, look down and have pity on me. Sister Bernadette warns him if he doesn't mind his language they'll put him in a ward alone and he says, Heavenly God, and that isn't as bad as Jesus Christ so she's satisfied.

In the morning I have to go downstairs for drops. The nurse says, Sit in this high chair and here's a nice sweet. The doctor has a bottle with brown stuff in it. He tells me put my head back, thats right, now open up, open your eyes and he pours the stuff into my right eye and it's a flame going through my skull. The nurse says, Open the other eye, come on be a good boy, and she has to force the eyelids open so the doctor can set fire to the other side of my skull. She wipes my cheeks and tells me run along upstairs but I can barely see and I want to stick my face into an icy stream. The doctor says, Run along, be a man, be a good trooper.

The whole world is brown and blurry on the stairs. The other patients are sitting by their beds with dinner trays and mine is there too but I don't want it with the way my skull is raging. I sit by my bed and a boy across the way says, Hoi, don't you want your dinner? I'll take it, and he comes for it.

I try to lie on the bed but a nurse says, Now, now, no lying on the bed in the middle of the day. Your case isn't that serious.

I have to sit with my eyes closed and everything going brown and black, black and brown and I'm sure I must be having a dream because Lord God above, is that the little fella with the typhoid, little Frankie, the moon was a ghostly galleon tossed upon cloudy seas, is that yourself, Frankie, for wasn't I promoted out of the Fever Hospital, thank God, where there's every class of disease and you never know what germs you might be bringing home to the wife in your clothes and what's up with you, Frankie, and the two eyes in your head all gone brown?

I have an infection, Seamus.

Yerra, you'll be over that before you're married, Frankie. The eyes need exercise. The blink is great value for the eyes. I had an uncle with bad eyes and the blink saved him. He

260

sat an hour ever day and blinked and it stood to him in the end. Wound up with powerful eyes, so he did.

I want to ask him more about the blink and the powerful eyes but he says, Now do you remember the poem, Frankie, the lovely poem of Patricia?

He stands in the aisle between the beds with his mop and his bucket and says the highwayman poem and all the patients stop their moaning and the nuns and nurses stand and listen and on and on goes Seamus till he comes to the end and everyone goes mad clapping and cheering him and he tells the world he loves that poem he'll have it in his head forever no matter where he goes and if it wasn't for Frankie McCourt and his typhoid there and poor Patricia Madigan with the dipteria that's gone God rest her he'd never know the poem and there I am famous in the eye ward of the City Home Hospital and all because of Seamus.

Mam can't come to visit everyday, it's a long way out, she doesn't always have the money for the bus and the walk is hard on her corns. She thinks my eyes look better though you can't tell with all that brown stuff, which looks and smells like iodine and if it's anything like iodine it must burn. Still, they say the bitterer the medicine the quicker the cure. She gets permission to take me for a walk around the grounds when the weather clears and there's a strange sight, Mr. Timoney standing against the wall where the old people are with his eyes raised to the sky. I want to talk to him and I have to ask Mam because you never know what's right or wrong in a hospital.

Mr. Timoney.

Who is it? Who do we have?

Frank McCourt, sir.

Francis, ah, Francis.

Mam says, I'm his mother, Mr. Timoney.

Well, then, the two of ye are blessed. I have neither kith nor kin nor Macushla my dog. And what are you doing in this place, Francis?

I have an infection in my eyes.

Ah, Jesus, Francis, not the eyes, not the eyes. Mother of Christ, you're too young for that.

Mr. Timoney, would you like me to read to you?

With them eyes, Francis? Ah, no, son, Save the eyes. I'm beyond reading. In my head I have everything I need. I was smart enough to put things in my head in my youth and now I have a library in my head. The English shot my wife. The Irish put down my poor innocent Macushla. Isn't it a joke of a world?

Mam says, Terrible world but God is good.

Indeed, missus. God made the world, it's a terrible world, but God is good. Good-bye, Francis. Rest your eyes and then read till they fall out of your head. We had good times with old Jonathan Swift, didn't we, Francis?

We did, Mr. Timoney.

Mam takes me back to the eye ward. She tells me, Don't be crying over Mr. Timoney, he's not even your father. Besides you'll be ruining your eyes.

Seamus comes to the ward three times a week and brings new poems in his head. He says, You made Patricia sad, Frankie, when you didn't like the one about the owl and the pussycat.

I'm sorry, Seamus.

I have it in my head, Frankie, and I'll say it for you if you don't say 'tis foolish.

I won't, Seamus.

He says the poem and everyone in the ward loves it. They want the words and he says it three more times till the whole ward is saying,

> The Owl and the Pussy-cat went to sea
> In a beautiful pea-green boat.
> They took some honey, and plenty of money
> Wrapped up in a five-pound note.
> The Owl looked up to the stars above,

And sang to a small guitar,
O lovely Pussy, O Pussy, my love,
What a beautiful Pussy you are,
You are,
You are.
What a beautiful Pussy you are.

They say it along with Seamus now and when it's finished they cheer and clap and Seamus laughs, delighted with himself. When he's gone with his mop and bucket you can hear them at all hours of the day and night

O lovely Pussy, O Pussy, my love,
What a beautiful Pussy you are,
You are,
You are.
What a beautiful Pussy you are.

Then Seamus comes with no mop and no bucket and I'm afraid he's sacked over the poetry but he's smiling and telling me he's off to England to work in a factory and earn decent wages for a change. He'll work for two months and bring the wife over and God might be pleased to send them children for he has to do something with all the poems in his head and what better than saying them to small ones in memory of that sweet Patricia Madigan dead of the dipteria.

Good-bye, Francis. If I had the right fist I'd write to you but I'll get the wife to write when she comes over. I might even learn to read and write myself so that the child that comes won't have a fool for a father.

I want to cry but you can't cry in the eye ward with brown stuff in your eyes and nurses saying, What's this what's this be a man, and nuns going on, Offer it up, think of the sufferings of Our Lord on the cross, the crown of thorns, the lance in the side, the hands and feet torn to bits with nails.

I'm a month in the hospital and the doctor says I can go home even if there's still a bit of infection but if I keep the eyes clean with soap and clean towels and build up my health with nourishing food plenty of beef and eggs I'll have a pair of sparkling eyes in no time ha ha.

Mr. Downes across the way comes back from England for his mother's funeral. He tells Mrs. Downes about my father. She tells Bridey Hannon and Bridey tells my mother. Mr. Downes says that Malachy McCourt is gone pure mad with the drink, that he squanders his wages in pubs all over Coventry, that he sings Irish rebel songs which the English don't mind because they're used to the way the Irish carry on about the hundreds of years of suffering, but they won't put up with any man that stands up in a pub and insults the King and Queen of England, their two lovely daughters and the Queen Mother herself. Insulting the Queen Mother is going beyond the beyonds. What did she ever do to anyone, that poor old lady? Time after time Malachy drinks away his rent money and winds up sleeping in parks when the landlord throws him out. He's a regular disgrace, so he is, and Mr. Downes is glad McCourt is not a Limerickman bringing shame to this ancient city. The magistrates in Coventry are losing their patience and if Malachy McCourt doesn't stop the bloody nonsense he'll be kicked out of the country entirely.

Mam tells Bridey she doesn't know what she's going to do with these stories from England, she never felt so desperate in her life. She can see Kathleen O'Connell doesn't want to give any more credit at the shop and her own mother barks at her if she asks for the loan of a shilling and the St. Vincent de Paul Society want to know when she'll stop asking for charity especially with a husband in England. She's ashamed of the way we look with the dirty old torn shirts, raggedy ganseys, broken shoes, holes in our stockings. She lies awake at night thinking the most merciful thing of all would be to put the four boys in an orphanage so that she could go to England herself and find some type of work where she could bring us all over in a year for the better life. There might be bombs but she'd prefer bombs anytime to the shame of begging from this one and that one.

No, no matter what she can't bear the thought of putting us in the orphanage. That might be all right if you had the likes of Boys' Town in America with a nice priest like Spencer Tracy but you could never trust the Christian Brothers out in Glin who get their exercise beating boys and starving the life out of them.

Mam says there's nothing left but the Dispensary and the public assistance, the relief, and she's ashamed of her life to go and ask for it. It means you're at the end of your rope and maybe one level above tinkers, knackers and street beggars in general. It means you have to crawl before Mr. Coffey and Mr. Kane and thank God the Dispensary is at the other end of Limerick so that people in our lane won't know we're getting the relief.

She knows from other women it's wise to be there early in the morning when Mr. Coffey and Mr. Kane might be in a good mood. If you go late in the morning they're liable to be cranky after seeing hundreds of men women and children sick and asking for help. She will take us with her to prove she has four children to feed. She gets us up early and tells us for once in our lives don't wash our faces, don't comb our hair, dress in any old rag. She tells me give my sore eyes a good rub and make them as red as I can for the worse you look at the Dispensary the more pity you get and the better your chances of getting the public assistance. She complains that Malachy Michael and Alphie look too healthy and you'd wonder why on this day of days they couldn't have their usual scabby knees or the odd cut bruise or black eye. If we meet anyone in the lane or the streets of Limerick we are not to tell them where we're going. She feels ashamed enough without telling the whole world and wait till her own mother hears.

There is a queue already outside the Dispensary. There are women like Mam with children in their arms, babies like Alphie, and children playing on the pavement. The women comfort the babies against the cold and scream at the ones playing in case they run into the street and get hit by a motor car or a bicycle. There are old men and women huddled against the wall talking to themselves or not talking at all. Mam warns us not to wander from her and we wait half an hour for the big door to open. A man tells us move inside in proper order and queue up before the platform, that Mr. Coffey and Mr. Kane will be there in a minute when they finish their tea in the room beyond. A woman complains her children are freezing with the cold and couldn't Coffey and Kane bloody well hurry up with their tea. The man says she's a troublemaker but he won't take her name this time with the cold that's in the morning but if there's another word she'll be a sorry woman.

Mr. Coffey and Mr. Kane get up on the platform and pay no attention to the people. Mr. Kane puts on his glasses, takes them off, polishes them, puts them on, looks at the ceiling. Mr. Coffey reads papers, writes something, passes papers to Mr. Kane. They whisper to each other. They take their time. They don't look at us.

Then Mr. Kane calls the first old man to the platform. What's your name?

Timothy Creagh, sir.

Creagh, hah? A fine old Limerick name you have there.

I do, sir. Indeed I do.

And what do you want, Creagh?

Ah, sure, I do be havin' them pains in me stomach again an' I'd like to see Dr. Feeley.

Well, now, Creagh, are you sure it's not the pints of porter that are going against your stomach.

Ah, no, indeed, sir. Sure I hardly touch the pint at all with the pains. My wife is home in the bed and I have to take care of her too.

There's great laziness in the world, Creagh. And Mr. Kane says to the people on the queue, Did ye hear that, ladies? Great laziness, isn't there?

And the women say, Oh, there is, indeed, Mr. Kane, great laziness.

Mr. Creagh gets his docket to see the doctor, the queue moves ahead and Mr. Kane is ready for Mam.

The public assistance, is that what you want, woman, the relief?

'Tis, Mr. Kane.

And where's your husband?

Oh, he's in England, but—

England, is it? And where is the weekly telegram, the big five pounds?

He didn't send us a penny in months, Mr. Kane.

Is that a fact? Well, we know why, don't we? We know what the men of Ireland are up to in England. We know there's the occasional Limerickman seen trotting around with a Piccadilly tart, don't we?

He looks out at the people on the queue and they know they're supposed to say, We do, Mr. Kane, and they know they're supposed to smile and laugh or things will go hard with them when they reach the platform. They know he might turn them over to Mr. Coffey and he's notorious for saying no to everything.

Mam tells Mr. Kane that Dad is in Coventry and nowhere near Piccadilly and Mr. Kane takes off his glasses and stares at her. What's this? Are we having a little contradiction here?

Oh, no, Mr. Kane, God no.

I want you to know, woman, that it is the policy here to give no relief to women with husbands in England. I want you to know you're taking the bread from the mouths of more deserving people who stayed in this country to do their bit.

Oh, yes, Mr. Kane.

And what's your name?

McCourt, sir.

That's not a Limerick name. Where did you get a name like that?

My husband, sir. He's from the North.

He's from the North and he leaves you here to get the relief from the Irish Free State. Is this what we fought for, is it?

I don't know, sir.

Why don't you go up to Belfast and see what the Orangemen will do for you, ah?

I don't know, sir.

You don't know. Of course you don't know. There's great ignorance in the world.

He looks out at the people, I said there's great ignorance in the world, and the people nod their heads and agree there's great ignorance in the world.

He whispers to Mr. Coffey and they look at Mam, they look at us. He tells Mam at last that she can have the public assistance but if she gets a single penny from her husband she's to drop all claims and give the money back to the Dispensary. She promises she will and we leave.

We follow her to Kathleen O'Connell's shop to get tea and bread and a few sods of turf for the fire. We climb the stairs to Italy and get the fire going and it's cozy when we have our tea. We're all very quiet, even the baby Alphie, because we know what Mr. Kane did to our mother.

X

It's cold and wet down in Ireland but we're up in Italy. Mam says we should bring the poor Pope up to hang on the wall opposite the window. After all he's a friend of the working-man, he's Italian, and they're a warm weather people. Mam sits by the fire, shivering, and we know something is wrong when she makes no move for a cigarette. She says she feels a cold coming and she'd love to have a tarty drink, a lemon-ade. But there's no money in the house, not even for bread in the morning. She drinks tea and goes to bed.

The bed creaks all night with her twistings and turnings and she keeps us awake with her moaning for water. In the morning, she stays in bed, still shivering, and we keep quiet. If she sleeps long enough Malachy and I will be too late for school. Hours pass and still she makes no move and when I know it's well past school time I start the fire for the kettle. She stirs and calls for lemonade but I give her a jam jar of water. I ask her if she'd like some tea and she acts like a woman gone deaf. She looks flushed and it's odd she doesn't even mention cigarettes.

We sit quietly by the fire, Malachy, Michael, Alphie, myself. We drink our tea while Alphie chews the last bit of bread covered with sugar. He makes us laugh the way he smears the sugar all over his face and grins at us with his fat sticky cheeks. But we can't laugh too much or Mam will jump out of the bed and order Malachy and me off to school where we'll be killed for being late. We don't laugh long, there is no more bread and we're hungry, the four of us. We can get no more credit at O'Connell's shop. We can't go near Grandma, either. She yells at us all the time because Dad is from the North and he never sends money home from England where he is working in a munitions factory. Grandma says we could starve to death for all he cares. That would teach Mam a lesson for marrying a man from the North with sallow skin, an odd manner and a look of the Presbyterian about him.

Still, I'll have to try Kathleen O'Connell once more. I'll tell her my mother is sick above in the bed, my brothers are starving and we'll all be dead for the want of bread.

I put on my shoes and run quickly through the streets of Limerick to keep myself warm against the February frost. You can look in people's windows and see how cozy it is in their kitchens with fires glowing or ranges black and hot everything bright in the electric light cups and saucers on the tables with plates of sliced bread pounds of butter jars of jam smells of fried eggs and rashers coming through the windows enough to make the water run in your mouth and families sitting there digging in all smiling the mother crisp and clean in her apron everyone washed and the Sacred Heart of Jesus looking down on them from the wall suffering and sad but still happy with all that food and light and good Catholics at their breakfast.

I try to find music in my own head but all I can find is my mother moaning for lemonade.

Lemonade. There's a van pulling away from South's pub leaving crates of beer and lemonade outside and there isn't a soul on the street. In a second I have two bottles of lemonade up under my jersey and I saunter away trying to look innocent.

There's a bread van outside Kathleen O'Connell's shop. The back door is open on shelves of steaming newly baked bread. The van driver is inside the shop having tea and a bun with Kathleen and it's no trouble for me to help myself to a loaf of bread. It's wrong to steal from Kathleen with the way she's always good to us but if I go in and ask her for bread she'll be annoyed and tell me I'm ruining her morning cup of tea, which she'd like to have in peace ease and comfort thank you. It's easier to stick the bread up under my jersey with the lemonade and promise to tell everything in confession.

My brothers are back in bed playing games under the overcoats but they jump when they see the bread. We tear at the loaf because we're too hungry to slice it and we make tea from this morning's leaves. When my mother stirs Malachy holds the lemonade bottle to her lips and she gasps till she finishes it. If she likes it that much I'll have to find more lemonade.

We put the last of the coal on the fire and sit around telling stories which we make up the way Dad did. I tell my brothers about my adventures with the lemonade and bread and I make up stories about how I was chased by pub owners and shopkeepers and how I ran into St. Joseph's Church where no one can follow you if you're a criminal, not even if you killed your own mother. Malachy and Michael look shocked over the way I got the bread and lemonade but then Malachy says it was only what Robin Hood would have done, rob the rich and give to the poor. Michael says I'm an outlaw and if they catch me they'll hang me from the highest tree in the People's Park the way outlaws are hanged in films at the Lyric Cinema. Malachy says I should make sure I'm in a state of grace because it might be hard to find a priest to come to my hanging. I tell him a priest would have to come to the hanging. That's what priests are for. Roddy McCorley had a priest and so did Kevin Barry. Malachy says there were no priests at the hanging of Roddy McCorley and Kevin Barry because they're not mentioned in the songs and he starts singing the songs to prove it till my mother groans in the bed and says shut up.

Alphie the baby is asleep on the floor by the fire. We put him into the bed with Mam so that he'll be warm though we don't want him to catch her disease and die. If she wakes up and finds him dead in the bed beside her there will be no end to the lamentations and she'll blame me on top of it.

The three of us get back into our own bed, huddling under the overcoats and trying not to roll into the hole in the mattress. It's pleasant there till Michael starts to worry over Alphie getting Mam's disease and me getting hanged for an outlaw. He says it isn't fair because that would leave him with only one brother and everyone in the world has brothers galore. He falls asleep from the worry and soon Malachy drifts off and I lie there thinking of jam. Wouldn't it be lovely to have another loaf of bread and a jar of strawberry jam or any kind of jam. I can't remember ever seeing a jam van making a delivery and I wouldn't want to be like Jesse James blasting my way into a shop demanding jam. That would surely lead to a hanging.

There's a cold sun coming through the window and I'm sure it must be warmer outside and wouldn't my brothers be surprised if they woke and found me there with more bread and jam. They'd gobble everything and then go on about my sins and the hanging.

Mam is still asleep though her face is red and there's a strangling sound when she snores.

I have to be careful going through the street because it's a school day and if Guard Dennehy sees me he'll drag me off to school and Mr. O'Halloran will knock me all over the classroom. The guard is in charge of school attendance and he loves chasing you on his bicycle and dragging you off to school by the ear.

There's a box sitting outside the door of one of the big houses on Barrington Street. I pretend to knock on the door so that I can see what's in the box, a bottle of milk, a loaf of bread, cheese, tomatoes and, oh, God, a jar of marmalade. I can't shove all that under my jersey. Oh, God. Should I take the whole box? The people passing by pay me no attention. I might as well take the whole box. My mother

272

would say you might as well be hung for a sheep as a lamb. I lift the box and try to look like a messenger boy making a delivery and no one says a word.

Malachy and Michael are beside themselves when they see what's in the box and they're soon gobbling thick cuts of bread slathered with golden marmalade. Alphie has the marmalade all over his face and hair and a good bit on his legs and belly. We wash down the food with cold tea because we have no fire to heat it.

Mam mumbles again for lemonade and I give her half the second bottle to keep her quiet. She calls for more and I mix it with water to stretch it because I can't be spending my life running around lifting lemonade from pubs. We're having a fine time of it till Mam begins to rave in the bed about her lovely little daughter taken from her and her twin boys gone before they were three and why couldn't God take the rich for a change and is there any lemonade in the house? Michael wants to know if Mam will die and Malachy tells him you can't die till a priest comes. Then Michael wonders if we'll ever have a fire and hot tea again because he's freezing in the bed even with the overcoats left over from olden times. Malachy says we should go from house to house asking for turf and coal and wood and we could use Alphie's pram to carry the load. We should take Alphie with us because he's small and he smiles and people will see him and feel sorry for him and us. We try to wash all the dirt and lint and feathers and sticky marmalade but when we touch him with water he howls. Michael says he'll only get dirty again in the pram so what's the use of washing him. Michael is small but he's always saying remarkable things like that.

We push the pram out to the rich avenues and roads but when we knock on the doors the maids tell us go away or they'll call the proper authorities and it's a disgrace to be dragging a baby around in a wreck of a pram that smells to the heavens a filthy contraption that you wouldn't use to haul a pig to the slaughterhouse and this is a Catholic country

273

where babies should be cherished and kept alive to hand down the faith from generation to generation. Malachy tells one maid to kiss his arse and she gives him such a clout the tears leap to his eyes and he says he'll never in his life ask the rich for anything again. He says there's no use asking anymore, that we should go around the backs of the houses and climb over the walls and take what we want. Michael can ring the front doorbells to keep the maids busy and Malachy and I can throw coal and turf over the walls and fill the pram all around Alphie.

We collect that way from three houses but then Malachy throws a piece of coal over a wall and hits Alphie and he starts screaming and we have to run forgetting Michael, still ringing doorbells and getting abuse from maids. Malachy says we should take the pram home first and then go back for Michael. We can't stop now with Alphie bawling and people giving us dirty looks and telling us we're a disgrace to our mother and Ireland in general.

When we're back home it takes a while to dig Alphie out from under the load of coal and turf and he won't stop screaming till I give him bread and marmalade. I'm afraid Mam will leap from her bed but she only mumbles on about Dad and drink and babies dead.

Malachy is back with Michael, with stories of his adventures ringing doorbells. One rich woman answered the door herself and invited him into the kitchen for cake and milk and bread and jam. She asked him all about his family and he told her his father had a big job in England but his mother is in the bed with a desperate disease and calling for lemonade morning noon and night. The rich woman wanted to know who was taking care of us and Michael bragged we were taking care of ourselves, that there was no shortage of bread and marmalade. The rich woman wrote down Michael's name and address and told him be a good boy and go home to his brothers and his mother in the bed.

Malachy barks at Michael for being such a fool as to tell

a rich woman anything. She'll go now and tell on us and before we know it we'll have the priests of the world banging on the door and disturbing us.

There's the banging on the door already. But it isn't a priest, it's Guard Dennehy. He calls up, Hello, hello, is anybody home? Are you there, Mrs. McCourt?

Michael knocks on the window and waves at the guard. I give him a good kick for himself and Malachy thumps him on the head and he yells, I'll tell the guard. I'll tell the guard. They're killing me, guard. They're thumping and kicking.

He won't shut up and Guard Dennehy shouts at us to open the door. I call out the window and tell him I can't open the door because my mother is in bed with a terrible disease.

Where's your father?

He's in England.

Well, I'm coming in to talk to your mother.

You can't. You can't. She has the disease. We all have the disease. It might be the typhoid. It might be the galloping consumption. We're getting spots already. The baby has a lump. It could kill.

He pushes in the door and climbs the stairs to Italy just as Alphie crawls out from under the bed covered with marmalade and dirt. He looks at him and my mother and us, takes off his cap and scratches his head. He says, Jesus, Mary and Joseph, this is a desperate situation. How did your mother get sick like that?

I tell him he shouldn't go near her and when Malachy says we might not be able to go to school for ages the guard says we'll go to school no matter what, that we're on the earth to go to school the way he's on the earth to make sure we go to school. He wants to know if we have any relations and he sends me off to tell Grandma and Aunt Aggie to come to our house.

They scream at me and tell me I'm filthy. I try to explain

that Mam has the disease and I'm worn out trying to make ends meet, keeping the home fires burning, getting lemonade for Mam and bread for my brothers. There's no use telling them about the marmalade for they'll only scream again. There's no use telling them about the nastiness of rich people and their maids.

They push me all the way back to the lane, barking at me and disgracing me on the streets of Limerick. Guard Dennehy is still scratching his poll. He says, Look at this, a disgrace. You wouldn't see the likes of this in Bombay or the Bowery of New York itself.

Grandma is wailing at my mother, Mother o' God, Angela, what's up with you in the bed? What did they do to you?

My mother runs her tongue over her dry lips and gasps for more lemonade.

She wants lemonade, says Michael, and we got it for her and bread and marmalade and we're all outlaws now. Frankie was the first outlaw till we went raiding for coal all over Limerick.

Guard Dennehy looks interested and takes Michael downstairs by the hand and in a few minutes we hear him laughing. Aunt Aggie says that's a disgraceful way to behave with my mother sick in the bed. The guard comes back and tells her go for a doctor. He keeps covering his face with his cap whenever he looks at me or my brothers. Desperadoes, he says, desperadoes.

The doctor comes with Aunt Aggie in his motor car and he has to rush my mother to the hospital with her pneumonia. We'd all like to go riding in the doctor's car but Aunt Aggie says, No, ye are all coming to my house till yeer mother comes home from the hospital.

I tell her not to bother. I'm eleven and I can easily look after my brothers. I'd be glad to stay at home from school and make sure everyone is fed and washed. But Grandma screams I will do no such a thing and Aunt Aggie gives me a thump for myself. Guard Dennehy says I'm too young yet to be an outlaw and a father but I have a promising future in both departments.

Get your clothes, says Aunt Aggie, ye are coming to my house till yeer mother is out of the hospital. Jesus above, that baby is a disgrace.

She finds a rag and ties it around Alphie's bottom for fear he might shit all over the pram. Then she looks at us and wants to know why we're standing there with our faces hanging out after she told us get our clothes. I'm afraid she'll hit me or yell at me when I tell her it's all right, we have our clothes, they're on us. She stares at me and shakes her head. Here, she says, put some sugar and water in the child's bottle. She tells me I have to push Alphie through the streets, she can't manage the pram with that bockety wheel that makes it rock back and forth and besides 'tis a disgraceful-looking object she'd be ashamed to put a mangy dog in. She takes the three old coats from our bed and piles them on the pram till you can hardly see Alphie at all.

Grandma comes with us and barks at me all the way from Roden Lane to Aunt Aggie's flat in Windmill Street. Can't you push that pram properly? Jesus, you're going to kill that child. Stop goin' from side to side or I'll give you a good clitther on the gob. She won't come into Aunt Aggie's flat. She can't stand the sight of us one more minute. She's fed up with the whole McCourt clan from the days when she had to send six fares to bring us all back from America, dishing out more money for funerals for dead children, giving us food every time our father drank the dole or the wages, helping Angela carry on while that blaguard from the North drinks his wages all over England. Oh, she's fed up, so she is, and off she goes across Henry Street with her black shawl pulled up around her white head, limping along in her black high-laced boots.

When you're eleven and your brothers are ten, five and one, you don't know what to do when you go to someone's house even if she's your mother's sister. You're told to leave the pram in the hall and bring the baby into the kitchen but if it's not your house you don't know what to do once you get into the kitchen for fear the aunt will yell at you or hit you on the skull. She takes off her coat and takes it to the bedroom and you stand with the baby in your arms waiting to be told. If you take one step forward or one step to the side she might come out and say where are you going and you don't know what to answer because you don't know yourself. If you say anything to your brothers she might say who do you think you're talking to in my kitchen? We have to stand and be quiet and that's hard when there's a tinkling sound from the bedroom and we know she's on the chamber pot peeing away. I don't want to look at Malachy. If I do I'll smile and he'll smile and Michael will smile and there's danger we'll start laughing and if we do we won't be able to stop for days at the picture in our heads of Aunt Aggie's big white bum perched on a flowery little chamber pot. I'm able to control myself. I won't laugh. Malachy and Michael won't laugh and it's easy to see we're all proud of ourselves for not laughing and getting into trouble with Aunt Aggie till Alphie in my arms smiles and says Goo goo and that sets us off. The three of us burst out laughing and Alphie grins with his dirty face and says Goo goo again till we're helpless and Aunt Aggie roars out of the room pulling her dress down and gives me a thump on the head that sends me against the wall baby and all. She hits Malachy too and she tries to hit Michael but he runs to the other side of her round table and she can't get at him. Come over here, she says, and I'll wipe that grin off your puss, but Michael keeps running around the table and she's too fat to catch him. I'll get you later, she says, I'll warm your arse, and you, Lord Muck, she says to me, put that child down on the floor over there by the range. She puts the old coats from the pram on the floor and Alphie lies there with his sugary water and says Goo goo and smiles. She tells us take off every scrap of our clothes, get out to the tap in the backyard and scrub every inch of our

278

bodies. We are not to come back into this house till we're spotless. I want to tell her it's the middle of February, it's freezing outside, we could all die, but I know if I open my mouth I might die right here on the kitchen floor.

We're out in the yard naked dousing ourselves with icy water from the tap. She opens the kitchen window and throws out a scrub brush and a big bar of brown soap like the one they used on Finn the Horse. She orders us to scrub each other's backs and don't stop till she tells us. Michael says his hands and feet are falling off with the cold but she doesn't care. She keeps telling us we're still dirty and if she has to come out to scrub us we'll rue the day. Another rue. I scrub myself harder. We all scrub till we're pink and our jaws chatter. It's not enough for Aunt Aggie. She comes out with a bucket and sloshes cold water all over us. Now, she says, get inside and dry yeerselves. We stand in the little shed next to her kitchen drying ourselves with one towel. We stand and shiver and wait because you can't go marching into her kitchen till she tells you. We hear her inside starting the fire, rattling the poker in the range, then yelling at us, Are ye goin' to stand in there all day? Come in here and put on yeer clothes.

She gives us mugs of tea and cuts of fried bread and we sit at the table eating quietly because you're not supposed to say a word unless she tells you. Michael asks her for a second cut of fried bread and we expect her to knock him off the chair for his cheek but she just grumbles, 'Tis far from two cuts of fried bread ye were brought up, and gives each of us another cut. She tries to feed Alphie bread soaked in tea but he won't eat it till she sprinkles it with sugar and when he's finished he smiles and pees all over her lap and we're delighted. She runs out to the shed to dab at herself with a towel and we're able to grin at each other at the table and tell Alphie he's the champion baby in the world. Uncle Pa Keating comes in the door all black from his job at the gas works. Oh, bejay, he says, what's this?

Michael says, My mother is in the hospital, Uncle Pa.

Is that so? What's up with her?

Pneumonia, says Malachy.

Well, now, that's better than oldmonia.

We don't know what he's laughing at and Aunt Aggie comes in from the shed and tells him how Mam is in the hospital and we're to stay with them till she gets out. He says, Grand, grand, and goes to the shed to wash himself though when he comes back you'd never know he touched himself with water at all he's that black.

He sits at the table and Aunt Aggie gives him his supper, which is fried bread and ham and sliced tomatoes. She tells us get away from the table and stop gawking at him having his tea and tells him to stop giving us bits of ham and tomato. He says, Arrah, for Jaysus sake, Aggie, the children are hungry, and she says, 'Tis none of your business. They're not yours. She tells us go out and play and be home for bed by half-past eight. We know it's freezing outside and we'd like to stay in by that warm range but it's easier to be in the streets playing than inside with Aunt Aggie and her nagging.

She calls me in later and sends me upstairs to borrow a rubber sheet from a woman who had a child that died. The woman says tell your aunt I'd like that rubber sheet back for the next child. Aunt Aggie says, Twelve years ago that child died and she still keeps the rubber sheet. Forty-five she is now and if there's another child we'll have to look for a star in the East. Malachy says, What's that? and she tells him mind his own business, he's too young.

Aunt Aggie places the rubber sheet on her bed and puts Alphie on it between herself and Uncle Pa. She sleeps inside against the wall and Uncle Pa outside because he has to get up in the morning for work. We are to sleep on the floor against the opposite wall with one coat under us and two over. She says if she hears a word out of us during the night she'll warm our arses and we're to be up early in the morning because it's Ash Wednesday and it wouldn't do us any harm

280

to go to Mass and pray for our poor mother and her pneumonia.

The alarm clock shocks us out of our sleep. Aunt Aggie calls from her bed, The three of ye are to get up and go to Mass. Do ye hear me? Up. Wash yeer faces and go to the Jesuits.

Her backyard is all frost and ice and our hands sting from the tap water. We throw a little on our faces and dry with the towel that's still damp from yesterday. Malachy whispers our wash was a lick and a promise, that's what Mam would say.

The streets are frosty and icy, too, but the Jesuit church is warm. It must be grand to be a Jesuit, sleeping in a bed with sheets blankets pillows and getting up to a nice warm house and a warm church with nothing to do but say Mass hear confessions and yell at people for their sins have your meals served up to you and read your Latin office before you go to sleep. I'd like to be a Jesuit some day but there's no hope of that when you grow up in a lane. Jesuits are very particular. They don't like poor people. They like people with motor cars who stick out their little fingers when they pick up their teacups.

The church is crowded with people at seven o'clock Mass getting the ashes on their foreheads. Malachy whispers that Michael shouldn't get the ashes because he won't be making his First Communion till May and it would be a sin. Michael starts to cry, I want the ashes, I want the ashes. An old woman behind us says, What are ye doin' to that lovely child? Malachy explains the lovely child never made his First Communion and he's not in a state of grace. Malachy is getting ready for Confirmation himself, always showing off his knowledge of the catechism, always going on about state of grace. He won't admit I knew all about the state of grace a year ago, so long ago I'm starting to forget it. The old woman says you don't have to be in a state of grace to get a few ashes on your forehead and tells Malachy stop tormenting his poor little brother. She pats Michael on the head and tells him he's a lovely child and go up there and get your ashes. He runs to the altar and when he comes back the woman gives him a penny to go with his ashes.

Aunt Aggie is still in the bed with Alphie. She tells Malachy to fill Alphie's bottle with milk and bring it to him. She tells me to start the fire in the range, that there's paper and wood in a box and coal in the coal scuttle. If the fire won't start sprinkle it with a little paraffin oil. The fire is slow and smoky and I sprinkle it with the paraffin oil, it flares up, whoosh, and nearly takes my eyebrows off. There is smoke everywhere and Aunt Aggie rushes into the kitchen. She shoves me away from the range. Jesus above, can't you do anything right? You're supposed to open the damper, you eejit.

I don't know anything about dampers. In our house we have a fireplace in Ireland downstairs and a fireplace in Italy upstairs and no sign of a damper. Then you go to your aunt's house and you're supposed to know all about dampers. There's no use telling her this is the first time you ever lit a fire in a range. She'll just give you another thump on the skull and send you flying. It's hard to know why grown people get so angry over little things like dampers. When I'm a man I won't go around thumping small children over dampers or anything else. Now she yells at me, Look at Lord Muck standing there. Would you ever think of opening the window and letting out the smoke? Of course you wouldn't. You have a puss on you like your father from the North. Do you think now you can boil the water for the tea without burning the house down?

She cuts three slices from a loaf, smears them with margarine for us and goes back to bed. We have the tea and bread and it's one morning we're glad to go to school where it's warm and there are no yelling aunts.

After school she tells me sit at the table and write my father a letter about Mam in the hospital and how we're all at Aunt Aggie's till Mam comes home. I'm to tell him we're all happy and in the best of health, send money, food is very dear, growing boys eat a lot, ha ha, Alphie the baby needs clothes and nappies.

I don't know why she's always angry. Her flat is warm and dry. She has electric light in the house and her own lavatory in the backyard. Uncle Pa has a steady job and he brings home his wages every Friday. He drinks his pints at South's pub but never comes home singing songs of Ireland's long woeful history. He says, A pox on all their houses, and he says the funniest thing in the world is that we all have arses that have to be wiped and no man escapes that. The minute a politician or a Pope starts his blather Uncle Pa thinks of him wiping his arse. Hitler and Roosevelt and Churchill all wipe their arses. De Valera, too. He says the only people you can trust in that department are the Mahommedans for they eat with one hand and wipe with the other. The human hand itself is a sneaky bugger and you never know what it's been up to.

There are good times with Uncle Pa when Aunt Aggie goes to the Mechanics' Institute to play cards, forty-five. He says, To hell with the begrudgers. He gets himself two bottles of stout from South's, six buns and a half pound of ham from the shop on the corner. He makes tea and we sit by the range drinking it, eating our ham sandwiches and buns and laughing over Uncle Pa and the way he goes on about the world. He says, I swallowed the gas, I drink the pint, I don't give a fiddler's fart about the world and its cousin. If little Alphie gets tired and cranky and cries Uncle Pa pulls his shirt back from his chest and tells him, Here, have a suck of diddy momma. The sight of that flat chest and the nipple shocks Alphie and makes him good again.

Before Aunt Aggie comes home we have to wash the mugs and clean up so she won't know we were stuffing ourselves with buns and ham sandwiches. She'd nag Uncle Pa for a month if she ever found out and that's what I don't understand. Why does he let her nag him like that? He went to the Great War, he was gassed, he's big, he has a job, he makes the world laugh. It's a mystery. That's what the priests and the masters tell you, everything is a mystery and you have to believe what you're told.

I could easily have Uncle Pa for a father. We'd have great times sitting by the fire in the range drinking tea and laughing over the way he farts and says, Light a match. That's a present from the Germans.

Aunt Aggie torments me all the time. She calls me scabby eyes. She says I'm the spitting image of my father, I have the odd manner, I have the sneaky air of a northern Presbyterian, I'll probably grow up and build an altar to Oliver Cromwell himself, I'll run off and marry an English tart and cover my house with pictures of the royal family.

I want to get away from her and I can think of only one way, to make myself sick and go to the hospital. I get up in the middle of the night and go to her backyard. I can pretend I'm going to the lavatory. I stand out in the open in the freezing weather and hope I'll catch pneumonia or the galloping consumption so that I'll go to the hospital with the nice clean sheets and the meals in the bed and books brought by the girl in the blue dress. I might meet another Patricia Madigan and learn a long poem. I stand in the backyard for ages in my shirt and bare feet looking up at the moon which is a ghostly galleon riding upon cloudy seas and go back to bed shivering hoping I'll wake up in the morning with a terrible cough and flushed cheeks. But I don't. I feel fresh and lively and I'd be in great form if I could be at home with my mother and brothers.

There are days when Aunt Aggie tells us she can't stand the sight of us another minute, Get away from me. Here, scabby eyes, take Alphie out in his pram, take your brothers, go to the park and play, do anything ye like and don't come back till teatime when the Angelus is ringing, not a minute later, do ye hear me, not a minute later. It's cold but we don't care. We push the pram up O'Connell Avenue out to

Ballinacurra or the Rosbrien Road. We let Alphie crawl around in fields to look at cows and sheep and we laugh when the cows nuzzle him. I get under the cows and squirt the milk into Alphie's mouth till he's full and throws it up. Farmers chase us till they see how small Michael and Alphie are. Malachy laughs at the farmers. He says, Hit me now with the child in me arms. Then he has a great notion, Why can't we go to our own house and play a while? We find twigs and bits of wood in the fields and rush to Roden Lane. There are matches by the fireplace in Italy and we have a good fire going in no time. Alphie falls asleep and soon the rest of us drift off till the Angelus booms out of the Redemptorist church and we know we're in trouble with Aunt Aggie for being late.

We don't care. She can yell at us all she wants but we had a grand time out the country with the cows and the sheep and then the lovely fire above in Italy.

You can tell she never has grand times like that. Electric light and a lavatory but no grand times.

Grandma comes for her on Thursdays and Sundays and they take the bus to the hospital to see Mam. We can't go because children are not allowed and if we say, How's Mam? they look cranky and tell us she's all right, she'll live. We'd like to know when she's getting out of hospital so that we can all go back home but we're afraid to open our mouths.

Malachy tells Aunt Aggie one day he's hungry and could he have a piece of bread. She hits him with a rolled-up *Little Messenger of the Sacred Heart* and there are tears on his eyelashes. He doesn't come home from school the next day and he's still gone at bedtime. Aunt Aggie says, Well, I suppose he ran away. Good riddance. If he was hungry he'd be here. Let him find comfort in a ditch.

Next day Michael runs in from the street, Dad's here, Dad's here, and runs back out and there's Dad sitting on the hall floor hugging Michael, crying, Your poor mother, your poor mother, and there's a smell of drink on him. Aunt

Aggie is smiling, Oh, you're here, and she makes tea and eggs and sausages. She sends me out for a bottle of stout for Dad and I wonder why she's so pleasant and generous all of a sudden. Michael says, Are we going to our own house, Dad?

We are, son.

Alphie is back in the pram with the three old coats and coal and wood for the fire. Aunt Aggie stands at her door and tells us be good boys, come back for tea anytime, and there's a bad word for her in my head, Oul'bitch. It's in my head and I can't help it and I'll have to tell the priest in confession.

Malachy isn't in a ditch, he's there in our own house eating fish and chips a drunken soldier dropped at the gate of the Sarsfield Barracks.

Mam comes home in two days. She's weak and white and walks slowly. She says, The doctor told me keep warm, have plenty of rest and nourishing food, meat and eggs three times a week. God help us, those poor doctors don't have a notion of not having. Dad makes tea and toasts bread for her on the fire. He fries bread for the rest of us and we have a lovely night up in Italy where it's warm. He says he can't stay forever, he has to go back to work in Coventry. Mam wonders how he'll get to Coventry without a penny in his pocket. He's up early on Holy Saturday and I have tea with him by the fire. He fries four cuts of bread and wraps them in pages of the *Limerick Chronicle*, two cuts in each coat pocket. Mam is still in bed and he calls to her from the bottom of the stairs, I'm going now. She says, All right. Write when you land. My father is going to England and she won't even get out of the bed. I ask if I can go with him to the railway station. No, he's not going there. He's going to the Dublin road to see if he can get a lift. He pats my head, tells me take care of my mother and brothers and goes out the door. I watch him go up the lane till he turns the corner. I run up the lane to see him go down Barrack

Hill and down St. Joseph's Street. I run down the hill and follow him as far as I can. He must know I'm following him because he turns and calls to me, Go home, Francis. Go home to your mother.

In a week there's a letter to say he arrived safely, that we are to be good boys, attend to our religious duties and above all obey our mother. In another week there's a telegram money order for three pounds and we're in heaven. We'll be rich, there will be fish and chips, jelly and custard, films every Saturday at the Lyric, the Coliseum, the Carlton, the Atheneum, the Central and the fanciest of all, the Savoy. We might even wind up having tea and cakes at the Savoy Café with the nobs and toffs of Limerick. We'll be sure to hold our teacups with our little fingers sticking out.

The next Saturday there's no telegram nor the Saturday after nor any Saturday forever. Mam begs again at the St. Vincent de Paul Society and smiles at the Dispensary when Mr. Coffey and Mr. Kane have their bit of a joke about Dad having a tart in Piccadilly. Michael wants to know what a tart is and she tells him it's something you have with tea. She spends most of the day by the fire with Bridey Hannon puffing on her Woodbines, drinking weak tea. The bread crumbs from the morning are always on the table when we come home from school. She never washes the jam jars or mugs and there are flies in the sugar and wherever there is sweetness.

She says Malachy and I have to take turns looking after Alphie, taking him out in the pram for a bit of fresh air. The child can't be kept in Italy from October to April. If we tell her we want to play with our pals she might let fly with a right cross to the head that stings the ears.

We play games with Alphie and the pram. I stand at the top of Barrack Hill and Malachy is at the bottom. When I give the pram a push down the hill Malachy is supposed to stop it but he's looking at a pal on roller skates and it speeds by him across the street and through the doors of Leniston's pub where men are having a peaceful pint and not expecting a pram with a dirty-faced child saying Goo goo goo goo. The barman shouts this is a disgrace, there must be a law against this class of behavior, babies roaring through the door in bockety prams, he'll call the guards on us, and Alphie waves at him and smiles and he says, all right, all right, the child can have a sweet and a lemonade, the brothers can have lemonade too, that raggedy pair, and God above, 'tis a hard world, the minute you think you're getting ahead a pram comes crashing through the door and you're dishing out sweets and lemonade right and left, the two of ye take that child and go home to yeer mother.

Malachy has another powerful idea, that we could go around Limerick like tinkers pushing Alphie in his pram into pubs for the sweets and lemonade, but I don't want Mam finding out and hitting me with her right cross. Malachy says I'm not a sport and runs off. I push the pram over to Henry Street and up by the Redemptorist church. It's a gray day, the church is gray and the small crowd of people outside the door of the priests' house is gray. They're waiting to beg for any food left over from the priests' dinner.

There in the middle of the crowd in her dirty gray coat is my mother.

This is my own mother, begging. This is worse than the dole, the St. Vincent de Paul Society, the Dispensary. It's the worst kind of shame, almost as bad as begging on the streets where the tinkers hold up their scabby children, Give us a penny for the poor child, mister, the poor child is hungry, missus.

My mother is a beggar now and if anyone from the lane or my school sees her the family will be disgraced entirely. My pals will make up new names and torment me in the schoolyard and I know what they'll say,

Frankie McCourt
beggar woman's boy
scabby-eyed
dancing
blubber-gob
Jap

The door of the priests' house swings open and the people rush with their hands out. I can hear them, Brother, brother, here, brother, ah, for the love o' God, brother. Five children at home, brother. I can see my own mother pushed along. I can see the tightness of her mouth when she snatches at a bag and turns from the door and I push the pram up the street before she can see me.

I don't want to go home anymore. I push the pram down to the Dock Road, out to Corkanree where all the dust and garbage of Limerick is dumped and burned. I stand a while and look at boys chase rats. I don't know why they have to torture rats that are not in their houses. I'd keep going on into the country forever if I didn't have Alphie bawling with the hunger, kicking his chubby legs, waving his empty bottle.

Mam has the fire going and something boiling in a pot. Malachy smiles and says she brought home corned beef and a few spuds from Kathleen O'Connell's shop. He wouldn't be so happy if he knew he was the son of a beggar. She calls us in from the lane and when we sit at the table it's hard for me to look at my mother the beggar. She lifts the pot to the table, spoons out the potatoes one each and uses a fork to lift out the corned beef.

It isn't corned beef at all. It's a great lump of quivering gray fat and the only sign of corned beef is a little nipple of red meat on top. We stare at that bit of meat and wonder who will get it. Mam says, That's for Alphie. He's a baby, he's growing fast, he needs it. She puts it on a saucer in front of him. He pushes it away with his finger, then pulls it back.

He lifts it to his mouth, looks around the kitchen, sees Lucky the dog and throws it to him.

There's no use saying anything. The meat is gone. We eat our potatoes with plenty of salt and I eat my fat and pretend it's that nipple of red meat.

XI

Mam warns us, Ye are to keep yeer paws out of that trunk for there's nothing in there that's of the slightest interest or any of yeer business.

All she has in that trunk is a lot of papers, certificates of birth and baptism, her Irish passport, Dad's English passport from Belfast, our American passports and her bright red flapper dress with spangles and black frills she brought all the way from America. She wants to keep that dress forever to remind herself she was young and dancing.

I don't care what she has in the trunk till I start a football team with Billy Campbell and Malachy. We can't afford uniforms or boots and Billy says, How will the world know who we are? We don't even have a name.

I remember the red dress and a name comes to me, The Red Hearts of Limerick. Mam never opens the trunk so what does it matter if I cut off a piece of the dress to make seven red hearts we can stick on our chests? What you don't know won't bother you, she always says herself.

The dress is buried under the papers. I look at my passport picture when I was small and I can see why they call me Jap. There's a paper that says Marriage Certificate, that Malachy McCourt and Angela Sheehan were joined in Holy Matrimony on the twenty-eighth of March, 1930. How could that be? I was born on the nineteenth of August and Billy Campbell told me the father and mother have to be married nine months before there's a sign of a child. Here I am born into the world in half the time. That means I must be a miracle and I might grow up to be a saint with people celebrating the feast of St. Francis of Limerick.

I'll have to ask Mikey Molloy, still the expert on Girls' Bodies and Dirty Things in General.

Billy says if we're to be great soccer players we have to practice and we're to meet over in the park. The boys complain when I hand out the hearts and I tell them if they don't like it they can go home and cut up their own mother's dresses and blouses.

We have no money for a proper ball so one of the boys brings a sheep's bladder stuffed with rags. We kick the bladder up and down the meadow till there are holes and rags start falling out and we get fed up kicking a bladder that's hardly there anymore. Billy says we're to meet tomorrow morning which is Saturday and go out Ballinacurra to see if we can challenge rich Crescent College boys to a proper game, seven a side. He says we're to pin our red hearts to our shirts even if they're red rags.

Malachy is going home for tea but I can't go because I have to see Mikey Molloy and find out why I was born in half the time. Mikey is coming out of his house with his father, Peter. It's Mikey's sixteenth birthday and his father is taking him to Bowles's pub for his first pint. Nora Molloy is inside screeching after Peter that if they go they can stay gone, she's done baking bread, she's never going to the lunatic asylum again, if he brings that child home drunk she'll go to Scotland and disappear from the face of the earth.

Peter tells Mikey, Pay no attention to her, Cyclops. The mothers of Ireland are always enemies of the first pint. My own mother tried to kill my father with a frying pan when he took me for the first pint.

Mikey asks Peter if I can come with them and have a lemonade.

Peter tells everyone in the pub that Mikey is there for his first pint and when all the men want to stand Mikey a pint

Peter says, Ah, no, 'twould be a terrible thing if he had too much and turned against it entirely.

The pints are drawn and we sit against the wall, the Molloys with their pints and I with my lemonade. The men wish Mikey all the best in the life to come and wasn't it a gift from God that he fell off that spout years ago and never had the fit since and wasn't it a great pity about that poor little bugger, Quasimodo Dooley, carried off with the consumption after all his trouble talking for years like an Englishman so he could be on the BBC which is no fit place for an Irishman anyway.

Peter is talking to the men and Mikey, sipping his first pint, whispers to me, I don't think I like it, but don't tell my father. Then he tells me how he practices the English accent in secret so that he can be a BBC announcer, Quasimodo's dream. He tells me I can have Cuchulain back, that he's no use to you when you're reading the news on the BBC. Now that he's sixteen he wants to go to England and if ever I get a wireless that will be him on the BBC Home Service.

I tell him about the marriage certificate, how Billy Campbell said it has to be nine months but I was born in half the time and would he know if I was some class of a miracle.

Naw, he says, naw. You're a bastard. You're doomed.

You don't have to be cursing me, Mikey.

I'm not. That's what they call people who aren't born inside the nine months of the marriage, people conceived beyond the blanket.

What's that?

What's what?

Conceived.

That's when the sperm hits the egg and it grows and there you are nine months later.

I don't know what you're talking about.

He whispers, The thing between your legs is the excitement.

I don't like the other names, the dong, the prick, the dick, the langer. So your father shoves his excitement into your mother and there's a spurt and these little germs go up into your mother where there's an egg and that grows into you.

I'm not an egg.

You are an egg. Everyone was an egg once.

Why am I doomed? 'Tisn't my fault I'm a bastard.

All bastards are doomed. They're like babies that weren't baptized. They're sent to Limbo for eternity and there's no way out and it's not their fault. It makes you wonder about God up there on His throne with no mercy for the little unbaptized babies. That's why I don't go near the chapel anymore. Anyway, you're doomed. Your father and mother had the excitement and they weren't married so you're not in a state of grace.

What am I going to do?

Nothing. You're doomed.

Can't I light a candle or something.

You could try the Blessed Virgin. She's in charge of the doom.

But I don't have a penny for the candle.

All right, all right, here's a penny. You can give it back when you get a job a million years from now. 'Tis costing me a fortune to be the expert on Girls' Bodies and Dirty Things in General.

The barman is doing a crossword puzzle and he says to Peter, What's the opposite of advance?

Retreat, says Peter.

That's it, says the barman. Everything has an opposite.

Mother o' God, says Peter.

What's up with you, Peter? says the barman.

What was that you said before, Tommy?

Everything has an opposite.

Mother o' God.

Are you all right, Peter? Is the pint all right?

294

The pint is grand, Tommy, and I'm the champion of all pint drinkers, amn't I?

Begod an' you are, Peter. No denyin' that to you.

That means I could be the champion in the opposite department.

What are you talking about, Peter?

I could be the champion of no pints at all.

Ah, now, Peter, I think you're going a bit far. Is the wife all right at home?

Tommy, take this pint away from me. I'm the champion of no pints at all.

Peter turns and takes the glass from Mikey. We're going home to your mother, Mikey.

You didn't call me Cyclops, Dad.

You're Mikey. You're Michael. We're going to England. No more pints for me, no pints for you, no more bread baking for your mother. Come on.

We're leaving the pub and Tommy the barman calls after us, You know what 'tis, Peter. 'Tis all them bloody books you're reading. They have your head destroyed.

Peter and Mikey turn to go home. I have to go to St. Joseph's to light the candle that will save me from the doom but I look in the window of Counihan's shop and there in the middle is a great slab of Cleeves' toffee and a sign, TWO PIECES FOR A PENNY. I know I'm doomed but the water is running along the sides of my tongue and when I put my penny on the counter for Miss Counihan I promise the Virgin Mary the next penny I get I'll be lighting a candle and would she please talk to her Son and delay the doom for awhile.

A penn'orth of Cleeves' toffee doesn't last forever and when it's gone I have to think of going home to a mother who let my father push his excitement into her so that I could be born in half the time and grow up to be a bastard. If she ever says a word about the red dress or anything I'll tell her I know all about the excitement and she'll be shocked.

Saturday morning I meet The Red Hearts of Limerick and we wander out the road looking for a football challenge. The boys are still grousing that the bits of red dress don't look like hearts till Billy tells them if they don't want to play football go home and play with their sisters' dolls.

There are boys playing football in a field in Ballinacurra and Billy challenges them. They have eight players and we have only seven but we don't mind because one of them has one eye and Billy tells us stay on his blind side. Besides, he says, Frankie McCourt is nearly blind with his two bad eyes and that's worse. They're all togged out in blue and white jerseys and white shorts and proper football boots. One of them says we look like something the cat brought in and Malachy has to be held back from fighting them. We agree to play half an hour because the Ballinacurra boys say they have to go to lunch. Lunch. The whole world has dinner in the middle of the day but they have lunch. If no one scores in half an hour it's a draw. We play back and forth till Billy gets the ball and goes speeding and dancing up the sideline so fast no one can catch him and in goes the ball for a goal. The half hour is nearly up but the Ballinacurra boys want another half hour and they manage to score well into the second half hour. Then the ball goes over the line for touch. It's our ball. Billy stands on the touch line with the ball over his head. He pretends to look at Malachy but throws the ball to me. It comes to me as if it's the only thing that exists in the whole world. It comes straight to my foot and all I have to do is swivel to the left and swing that ball straight into the goal. There's a whiteness in my head and I feel like a boy in heaven. I'm floating over the whole field till The Red Hearts of Limerick clap me on the back and tell me that was a great goal, Frankie, you too, Billy.

We walk back along O'Connell Avenue and I keep thinking of the way the ball came to my foot and surely it was sent by God or the Blessed Virgin Mary who would never send such a blessing to one doomed for being born in half the time and I know as long as I live I'll never forget that ball coming from Billy Campbell, that goal.

Mam meets Bridey Hannon and her mother going up the lane and they tell her about Mr. Hannon's poor legs. Poor John, it's a trial for him to cycle home every night after delivering coal and turf all day on the great float for the coal merchants on the Dock Road. He's paid from eight in the morning till half five in the evening though he has to get the horse ready well before eight and settle him for the night well after half five. He's up and down on that float all day hoisting bags of coal and turf, desperate to keep the bandages in place on his legs so the dirt won't get into the open sores. The bandages are forever sticking and have to be ripped away and when he comes home she washes the sores with warm water and soap, covers them with ointment and wraps them in clean bandages. They can't afford new bandages every day so she keeps washing the old ones over and over till they're gray.

Mam says Mr. Hannon should see the doctor and Mrs. Hannon says, Sure, he seen the doctor a dozen times and the doctor says he has to stay off them legs. That's all. Stay off them legs. Sure how can he stay off them legs? He has to work. What would we live on if he didn't work?

Mum says maybe Bridey could get some kind of a job herself and Bridey is offended. Don't you know I have a weak chest, Angela? Don't you know I had rheumatic fever an' I could go at any time? I have to be careful.

Mam often talks about Bridey and her rheumatic fever and weak chest. She says, That one is able to sit here by the hour and complain about her ailments but it doesn't stop her from puffing away on the Woodbines.

Mam tells Bridey she's very sorry over the weak chest and it's terrible the way her father suffers. Mrs. Hannon tells my mother that John is getting worse every day, And what would

297

you think, Mrs. McCourt, if your boy Frankie went on the float with him a few hours a week and helped him with the bags? We can barely afford it but Frankie could earn a shilling or two and John could rest his poor legs.

Mam says, I don't know, he's only eleven and he had that typhoid and the coal dust wouldn't be good for his eyes.

Bridey says, He'd be out in the air and there's nothing like fresh air for someone with bad eyes or getting over the typhoid, isn't that right, Frankie?

'Tis, Bridey.

I'm dying to go around with Mr. Hannon on the great float like a real workingman. If I'm good at it they might let me stay at home from school forever but Mam says, He can do it as long as it doesn't interfere with school and he can start on a Saturday morning.

I'm a man now so I light the fire early on Saturday morning and make my own tea and fried bread. I wait next door for Mr. Hannon to come out with his bicycle and there's a lovely smell of rashers and eggs coming through the window. Mam says Mr. Hannon gets the best of food because Mrs. Hannon is as mad about him as she was the day she married him. They're like two lovers out of an American film the way they go on. Here he is pushing the bicycle and puffing away on the pipe in his mouth. He tells me climb up on the bar of his bike and off we go to my first job as a man. His head is over mine on the bike and the smell of the pipe is lovely. There's a coal smell on his clothes and that makes me sneeze.

Men are walking or cycling toward the coal yards and Rank's Flour Mills and the Limerick Steamship Company on the Dock Road. Mr. Hannon takes his pipe from his mouth and tells me this is the best morning of all, Saturday, half day. We'll start at eight and be finished by the time the Angelus rings at twelve.

First we get the horse ready, give him a bit of a rub, fill the wooden tub with oats and the bucket with water. Mr. Hannon shows me how to put on the harness and lets me back the horse into the shafts of the float. He says, Jaysus, Frankie, you have the knack of it.

That makes me so happy I want to jump up and down and drive a float the rest of my life.

There are two men filling bags with coal and turf and weighing them on the great iron scale, a hundredweight in each bag. It's their job to stack the bags on the float while Mr. Hannon goes to the office for the delivery dockets. The bag men are fast and we're ready for our rounds. Mr. Hannon sits up on the left side of the float and flicks the whip to show where I'm to sit on the right side. It's hard to climb up the way the float is so high and packed with bags and I try to get up by climbing the wheel. Mr. Hannon says I should never do the likes of that again. Never put your leg or hand near a wheel when the horse is harnessed in the shafts. A horse might take a notion to go for a walk for himself and there you are with the leg or the arm caught in the wheel and twisted off your body and you looking at it. He says to the horse, G'up ower that, and the horse shakes his head and rattles the harness and Mr. Hannon laughs. That fool of a horse loves to work, he says. He won't be rattling his harness in a few hours.

When the rain starts we cover ourselves with old coal bags and Mr. Hannon turns his pipe upside down in his mouth to keep the tobacco dry. He says the rain makes everything heavier but what's the use of complaining. You might as well complain about the sun in Africa.

We cross the Sarsfield Bridge for deliveries to the Ennis Road and the North Circular Road. Rich people, says Mr. Hannon, and very slow to put their hands in their pockets for a tip.

We have sixteen bags to deliver. Mr. Hannon says we're lucky today because some houses get more than one and he doesn't have to be climbing on and off that float destroying his legs. When we stop he gets down and I pull the bag to the edge and lay it on his shoulders. Some houses have areas outside where you pull up a trap door and tip the bag till it empties and that's easy. There are other houses with long backyards and you can see Mr. Hannon suffering with his legs when he has to carry the bags from the float to the sheds near the back doors. Ah, Jaysus, Frankie, ah, Jaysus, is the only complaint out of him and he asks me to give him a hand to climb back on the float. He says if he had a handcart he could wheel the bags from float to house and that would be a blessing but a handcart would cost two weeks' wages and who could afford that?

The bags are delivered and the sun is out, the float is empty, and the horse knows his workday is over. It's lovely to sit on the float looking along the length of the horse from his tail to his head rocking along the Ennis Road over the Shannon and up the Dock Road. Mr. Hannon says the man who delivered sixteen hundredweights of coal and turf deserves a pint and the boy who helped him deserves a lemonade. He tells me I should go to school and not be like him working away with the two legs rotting under him. Go to school, Frankie, and get out of Limerick and Ireland itself. This war will be over some day and you can go to America or Australia or any big open country where you can look up and see no end to the land. The world is wide and you can have great adventures. If I didn't have these two legs I'd be over in England making a fortune in the factories like the rest of the Irishmen, like your father. No, not like your father. I hear he left you high and dry, eh? I don't know how a man in his right mind can go off and leave a wife and family to starve and shiver in a Limerick winter. School, Frankie, school. The books, the books, the books. Get out of Limerick before your legs rot and your mind collapses entirely.

The horse clops along and when we get to the coal yard we feed and water him and give him a rubdown. Mr. Hannon talks to him all the time and calls him Me oul' segosha, and the horse snuffles and pushes his nose against Mr. Hannon's chest. I'd love to bring this horse home and let him stay downstairs when we're up in Italy but even if I could get him in the door my mother would yell at me that the last thing we need in this house is a horse.

The streets going up from the Dock Road are too hilly for Mr. Hannon to ride the bicycle and carry me, so we walk. His legs are sore from the day and it takes a long time to get up to Henry Street. He leans on the bicycle or sits, on the steps outside houses, grinding down on the pipe in his mouth.

I'm wondering when I'll get the money for the day's work because Mam might let me go to the Lyric Cinema if I get home in time with my shilling or whatever Mr. Hannon gives me. Now we're at the door of South's pub and he tells me come in, didn't he promise me a lemonade?

Uncle Pa Keating is sitting in the pub. He's all black as usual and he's sitting next to Bill Galvin, all white as usual, snuffling and taking great slugs out of his black pint. Mr. Hannon says, How're you? and sits on the other side of Bill Galvin and everyone in the pub laughs. Jaysus, says the barman, look at that, two lumps of coal and a snowball. Men come in from other parts of the pub to see the two coal-black men with the lime-white man in the middle and they want to send down to the *Limerick Leader* for a man with a camera.

Uncle Pa says, What are you doing all black yourself, Frankie? Did you fall down a coal mine?

I was helping Mr. Hannon on the float.

Your eyes look atrocious, Frankie. Piss holes in the snow.

'Tis the coal dust, Uncle Pa.

Wash them when you go home.

I will, Uncle Pa.

Mr. Hannon buys me a lemonade, gives me the shilling for my morning's work and tells me I can go home now, I'm a great worker and I can help him again next week after school.

On the way home I see myself in the glass of a shop

window all black from the coal, and I feel like a man, a man with a shilling in his pocket, a man who had a lemonade in a pub with two coal men and a lime man. I'm not a child anymore and I could easily leave Leamy's School forever. I could work with Mr. Hannon every day and when his legs got too bad I could take over the float and deliver coal to the rich people the rest of my life and my mother wouldn't have to be a beggar at the Redemptorist priests' house.

People on the streets and lanes give me curious looks. Boys and girls laugh and call out, Here's the chimney sweep. How much do you want for cleaning our chimney? Did you fall into a coal hole? Were you burned by the darkness?

They're ignorant. They don't know I spent the day delivering hundredweights of coal and turf. They don't know I'm a man.

Mam is sleeping up in Italy with Alphie and there's a coat over the window to keep the room dark. I tell her I earned a shilling and she says I can go to the Lyric, I deserve it. Take tuppence and leave the rest of the shilling on the mantelpiece downstairs so that she can send out for a loaf of bread for the tea. The coat suddenly drops from the window and the room is bright. Mam looks at me, God above, look at your eyes. Go downstairs and I'll be down in a minute to wash them.

She heats water in the kettle and dabs at my eyes with boric acid powder and tells me I can't go to the Lyric Cinema today or any day till my eyes clear up though God knows when that will be. She says, You can't be delivering coal with the state of your eyes. The dust will surely destroy them.

I want the job. I want to bring home the shilling. I want to be a man.

You can be a man without bringing home a shilling. Go upstairs and lie down and rest your two eyes or it's a blind man you'll be.

I want that job. I wash my eyes three times a day with the boric acid powder. I remember Seamus in the hospital and how his uncle's eyes were cured with the blink exercise and I make sure to sit and blink for an hour every day. You can't beat the blink for the strong eye, he said. And now I blink and blink till Malachy runs to my mother, talking out in the lane with Mrs. Hannon, Mam, something is up with Frankie, he's upstairs blinking and blinking.

She comes running up. What's wrong with you?

I'm making my eyes strong with the exercise.

What exercise?

The blinking.

Blinking is not exercise.

Seamus in the hospital says you can't beat the blink for the strong eye. His uncle had powerful eyes from the blinking.

She says I'm getting odd and goes back to the lane and her chat with Mrs. Hannon and I blink and bathe my eyes with the boric acid powder in warm water. I can hear Mrs. Hannon through the window, Your little Frankie is a god-send to John for 'tis the climbing up and down on that float that was ruining his legs entirely.

Mam doesn't say anything and that means she feels so sorry for Mr. Hannon she'll let me help him again on his heavy delivery day, Thursday. I wash my eyes three times a day and I blink till I get a pain in my eyebrows. I blink in school when the master isn't looking and all the boys in my class are calling me Blinky and adding that to the list of names.

> *Blinky McCourt*
> *beggar woman's son*
> *scabby-eyed*
> *blubber gob*
> *dancing*
> *Jap.*

I don't care what they call me anymore as long as my eyes are clearing up and I have a regular job lifting hundredweights of coal on a float. I wish they could see me on Thursday after school when I'm on the float and Mr. Hannon hands me the reins so that he can smoke his pipe in comfort. Here you are, Frankie, nice and gentle for this is a good horse and he doesn't need to be pulled at.

He hands me the whip too but you never need the whip with this horse. It's all for show and I just flick it at the air like Mr. Hannon or I might knock a fly off the horse's great golden rump swinging between the shafts.

Surely the world is looking at me and admiring the way I rock with the float, the cool way I have with the reins and the whip. I wish I had a pipe like Mr. Hannon and a tweed cap. I wish I could be a real coal man with black skin like Mr. Hannon and Uncle Pa Keating so that people would say, There goes Frankie McCourt that delivers all the coal in Limerick and drinks his pint in South's pub. I'd never wash my face. I'd be black every day of the year even Christmas when you're supposed to give yourself a good wash for the coming of the Infant Jesus. I know He wouldn't mind because I saw the Three Wise Men in the Christmas crib at the Redemptorist church and one of them was blacker than Uncle Pa Keating, the blackest man in Limerick, and if a Wise Man is black it means that everywhere you go in the world someone is delivering coal.

The horse lifts his tail and great lumps of steaming yellow shit drop from his behind. I start to pull on the reins so that he can stop and have a bit of comfort for himself but Mr. Hannon says, No, Frankie, let him trot. They always shit on the trot. That's one of the blessings horses have, they shit on the trot, and they're not dirty and stinking like the human race, not at all, Frankie. The worst thing in the world is to go into a lavatory after a man that had a feed of pig's feet and a night of pints. The stink from that could twist the nostrils of a strong man. Horses are different. All they have is oats and hay and what they drop is clean and natural.

I work with Mr. Hannon after school on Tuesdays and Thursdays and the half day on Saturday morning and that means three shillings for my mother though she worries all the time over my eyes. The minute I get home she washes them and makes me rest them for half an hour.

Mr. Hannon says he'll wait near Leamy's School for me on Thursdays after his deliveries on Barrington Street. Now the boys will see me. Now they'll know I'm a workingman and more than a scabby-eyed blubber gob dancing Jap. Mr. Hannon says, Up you get, and I climb up on the float like any workingman. I look at the boys gawking at me. Gawking. I tell Mr. Hannon if he wants to smoke his pipe in comfort I'll take the reins and when he hands them over I'm sure I hear the boys gasping. I tell the horse, G'up ower that, like Mr. Hannon. We trot away and I know dozens of Leamy's boys are committing the deadly sin of envy. I tell the horse again, G'up ower that, to make sure everyone heard, to make sure they know I'm driving that float and no one else, to make sure they'll never forget it was me they saw on that float with the reins and the whip. It's the best day of my life, better than my First Communion day, which Grandma ruined, better than my Confirmation day when I had the typhoid.

They don't call me names anymore. They don't laugh at my scabby eyes. They want to know how I got such a good job at eleven years of age and what I'm paid and if I'll have that job forever. They want to know if there are any other good jobs going in the coal yards and would I put in a good word for them.

Then there are big boys of thirteen who stick their faces in mine and say they should have that job because they're bigger and I'm nothing but a scrawny little runt with no shoulders. They can talk as much as they like. I have the job and Mr. Hannon tells me I'm powerful.

There are days his legs are so bad he can hardly walk at all and you can see Mrs. Hannon worries. She gives me a mug of tea and I watch her roll up his trouser legs and peel away the dirty bandages. The sores are red and yellow and clogged with coal dust. She washes them with soapy water and smears them with a yellow ointment. She props the legs up on a chair and that's where he stays the rest of the night reading the paper or a book from the shelf above his head.

The legs are getting so bad he has to get up an hour earlier in the morning to get the stiffness out, to put on another dressing. It's still dark one Saturday morning when Mrs. Hannon knocks at our door and asks me if I'd go to a neighbor and borrow their handcart to take on the float for Mr. Hannon will never be able to carry the bags today and maybe I'd just roll them on the handcart for him. He won't be able to carry me on his bicycle so I can meet him at the yard with the handcart.

The neighbor says, Anything for Mr. Hannon, God bless him.

I wait at the gate of the coal yard and watch him cycle toward me, slower than ever. He's so stiff he can hardly get off the bike and he says, You're a great man, Frankie. He lets me get the horse ready though I still have trouble getting on the harness. He lets me handle the float out of the yard and into the frosty streets and I wish I could drive forever and never go home. Mr. Hannon shows me how to pull the bags to the edge of the float and drop them on the ground so that I can pull them on to the handcart and push them to the houses. He tells me how to lift and push the bags without straining myself and we have the sixteen bags delivered by noon.

I wish the boys at Leamy's could see me now, the way I drive the horse and handle the bags, the way I do everything while Mr. Hannon rests his legs. I wish they could see me pushing the handcart to South's pub and having my lemonade with Mr. Hannon and Uncle Pa and me all black and Bill Galvin all white. I'd like to show the world the tips Mr. Hannon lets me keep, four shillings, and the shilling he gives me for the morning's work, five shillings altogether.

Mam is sitting by the fire and when I hand her the

money she looks at me, drops it in her lap and cries. I'm puzzled because money is supposed to make you happy. Look at your eyes, she says. Go to that glass and look at your eyes.

My face is black and the eyes are worse than ever. The whites and the eyelids are red, and the yellow stuff oozes to the corners and out over the lower lids. If the ooze sits a while it forms a crust that has to be picked off or washed away.

Mam says that's the end of it. No more Mr. Hannon. I try to explain that Mr. Hannon needs me. He can barely walk anymore. I had to do everything this morning, drive the float, wheel the handcart with the bags, sit in the pub, drink lemonade, listen to the men discussing who is the best, Rommel or Montgomery.

She says she's sorry for Mr. Hannon's troubles but we have troubles of our own and the last thing she needs now is a blind son stumbling through the streets of Limerick. Bad enough you nearly died of typhoid, now you want to go blind on top of it.

And I can't stop crying now because this was my one chance to be a man and bring home the money the telegram boy never brought from my father. I can't stop crying because I don't know what Mr. Hannon is going to do on Monday morning when he has no one to help him pull the bags to the edge of the float, to push the bags into the houses. I can't stop crying because of the way he is with that horse he calls sweet because he's so gentle himself and what will the horse do if Mr. Hannon isn't there to take him out, if I'm not there to take him out? Will that horse fall down hungry for the want of oats and hay and the odd apple?

Mam says I shouldn't be crying, it's bad for the eyes. She says, We'll see. That's all I can tell you now. We'll see.

She washes my eyes and gives me sixpence to take Malachy to the Lyric to see Boris Karloff in *The Man They Could Not*

Hang and have two pieces of Cleeves' toffee. It's hard to see the screen with the yellow stuff oozing from my eyes and Malachy has to tell me what's happening. People around us tell him shut up, they'd like to hear what Boris Karloff is saying, and when Malachy talks back to them and tells them he's only helping his blind brother they call the man in charge, Frank Goggin, and he says if he hears another word out of Malachy he'll throw the two of us out.

I don't mind. I have a way of squeezing the stuff out of one eye and clearing it so that I can see the screen while the other eye fills up and I go back and forth, squeeze, look, squeeze, look, and everything I see is yellow.

Monday morning Mrs. Hannon is knocking on our door again. She asks Mam if Frank would ever go down to the coal yard and tell the man in the office that Mr. Hannon can't come in today, that he has to see a doctor about his legs, that he'll surely be in tomorrow and what he can't deliver today he will tomorrow. Mrs. Hannon always calls me Frank now. Anyone that delivers hundredweights of coal is not a Frankie.

The man in the office says, Humph. I think we're very tolerant with Hannon. You, what's your name?

McCourt, sir.

Tell Hannon we'll need a note from the doctor. Do you understand that?

I do, sir.

The doctor tells Mr. Hannon he has to go to the hospital or it's a case of gangrene he'll have and the doctor won't be responsible. The ambulance takes Mr. Hannon away and my big job is gone. Now I'll be white like everyone else in Leamy's, no float, no horse, no shillings to bring home to my mother.

In a few days Bridey Hannon comes to our door. She says her mother would like me to come and see her, have a cup of tea with her. Mrs. Hannon is sitting by the fire with her hand on the seat of Mr. Hannon's chair. Sit down, Frank, she says, and when I go to sit on one of the ordinary kitchen chairs she says, No, sit here. Sit here on the chair of himself. Do you know how old he is, Frank?

Oh, he must be very old, Mrs. Hannon. He must be thirty-five.

She smiles. She has lovely teeth. He's forty-nine, Frank, and a man that age shouldn't have legs like that.

He shouldn't, Mrs. Hannon.

Did you know you were a joy to him going around on that float?

I didn't, Mrs. Hannon.

You were. We had two daughters, Bridey that you know, and Kathleen, the nurse above in Dublin. But no son and he said you gave him the feeling of a son.

I feel my eyes burning and I don't want her to see me crying especially when I don't know why I'm crying. That's all I do lately. Is it the job? Is it Mr. Hannon? My mother says, Oh, your bladder is near your eye.

I think I'm crying because of the quiet way Mrs. Hannon is talking and she's talking like that because of Mr. Hannon.

Like a son, she says, and I'm glad he had that feeling. His working days are over, you know. He has to stay at home from this out. There might be a cure and if there is sure he might be able to get a job as a watchman where he doesn't have to be lifting and hauling.

I won't have a job anymore, Mrs. Hannon.

You have a job, Frank. School. That's your job.

That's not a job, Mrs. Hannon.

You'll never have another job like it, Frank. It breaks Mr. Hannon's heart to think of you dragging bags of coal off a float and it breaks your mother's heart and 'twill destroy your eyes. God knows I'm sorry I ever got you into this for it had your poor mother caught between your eyes and Mr. Hannon's legs.

Can I go to the hospital to see Mr. Hannon?

They might not let you in but surely you can come here

309

to see him. God knows he won't be doing much but reading and looking out the window.

Mam tells me at home, You shouldn't cry but then again tears are salty and they'll wash the bad stuff from your eyes.

XII

There's a letter from Dad. He's coming home two days before Christmas. He says everything will be different, he's a new man, he hopes we're good boys, obeying our mother, attending to our religious duties, and he's bringing us all something for Christmas.

Mam takes me to the railway station to meet him. The station is always exciting with all the coming and going, people leaning from carriages, crying, smiling, waving good-bye, the train hooting and calling, chugging away in clouds of steam, people sniffling on the platform, the railway tracks silvering into the distance, on to Dublin and the world beyond.

Now it's near midnight and cold on the empty platform. A man in a railway cap asks us if we'd like to wait in a warm place. Mam says, Thank you very much, and laughs when he leads us to the end of the platform where we have to climb a ladder to the signal tower. It takes her a while because she's heavy and she keeps saying, Oh, God, oh, God.

We're above the world and it's dark in the signal tower except for the lights that blink red and green and yellow when the man bends over the board. He says, I'm just having a bit of supper and you're welcome.

Mam says, Ah, no, thanks, we couldn't take your supper from you.

He says, The wife always makes too much for me and if I was up in this tower for a week I wouldn't be able to eat it. Sure it's not hard work looking at lights and pulling on the odd lever.

He takes the top off a flask and pours cocoa into a mug. Here, he says to me, put yourself outside that cocoa.

He hands Mam half a sandwich. Ah, no, she says, surely you could take that home to your children.

I have two sons, missus, and they're off there fighting in the forces of His Majesty, the King of England. One did his bit with Montgomery in Africa and the other is over in Burma or some other bloody place, excuse the language. We get our freedom from England and then we fight her wars. So here, missus, take the bit of sandwich.

Lights on the board are clicking and the man says, Your train is coming, missus.

Thank you very much and Happy Christmas.

Happy Christmas to yourself, missus, and a Happy New Year, too. Mind yourself on that ladder, young fella. Help your mother.

Thank you very much, sir.

We wait again on the platform while the train rumbles into the station. Carriage doors open and a few men with suitcases step to the platform and hurry toward the gate. There is a clanking of milk cans dropped to the platform. A man and two boys are unloading newspapers and magazines.

There is no sign of my father. Mam says he might be asleep in one of the carriages but we know he hardly sleeps even in his own bed. She says the boat from Holyhead might have been late and that would make him miss the train. The Irish Sea is desperate at this time of the year.

He's not coming, Mam. He doesn't care about us. He's just drunk over there in England.

Don't talk about your father like that.

I say no more to her. I don't tell her I wish I had a father like the man in the signal tower who gives you sandwiches and cocoa.

Next day Dad walks in the door. His top teeth are missing and there's a bruise under his left eye. He says the Irish Sea was rough and when he leaned over the side his teeth dropped out. Mam says, It wouldn't be the drink, would it? It wouldn't be a fight?

Och, no, Angela.

Michael says, You said you'd have something for us, Dad.

Oh, I do.

He takes a box of chocolates from his suitcase and hands it to Mam. She opens the box and shows us the inside where half the chocolates are gone.

Could you spare it? she says.

She shuts the box and puts it on the mantelpiece. We'll have chocolates after our Christmas dinner tomorrow.

Mam asks him if he brought any money. He tells her times are hard, jobs are scarce, and she says, Is it coddin' me you are? There's a war on and there's nothing but jobs in England. You drank the money, didn't you?

You drank the money, Dad.

You drank the money, Dad.

You drank the money, Dad.

We're shouting so loud Alphie begins to cry. Dad says, Och, boys, now boys. Respect for your father.

He puts on his cap. He has to see a man. Mam says, Go see your man but don't come drunk to this house tonight singing Roddy McCorley or anything else.

He comes home drunk but he's quiet and passes out on the floor next to Mam's bed.

We have a Christmas dinner next day because of the food voucher Mam got from the St. Vincent de Paul Society. We have sheep's head, cabbage, floury white potatoes, and a bottle of cider because it's Christmas. Dad says he's not hungry, he'll have tea, borrows a cigarette from Mam. She says, Eat something. It's Christmas.

He tells her again he's not hungry but if no one else wants them he'll eat the sheep's eyes. He says there's great nourishment in the eye and we all make sounds of disgust. He washes them down with his tea and smokes the rest of his Woodbine. He puts on his cap and goes upstairs for his suitcase.

Mam says, Where are you going?

London.

On this day of Our Lord? Christmas Day?

It's the best day for travel. People in motor cars will always give the workingman a lift to Dublin. They think of the hard times of the Holy Family.

And how will you get on the boat to Holyhead without a penny in your pocket?

The way I came. There's always a time when they're not looking.

He kisses each of us on the forehead, tells us be good boys, obey Mam, say our prayers. He tells Mam he'll write and she says, Oh, yes, the way you always did. He stands before her with his suitcase. She gets up, takes down the box of chocolates and hands them around. She puts a chocolate in her mouth and takes it out again because it's too hard and she can't chew it. I have a soft one and I offer it for the hard one, which will last longer. It's creamy and rich and there's a nut in the middle. Malachy and Michael complain they didn't get a nut and why is it Frank always gets the nut? Mam says, What do you mean, always? This is the first time we ever had a box of chocolates.

Malachy says, He got the raisin in the bun at school and all the boys said he gave it to Paddy Clohessy, so why couldn't he give us the nut?

Mam says, Because 'tis Christmas and he has sore eyes and the nut is good for the sore eyes.

Michael says, Will the nut make his eyes better?

'Twill.

Will it make one eye better or will it make two eyes better?

The two eyes, I think.

Malachy says, If I had another nut I'd give it to him for his eyes.

Mam says, I know you would.

Dad watches us a moment eating our chocolates. He lifts the latch, goes out the door and pulls it shut.

Mam tells Bridey Hannon, Days are bad but nights are worse and will this rain ever stop? She tries to ease the bad days by staying in bed and letting Malachy and me light the fire in the morning while she sits up in the bed passing Alphie bits of bread and holding the mug to his mouth for the tea that's in it. We have to go downstairs to Ireland to wash our faces in the basin under the tap and try to dry ourselves in the old damp shirt that hangs over the back of a chair. She makes us stand by the bed to see if we left rings of dirt around our necks and if we did it's back down to the tap and the damp shirt. When there's a hole in a pair of pants she sits up and patches it with any rag she can find. We wear short pants till we're thirteen or fourteen and our long stockings always have holes to be darned. If she has no wool for the darning and the stockings are dark we can blacken our ankles with shoe polish for the respectability that's in it. It's a terrible thing to walk the world with skin showing through the holes of our stockings. When we wear them week after week the holes grow so big we have to pull the stocking forward under the toes so that the hole in the back is hidden in the shoe. On rainy days the stockings are soggy and we have to hang them before the fire at night and hope they'll dry by morning. Then they're hard with dirt cake and we're afraid to pull them on our feet for fear they'll fall on the floor in bits before our eyes. We might be lucky enough to get our stockings on but then we have to block the holes in our shoes and I fight with my brother, Malachy, over any scrap of cardboard or paper in the house. Michael is only six and he has to wait for anything left over unless Mam threatens us from the bed that we're to help our small brother. She says, If ye don't fix yeer brother's shoes an' I have to get out of this bed there will be wigs on the green. You'd have to feel sorry for Michael because he's too old to play with Alphie and too young to play with us and he can't fight with anyone for the same reasons.

The rest of the dressing is easy, the shirt I wore to bed is the shirt I wear to school. I wear it day in day out. It's the shirt for football, for climbing walls, for robbings orchards. I go to Mass and the Confraternity in that shirt and people sniff the air and move away. If Mam gets a docket for a new one at the St. Vincent de Paul the old shirt is promoted to towel and hangs damp on the chair for months or Mam might use bits of it to patch other shirts. She might even cut it up and let Alphie wear it a while before it winds up on the floor pushed against the bottom of the door to block the rain from the lane.

We go to school through lanes and back streets so that we won't meet the respectable boys who go to the Christian Brothers' School or the rich ones who go to the Jesuit school, Crescent College. The Christian Brothers' boys wear tweed jackets, warm woolen sweaters, shirts, ties and shiny new boots. We know they're the ones who will get jobs in the civil service and help the people who run the world. The Crescent College boys wear blazers and school scarves tossed around their necks and over their shoulders to show they're cock o' the walk. They have long hair which falls across their foreheads and over their eyes so that they can toss their quiffs like Englishmen. We know they're the ones who will go to university, take over the family business, run the government, run the world. We'll be the messenger boys on bicycles who deliver their groceries or we'll go to England to work on the building sites. Our sisters will mind their children and scrub their floors unless they go off to England, too. We know that. We're ashamed of the way we look and if boys from the rich schools pass remarks we'll get into a fight and wind up with bloody noses or torn clothes. Our masters will have no patience with us and our fights because their sons go to the rich schools and, Ye have no right to raise your hands to a better class of people so ye don't.

You never know when you might come home and find Mam sitting by the fire chatting with a woman and a child, strangers. Always a woman and child. Mam finds them wandering the streets and if they ask, Could you spare a few pennies, miss? her heart breaks. She never has money so she invites them home for tea and a bit of fried bread and if it's a bad night she'll let them sleep by the fire on a pile of rags in the corner. The bread she gives them always means less for us and if we complain she says there are always people worse off and we can surely spare a little from what we have.

Michael is just as bad. He brings home stray dogs and old men. You never know when you'll find a dog in the bed with him. There are dogs with sores, dogs with no ears, no tails. There's a blind greyhound he found in the park tormented by children. Michael fought off the children, picked up the greyhound that was bigger than himself and told Mam the dog could have his supper. Mam says, What supper? We're lucky if there's a cut of bread in the house. Michael tells her the dog can have his bread. Mam says that dog has to go tomorrow and Michael cries all night and cries worse in the morning when he finds the dog dead in the bed beside him. He won't go to school because he has to dig a grave outside where the stable was and he wants all of us to dig with him and say the rosary. Malachy says it's useless saying prayers for a dog, how do you know he was even a Catholic? Michael says, Of course he was a Catholic dog. Didn't I have him in my arms? He cries so hard over the dog Mam lets us all stay at home from school. We're so delighted we don't mind helping Michael with the grave and we say three Hail Marys. We're not going to stand there wasting a good day off from school saying the rosary for a dead greyhound. Michael is only six but when he brings old men home he

317

manages to get the fire going and give them tea. Mam says it's driving her crazy to come home and find these old men drinking out of her favorite mug and mumbling and scratching by the fire. She tells Bridey Hannon that Michael has a habit of bringing home old men all a bit gone in the head and if he doesn't have a bit of bread for them he knocks on neighbors' doors and has no shame begging for it. In the end she tells Michael, No more old men. One of them left us with lice and we're plagued.

The lice are disgusting, worse than rats. They're in our heads and ears and they sit in the hollows of our collarbones. They dig into our skin. They get into the seams of our clothes and they're everywhere in the coats we use as blankets. We have to search every inch of Alphie's body because he's a baby and helpless.

The lice are worse than the fleas. Lice squat and suck and we can see our blood through their skins. Fleas jump and bite and they're clean and we prefer them. Things that jump are cleaner than things that squat.

We all agree there will be no more stray women and children, dogs and old men. We don't want any more diseases and infections.

Michael cries.

Grandma's next door neighbor, Mrs. Purcell, has the only wireless in her lane. The government gave it to her because she's old and blind. I want a radio. My grandmother is old but she's not blind and what's the use of having a grandmother who won't go blind and get a government radio?

Sunday nights I sit outside on the pavement under Mrs. Purcell's window listening to plays on the BBC and Radio Eireann, the Irish station. You can hear plays by O'Casey, Shaw, Ibsen and Shakespeare himself, the best of all, even if he is English. Shakespeare is like mashed potatoes, you can never get enough of him. And you can hear strange plays about Greeks plucking out their eyes because they married their mothers by mistake.

One night I'm sitting under Mrs. Purcell's window listening to *Macbeth*. Her daughter, Kathleen, sticks her head out the door. Come in, Frankie. My mother says you'll catch the consumption sitting on the ground in this weather.

Ah, no, Kathleen. It's all right.

No. Come in.

They give me tea and a grand cut of bread slathered with blackberry jam. Mrs. Purcell says, Do you like the Shakespeare, Frankie?

I love the Shakespeare, Mrs. Purcell.

Oh, he's music, Frankie, and he has the best stories in the world. I don't know what I'd do with meself of a Sunday night if I didn't have the Shakespeare.

When the play finishes she lets me fiddle with the knob on the radio and I roam the dial for distant sounds on the shortwave band, strange whispering and hissing, the whoosh of the ocean coming and going and the Morse Code dit dit dit dot. I hear mandolins, guitars, Spanish bagpipes, the drums of Africa, boatmen wailing on the Nile. I see sailors on watch sipping mugs of hot cocoa. I see cathedrals, skyscrapers, cottages. I see Bedouins in the Sahara and the French Foreign Legion, cowboys on the American prairie. I see goats skipping along the rocky coast of Greece where the shepherds are blind because they married their mothers by mistake. I see people chatting in cafés, sipping wine, strolling on boulevards and avenues. I see night women in doorways, monks chanting vespers, and here is the great boom of Big Ben, This is the BBC Overseas Service and here is the news.

Mrs. Purcell says, Leave that on, Frankie, so we'll know the state of the world.

After the news there is the American Armed Forces Network and it's lovely to hear the American voices easy and cool and here is the music, oh, man, the music of Duke

Ellington himself telling me take the A train to where Billie Holiday sings only to me,

> *I can't give you anything but love, baby.*
> *That's the only thing I've plenty of, baby.*

Oh, Billie, Billie, I want to be in America with you and all that music, where no one has bad teeth, people leave food on their plates, every family has a lavatory, and everyone lives happily ever after.

And Mrs. Purcell says, Do you know what, Frankie?

What, Mrs. Purcell?

That Shakespeare is that good he must have been an Irishman.

The rent man is losing his patience. He tells Mam, Four weeks behind you are, missus. That's one pound two shillings. This has to stop for I have to go back to the office and report to Sir Vincent Nash that the McCourts are a month behind. Where am I then, missus? Out on my arse jobless and a mother to support that's ninety-two and a daily communicant in the Franciscan church. The rent man collects the rents, missus, or he loses the job. I'll be back next week and if you don't have the money, one pound eight shillings and sixpence total, 'tis out on the pavement you'll be with the skies dripping on your furniture.

Mam comes back up to Italy and sits by the fire wondering where in God's name she'll get the money for a week's rent never mind the arrears. She'd love a cup of tea but there's no way of boiling the water till Malachy pulls a loose board off the wall between the two upstairs rooms. Mam says, Well, 'tis off now and we might as well chop it up for the fire. We boil the water and use the rest of the wood for the morning tea but what about tonight and tomorrow and ever after? Mam says, One more board from that wall, one more and not another one. She says that for two weeks till there's nothing left but the beam frame. She warns us we are not to touch the beams for they hold up the ceiling and the house itself.

Oh, we'd never touch the beams.

She goes to see Grandma and it's so cold in the house I take the hatchet to one of the beams. Malachy cheers me on and Michael claps his hands with excitement. I pull on the beam, the ceiling groans and down on Mam's bed there's a shower of plaster, slates, rain. Malachy says, Oh, God, we'll all be killed, and Michael dances around singing, Frankie broke the house, Frankie broke the house.

We run through the rain to tell Mam the news. She looks puzzled with Michael chanting, Frankie broke the house, till I explain there's a hole in the house and it's falling down. She says, Jesus, and runs through the streets with Grandma trying to keep up.

Mam sees her bed buried under plaster and slates and pulls at her hair, What'll we do at all, at all? and screams at me for interfering with the beams. Grandma says, I'll go to the landlord's office and tell them fix this before ye are all drowned entirely.

She's back in no time with the rent man. He says, Great God in heaven, where's the other room?

Grandma says, What room?

I rented ye two rooms up here and one is gone. Where is that room?

Mam says, What room?

There were two rooms up here and now there's one. And what happened to the wall? There was a wall. Now there's no wall. I distinctly remember a wall because I distinctly remember a room. Now where is that wall? Where is that room?

Grandma says, I don't remember a wall and if I don't remember a wall how can I remember a room?

Ye don't remember? Well, I remember. Forty years a

landlord's agent and I never seen the likes of this. By God, 'tis a desperate situation altogether when you can't turn your back but tenants are not paying their rent and making walls and rooms disappear on top of it. I want to know where that wall is and what ye did with the room, so I do.

Mam turns to us. Do any of ye remember a wall?

Michael pulls at her hand. Is that the wall we burned in the fire?

The rent man says, Dear God in heaven, this beats Banagher, this takes the bloody biscuit, this is goin' beyond the beyonds. No rent and what am I to tell Sir Vincent below in the office? Out, missus, I'm puttin' ye out. One week from today I'll knock on this door and I want to find nobody at home, everybody out never to return. Do you have me, missus?

Mam's face is tight. 'Tis a pity you weren't alive in the times when the English were evicting us and leaving us on the side of the road.

No lip, missus, or I'll send the men to put ye out tomorrow.

He goes out the door and leaves it open to show what he thinks of us. Mam says, I don't know in God's name what I'm going to do. Grandma says, Well, I don't have room for ye but your cousin, Gerard Griffin, is living out the Rosbrien Road in that little house of his mother's and he'd surely be able to take ye in till better times come. 'Tis all hours of the night but I'll go up and see what he says and Frank can come with me.

She tells me put on a coat but I don't have one and she says, I suppose there's no use in asking if ye have an umbrella either. Come on.

She pulls the shawl over her head and I follow her out the door, up the lane, through the rain to Rosbrien Road nearly two miles away. She knocks on the door of a little cottage in a long row of little cottages. Are you there, Laman? I know you're in there. Open the door.

Grandma, why are you calling him Laman? Isn't his name Gerard?

How would I know? Do I know why the world calls your uncle Pat Ab? Everyone calls this fella Laman. Open the door. We'll go in. He might be working overtime.

She pushes the door. It's dark and there's a damp sweet smell in the room. This room looks like the kitchen and there's a smaller room next to it. There's a little loft above the bedroom with a skylight where the rain is beating. There are boxes everywhere, newspapers, magazines, bits of food, mugs, empty tins. We can see two beds taking up all the space in the bedroom, a great acre of a bed and a smaller one near the window. Grandma pokes at a lump in the big bed. Laman, is that you? Get up, will you, get up.

What? What? What? What?

There's trouble. Angela is gettin' evicted with the children an' 'tis delvin' out of the heavens. They need a bit of shelter till they get on their feet an' I have no room for them. You can put them up in the loft if you like but that wouldn't do because the small ones wouldn't be able to climb and they'd fall down an' get killed so you go up there an' they can move in here.

All right, all right, all right, all right.

He hoists himself from the bed and there's a whiskey smell. He goes to the kitchen and pulls the table to the wall for his climb to the loft. Grandma says, That's fine now. Ye can move up here tonight an' ye won't have the eviction men coming after ye.

Grandma tells Mam she's going home. She's tired and drenched and she's not twenty-five anymore. She says there's no need to be taking beds or furniture with all the stuff that's up in Laman Griffin's. We put Alphie in the pram and pile around him the pot, the pan, the kettle, the jam jars and mugs, the Pope, two bolsters and the coats from the beds. We drape the coats over our heads and push the pram through the streets. Mam tells us be quiet going up the lane or the neighbors will know we got the eviction and there will be shame. The pram has a bockety wheel which tilts it and makes it go in different directions. We try to keep it straight and we're having a great time because it must be after midnight and surely Mam won't make us go to school tomorrow. We're moving so far from Leamy's School now maybe we'll never have to go again. Once we get away from the lane Alphie bangs on the pot with the spoon and Michael sings a song he heard in a film with Al Jolson, Swanee, how I love ya, how I love ya, my dear ol' Swanee. He makes us laugh the way he tries to sing in a deep voice like Al Jolson.

Mam says she's glad it's late and there's no one on the streets to see our shame.

Once we get to the house we take Alphie and everything else from the pram so that Malachy and I can run back down to Roden Lane for the trunk. Mam says she'd die if she lost that trunk and everything in it.

Malachy and I sleep at opposite ends of the small bed. Mam takes the big bed with Alphie beside her and Michael at the bottom. Everything is damp and musty and Laman Griffin snores over our heads. There are no stairs in this house and that means no angel ever on the seventh step.

But I'm twelve going on thirteen and I might be too old for angels.

It's still dark when the alarm goes off in the morning and Laman Griffin snorts and blows his nose and hawks the stuff from his chest. The floor creaks under him and when he pisses for ages into the chamber pot we have to stuff our mouths with coats to stop the laughing and Mam hisses at us to be quiet. He grumbles away above us before he climbs down to get his bicycle and bang his way out the door. Mam whispers, The coast is clear, go back to sleep. Ye can stay at home today.

We can't sleep. We're in a new house, we have to pee

and we want to explore. The lavatory is outside, about ten steps from the back door, our own lavatory, with a door you can close and a proper seat where you can sit and read squares of the *Limerick Leader* Laman Griffin left behind for wiping himself. There is a long backyard, a garden with tall grass and weeds, an old bicycle that must have belonged to a giant, tin cans galore, old papers and magazines rotting into the earth, a rusted sewing machine, a dead cat with a rope around his neck that somebody must have thrown over the fence.

Michael gets a notion in his head that this is Africa and keeps asking, Where's Tarzan? Where's Tarzan? He runs up and down the backyard with no pants on trying to imitate Tarzan yodeling from tree to tree. Malachy looks over the fences into the other yards and tells us, They have gardens. They're growing things. We can grow things. We can have our own spuds and everything.

Mam calls from the back door, See if ye can find anything to start the fire in here.

There's a wooden shed built against the back of the house. It's collapsing and surely we could use some of the wood for the fire. Mam is disgusted with the wood we bring in. She says it's rotten and full of white maggots but beggars can't be choosers. The wood sizzles above the burning paper and we watch the white maggots try to escape. Michael says he feels sorry for the white maggots but we know he's sorry for everything in the world.

Mam tells us this house used to be a shop, that Laman Griffin's mother sold groceries through the little window and that's how she was able to send Laman away to Rockwell College so that he could wind up as an officer in the Royal Navy. Oh, he was, indeed. An officer in the Royal Navy, and here's a picture of him with other officers all having dinner with a famous American film star Jean Harlow. He was never the same after he met Jean Harlow. He fell madly in love with her but what was the use? She was Jean Harlow and he was nothing but an officer in the Royal Navy and it drove him to drink and they threw him out of the Navy. Now look at him, a common laborer for the Electricity Supply Board and a house that's a disgrace. You'd look at this house and never know there was a human being living in it. You can see Laman never moved a thing since his mother died and now we have to clean up so that we can live in this place.

There are boxes packed with bottles of purple hair oil. While Mam is out in the lavatory we open a bottle and smear it on our heads. Malachy says the smell is gorgeous but when Mam comes back she says, What's that horrible stink? and wants to know why our heads are suddenly greasy. She makes us stick our heads under the tap outside and dry ourselves with an old towel pulled out from under a pile of magazines called *The Illustrated London News* so old they have pictures of Queen Victoria and Prince Edward waving. There are bars of Pear's soap and a thick book called *Pear's Encyclopedia*, which keeps me up day and night because it tells you everything about everything and that's all I want to know.

There are bottles of Sloan's Liniment, which Mam says will come in handy when we get cramps and pains from the damp. The bottles say, Here's the pain, Where's the Sloan's? There are boxes of safety pins and bags packed with women's hats that crumble when you touch them. There are bags with corsets, garters, women's high button shoes and different laxatives that promise glowing cheeks, bright eyes and a curl in your hair. There are letters from General Eoin O'Duffy to Gerard Griffin, Esq., saying welcome to the ranks of the National Front, the Irish Blueshirts, that it is a privilege to know a man like Gerard Griffin is interested in the movement with his excellent education, his Royal Navy training, his reputation as a great rugby player on the Young Munster team that won the national championship, the Bateman Cup. General O'Duffy is forming an Irish Brigade that will soon sail off to Spain to fight with that great Catholic Generalissimo Franco himself, and Mr. Griffin would be a powerful addition to the Brigade.

Mam says Laman's mother wouldn't let him go. She didn't spend all those years slaving away in a little shop to send him to college so that he could go gallivanting off to Spain for Franco so he stayed at home and got that job digging holes for the poles of the Electricity Supply Board along country roads and his mother was happy to have him home to herself every night but Friday when he drank his pint and moaned over Jean Harlow.

Mam is happy we'll have loads of paper for lighting the fire though the wood we burn from that collapsing shed leaves a sickening smell and she worries the white maggots will escape and breed.

We work all day moving boxes and bags to the shed outside. Mam opens all the windows to air the house and let out the smell of the hair oil and the years of no air. She says it's a relief to be able to see the floor again and now we can sit down and have a nice cup of tea in peace, ease and comfort, and won't it be lovely when the warm weather comes and we might be able to have a garden and sit outside with our tea the way the English do.

Laman Griffin comes home at six every night but Friday, has his tea and goes to bed till next morning. Saturdays he goes to bed at one in the afternoon and stays there till Monday morning. He pulls the kitchen table over to the wall under the loft, climbs up on a chair, pulls the chair up to the table, climbs up on the chair again, catches a leg of the bed, pulls himself up. If he's too drunk on Fridays he makes me climb up for his pillow and blankets and sleeps on the kitchen floor by the fire or falls into bed with me and my brothers and snores and farts all night.

When we first moved in he complained over how he gave up his room downstairs for the loft and he's worn out climbing up and down to go to the lavatory in the backyard. He calls down, Bring the table, the chair, I'm coming down, and we have to clear off the table and pull it to the wall. He's fed up, he's finished with the climbing, he's going to use his mother's lovely chamber pot. He lies in bed all day reading books from the library, smoking Gold Flake cigarettes and throwing Mam a few shillings to send one of us to the shop so that he can have scones with his tea or a nice bit of ham and sliced tomato. Then he calls to Mam, Angela, this chamber pot is full, and she drags chair and table to climb for the chamber pot, empty it in the lavatory outside, rinse it and climb back to the loft. Her face gets tight and she says, Is there anything else your lordship would like this day? and he laughs, Woman's work, Angela, woman's work and free rent.

Laman throws down his library card from the loft and tells me get him two books, one on angling, one on gardening. He writes a note to the librarian to say his legs are killing him from digging holes for the Electricity Supply Board and from now on Frank McCourt will be getting his books. He knows the boy is only thirteen going on fourteen and he knows the rules are strict about allowing children into the adult part of the library but the boy will wash his hands and behave himself and do what he's told, thank you.

The librarian reads the note and says 'tis an awful pity about Mr. Griffin, he's a true gentleman and a man of great learning, you wouldn't believe the books he reads, sometimes four a week, that one day he took home a book in French, French, if you don't mind, on the history of the rudder, the rudder, if you don't mind, she'd give anything for a look inside his head for it must be packed with all sorts of learning, packed, if you don't mind.

She picks out a gorgeous book with colored pictures about English gardens. She says, I know what he likes in the fishing department, and chooses a book called *In Search of the Irish Salmon* by Brigadier General Hugh Colton. Oh, says the librarian, he reads hundreds of books about English officers fishing in Ireland. I've read some myself out of pure curiosity and you can see why those officers are glad to be in Ireland after all they put up with in India and Africa and other desperate places. At least the people here are polite. We're known for that, the politeness, not running around throwing spears at people.

Laman lies in the bed, reads his books, talks down from the loft about the day his legs will heal and he'll be out there in the back planting a garden which will be famous far and wide for color and beauty and when he's not gardening he'll be roaming the rivers around Limerick and bringing home salmon that will make your mouth water. His mother left a recipe for salmon that's a family secret and if he had the time and his legs weren't killing him he'd find it someplace in this house. He says now that I'm reliable I can get a book for myself every week but he don't be bringing home filth. I want to know what the filth is but he won't tell me so I'll have to find out for myself.

Mam says she wants to join the library too but it's a long walk from Laman's house, two miles, and would I mind getting her a book every week, a romance by Charlotte M. Brame or any other nice writer. She doesn't want any books about English officers looking for salmon or books about people shooting each other. There's enough trouble in the world without reading about people bothering fish and each other.

Grandma caught a chill the night we had the trouble in the house in Roden Lane and the chill turned into pneumonia. They shifted her to the City Home Hospital and now she's dead.

Her oldest son, my uncle Tom, thought he'd go to England to work like other men in the lanes of Limerick but his consumption got worse and he came back to Limerick and now he's dead.

His wife, Galway Jane, followed him, and four of their six

children had to be put into orphanages. The oldest boy, Gerry, ran away and joined the Irish army, deserted and crossed to the English army. The oldest girl, Peggy, went to Aunt Aggie and lives in misery.

The Irish army is looking for boys who are musical and would like to train in the Army School of Music. They accept my brother, Malachy, and he goes off to Dublin to be a soldier and play the trumpet.

Now I have only two brothers at home and Mam says her family is disappearing before her very eyes.

Boys from my class at Leamy's School are going on a weekend cycling trip to Killaloe. They tell me I should borrow a
bicycle and come. All I need is a blanket, a few spoons of
tea and sugar and a few cuts of bread to keep me going. I'll
learn to cycle on Laman Griffin's bicycle every night after
he goes to bed and he'll surely let me borrow it for the two
days in Killaloe.

The best time to ask him for anything is Friday night when
he's in a good mood after his night of drinking and his dinner.
He brings home the same dinner in his overcoat pockets, a
big steak dripping blood, four potatoes, an onion, a bottle
of stout. Mam boils the potatoes and fries the steak with
sliced onion. He keeps his overcoat on, sits at the table and
eats the steak out of his hands. The grease and blood roll
down his chin and on to the overcoat where he wipes his
hands. He drinks his stout and laughs that there's nothing
like a great bloody steak of a Friday night and if that's the
worst sin he ever commits he'll float to heaven body and
soul, ha ha ha.

Of course you can have my bike, he says. Boy should be
able to get out and see the countryside. Of course. But you
have to earn it. You can't be getting something for nothing,
isn't that right?

'Tis.

And I have a job for you. You don't mind doing a bit of
a job, do you?

I don't.

And you'd like to help your mother?

I would.

Well, now, that very chamber pot is full since this morning. I want you to climb up and get it and take it to the lavatory and rinse it under the tap abroad and climb back up with it.

I don't want to empty his chamber pot but I dream of cycling miles on the road to Killaloe, fields and sky far from this house, a swim in the Shannon, a night sleeping in a barn. I pull the table and chair to the wall. I climb up and under the bed there's the plain white chamber pot streaked brown and yellow, brimming with piss and shit. I lay it gently at the edge of the loft so that it won't spill, climb down to the chair, reach for the chamber pot, bring it down, turn my face away, hold it while I step down to the table, place it on the chair, step to the floor, take the chamber pot to the lavatory, empty it, and get sick behind the lavatory till I get used to this job.

Laman says I'm a good boy and the bike is mine anytime I want it as long as the chamber pot is empty and I'm there to run to the shop for his cigarettes, go to the library for books and do whatever else he wants. He says, You have a great way with a chamber pot. He laughs and Mam stares into the dead ashes in the fireplace.

It's raining so hard one day, Miss O'Riordan the librarian says, Don't go out in that or you'll ruin the books you're carrying. Sit down over there and behave yourself. You can read all about the saints while you're waiting.

There are four big books, *Butler's Lives of the Saints*. I don't want to spend my life reading about saints but when I start I wish the rain would last forever. Whenever you see pictures of saints, men or women, they're always looking up to heaven where there are clouds filled with little fat angels carrying flowers or harps giving praise. Uncle Pa Keating says he can't think of a single saint in heaven he'd want to sit down and have a pint with. The saints in these books are different.

There are stories about virgins, martyrs, virgin martyrs and they're worse than any horror film at the Lyric Cinema.

I have to look in the dictionary to find out what a virgin is. I know the Mother of God is the Virgin Mary and they call her that because she didn't have a proper husband, only poor old St. Joseph. In the *Lives of the Saints* the virgins are always getting into trouble and I don't know why. The dictionary says, Virgin, woman (usually a young woman) who is and remains in a state of inviolate chastity.

Now I have to look up inviolate and chastity and all I can find here is that inviolate means not violated and chastity means chaste and that means pure from unlawful sexual inter-course. Now I have to look up intercourse and that leads to intromission, which leads to intromittent, the copulatory organ of any male animal. Copulatory leads to copulation, the union of the sexes in the art of generation and I don't know what that means and I'm too weary going from one word to another in this heavy dictionary which leads me on a wild goose chase from this word to that word and all because the people who wrote the dictionary don't want the likes of me to know anything.

All I want to know is where I came from but if you ask anyone they tell you ask someone else or send you from word to word.

All these virgin martyrs are told by Roman judges they have to give up their faith and accept the Roman gods but they say, Nay, and the judges have them tortured and killed. My favorite is St. Christina the Astonishing who takes ages to die. The judge says, Cut off her breast, and when they do she throws it at him and he goes deaf dumb and blind. Another judge is brought on the case and he says, Cut off the other breast, and the same thing happens. They try to kill her with arrows but they just bounce off her and kill the soldiers who shot them. They try to boil her in oil but she rocks in the vat and takes a nap for herself. Then the judges get fed up and have her head cut off and that does the job.

The feast of St. Christina the Astonishing is the twenty-fourth of July and I think I'll keep that for myself along with the feast of St. Francis of Assisi on the fourth of October.

The librarian says, You have to go home now, the rain is stopped, and when I'm going out the door she calls me back. She wants to write a note to my mother and she doesn't mind one bit if I read it. The note says, Dear Mrs. McCourt, Just when you think Ireland is gone to the dogs altogether you find a boy sitting in the library so absorbed in the *Lives of the Saints* he doesn't realize the rain has stopped and you have to drag him away from the aforesaid *Lives*. I think, Mrs. McCourt, you might have a future priest on your hands and I will light a candle in hopes it comes true. I remain, Yours truly, Catherine O'Riordan, Asst. Librarian.

Hoppy O'Halloran is the only master in Leamy's National School who ever sits. That's because he's the headmaster or because he has to rest himself from the twisting walk that comes from the short leg. The other masters walk back and forth in the front of the room or up and down the aisles and you never know when you'll get a whack of a cane or a slap of a strap for giving the wrong answer or writing something sloppy. If Hoppy wants to do anything to you he calls you to the front of the room to punish you before three classes.

There are good days when he sits at the desk and talks about America. He says, My boys, from the frozen wastes of North Dakota to the fragrant orange groves of Florida, Americans enjoy all climates. He talks about American history, If the American farmer, with flintlock and musket, could wrest from the English a continent, surely we, warriors ever, can recover our island.

If we don't want him tormenting us with algebra or Irish grammar all we have to do is ask him a question about America and that gets him so excited he might go on for the whole day.

He sits at his desk and recites the tribes and chiefs he loves. Arapaho, Cheyenne, Chippewa, Sioux, Apache, Iroquois. Poetry, my boys, poetry. And listen to the chiefs, Kicking Bear, Rain-in-the-Face, Sitting Bull, Crazy Horse, and the genius, Geronimo.

In seventh class he hands out a small book, a poem that goes on for pages and pages, *The Deserted Village*, by Oliver Goldsmith. He says that this seems to be a poem about England but it is a lament for the poet's native land, our own native land, Ireland. We are to get this poem by heart, twenty lines a night to be recited every morning. Six boys are called to the front of the room for reciting and if you miss a line you are slapped twice on each hand. He tells us put the books under the desks and the whole class chants the passage on the schoolmaster in the village.

> *Beside yon straggling fence that skirts the way,*
> *With blossomed furze unprofitably gay,*
> *There, in his noisy mansion, skilled to rule*
> *The village master taught his little school.*
> *A man severe he was and stern to view,*
> *I knew him well, and every truant knew.*
> *Full well the boding tremblers learned to trace*
> *The day's disaster in his morning face.*
> *Full well they laughed with counterfeited glee*
> *At all his jokes for many a joke had he.*
> *Full well the busy whisper circling round*
> *Conveyed the dismal tidings when he frowned.*

He always closes his eyes and smiles when we reach the last lines of the passage,

> *Yet he was kind, or, if severe in aught,*
> *The love he bore to learning was in fault.*
> *The village all declared how much he knew.*
> *'Twas certain he could write, and cipher too.*

Lands he could measure, terms and tides presage,
And even the story ran that he could gauge.
In arguing, too, the parson owned his skill,
For, even though vanquished, he could argue still,
While words of learned length and thundering sound
Amazed the gazing rustics ranged around.
And still they gazed, and still the wonder grew,
That one small head could carry all he knew.

We know he loves these lines because they're about a schoolmaster, about him, and he's right because we wonder how one small head could carry all he knows and we will remember him in these lines. He says, Ah, boys, boys, You can make up your own minds but first stock them. Are you listening to me? Stock your minds and you can move through the world resplendent. Clarke, define resplendent.

I think it's shining, sir.

Pithy, Clarke, but adequate. McCourt, give us a sentence with pithy.

Clarke is pithy but adequate, sir.

Adroit, McCourt. You have a mind for the priesthood, my boy, or politics. Think of that.

I will, sir.

Tell your mother come and see me.

I will, sir.

Mam says, No, I could never go near Mr. O'Halloran. I don't have a decent dress or a proper coat. What does he want to see me for?

I don't know.

Well, ask him.

I can't. He'll kill me. If he says bring your mother you have to bring your mother or out comes the stick.

She comes to see him and he talks to her in the hallway. He tells her that her son Frank must continue school. He must not fall into the messenger boy trap. That leads nowhere. Take him up to the Christian Brothers, tell them

336

I sent you, tell them he is a bright boy and ought to be going to secondary school and beyond that, university.

He tells her he did not become headmaster of Leamy's National School to preside over an academy of messenger boys.

Mam says, Thank you, Mr. O'Halloran.

I wish Mr. O'Halloran would mind his own business. I don't want to go to the Christian Brothers. I want to quit school forever and get a job, get my wages every Friday, go to the pictures on Saturday nights like everyone.

A few days later Mam tells me give my face and hands a good wash, we're going to the Christian Brothers. I tell her I don't want to go, I want to work, I want to be a man. She tells me stop the whining, I'm going to secondary school and we'll all manage somehow. I'm going to school if she has to scrub floors and she'll practice on my face.

She knocks on the door at the Christian Brothers and says she wants to see the superior, Brother Murray. He comes to the door, looks at my mother and me and says, What?

Mam says, This is my son, Frank. Mr. O'Halloran at Leamy's says he's bright and would there be any chance of getting him in here for secondary school?

We don't have room for him, says Brother Murray and closes the door in our faces.

Mam turns away from the door and it's a long silent walk home. She takes off her coat, makes tea, sits by the fire. Listen to me, she says. Are you listening?

I am.

That's the second time a door was slammed in your face by the Church.

Is it? I don't remember.

Stephen Carey told you and your father you couldn't be an altar boy and closed the door in your face. Do you remember that?

I do.

And now Brother Murray slams the door in your face.

I don't mind. I want to get a job.

Her face tightens and she's angry. You are never to let anybody slam the door in your face again. Do you hear me?

She starts to cry by the fire, Oh, God, I didn't bring ye into the world to be a family of messenger boys.

I don't know what to do or say, I'm so relieved I don't have to stay in school for five or six more years.

I'm free.

I'm thirteen going on fourteen and it's June, the last month of school forever. Mam takes me to see the priest, Dr. Cowpar, about getting a job as telegram boy. The supervisor in the post office, Mrs. O'Connell, says, Do you know how to cycle, and I lie that I do. She says I can't start till I'm fourteen so come back in August.

Mr. O'Halloran tells the class it's a disgrace that boys like McCourt, Clarke, Kennedy, have to hew wood and draw water. He is disgusted by this free and independent Ireland that keeps a class system foisted on us by the English, that we are throwing our talented children on the dungheap.

You must get out of this country, boys. Go to America, McCourt. Do you hear me?

I do, sir.

Priests come to the school to recruit us for the foreign missions, Redemptorists, Franciscans, Holy Ghost Fathers, all converting the distant heathen. I ignore them. I'm going to America till one priest catches my attention. He says he comes from the order of the White Fathers, missionaries to the nomadic Bedouin tribes and chaplains to the French Foreign Legion.

I ask for the application.

I will need a letter from the parish priest and a physical

examination by my family doctor. The parish priest writes the letter on the spot. He would have been glad to see me go last year. The doctor says, What's this?

That's an application to join the White Fathers, missionaries to the nomadic tribes of the Sahara and chaplains to the French Foreign Legion.

Oh, yeh? French Foreign Legion, is it? Do you know the preferred form of transportation in the Sahara Desert?

Trains?

No. It's the camel. Do you know what a camel is?

It has a hump.

It has more than a hump. It has a nasty, mean disposition and its teeth are green with gangrene and it bites. Do you know where it bites?

In the Sahara?

No, you omadhaun. It bites your shoulder, rips it right off. Leaves you standing there tilted in the Sahara. How would you like that, eh? And what class of a spectacle you'd be strolling down the street, lopsided in Limerick. What girl in her right mind will look at an ex–White Father with one miserable scrawny shoulder? And look at your eyes. They're bad enough here in Limerick. In the Sahara they'll fester and rot and fall out of your head. How old are you?

Thirteen.

Go home to your mother.

It's not our house and we don't feel free in it the way we did in Roden Lane, up in Italy or down in Ireland. When Laman comes home he wants to read in his bed or sleep and we have to be quiet. We stay in the streets till after dark and when we come inside there's nothing to do but go to bed and read a book if we have a candle or paraffin oil for the lamp.

Mam tells us go to bed, she'll be after us in a minute as soon as she climbs to the loft with Laman's last mug of tea.

We often fall asleep before she goes up but there are nights we hear them talking, grunting, moaning. There are nights when she never comes down and Michael and Alphie have the big bed to themselves. Malachy says she stays up there because it's too hard for her to climb down in the dark.

He's only twelve and he doesn't understand.

I'm thirteen and I think they're at the excitement up there.

I know about the excitement and I know it's a sin but how can it be a sin if it comes to me in a dream where American girls pose in swimming suits on the screen at the Lyric Cinema and I wake up pushing and pumping? It's a sin when you're wide awake and going at yourself the way the boys talked about it in Leamy's schoolyard after Mr. O'Dea roared the Sixth Commandment at us, Thou Shalt Not Commit Adultery, which means impure thoughts, impure words, impure deeds, and that's what adultery is, Dirty Things in General.

One Redemptorist priest barks at us all the time about the Sixth Commandment. He says impurity is so grave a sin the Virgin Mary turns her face away and weeps.

And why does she weep, boys? She weeps because of you and what you are doing to her Beloved Son. She weeps when she looks down the long dreary vista of time and beholds in horror the spectacle of Limerick boys defiling themselves, polluting themselves, interfering with themselves, abusing themselves, soiling their young bodies, which are the temples of the Holy Ghost. Our Lady weeps over these abominations knowing that every time you interfere with yourself you nail to the cross her Beloved Son, that once more you hammer into His dear head the crown of thorns, that you reopen those ghastly wounds. In an agony of thirst He hangs on the cross and what is He offered by those perfidious Romans? A lavatory sponge plunged into vinegar and gall and thrust into His poor mouth, a mouth that moves rarely except to pray, to pray even for you, boys, even for you who nailed Him to that cross. Consider Our Lord's suffering. Consider the crown of thorns. Consider a small pin driven into your skull, the agony of the piercing. Consider then twenty thorns driven into your head. Reflect, meditate on the nails tearing His hands, His feet. Could you endure a fraction of that agony? Take that pin again, that mere pin. Force it into your side. Enlarge that sensation a hundredfold and you are penetrated by that awful lance. Oh, boys, the devil wants your souls. He wants you with him in hell and know this, that every time you interfere with yourself, every time you succumb to the vile sin of self-abuse you not only nail Christ to the cross you take another step closer to hell itself. Retreat from the abyss, boys. Resist the devil and keep your hands to yourself.

I can't stop interfering with myself. I pray to the Virgin Mary and tell her I'm sorry I put her Son back on the cross and I'll never do it again but I can't help myself and swear I'll go to confession and after that, surely after that, I'll never never do it again. I don't want to go to hell with devils chasing me for eternity jabbing me with hot pitchforks.

The priests of Limerick have no patience with the likes of me. I go to confession and they hiss that I'm not in a proper spirit of repentance, that if I were I'd give up this hideous sin. I go from church to church looking for an easy priest till Paddy Clohessy tells me there's one in the Dominican church who's ninety years old and deaf as a turnip. Every few weeks the old priest hears my confession and mumbles that I should pray for him. Sometimes he falls asleep and I don't have the heart to wake him up so I go to Communion the next day without penance or absolution. It's not my fault if priests fall asleep on me and surely I'm in a state of grace just for going to confession. Then one day the little panel in the confession box slides back and it's not my man at all, it's a young priest with a big ear like a seashell. He'll surely hear everything.

Bless me, Father, for I have sinned, it's a fortnight since my last confession.

And what have you done since then, my child?

I hit my brother, I went on the mooch from school, I lied to my mother.

Yes, my child, and what else?

I—I—I did dirty things, Father.

Ah, my child, was that with yourself or with another or with some class of beast?

Some class of beast. I never heard of a sin like that before. This priest must be from the country and if he is he's opening up new worlds to me.

The night before I'm to go to Killaloe Laman Griffin comes home drunk and eats a great bag of fish and chips at the table. He tells Mam boil water for tea and when she says she has no coal or turf he yells at her and calls her a great lump living free under his roof with her pack of brats. He throws money at me to go to the shop for a few sods of turf and wood for kindling. I don't want to go. I want to hit him for the way he treats my mother but if I say anything he won't let me have the bicycle tomorrow after I've waited three weeks.

When Mam gets the fire going and boils the water I remind him of his promise to loan me the bike.

Did you empty the chamber pot today?

Oh, I forgot. I'll do it this minute.

He shouts, You didn't empty my damn chamber pot. I promise you the bike. I give you tuppence a week to run messages for me and empty the chamber pot and you stand there with your thick gob hanging out and tell me you didn't do it.

I'm sorry. I forgot. I'll do it now.

You will, will you? And how do you think you'll get up to the loft? Are you going to pull the table out from under my fish and chips?

Mam says, Sure, he was at school all day and he had to go to the doctor for his eyes.

Well, you can bloody well forget about the bicycle. You didn't live up to the bargain.

But he couldn't do it, says Mam.

He tells her shut up and mind her own business and she goes quiet by the fire. He goes back to his fish and chips but I tell him again, You promised me. I emptied that chamber pot and did your messages for three weeks.

Shut up and go to bed.

You can't tell me go to bed. You're not my father, and you promised me.

I'm telling you, as sure as God made little apples, that if I get up from this table you'll be calling for your patron saint.

You promised me.

He pushes the chair back from the table. He stumbles toward me and sticks his finger between my eyes. I'm telling you shut your gob, scabby eyes.

I won't. You promised me.

He punches my shoulders and when I won't stop moves to my head. My mother jumps up, crying, and tries to pull him away. He punches and kicks me into the bedroom but I keep saying, You promised me. He knocks me to my mother's bed and punches till I cover my face and head with my arms.

I'll kill you, you little shit.

Mam is screaming and pulling at him till he falls backward into the kitchen. She says, Come on, oh, come on. Eat your fish and chips. He's only a child. He'll get over it.

I hear him go back to his chair and pull it to the table. I hear him snuffle and slurp when he eats and drinks. Hand me the matches, he says. By Jesus, I need a fag after that. There's a put-put sound when he puffs on the cigarette and a whimper from my mother.

He says, I'm going to bed, and with the drink in him it

343

takes him a while to climb the chair to the table, pull up the chair, climb to the loft. The bed squeaks under him and he grunts when he pulls off his boots and drops them to the floor.

I can hear Mam crying when she blows into the globe of the paraffin oil lamp and everything goes dark. After what happened she'll surely want to get into her own bed and I'm ready to go to the small one against the wall. Instead, there's the sound of her climbing the chair, the table, the chair, crying up into the loft and telling Laman Griffin, He's only a boy, tormented with his eyes, and when Laman says, He's a little shit and I want him out of the house, she cries and begs till there's whispering and grunting and moaning and nothing.

In awhile they're snoring in the loft and my brothers are asleep around me. I can't stay in this house for if Laman Griffin comes at me again I'll take a knife to his neck. I don't know what to do or where to go.

I leave the house and follow the streets from the Sarsfield Barracks to the Monument Café. I dream of how I'll get back at Laman some day. I'll go to America and see Joe Louis. I'll tell him my troubles and he'll understand because he comes from a poor family. He'll show me how to build up my muscles, how to hold my hands and use my feet. He'll show me how to dig my chin into my shoulder the way he does and how to let go with a right uppercut that will send Laman flying. I'll drag Laman to the graveyard at Mungret where his family and Mam's family are buried and I'll cover him with earth all the way to his chin so that he won't be able to move and he'll beg for his life and I'll say, End of the road, Laman, you're going to meet your Maker, and he'll beg and beg while I trickle dirt on his face till it's covered completely and he's gasping and asking God for forgiveness for not giving me the bike and punching me all over the house and doing the excitement with my mother and I'll be laughing away because he's not in a state of grace after the excitement and he's going to hell as sure as God made little apples as he used to say himself.

The streets are dark and I have to keep an eye out in case I might be lucky like Malachy long ago and find fish and chips dropped by drunken soldiers. There's nothing on the ground. If I find my uncle, Ab Sheehan, he might give me some of his Friday night fish and chips, but they tell me in the café he came and went already. I'm thirteen now so I don't call him Uncle Pat anymore. I call him Ab or The Abbot like everybody else. Surely if I go to Grandma's house he'll give me a piece of bread or something and maybe he'll let me stay the night. I can tell him I'll be working in a few weeks delivering telegrams and getting big tips at the post office and ready to pay my own way.

He's sitting up in bed finishing his fish and chips, dropping to the floor the *Limerick Leader* they were wrapped in, wiping his mouth and hands with the blanket. He looks at me, That face is all swole. Did you fall on that face?

I tell him I did because there's no use telling him anything else. He wouldn't understand. He says, You can stay in me mother's bed tonight. You can't walk the streets with that face and them two red eyes in your head.

He says there's no food in the house, not a scrap of bread, and when he falls asleep I take the greasy newspaper from the floor. I lick the front page, which is all advertisements for films and dances in the city. I lick the headlines. I lick the great attacks of Patton and Montgomery in France and Germany. I lick the war in the Pacific. I lick the obituaries and the sad memorial poems, the sports pages, the market prices of eggs butter and bacon. I suck the paper till there isn't a smidgen of grease.

I wonder what I'll do tomorrow.

XIV

In the morning The Abbot gives me the money to go to Kathleen O'Connell's for bread, margarine, tea, milk. He boils water on the gas ring and tells me I can have a mug of tea and, Go aisy with the sugar, I'm not a millionaire. You can have a cut o' bread but don't make it too thick.

It's July and school is over forever. In a few weeks I'll be delivering telegrams at the post office, working like a man. In the weeks I'm idle I can do anything I like, get up in the morning, stay in bed, take long walks out the country like my father, wander around Limerick. If I had the money I'd go over to the Lyric Cinema, eat sweets, see Errol Flynn conquering everyone in sight. I can read the English and Irish papers The Abbot brings home or I can use the library cards of Laman Griffin and my mother till I'm found out.

Mam sends Michael with a milk bottle of warm tea, a few cuts of bread smeared with dripping, a note to say Laman Griffin isn't angry anymore and I can come back. Michael says, Are you coming home, Frankie?

No.

Ah, do, Frankie. Come on.

I live here now. I'm never going back.

But Malachy is gone to the army and you're here and I have no big brother. All the boys have big brothers and I only have Alphie. He's not even four and can't talk right.

I can't go back. I'm never going back. You can come here any time you like.

His eyes glint with tears and that gives me such a pain in

my heart I want to say, All right, I'll come with you. I'm only saying that. I know I'll never be able to face Laman Griffin again and I don't know if I can look at my mother. I watch Michael go up the lane with the sole of his shoe broken and clacking along the pavement. When I start that job at the post office I'll buy him shoes so I will. I'll give him an egg and take him to the Lyric Cinema for the film and the sweets and then we'll go to Naughton's and eat fish and chips till our bellies are sticking out a mile. I'll get money some day for a house or a flat with electric light and a lavatory and beds with sheets blankets pillows like the rest of the world. We'll have breakfast in a bright kitchen with flowers dancing in a garden beyond, delicate cups and saucers, eggcups, eggs soft in the yolk and ready to melt the rich creamery butter, a teapot with a cozy on it, toast with butter and marmalade galore. We'll take our time and listen to music from the BBC or the American Armed Forces Network. I'll buy proper clothes for the whole family so our arses won't be hanging out of our pants and we won't have the shame. The thought of the shame brings a pain in my heart and starts me sniffling. The Abbot says, What's up with you? Didn't you have your bread? Didn't you have your tay? What more do you want? 'Tis an egg you'll be lookin' for next.

There's no use talking to someone who was dropped on his head and sells papers for a living.

He complains he can't be feeding me forever and I'll have to get my own bread and tea. He doesn't want to come home and find me reading in the kitchen with the electric lightbulb blazing away. He can read numbers so he can and when he goes out to sell papers he reads the electric meter so he'll know how much I used and if I don't stop turning on that light he'll take the fuse out and carry it in his pocket and if I put another fuse in he'll have the electricity pulled out altogether and go back to gas, which was good enough for his poor dead mother and will surely suit him for all he does is sit up in the bed to eat his fish and chips and count his money before he goes to sleep.

I get up early like Dad and go on long walks into the country. I walk around the graveyard in the old abbey at Mungret where my mother's relations are buried and I go up the boreen to the Norman castle at Carrigogunnell where Dad brought me twice. I climb to the top and Ireland is spread out before me, the Shannon shining its way to the Atlantic. Dad told me this castle was built hundreds of years ago and if you wait for the larks to stop their singing over there you can hear the Normans below hammering and talking and getting ready for battle. Once he brought me here in the dark so that we could hear Norman and Irish voices down through the centuries and I heard them. I did.

Sometimes I'm up there alone on the heights of Carrigogunnell and there are voices of Norman girls from olden times laughing and singing in French and when I see them in my mind I'm tempted and I climb to the very top of the castle where once there was a tower and there in full view of Ireland I interfere with myself and spurt all over Carrigogunnell and fields beyond.

That's a sin I could never tell a priest. Climbing to great heights and going at yourself before all of Ireland is surely worse than doing it in a private place with yourself or with another or with some class of a beast. Somewhere down there in the fields or along the banks of the Shannon a boy or a milkmaid might have looked up and seen me in my sin and if they did I'm doomed because the priests are always saying that anyone who exposes a child to sin will have a millstone tied around his neck and be cast into the sea.

Still, the thought of someone watching me brings on the excitement again. I wouldn't want a small boy to be watching me. No, no, that would surely lead to the millstone, but if there was a milkmaid gawking up she'd surely get excited and go at herself though I don't know if girls can go at

348

themselves when they don't have anything to go at. No equipment, as Mikey Molloy used to say.

I wish that old deaf Dominican priest would come back so that I could tell him my troubles with the excitement but he's dead now and I'll have to face a priest who'll go on about the millstone and the doom.

Doom. That's the favorite word of every priest in Limerick.

I walk back along O'Connell Avenue and Ballinacurra where people have their bread and milk delivered early to their doorsteps and surely there's no harm if I borrow a loaf or a bottle with every intention of giving it back when I get my job at the post office. I'm not stealing, I'm borrowing, and that's not a mortal sin. Besides, I stood on top of a castle this morning and committed a sin far worse than stealing bread and milk and if you commit one sin you might as well commit a few more because you get the same sentence in hell. One sin, eternity. A dozen sins, eternity.

Might as well be hung for a sheep as a lamb, as my mother would say. I drink the odd pint of milk and leave the bottle so that the milkman won't be blamed for not delivering. I like milkmen because one of them gave me two broken eggs which I swallowed raw with bits of shells and all. He said I'd grow up powerful if I had nothing else but two eggs in a pint of porter every day. Everything you need is in the egg and everything you want is in the pint.

Some houses get better bread than others. It costs more and that's what I take. I feel sorry for the rich people who will get up in the morning and go to the door and find their bread missing but I can't let myself starve to death. If I starve I'll never have the strength for my telegram boy job at the post office, which means I'll have no money to put back all that bread and milk and no way of saving to go to America and if I can't go to America I might as well jump into the River Shannon. It's only a few weeks till I get my first wages in the post office and surely these rich people won't collapse with the hunger till then. They can always send the maid out for more. That's the difference between the poor and the rich. The poor can't send out for more because there's no money to send out for more and if there was they wouldn't have a maid to send. It's the maids I have to worry about. I have to be careful when I borrow the milk and the bread and they're at the front doors polishing knobs, knockers and letter boxes. If they see me they'll be running to the woman of the house, Oh, madam, madam, there's an urchin beyant that's makin' off with all the milk and bread.

Beyant. Maids talk like that because they're all from the country, Mullingar heifers, says Paddy Clohessy's uncle, beef to the heels, and they wouldn't give you the steam of their piss.

I bring home the bread and even if The Abbot is surprised he doesn't say, Where did you get it? because he was dropped on his head and that knocks the curiosity out of you. He just looks at me with his big eyes that are blue in the middle and yellow all around and slurps his tea from the great cracked mug his mother left behind. He tells me, That's me mug and don't be drinkin' your tay oush of ish.

Oush of ish. That's the Limerick slum talk that always worried Dad. He said, I don't want my sons growing up in a Limerick lane saying, Oush of ish. It's common and low class. Say out of it properly.

And Mam said, I hope it keeps fine for you but you're not doing much to get us oush of ish.

Out beyond Ballinacurra I climb orchard walls for apples. If there's a dog I move on because I don't have Paddy Clohessy's way of talking to them. Farmers come at me but they're always slow in their rubber boots and even if they jump on a bicycle to chase me I jump over walls where they can't take a bike.

The Abbot knows where I got the apples. If you grow up

in the lanes of Limerick you're bound to rob the odd orchard sooner or later. Even if you hate apples you have to rob orchards or your pals will say you're a sissy.

I always offer The Abbot an apple but he won't eat it because of the scarcity of teeth in his head. He has five left and he won't risk leaving them in an apple. If I cut the apple into slices he still won't eat it because that's not the proper way to eat an apple. That's what he says and if I say, You slice bread before you eat it, don't you? he says, Apples is apples and bread is bread.

That's how you talk when you're dropped on your head.

Michael comes again with warm tea in a milk bottle and two cuts of fried bread. I tell him I don't need it anymore. Tell Mam I'm taking care of myself and I don't need her tea and fried bread, thank you very much. Michael is delighted when I give him an apple and I tell him come every second day and he can have more. That stops him from asking me to go back to Laman Griffin's and I'm glad it stops his tears.

There's a market down in Irishtown where the farmers come on Saturdays with their vegetables, hens, eggs, butter. If I'm there early they'll give me a few pennies for helping unload their carts or motor cars. At the end of the day they'll give me vegetables they can't sell, anything crushed, bruised or rotten in parts. One farmer's wife always gives me cracked eggs and tells me, Fry them eggs tomorrow when you come back from Mass in a state of grace for if you ate them eggs with a sin on your sowl they'll stick in your gullet, so they will.

She's a farmer's wife and that's how they talk.

I'm not much better than a beggar now myself the way I stand at the doors of fish and chip shops when they're closing in hopes they might have burnt chips left over or bits of fish floating around in the grease. If they're in a hurry the shop owners will give me the chips and a sheet of paper for wrapping.

The paper I like is the *News of the World*. It's banned in

Ireland but people sneak it in from England for the shocking pictures of girls in swimming suits that are almost not there. Then there are stories of people committing all kinds of sins you wouldn't find in Limerick, getting divorces, committing adultery.

Adultery. I still have to find out what that word means, look it up in the library. I'm sure it's worse than what the masters taught us, bad thoughts, bad words, bad deeds.

I take my chips home and get into bed like The Abbot. If he has a few pints taken he sits up eating his chips from the *Limerick Leader* and singing "The Road to Rasheen." I eat my chips. I lick the *News of the World*. I lick the stories about people doing shocking things. I lick the girls in their bathing suits and when there's nothing left to lick I look at the girls till The Abbot blows out the light and I'm committing a mortal sin under the blanket.

I can go to the library any time with Mam's card or Laman Griffin's. I'll never be caught because Laman is too lazy to get out of bed on a Saturday and Mam will never go near a library with the shame of her clothes.

Miss O'Riordan smiles. The *Lives of the Saints* are waiting for you, Frank. Volumes and volumes. Butler, O'Hanlon, Baring-Gould. I've told the head librarian all about you and she's so pleased she's ready to give you your own grown-up card. Isn't that wonderful?

Thanks, Miss O'Riordan.

I'm reading all about St. Brigid, virgin, February first. She was so beautiful that men from all over Ireland panted to marry her and her father wanted her to marry someone important. She didn't want to marry anyone so she prayed to God for help and He caused her eye to melt in her head so that it dribbled down her cheek and left such a great welt the men of Ireland lost interest.

Then there's St. Wilgefortis, virgin martyr, July twentieth.

Her mother had nine children, all at the same time, four sets of twins and Wilgefortis the odd one, all winding up martyrs for the faith. Wilgefortis was beautiful and her father wanted to marry her off to the King of Sicily. Wilgefortis was desperate and God helped her by allowing a beard and a mustache to grow on her face, which made the King of Sicily think twice but sent her father into such a rage he had her crucified beard and all.

St. Wilgefortis is the one you pray to if you're an English-woman with a troublesome husband.

The priests never tell us about virgin martyrs like St. Agatha, February fifth. February is a powerful month for virgin martyrs. Sicilian pagans ordered Agatha to give up her faith in Jesus and like all the virgin martyrs she said, Nay. They tortured her, stretched her on the rack, tore her sides with iron hooks, burned her with blazing torches, and she said, Nay, I will not deny Our Lord. They crushed her breasts and cut them off but when they rolled her over hot coals it was more than she could bear so she expired, giving praise.

Virgin martyrs always died singing hymns and giving praise not minding one bit if lions tore big chunks from their sides and gobbled them on the spot.

How is it the priests never told us about St. Ursula and her eleven thousand maiden martyrs, October twenty-first? Her father wanted her to marry a pagan king but she said, I'll go away for awhile, three years, and think about it. So off she goes with her thousand noble ladies-in-waiting and their companions, ten thousand. They sailed around for awhile and traipsed through various countries till they stopped in Cologne where the chief of the Huns asked Ursula to marry him. Nay, she said, and the Huns killed her and the maidens with her. Why couldn't she say yes and save the lives of eleven thousand virgins? Why did virgin martyrs have to be so stubborn?

I like St. Moling, an Irish bishop. He didn't live in a palace like the bishop of Limerick. He lived in a tree and when other saints visited him for dinner they would sit around on branches like birds having a grand time with their water and dry bread. He was walking along one day and a leper said, Hoy, St. Moling, where are you going? I'm going to Mass, says St. Moling. Well, I'd like to go to Mass too, so why don't you hoist me up on your back and carry me? St. Moling did but he no sooner had the leper up on his back than the leper started to complain. Your hair shirt, he said, is hard on my sores, take it off. St. Moling took off the shirt and off they went again. Then the leper says, I need to blow my nose. St. Moling says, I don't have any class of a handkerchief, use your hand. The leper says, I can't hold on to you and blow my nose at the same time. All right, says St. Moling, you can blow into my hand. That won't do, says the leper, I barely have a hand left with the leprosy and I can't hold on and blow into your hand. If you were a proper saint you'd twist around here and suck the stuff out of my head. St. Moling didn't want to suck the leper's snot but he did and offered it up and praised God for the privilege.

I could understand my father sucking the bad stuff out of Michael's head when he was a baby and desperate but I don't understand why God wanted St. Moling to go around sucking the snot out of leper's heads. I don't understand God at all and even if I'd like to be a saint and have everyone adore me I'd never suck the snot of a leper. I'd like to be a saint but if that's what you have to do I think I'll stay the way I am.

Still, I'm ready to spend my life in this library reading about virgins and virgin martyrs till I get into trouble with Miss O'Riordan over a book someone left on the table. The author is Lin Yütang. Anyone can tell this is a Chinese name and I'm curious to know what the Chinese talk about. It's a book of essays about love and the body and one of his words sends me to the dictionary. Turgid. He says, The male organ of copulation becomes turgid and is inserted into the receptive female orifice.

Turgid. The dictionary says swollen and that's what I am, standing there looking at the dictionary because I know now what Mikey Molloy was talking about all along, that we're no different from the dogs that get stuck in each other in the streets and it's shocking to think of all the mothers and fathers doing the likes of this.

My father lied to me for years about the Angel on the Seventh Step.

Miss O'Riordan wants to know what word I'm looking for. She always looks worried when I'm at the dictionary so I tell her I'm looking for canonize or beatific or any class of a religious word.

And what's this? she says. This is not the *Lives of the Saints*.

She picks up Lin Yütang and starts reading the page where I left the book face down on the table.

Mother o' God. Is this what you were reading? I saw this in your hand.

Well, I—I—only wanted to see if the Chinese, if the Chinese, ah, had any saints.

Oh, indeed, you did. This is disgraceful. Filth. No wonder the Chinese are the way they are. But what could you expect of slanty eyes and yellow skin and you, now that I look at you, have a bit of the slanty eye yourself. You are to leave this library at once.

But I'm reading the *Lives of the Saints*.

Out or I'll call the head librarian and she'll have the guards on you. Out. You should be running to the priest and confessing your sins. Out, and before you go hand me the library cards of your poor mother and Mr. Griffin. I have a good mind to write to your poor mother and I would if I thought it wouldn't destroy her entirely. Lin Yütang, indeed. Out.

There's no use trying to talk to librarians when they're in that state. You could stand there for an hour telling them all you've read about Brigid and Wilgefortis and Agatha and Ursula and the maiden martyrs but all they think about is one word on one page of Lin Yütang.

The People's Park is behind the library. It's a sunny day, the grass is dry, and I'm worn out begging for chips and putting up with librarians who get into a state over turgid and I'm looking at the clouds drifting above the monument and drifting off myself all turgid till I'm having a dream about virgin martyrs in bathing suits in the *News of the World* pelting Chinese writers with sheeps' bladders and I wake up in a state of excitement with something hot and sticky pumping out of me oh God my male organ of copulation sticking out a mile people in the park giving me curious looks and mothers telling their children come over here love come away from that fella someone should call the guards on him.

The day before my fourteenth birthday I see myself in the glass in Grandma's sideboard. The way I look how can I ever start my job at the post office. Everything is torn, shirt, gansey, short pants, stockings, and my shoes are ready to fall off my feet entirely. Relics of oul' decency, my mother would call them. If my clothes are bad I'm worse. No matter how I drench my hair under the tap it sticks out in all directions. The best cure for standing up hair is spit, only it's hard to spit on your own head. You have to let go with a good one up in the air and duck to catch it on your poll. My eyes are red and oozing yellow, there are matching red and yellow pimples all over my face and my front teeth are so black with rot I'll never be able to smile in my life.

I have no shoulders and I know the whole world admires shoulders. When a man dies in Limerick the women always say, Grand man he was, shoulders that big and wide he wouldn't come in the door for you, had to come in sideways. When I die they'll say, Poor little devil, died without a sign of a shoulder. I wish I had some sign of a shoulder so that people would know I was at least fourteen years of age. All the boys in Leamy's had shoulders except for Fintan Slattery and I don't want to be like him with no shoulders and knees worn away from prayer. If I had any money left I'd light a candle to St. Francis and ask him if there's any chance God could be persuaded to perform a miracle on my shoulders. Or if I had a stamp I could write to Joe Louis and say, Dear Joe, Is there any chance you could tell me where you got your powerful shoulders even though you were poor?

I have to look decent for my job so I take off all my clothes and stand naked in the backyard washing them under the tap with a bar of carbolic soap. I hang them on Grandma's clothesline, shirt, gansey, pants, stockings, and pray to God it won't rain, pray they'll be dry for tomorrow, which is the start of my life.

I can't go anywhere in my pelt so I stay in bed all day reading old newspapers, getting excited with the girls in the *News of the World* and thanking God for the drying sun. The Abbot comes home at five and makes tea downstairs and even though I'm hungry I know he'll grumble if I ask him for anything. He knows the one thing that worries me is he might go to Aunt Aggie and complain I'm staying in Grandma's house and sleeping in her bed and if Aunt Aggie hears that she'll come over and throw me into the street.

He hides the bread when he's finished and I can never find it. You would think that one who was never dropped on his head would be able to find the hidden bread of one who was dropped on his head. Then I realize if the bread is not in the house he must take it with him in the pocket of the overcoat he wears winter and summer. The minute I hear him clumping from the kitchen to the backyard lavatory I run downstairs, pull the loaf from the pocket, cut off a thick slice, back into the pocket, up the stairs and into bed. He can never say a word, never accuse me. You'd have to be a thief of the worst class to steal one slice of bread and no one would ever believe him, not even Aunt Aggie. Besides, she'd bark at him and say, What are you doing anyway going around with a loaf of bread in your pocket? That's no place for a loaf of bread.

I chew the bread slowly. One mouthful every fifteen minutes will make it last and if I wash it down with water the bread will swell in my belly and give me the full feeling.

I look out the back window to make sure the evening sun is drying my clothes. Other backyards have lines with clothes that are bright and colorful and dance in the wind. Mine hang from the line like dead dogs.

The sun is bright but it's cold and damp in the house and I wish I had something to wear in the bed. I have no other clothes and if I touch anything of The Abbot's he'll surely run to Aunt Aggie. All I can find in the wardrobe is Grandma's old black woolen dress. You're not supposed to wear your Grandmother's old dress when she's dead and you're a boy but what does it matter if it keeps you warm and you're in bed under the blankets where no one will ever know. The dress has the smell of old dead grandmother and I worry she might rise from the grave and curse me before the whole family and all assembled. I pray to St. Francis, ask him to keep her in the grave where she belongs, promise him a candle when I start my job, remind him the robe he wore himself wasn't too far from a dress and no one ever tormented him over it and fall asleep with the image of his face in my dream.

The worst thing in the world is to be sleeping in your dead grandmother's bed wearing her black dress when your uncle The Abbot falls on his arse outside South's pub after a night of drinking pints and people who can't mind their own business rush to Aunt Aggie's house to tell her so that she gets Uncle Pa Keating to help her carry The Abbot home and upstairs to where you're sleeping and she barks at you, What are you doin' in this house, in that bed? Get up and put on the kettle for tea for your poor uncle Pat that fell down, and when you don't move she pulls the blankets and falls backward like one seeing a ghost and yelling Mother o'God what are you doin' in me dead mother's dress?

That's the worst thing of all because it's hard to explain

that you're getting ready for the big job in your life, that you washed your clothes, they're drying abroad on the line, and it was so cold you had to wear the only thing you could find in the house, and it's even harder to talk to Aunt Aggie when The Abbot is groaning in the bed, Me feet is like a fire, put water on me feet, and Uncle Pa Keating is covering his mouth with his hand and collapsing against the wall laughing and telling you that you look gorgeous and black suits you and would you ever straighten your hem. You don't know what to do when Aunt Aggie tells you, Get out of that bed and put the kettle on downstairs for tea for your poor uncle. Should you take off the dress and put on a blanket or should you go as you are? One minute she's screaming, What are you doin' in me poor mother's dress? the next she's telling you put on that bloody kettle. I tell her I washed my clothes for the big job.

What big job?

Telegram boy at the post office.

She says if the post office is hiring the likes of you they must be in a desperate way altogether, go down and put on that kettle.

The next worse thing is to be out in the backyard filling the kettle from the tap with the moon beaming away and Kathleen Purcell from next door perched up on the wall looking for her cat. God, Frankie McCourt, what are you doin' in your grandmother's dress? and you have to stand there in the dress with the kettle in your hand and explain how you washed your clothes which are hanging there on the line for all to see and you were so cold in the bed you put on your grandmother's dress and your uncle Pat, The Abbot, fell down and was brought home by Aunt Aggie and her husband, Pa Keating, and she drove you into the backyard to fill this kettle and you'll take off this dress as soon as ever your clothes are dry because you never had any desire to go through life in your dead grandmother's dress.

Now Kathleen Purcell lets out a scream, falls off the wall,

359

forgets the cat, and you can hear her giggling into her blind mother, Mammy, Mammy, wait till I tell you about Frankie McCourt abroad in the backyard in his dead grandmother's dress. You know that once Kathleen Purcell gets a bit of scandal the whole lane will know it before morning and you might as well stick your head out the window and make a general announcement about yourself and the dress problem.

By the time the kettle boils The Abbot is asleep from the drink and Aunt Aggie says she and Uncle Pa will have a drop of tea themselves and she doesn't mind if I have a drop myself. Uncle Pa says on second thought the black dress could be the cassock of a Dominican priest and he goes down on his knees and says, Bless me, Father, for I have sinned. Aunt Aggie says, Get up, you oul' eejit, and stop makin' a feck of religion. Then she says, And you what are you doin' in this house?

I can't tell her about Mam and Laman Griffin and the excitement in the loft. I tell her I was thinking of staying here a while because of the great distance from Laman Griffin's house to the post office and as soon as I get on my feet we'll surely find a decent place and we'll all move on, my mother and brothers and all.

Well, she says, that's more than your father would do.

XV

It's hard to sleep when you know the next day you're four-teen and starting your first job as a man. The Abbot wakes at dawn moaning. Would I ever make him some tay and if I do I can have a big cut of bread from the half loaf in his pocket which he was keeping there out of the way of the odd rat and if I look in Grandma's gramophone where she used to keep the records I'll find a jar of jam.

He can't read, he can't write, but he knows where to hide the jam.

I bring The Abbot his tea and bread and make some for myself. I put on my damp clothes and get into the bed hoping that if I stay there the clothes will dry from my own heat before I go to work. Mam always says it's the damp clothes that give you the consumption and an early grave. The Abbot is sitting up telling me he has a terrible pain in his head from a dream where I was wearing his poor mother's black dress and she flying around screaming, Sin, sin, 'tis a sin. He finishes his tea and falls into a snore sleep and I wait for his clock to say half-past eight, time to get up and be at the post office at nine even if the clothes are still damp on my skin.

On my way out I wonder why Aunt Aggie is coming down the lane. She must be coming to see if The Abbot is dead or needing a doctor. She says, What time do you have to be at that job?

Nine.

All right.

She turns and walks with me to the post office on Henry

Street. She doesn't say a word and I wonder if she's going to the post office to denounce me for sleeping in my grandmother's bed and wearing her black dress. She says, Go up and tell them your aunt is down here waiting for you and you'll be an hour late. If they want to argue I'll go up and argue.

Why do I have to be an hour late?

Do what you're bloody well told.

There are telegram boys sitting on a bench along a wall. There are two women at a desk, one fat, one thin. The thin one says, Yes?

My name is Frank McCourt, miss, and I'm here to start work.

What kind of work would that be now?

Telegram boy, miss.

The thin one cackles, Oh, God, I thought you were here to clean the lavatories.

No, miss. My mother brought a note from the priest, Dr. Cowpar, and there's supposed to be a job.

Oh, there is, is there? And do you know what day this is?

I do, miss. 'Tis my birthday. I'm fourteen.

Isn't that grand, says the fat woman.

Today is Thursday, says the thin woman. Your job starts on Monday. Go away and wash yourself and come back then.

The telegram boys along the wall are laughing. I don't know why but I feel my face turning hot. I tell the women, Thank you, and on the way out I hear the thin one, Jesus above, Maureen, who dragged in that specimen? and they laugh along with the telegram boys.

Aunt Aggie says, Well? and I tell her I don't start till Monday. She says my clothes are a disgrace and what did I wash them in.

Carbolic soap.

They smell like dead pigeons and you're making a laughingstock of the whole family.

She takes me to Roche's Stores and buys me a shirt, a gansey, a pair of short pants, two pairs of stockings and a pair of summer shoes on sale. She gives me two shillings to have tea and a bun for my birthday. She gets on the bus to go back up O'Connell Street too fat and lazy to walk. Fat and lazy, no son of her own, and still she buys me the clothes for my new job.

I turn toward Arthur's Quay with the package of new clothes under my arm and I have to stand at the edge of the River Shannon so that the whole world won't see the tears of a man the day he's fourteen.

Monday morning I'm up early to wash my face and flatten my hair with water and spit. The Abbot sees me in my new clothes. Jaysus, he says, is it gettin' married you are? and goes back to sleep.

Mrs. O'Connell, the fat woman, says, Well, well, aren't we the height of fashion, and the thin one, Miss Barry, says, Did you rob a bank on the weekend? and there's a great laugh from the telegram boys sitting on the bench along the wall.

I'm told to sit at the end of the bench and wait for my turn to go out with telegrams. Some telegram boys in uniforms are the permanent ones who took the exam. They can stay in the post office forever if they like, take the next exam for postman and then the one for clerk that lets them work inside selling stamps and money orders behind the counter downstairs. The post office gives permanent boys big water-proof capes for the bad weather and they get two weeks holiday every year. Everyone says these are good jobs, steady and pensionable and respectable, and if you get a job like this you never have to worry again in your whole life, so you don't.

Temporary telegram boys are not allowed to stay in the job beyond the age of sixteen. There are no uniforms, no holidays, the pay is less, and if you stay out sick a day you can be fired. No excuses. There are no waterproof capes. Bring your own raincoat or dodge the raindrops.

Mrs. O'Connell calls me to her desk to give me a black leather belt and pouch. She says there's a great shortage of bicycles so I'll have to walk my first batch of telegrams. I'm to go to the farthest address first, work my way back, and don't take all day. She's long enough in the post office to know how long it takes to deliver six telegrams even by foot. I'm not to be stopping in pubs or bookies or even home for a cup of tea and if I do I'll be found out. I'm not to be stopping in chapels to say a prayer. If I have to pray do it on the hoof or on the bicycle. If it rains pay no attention. Deliver the telegrams and don't be a sissy.

One telegram is addressed to Mrs. Clohessy of Arthur's Quay and that couldn't be anyone but Paddy's mother.

Is that you, Frankie McCourt? she says. God, I wouldn't know you you're that big. Come in, will you.

She's wearing a bright frock with flowers all over and shiny new shoes. There are two children on the floor playing with a toy train. On the table there is a teapot, cups with saucers, a bottle of milk, a loaf of bread, butter, jam. There are two beds over by the window where there were none before. The big bed in the corner is empty and she must know what I'm wondering. He's gone, she says, but he's not dead. Gone t' England with Paddy. Have a cup o' tay an' a bit o' bread. You need it, God help us. You look like one left over from the Famine itself. Ate that bread an' jam an' build yourself up. Paddy always talked about you and Dennis, my poor husband that was in the bed, never got over the day your mother came an' sang the song about the Kerry dancing. He's over in England now making sandwiches in a canteen and sending me a few bob every week. You'd wonder what the English are thinking about when they take a man that has the consumption and give him a job making sandwiches. Paddy has a grand job in a pub in Cricklewood, which is in England. Dennis would still be here if it wasn't for Paddy climbin' the wall for the tongue.

Tongue?

Dennis had the craving, so he did, for a nice sheep's head with a bit of cabbage and a spud so up with me to Barry the butcher with the last few shillings I had. I boiled that head an' sick an' all as he was Dennis couldn't wait for it to be done. He was a demon there in the bed callin' for the head an' when I gave it to him on the plate he was delighted with himself suckin' the marrow outa every inch of that head. Then he finishes an' he says, Mary, where is the tongue?

What tongue? says I.

The tongue of this sheep. Every sheep is born with a tongue that lets him go ba ba ba and there's a great lack of tongue in this head. Go up to Barry the butcher and demand it.

So up with me to Barry the butcher and he said, That bloody sheep came in here bleatin' an' cryin' so much we cut the tongue from her and thrun it to the dog who gobbled it up and ever since ba bas like a sheep and if he doesn't quit I'll cut his tongue and throw it to the cat.

Back I go to Dennis and he gets frantic in the bed. I want that tongue, he says. All the nourishment is in the tongue. And what do you think happens next but my Paddy, that was your friend, goes up to Barry the butcher after dark, climbs the wall, cuts the tongue of a sheep's head that's on a hook on the wall and brings it back to his poor father in the bed. Of course I have to boil that tongue with salt galore and Dennis, God love him, ates it, lies back in the bed a minute, throws back the blanket and stands out on his two feet announcing to the world that consumption or no consumption, he's not going to die in that bed, if he's going to die at all it might as well be under a German bomb with him making a few pounds for his family instead of whining in the bed there beyond.

She shows me a letter from Paddy. He's working in his uncle Anthony's pub twelve hours a day, twenty-five shillings a week and every day soup and a sandwich. He's delighted when the Germans come over with the bombs so that he can sleep while the pub is closed. At night he sleeps on the floor of the hallway upstairs. He will send his mother two pounds every month and he's saving the rest to bring her and the family to England where they'll be much better off in one room in Cricklewood than ten rooms in Arthur's Quay. She'll be able to get a job no bother. You'd have to be a sad case not to be able to get a job in a country that's at war especially with Yanks pouring in and spending money right and left. Paddy himself is planning to get a job in the middle of London where Yanks leave tips big enough to feed an Irish family of six for a week.

Mrs. Clohessy says, We have enough money for food and shoes at last, thanks be to God and His Blessed Mother. You'll never guess who Paddy met over there in England fourteen years of age an' workin' like a man. Brendan Kiely, the one ye used to call Question. Workin' he is an' savin' so he can go an' join the Mounties an' ride all over Canada like Nelson Eddy singin' I'll be callin' you ooh ooh ooh ooh ooh ooh. If it wasn't for Hitler we'd all be dead an' isn't that a terrible thing to say. And how's your poor mother, Frankie?

She's grand, Mrs. Clohessy.

No, she's not. I seen her in the Dispensary and she looks worse than my Dennis did in the bed. You have to mind your poor mother. You look desperate too, Frankie, with them two red eyes starin' outa your head. Here's a little tip for you. Thruppence. Buy yourself a sweet.

I will, Mrs. Clohessy.

Do.

*   *   *

At the end of the week Mrs. O'Connell hands me the first wages of my life, a pound, my first pound. I run down the stairs and up to O'Connell Street, the main street, where the lights are on and people are going home from work, people like me with wages in their pockets. I want them to know I'm like them, I'm a man, I have a pound. I walk up one side of O'Connell Street and down the other and hope they'll notice me. They don't. I want to wave my pound note at the world so they'll say, There he goes, Frankie McCourt the workingman, with a pound in his pocket.

It's Friday night and I can do anything I like. I can have fish and chips and go to the Lyric Cinema. No, no more Lyric. I don't have to sit up in the gods anymore with people all around me cheering on the Indians killing General Custer and the Africans chasing Tarzan all over the jungle. I can go to the Savoy Cinema now, pay sixpence for a seat down front where there's a better class of people eating boxes of chocolates and covering their mouths when they laugh. After the film I can have tea and buns in the restaurant upstairs.

Michael is across the street calling me. He's hungry and wonders if there's any chance he could go to The Abbot's for a bit of bread and stay there for the night instead of going all the way to Laman Griffin's. I tell him he doesn't have to worry about a bit of bread. We'll go to the Coliseum Café and have fish and chips, all he wants, lemonade galore, and then we'll go to see *Yankee Doodle Dandy* with James Cagney and eat two big bars of chocolate. After the film we have tea and buns and we sing and dance like Cagney all the way to The Abbot's. Michael says it must be great to be in America where people have nothing else to do but sing and dance. He's half asleep but he says he's going there some day to sing and dance and would I help him go and when he's asleep I start thinking about America and how I have to save money for my fare instead of squandering it on fish and chips and tea and buns. I'll have to save a few shillings from my pound because if I don't I'll be in Limerick forever. I'm fourteen now and if I save something every week surely I should be able to go to America by the time I'm twenty.

There are telegrams for offices, shops, factories where there's no hope of a tip. Clerks take the telegrams without a look at you or a thank you. There are telegrams for the respectable people with maids along the Ennis Road and the North Circular Road where there's no hope of a tip. Maids are like clerks, they don't look at you or say thank you. There are telegrams for the houses of priests and nuns and they have maids, too, even if they say poverty is noble. If you waited for tips from priests or nuns you'd die on their doorstep. There are telegrams for people miles outside the city, farmers with muddy yards and dogs who want to eat your legs. There are telegrams for rich people in big houses with gate lodges and miles of land surrounded by walls. The gatekeeper waves you in and you have to cycle for miles up long drives past lawns, flower beds, fountains to reach the big house. If the weather is fine people are playing croquet, the Protestant game, or strolling around, talking and laughing, all decked out in flowery dresses and blazers with crests and golden buttons and you'd never know there was a war on. There are Bentleys and Rolls-Royces parked outside the great front door where a maid tells you go around to the servants' entrance don't you know any better.

People in the big houses have English accents and they don't tip telegram boys.

The best people for tips are widows, Protestant ministers' wives and the poor in general. Widows know when the telegram money order is due from the English government and they wait by the window. You have to be careful if they ask you in for a cup of tea because one of the temporary boys, Scrawby Luby, said an old widow of thirty-five had him in for tea and tried to take down his pants and he had to run out of the house though he was really tempted and had to go to confession the next Saturday. He said it was very awkward hopping up on the bike with his thing sticking out but if you cycle very fast and think of the sufferings of the Virgin Mary you'll go soft in no time.

Protestant ministers' wives would never carry on like Scrawby Luby's old widow unless they're widows themselves. Christy Wallace, who is a permanent telegram boy and ready to be a postman any day, says Protestants don't care what they do even if they're ministers' wives. They're doomed anyway, so what does it matter if they have a bit of a romp with a telegram boy. All the telegram boys like Protestant ministers' wives. They might have maids but they answer doors themselves and say, One moment, please, and give you sixpence. I'd like to talk to them and ask them how it feels to be doomed but they might get offended and take back the sixpence.

The Irishmen working in England send their telegram money orders on Friday nights and all day Saturday and that's when we get the good tips. The minute we deliver one batch we're out with another.

The worst lanes are in the Irishtown, off High Street or Mungret Street, worse than Roden Lane or O'Keeffe's Lane or any lane I lived in. There are lanes with channels running down the middle. Mothers stand at doors and yell gardyloo when they empty their slop buckets. Children make paper boats or float matchboxes with little sails on the greasy water.

When you ride into a lane the children call out, Here's the telegram boy, here's the telegram boy. They run to you and the women wait at the door. If you give a small child a telegram for his mother he's the hero of the family. Little girls know they're supposed to wait till the boys get their chance though they can get the telegram if they have no brothers. Women at the door will call to you that they have no money now but if you're in this lane tomorrow knock on the door for your tip, God bless you an' all belongin' to you.

Mrs. O'Connell and Miss Barry at the post office tell us every day our job is to deliver telegrams and nothing else.

We are not to be doing things for people, going to the shop for groceries or any other kind of message. They don't care if people are dying in the bed. They don't care if people are legless, lunatic or crawling on the floor. We are to deliver the telegram and that's all. Mrs. O'Connell says, I know everything ye do, everything, for the people of Limerick have their eye on ye and there are reports which I have here in my drawers.

A fine place to keep reports, says Toby Mackey under his breath.

But Mrs. O'Connell and Miss Barry don't know what it's like in the lane when you knock on a door and someone says come in and you go in and there's no light and there's a pile of rags on a bed in a corner the pile saying who is it and you say telegram and the pile of rags tells you would you ever go to the shop for me I'm starving with the hunger and I'd give me two eyes for a cup of tea and what are you going to do say I'm busy and ride off on your bike and leave the pile of rags there with a telegram money order that's pure useless because the pile of rags is helpless to get out of the bed to go to the post office to cash the bloody money order.

What are you supposed to do?

You're told never never go to the post office to cash one of those money orders for anyone or you'll lose your job forever. But what are you supposed to do when an old man that was in the Boer War hundreds of years ago says his legs are gone and he'd be forever grateful if you'd go to Paddy Considine in the post office and tell him the situation and Paddy will surely cash the money order and keep two shillings for yourself grand boy that you are. Paddy Considine says no bother but don't tell anyone or I'd be out on my arse and so would you, son. The old man from the Boer War says he knows you have telegrams to deliver now but would you ever come back tonight and maybe go to the shop for him for he doesn't have a thing in the house and he's freezing on top of it. He sits in an old armchair in the corner covered with bits of blankets and a bucket behind the chair that stinks enough to make you sick and when you look at that old man in the dark corner you want to get a hose with hot water and strip him and wash him down and give him a big feed of rashers and eggs and mashed potatoes with loads of butter salt and onions.

I want to take the man from the Boer War and the pile of rags in the bed and put them in a big sunny house in the country with birds chirping away outside the window and a stream gurgling.

Mrs. Spillane in Pump Lane off Carey's Road has two crippled twin children with big blond heads, small bodies, and bits of legs that dangle over the edges of the chairs. They look into the fire all day and say, Where's Daddy? They speak English like everybody else but they babble away to one another in a language they made up, Hung sup tea tea sup hung. Mrs. Spillane says that means, When are we getting our supper? She tells me she's lucky if her husband sends four pounds a month and she's beside herself with the abuse she gets from the Dispensary over him being in England. The children are only four and they're very bright even if they can't walk or take care of themselves. If they could walk, if they were any way normal, she'd pack up and move to England out of this godforsaken country that fought so long for freedom and look at the state of us, de Valera in his mansion above in Dublin the dirty oul' bastard and the rest of the politicians that can all go to hell, God forgive me. The priests can go to hell too and I won't ask God to forgive me for saying the likes of that. There they are, the priests and the nuns telling us Jesus was poor and 'tis no shame, lorries driving up to their houses with crates and barrels of whiskey and wine, eggs galore and legs of ham and they telling us what we should give up for Lent. Lent, my arse. What are we to give up when we have Lent all year long?

I want to take Mrs. Spillane and her two blond crippled children and put them in that house in the country with the pile of rags and the man from the Boer War and wash everyone and let them all sit in the sun with the birds singing and the streams gurgling.

I can't leave the pile of rags alone with a useless money order because the pile is an old woman, Mrs. Gertrude Daly, all twisted with every class of disease you can get in a Limerick lane, arthritis, rheumatism, falling hair, a nostril half gone from her jabbing at it with her finger, and you wonder what kind of a world is it when this old woman sits up from the rags and smiles at you with teeth that gleam white in the dark, her own teeth and perfect.

That's right, she says, me own teeth, and when I rot in the grave they'll find me teeth a hundred years from now all white an' shiny an' I'll be declared a saint.

The telegram money order, three pounds, is from her son. It has a message, Happy Birthday, Mammy, Your fond son, Teddy. She says, A wonder he can spare it, the little shit, trottin' around with every tart in Piccadilly. She asks if I'd ever do her a favor and cash the money order and get her a little Baby Powers whiskey at the pub, a loaf of bread, a pound of lard, seven potatoes, one for each day of the week. Would I boil a potato for her, mash it up with a lump of lard, give her a cut of bread, bring her a drop of water to go with the whiskey? Would I go to O'Connor the chemist for ointment for her sores and while I'm at it bring some soap so she can give her body a good scrub and she'll be forever grateful and say a prayer for me and here's a couple of shillings for all my troubles.

Ah, no thanks, ma'am.

Take the money. Little tip. You did me great favors.

I couldn't, ma'am, the way you are.

Take the money or I'll tell the post office you're not to deliver my telegram anymore.

Oh, all right, ma'am. Thanks very much.

Good night, son. Be good to your mother.

Good night, Mrs. Daly.

School starts in September and some days Michael stops at The Abbot's before the walk home to Laman Griffin's. On rainy days he says, Can I stay here tonight? and soon he doesn't want to go back to Laman Griffin's at all. He's worn out and hungry with two miles out and two miles back.

When Mam comes looking for him I don't know what to say to her. I don't know how to look at her and I keep my eyes off to one side. She says, How's the job? as if nothing ever happened in Laman Griffin's and I say, Grand, as if nothing ever happened in Laman Griffin's. If the rain is too heavy for her to go home she stays in the small room upstairs with Alphie. She goes back to Laman's the next day but Michael stays and soon she's moving in herself bit by bit till she stops going to Laman's altogether.

The Abbot pays the rent every week. Mam gets the relief and the food dockets till someone informs on her and she's cut off from the Dispensary. She's told that if her son is bringing in a pound a week that's more than some families get on the dole and she should be grateful he has a job. Now I have to hand over my wages. Mam says, A pound? Is that all you get for riding around in all kinds of weather? This would be four dollars in America. Four dollars. And you couldn't feed a cat for four dollars in New York. If you were delivering telegrams for Western Union in New York you'd be earning twenty-five dollars a week and living in luxury. She always translates Irish money into American so that she won't forget and tries to convince everyone times were better over there. Some weeks she lets me keep two shillings but if I go to a film or buy a secondhand book there's nothing left, I won't be able to save for my fare, and I'll be stuck in Limerick till I'm an old man of twenty-five.

Malachy writes from Dublin to say he's fed up and doesn't want to spend the rest of his life blowing a trumpet in the army band. He's home in a week and complains when he has to share the big bed with Michael, Alphie and me. He had his own army cot up there in Dublin with sheets and blankets and a pillow. Now he's back to overcoats and a bolster that sends up a cloud of feathers when you touch it. Mam says, Pity about you. I'm sorry for your troubles. The Abbot has his own bed, and my mother has the small room. We're all together again, no Laman tormenting us. We make tea and fried bread and sit on the kitchen floor. The Abbot says you're not supposed to be sitting on kitchen floors, what are tables and chairs for? He tells Mam that Frankie is not right in the head and Mam says we'll all catch our death from the damp of the floor. We sit on the floor and sing and Mam and The Abbot sit on chairs. She sings,

> *Are you lonesome tonight?*
> *Do you miss me tonight?*
> *Are you sorry we drifted apart?*
> *Does your memory stray*
> *To that bright summer's day*
> *When I kissed you*
> *And called you sweetheart?*

The Abbot sings "The Road to Rasheen" and we still don't know what the song is about. We sit on the floor and tell stories about things that happened, things that never happened and things that will happen when we all go to America.

There are slow days at the post office and we sit on the bench and talk. We can talk but we are not to laugh. Miss

Barry says we should be grateful we're getting paid to sit there, bunch of idlers and streetboys that we are, and that there is to be no laughing. Getting paid for sitting and chatting is no laughing matter and the first titter out of any of us and out we go till we come to our senses and if the tittering continues we'll be reported to the proper authorities.

The boys talk about her under their breath. Toby Mackey says, What that oul' bitch needs is a good rub o' the relic, a good rub o' the brush. Her mother was a streetwalking flaghopper and her father escaped from a lunatic asylum with bunions on his balls and warts on his wank.

There is laughing along the bench and Miss Barry calls to us, I warned ye against the laughing. Mackey, what is it you're prattling about over there?

I said we'd all be better off out in the fresh air on this fine day delivering telegrams, Miss Barry.

I'm sure you did, Mackey. Your mouth is a lavatory. Did you hear me?

I did, Miss Barry.

You have been heard on the stairs, Mackey.

Yes, Miss Barry.

Shut up, Mackey.

I will, Miss Barry.

Not another word, Mackey.

No, Miss Barry.

I said shut up, Mackey.

All right, Miss Barry.

That's the end of it, Mackey. Don't try me.

I won't, Miss Barry.

Mother o' God give me patience.

Yes, Miss Barry.

Take the last word, Mackey. Take it, take it, take it.

I will, Miss Barry.

Toby Mackey is a temporary telegram boy like me. He saw a film called *The Front Page* and now he wants to go to America some day and be a tough newspaper reporter with a hat and a cigarette. He keeps a notebook in his pocket because a good reporter has to write down what happens. Facts. He has to write down facts not a lot of bloody poetry, which is all you hear in Limerick with men in pubs going on about our great sufferings under the English. Facts, Frankie. He writes down the number of telegrams he delivers and how far he travels. We sit on the bench making sure we don't laugh and he tells me that if we deliver forty telegrams a day that's two hundred a week and that's ten thousand a year and twenty thousand in our two years at the job. If we cycle one hundred and twenty-five miles in a week that's thirteen thousand miles in two years and that's halfway around the world, Frankie, and no wonder there isn't a scrap of flesh on our arses.

Toby says nobody knows Limerick like the telegram boy. We know every avenue, road, street, terrace, mews, place, close, lane. Jasus, says Toby, there isn't a door in Limerick we don't know. We knock on all kinds of doors, iron, oak, plywood. Twenty thousand doors, Frankie. We rap, kick, push. We ring and buzz bells. We shout and whistle, Telegram boy, telegram boy. We drop telegrams in letter boxes, shove them under doors, throw them over the transom. We climb in windows where people are bedridden. We fight off every dog who wants to turn us into dinner. You never know what's going to happen when you hand people their telegrams. They laugh and sing and dance and cry and scream and fall down in a weakness and you wonder if they'll wake up at all and give you the tip. It's not a bit like delivering telegrams in America where Mickey Rooney rides around in a film called *The Human Comedy* and people are pleasant and falling over themselves to give you a tip, inviting you in, giving you a cup of tea and a bun.

Toby Mackey says he has facts galore in his notebook and he doesn't give a fiddler's fart about anything and that's the way I'd like to be myself.

Mrs. O'Connell knows I like the country telegrams and

if a day is sunny she gives me a batch of ten that will keep me away all morning and I don't have to return till after the dinner hour at noon. There are fine autumn days when the Shannon sparkles and the fields are green and glinting with silver morning dew. Smoke blows across fields and there's the sweet smell of turf fires. Cows and sheep graze in the fields and I wonder if these are the beasts the priest was talking about. I wouldn't be surprised because there's no end to the bulls climbing on cows, rams on sheep, stallions on mares, and they all have such big things it makes me break out in a sweat to look at them and I feel sorry for all the female creatures in the world who have to suffer like that though I wouldn't mind being a bull myself because they can do what they like and it's never a sin for an animal. I wouldn't mind going at myself here but you never know when a farmer might come along the road driving cows and sheep to a fair or to another field raising his stick and bidding you, Good day, young fella, grand morning, thank God and His Blessed Mother. A farmer that religious might be offended if he saw you breaking the sixth Commandment forninst his field. Horses like to stick their heads over fences and hedges to see what's passing by and I stop and talk to them because they have big eyes and long noses that show how intelligent they are. Sometimes two birds will be singing to each other across a field and I have to stop and listen to them and if I stay long enough more birds will join till every tree and bush is alive with birdsong. If there's a stream gurgling under a bridge on the road, birds singing and cows mooing and lambs baaing, that's better than any band in a film. The smell of dinner bacon and cabbage wafting from a farmhouse makes me so weak with the hunger I climb into a field and stuff myself with blackberries for half an hour. I stick my face into the stream and drink icy water that's better than the lemonade in any fish and chip shop.

When I'm finished delivering the telegrams there's enough time to go to the ancient monastery graveyard where my mother's relations are buried, the Guilfoyles and the Shee-hans, where my mother wants to be buried. I can see from here the high ruins of Carrigogunnell Castle and there's plenty of time to cycle there, sit up on the highest wall, look at the Shannon flowing out to the Atlantic on its way to America and dream of the day I'll be sailing off myself.

The boys at the post office tell me I'm lucky to get the Carmody family telegram, a shilling tip, one of the biggest tips you'll ever get in Limerick. So why am I getting it? I'm the junior boy. They say, Well, sometimes Theresa Carmody answers the door. She has the consumption and they're afraid of catching it from her. She's seventeen, in and out of the sanatorium, and she'll never see eighteen. The boys at the post office say sick people like Theresa know there's little time left and that makes them mad for love and romance and everything. Everything. That's what the consumption does to you, say the boys at the post office.

I cycle through wet November streets thinking of that shilling tip, and as I turn into the Carmody street the bicycle slides out from under me and I skid along the ground scraping my face and tearing open the back of my hand. Theresa Carmody opens the door. She has red hair. She had green eyes like the fields beyond Limerick. Her cheeks are bright pink and her skin is a fierce white. She says, Oh, you're all wet and bleeding.

I skidded on my bike.

Come in and I'll put something on your cuts.

I wonder, Should I go in? I might get the consumption and that will be the end of me. I want to be alive when I'm fifteen and I want the shilling tip.

Come in. You'll perish standing there.

She puts on the kettle for the tea. Then she dabs iodine on my cuts and I try to be a man and not whimper. She says, Oh, you're a great bit of a man. Go into the parlor and dry yourself before the fire. Look, why don't you take off your pants and dry them on the screen of the fire?

Ah, no.

Ah, do.

I will.

I drape my pants over the screen. I sit there watching the steam rise and I watch myself rise and I worry she might come in and see me in my excitement.

There she is with a plate of bread and jam and two cups of tea. Lord, she says, you might be a scrawny bit of a fellow but that's a fine boyo you have there.

She puts the plate and the cups on a table by the fire and there they stay. With her thumb and forefinger she takes the tip of my excitement and leads me across the room to a green sofa against the wall and all the time my head is filled with sin and iodine and fear of consumption and the shilling tip and her green eyes and she's on the sofa don't stop or I'll die and she's crying and I'm crying for I don't know what's happening to me if I'm killing myself catching consumption from her mouth I'm riding to heaven I'm falling off a cliff and if this is a sin I don't give a fiddler's fart.

We take our ease on the sofa a while till she says, Don't you have more telegrams to deliver? and when we sit up she gives a little cry, Oh, I'm bleeding.

What's up with you?

I think it's because it's the first time.

I tell her, Wait a minute. I bring the bottle from the kitchen and splash the iodine on her injury. She leaps from the sofa, dances around the parlor like a wild one and runs into the kitchen to douse herself with water. After she dries herself she says, Lord, you're very innocent. You're not supposed to be pouring iodine on girls like that.

I thought you were cut.

For weeks after that I deliver the telegram. Sometimes we have the excitement on the sofa but there are other days she has the cough and you can see the weakness on her. She never tells me she has the weakness. She never tells me she has the consumption. The boys at the post office say I must have been having a great time with the shilling tip and Theresa Carmody. I never tell them I stopped taking the shilling tip. I never tell them about the green sofa and the excitement. I never tell them of the pain that comes when she opens the door and I can see the weakness on her and all I want to do then is make tea for her and sit with my arms around her on the green sofa.

One Saturday I'm told to deliver the telegram to Theresa's mother at her job in Woolworth's. I try to be casual. Mrs. Carmody, I always deliver the telegram to your, I think your daughter, Theresa?

Yes, she's in the hospital.

Is she in the sanatorium?

I said she's in the hospital.

She's like everyone else in Limerick, ashamed of the TB, and she doesn't give me a shilling or any kind of tip. I cycle out to the sanatorium to see Theresa. They say you have to be a relation and you have to be adult. I tell them I'm her cousin and I'll be fifteen in August. They tell me go away. I cycle to the Franciscan church to pray for Theresa. St. Francis, would you please talk to God. Tell Him it wasn't Theresa's fault. I could have refused that telegram Saturday after Saturday. Tell God Theresa was not responsible for the excitement on the sofa because that's what the consumption does to you. It doesn't matter anyway, St. Francis, because I love Theresa. I love her as much as you love any bird or beast or fish and will you tell God take the consumption away and I promise I'll never go near her again.

The next Saturday they give me the Carmody telegram. From halfway up the street I can see the blinds are drawn. I can see the black crepe wreath on the door. I can see the white purple-lined mourning card. I can see beyond the door and walls where Theresa and I tumbled naked and wild on the green sofa and I know now she is in hell and all because of me.

I slip the telegram under the door and cycle back down to the Franciscan church to beg for the repose of Theresa's soul. I pray to every statue, to the stained glass windows, the Stations of the Cross. I swear I'll lead a life of faith, hope and charity, poverty, chastity and obedience.

Next day, Sunday, I go to four Masses. I do the Stations of the Cross three times. I say rosaries all day. I go without food and drink and wherever I find a quiet place I cry and beg God and the Virgin Mary to have mercy on the soul of Theresa Carmody.

On Monday I follow the funeral to the graveyard on my post office bicycle. I stand behind a tree a distance from the grave. Mrs. Carmody weeps and moans. Mr. Carmody snuffles and looks puzzled. The priest recites the Latin prayers and sprinkles the coffin with holy water.

I want to go to the priest, to Mr. and Mrs. Carmody. I want to tell them how I'm the one who sent Theresa to hell. They can do whatever they like with me. Abuse me. Revile me. Throw grave dirt at me. But I stay behind the tree till the mourners leave and the grave diggers fill in the grave.

Frost is already whitening the fresh earth on the grave and I think of Theresa cold in the coffin, the red hair, the green eyes. I can't understand the feelings going through me but I know that with all the people who died in my family and all the people who died in the lanes around me and all the people who left I never had a pain like this in my heart and I hope I never will again.

It's getting dark. I walk my bicycle out of the graveyard. I have telegrams to deliver.

XVI

Mrs. O'Connell gives me telegrams to deliver to Mr. Harrington, the Englishman with the dead wife that was born and bred in Limerick. The boys at the post office say sympathy telegrams are a waste of time. People just cry and moan with the grief and they think they're excused from the tip. They'll ask you if you'd like to come in for a look at the departed and a prayer by the bed. That wouldn't be so bad if they offered you a drop of sherry and a ham sandwich. Oh, no, they're happy to get your prayer but you're only a telegram boy and you're lucky if you get a dry biscuit. Older boys at the post office say you have to play your cards right to get the grief tip. If you're asked in to say a prayer you have to kneel by the corpse, give a powerful sigh, bless yourself, drop your forehead to the bedclothes so they won't see your face, let your shoulders shake like one collapsing with sorrow, hold on to the bed with your two hands as if they're going to have to tear you away to deliver the rest of your telegrams, make sure your cheeks are glinting with tears or the spit you dabbed on, and if you don't get a tip after all that push the next batch of telegrams under the door or fire them over the transom and leave them to their grief.

This isn't my first time delivering telegrams to the Harrington house. Mr. Harrington is always away on business for the insurance company and Mrs. Harrington is generous with the tip. But she's gone and Mr. Harrington answers the doorbell. His eyes are red and he sniffles. He says, Are you Irish?

Irish? What else would I be standing there on his doorstep in Limerick with a batch of telegrams in my hand? I am, sir. He says, Come in. Put the telegrams on the hall stand. He shuts the hall door, locks it, puts the key in his pocket and I think, Aren't Englishmen very peculiar.

You'll want to see her, of course. You'll want to see what you people have done to her with your damn tuberculosis. Race of ghouls. Follow me.

He leads me first to the kitchen where he picks up a plate of ham sandwiches and two bottles, and then upstairs. Mrs. Harrington looks lovely in the bed, blond, pink, peaceful.

This is my wife. She may be Irish but she doesn't look it, thank God. Like you. Irish. You'll need a drink, of course. You Irish quaff at every turn. Barely weaned before you clamor for the whiskey bottle, the pint of stout. You'll have what, whiskey, sherry?

Ah, a lemonade will be lovely.

I am mourning my wife not celebrating the bloody citrus. You'll have a sherry. Swill from bloody Catholic fascist Spain.

I gulp the sherry. He refills my glass and goes to refill his own with whiskey. Damn. Whiskey all gone. Stay here. Do you hear me? I'm going to the pub for another bottle of whiskey. Stay till I come back. Don't move.

I'm confused, dizzy from the sherry. I don't know what you're supposed to do with grieving Englishmen. Mrs. Harrington, you look lovely in the bed. But you're a Protestant, already doomed, in hell, like Theresa. Priest said, Outside the Church there is no salvation. Wait, I might be able to save your soul. Baptize you Catholic. Make up for what I did to Theresa. I'll get some water. Oh, God, the door is locked. Why? Maybe you're not dead at all? Watching me. Are you dead, Mrs. Harrington? I'm not afraid. Your face is icy. Oh, you're dead all right. I'll baptize you with sherry from bloody Catholic fascist Spain. I baptize thee in the name of the Father, the Son, the—

What the bloody hell are you doing? Get off my wife,

you wretched Papist twit. What primitive Paddy ritual is this? Did you touch her? Did you? I'll wring your scrawny neck.

I—I,—

Oi, Oi, speak English, you scrap.

I was just, a little sherry to get her into heaven.

Heaven? We had heaven, Ann, I, our daughter, Emily. You'll never lay your pink piggy eyes on her. Oh, Christ, I can't stand it. Here, more sherry.

Ah, no, thanks.

Ah, no thanks. That puny Celtic whine. You people love your alcohol. Helps you crawl and whine better. Of course you want food. You have the collapsed look of a starving Paddy. Here. Ham. Eat.

Ah, no thanks.

Ah, no thanks. Say that again and I'll ram the ham up your arse.

He waves a ham sandwich at me, with the heel of his hand pushes it into my mouth.

He collapses into a chair. Oh, God, God, what am I to do? Must rest a moment.

My stomach heaves. I rush to the window, stick my head out and throw up. He leaps from the chair and charges me.

You, you, God blast you to hell, you vomited on my wife's rosebush.

He lunges at me, misses, falls to the floor. I climb out the window, hang on to the ledge. He's at the window, grabbing at my hands. I let go, drop to the rosebush, into the ham sandwich and sherry I've just thrown up. I'm pricked by rose thorns, stung, my ankle is twisted. He's at the window, barking, Come back here, you Irish runt. He'll report me to the post office. He hits me in the back with the whiskey bottle, pleads, Will you not watch one hour with me?

He pelts me with sherry glasses, whiskey glasses, assorted ham sandwiches, items from his wife's dressing table, powders, creams, brushes.

I climb on my bike and wobble through the streets of Limerick, dizzy with sherry and pain. Mrs. O'Connell attacks me, Seven telegrams, one address, and you're gone all day.

I was, I was,

You was. You was. Drunk is what you was. Drunk is what you are. Reeking. Oh, we heard. That nice man rang, Mr. Harrington, lovely Englishman that sounds like James Mason. Lets you in to say a prayer for his poor wife and next thing you're out the window with the sherry and the ham. Your poor mother. What she brought into the world.

He made me eat the ham, drink the sherry.

Made you? Jesus, that's a good one. Made you. Mr. Harrington is a refined Englishman and there is no reason for him to lie and we don't want your kind in this post office, people that can't keep their hands off the ham and sherry, so hand in your telegram pouch and bicycle for your days are done in this post office.

But I need the job. I have to save and go to America.

America. Sad day when America lets in the likes of you.

I hobble through the streets of Limerick. I'd like to go back and throw a brick through Mr. Harrington's window. No. Respect for the dead. I'll go across the Sarsfield Bridge and out the riverbank where I can lie down somewhere in the bushes. I don't know how I can go home and tell my mother I lost my job. Have to go home. Have to tell her. Can't stay out the riverbank all night. She'd be frantic.

Mam begs the post office to take me back. They say no. They never heard the likes. Telegram boy mauling corpse. Telegram boy fleeing scene with ham and sherry. He will never set foot in the post office again. No.

She gets a letter from the parish priest. Take the boy back, says the parish priest. Oh, yes, Father, indeed, says the post office. They'll let me stay till my sixteenth birthday, not a minute longer. Besides, says Mrs. O'Connell, when you think of what the English did to us for eight hundred years that man had no right to complain over a little ham and sherry. Compare a little ham and sherry to the Great Famine and where are you? If my poor husband was alive and I told him what you did he'd say you struck a blow, Frank McCourt, struck a blow.

Every Saturday morning I swear I'll go to confession and tell the priest of my impure acts at home, on lonely boreens around Limerick with cows and sheep gawking, on the heights of Carrigogunnell with the world looking up.

I'll tell him about Theresa Carmody and how I sent her to hell, and that will be the end of me, driven from the Church.

Theresa is a torment to me. Every time I deliver a telegram to her street, every time I pass the graveyard I feel the sin growing in me like an abscess and if I don't go to confession soon I'll be nothing but an abscess riding around on a bicycle with people pointing and telling each other, There he is, there's Frankie McCourt, the dirty thing that sent Theresa Carmody to hell.

I look at people going to Communion on Sundays, everyone in a state of grace, returning to their seats with God in their mouths, peaceful, easy, ready to die at any moment and go straight to heaven or go home to their rashers and eggs without a worry in the world.

I'm worn out from being the worst sinner in Limerick. I want to get rid of this sin and have rashers and eggs and no guilt, no torment. I want to be ordinary.

The priests tell us all the time that God's mercy is infinite but how can any priest give absolution to someone like me who delivers telegrams and winds up in a state of excitement on a green sofa with a girl dying of the galloping consumption.

I cycle all around Limerick with telegrams and stop at

every church. I ride from Redemptorists to Jesuits to Augustinians to Dominicans to Franciscans. I kneel before the statue of St. Francis of Assisi and beg him to help me but I think he's too disgusted with me. I kneel with people in the pews next to confessionals but when my turn comes I can't breathe, my heart pounds, my forehead turns cold and clammy and I run from the church.

I swear I'll go to confession at Christmas. I can't. Easter. I can't. Weeks and months pass and it's a year since Theresa died. I'll go on her anniversary but I can't. I'm fifteen now and I pass churches without stopping. I'll have to wait till I go to America where there are priests like Bing Crosby in *Going My Way* who won't kick me out of the confessional like Limerick priests.

I still have the sin in me, the abscess, and I hope it doesn't kill me entirely before I see the American priest.

There's a telegram for an old woman, Mrs. Brigid Finucane. She says, How old are you, by?

Fifteen and a half, Mrs. Finucane.

Young enough to make a fool of yourself and ould enough to know better. Are you shmart, by? Are you anyway intelligent?

I can read and write, Mrs. Finucane.

Arrah, there are people above in the lunatic asylum can read and write. Can you write a letter?

I can.

She wants me to write letters to her customers. If you need a suit or dress for your child you can go to her. She gives you a ticket to a shop and they give you the clothes. She gets a discount and charges you the full price and interest on top. You pay her back weekly. Some of her customers fall behind in their payments and they need threatening letters. She says, I'll give you threepence for every letter you write and another threepence if it brings a payment. If you want the job come here on Thursday and Friday nights, and bring your own paper and envelopes.

I'm desperate for that job. I want to go to America. But I have no money for paper and envelopes. Next day I'm delivering a telegram to Woolworth's and there is the answer, a whole section packed with paper and envelopes. I have no money so I have to help myself. But how? Two dogs save the day for me, two dogs at the door of Woolworth's stuck together after the excitement. They yelp and run in circles. Customers and sales clerks giggle and pretend to be looking someplace else and while they're busy pretending I slip paper and envelopes under my sweater, out the door and off on my bike far from stuck dogs.

Mrs. Finucane looks suspicious. That's very fancy stationery you have there, by. Is that your mother's? You'll give that back when you get the money, won't you, by?

Oh, I will.

From now on I'm never to come to her front door. There's a lane behind her house and I'm to come in the back door for fear someone might see me.

In a large ledger she gives me the names and addresses of six customers behind in their payments. Threaten 'em, by. Frighten the life out of 'em.

My first letter,

Dear Mrs. O'Brien,

Inasmuch as you have not seen fit to pay me what you owe me I may be forced to resort to legal action. There's your son, Michael, parading around the world in his new suit which I paid for while I myself have barely a crust to keep body and soul together. I am sure you don't want to languish in the dungeons of Limerick jail far from friends and family.

I remain, yours in litigious anticipation,
Mrs. Brigid Finucane

She tells me, That's a powerful letter, by, better than anything you'd read in the *Limerick Leader*. That word, inasmuch, that's a holy terror of a word. What does it mean?

I think it means this is your last chance.

I write five more letters and she gives me money for stamps. On my way to the post office I think, Why should I squander money on stamps when I have two legs to deliver the letters myself in the dead of night? When you're poor a threatening letter is a threatening letter no matter how it comes in the door.

I run through the lanes of Limerick shoving letters under doors, praying no one will see me.

The next week Mrs. Finucane is squealing with joy. Four of 'em paid. Oh, sit down now and write more, by. Put the fear of God in 'em.

Week after week my threatening letters grow sharper and sharper. I begin to throw in words I hardly understand myself.

Dear Mrs. O'Brien,
     Inasmuch as you have not succumbed to the imminence of litigation in our previous epistle be advised that we are in consultation with our barrister above in Dublin.

Next week Mrs. O'Brien pays. She came in tremblin' with tears in her eyes, by, and she promised she'd never miss another payment.

On Friday nights Mrs. Finucane sends me to a pub for a bottle of sherry. You're too young for sherry, by. You can make yourself a nice cup of tea but you have to use the tea leaves left over from this morning. No, you can't have a piece of bread with the prices they're charging. Bread is it? Next thing you'll be asking for an egg.

She rocks by the fire, sipping her sherry, counting the money in the purse on her lap, entering payments in her ledger before she locks everything in the trunk under her bed upstairs. After a few sherries she tells me what a lovely thing it is to have a little money so you can leave it to the Church for Masses to be said for the repose of your soul. It makes her so happy to think of priests saying Masses for her years and years after she's dead and buried.

Sometimes she falls asleep and if the purse drops to the floor I help myself to an extra few shillings for the overtime and the use of all the big new words. There will be less money for the priests and their Masses but how many Masses does a soul need and surely I'm entitled to a few pounds after the way the Church slammed doors in my face? They wouldn't let me be an altar boy, a secondary school pupil, a missionary with the White Fathers. I don't care. I have a post office savings account and if I keep writing successful threatening letters, helping myself to the odd few shillings from her purse and keeping the stamp money, I'll have my escape money to America. If my whole family dropped from the hunger I wouldn't touch this money in the post office.

Often I have to write threatening letters to neighbors and friends of my mother and I worry they might discover me. They complain to Mam, That oul' bitch, Finucane, below in Irishtown, sent me a threatening letter. What kind of a demon outa hell would torment her own kind with a class of a letter that I can't make head nor tail of anyway with words never heard on land or sea. The person that would write that letter is worse than Judas or any informer for the English.

My mother says anyone that writes such letters should be boiled in oil and have his fingernails pulled out by blind people.

I'm sorry for their troubles but there's no other way for me to save the money for America. I know that someday I'll be a rich Yank and send home hundreds of dollars and my family will never have to worry about threatening letters again.

*   *   *

Some of the temporary telegram boys are taking the permanent exam in August. Mrs. O'Connell says, You should take that exam, Frank McCourt. You have a bit of a brain in your head and you'd pass it no bother. You'd be a postman in no time and a great help to your poor mother.

Mam says I should take it, too, become a postman, save up, go to America and be a postman over there and wouldn't that be a lovely life.

I'm delivering a telegram to South's pub on a Saturday and Uncle Pa Keating is sitting there, all black as usual. He says, Have a lemonade there, Frankie, or is it a pint you want now that you're near sixteen?

Lemonade, Uncle Pa, thanks.

You'll want your first pint the day you're sixteen, won't you?

I will but my father won't be here to get it for me.

Don't worry about that. I know 'tis not the same without your father but I'll get you the first pint. 'Tis what I'd do if I had a son. Come here the night before you're sixteen.

I will, Uncle Pa.

I hear you're taking that exam for the post office?

I am.

Why would you do a thing like that?

'Tis a good job and I'd be a postman in no time and it has the pension.

Ah, pension my arse. Sixteen years of age an' talking about the pension. Is it coddin' me you are? Do you hear what I said, Frankie? Pension my arse. If you pass the exam you'll stay in the post office nice and secure the rest of your life. You'll marry a Brigid and have five little Catholics and grow little roses in your garden. You'll be dead in your head before you're thirty and dried in your ballocks the year before. Make up your own bloody mind and to hell with the safeshots and the begrudgers. Do you hear me, Frankie McCourt?

I do, Uncle Pa. That's what Mr. O'Halloran said.

What did he say?

Make up your own mind.

True for Mr. O'Halloran. 'Tis your life, make your own decisions and to hell with the begrudgers, Frankie. In the heel o' the hunt you'll be going to America anyway, won't you?

I will, Uncle Pa.

The day of the exam I'm excused from work. There's a sign in an office window on O'Connell Street, SMART BOY WANTED, NEAT HANDWRITING, GOOD AT SUMS, APPLY HERE TO MANAGER, MR. MCCAFFREY, EASONS LTD.

I stand outside the place of the exam, the house of the Limerick Protestant Young Men's Association. There are boys from all over Limerick climbing the steps to take the exam and a man at the door is handing them sheets of paper and pencils and barking at them to hurry up, hurry up. I look at the man at the door, I think of Uncle Pa Keating and what he said, I think of the sign in Eason's office, SMART BOY WANTED. I don't want to go in that door and pass that exam for if I do I'll be a permanent telegram boy with a uniform, then a postman, then a clerk selling stamps for the rest of my life. I'll be in Limerick forever, growing roses with my head dead and my ballocks all dried up.

The man at the door says, You, are you coming in here or are you goin' to stand there with your face hanging out?

I want to say to the man, Kiss my arse, but I still have a few weeks left in the post office and he might report me. I shake my head and walk up the street where a smart boy is wanted.

The manager, Mr. McCaffrey, says, I would like to see a specimen of your handwriting, to see, in short, if you have a decent fist. Sit down there at that table. Write your name and address and write me a paragraph explaining why you came here for this job and how you propose to rise in the ranks of Eason and Son, Ltd., by dint of perseverance and assiduity where there is great opportunity in this company for a boy that will keep his eye on the guidon ahead and guard his flanks from the siren call of sin.

I write,

Frank McCourt,
4, Little Barrington Street,
Limerick City,
County Limerick,
Ireland

I am applying for this job so that I can rise to the highest ranks of Easons Ltd., by dint of perseverance and assadooty knowing that if I keep my eyes ahead and protect my flanks I'll be safe from all temptation and a credit to Easons and Ireland in general.

What's this? says Mr. McCaffrey. Do we have here a twisting of the truth?

I don't know, Mr. McCaffrey.

Little Barrington Street. That's a lane. Why are you calling it a street? You live in a lane, not a street.

They call it a street, Mr. McCaffrey.

Don't be getting above yourself, boy.

Oh, I wouldn't, Mr. McCaffrey.

You live in a lane and that means you have nowhere to go but up. Do you understand that, McCourt?

I do, sir.

You have to work your way out of the lane, McCourt.

I do, Mr. McCaffrey.

You have the cut and jib of a lane boy, McCourt.

Yes, Mr. McCaffrey.

You have the look of the lane all over you. All over you from poll to toe cap. Don't try to fool the populace,

McCourt. You'd have to rise early in the morning to fool the likes of me.

Oh, I wouldn't, Mr. McCaffrey.

Then there's the eyes. Very sore eyes you have there. Can you see?

I can, Mr. McCaffrey.

You can read and write but can you do addition and subtraction?

I can, Mr. McCaffrey.

Well, I don't know what the policy is on sore eyes. I would have to ring Dublin and see where they stand on sore eyes. But your writing is clear, McCourt. A good fist. We'll take you on pending the decision on the sore eyes. Monday morning. Half six at the railway station.

In the morning?

In the morning. We don't give out the bloody morning papers at night, do we?

No, Mr. McCaffrey.

Another thing. We distribute *The Irish Times*, a Protestant paper, run by the freemasons in Dublin. We pick it up at the railway station. We count it. We take it to the news-agents. But we don't read it. I don't want to see you reading it. You could lose the Faith and by the look of those eyes you could lose your sight. Do you hear me, McCourt?

I do, Mr. McCaffrey.

No *Irish Times*, and when you come in next week I'll tell you about all the English filth you're not to read in this office. Do you hear me?

I do, Mr. McCaffrey

Mrs. O'Connell has the tight mouth and she won't look at me. She says to Miss Barry, I hear a certain upstart from the lanes walked away from the post office exam. Too good for it, I suppose.

True for you, says Miss Barry.

Too good for us, I suppose.

True for you.

Do you think he'd ever tell us why he didn't take the exam?

Oh, he might, says Miss Barry, if we went down on our two knees.

I tell her, I want to go to America, Mrs. O'Connell.

Did you hear that, Miss Barry?

I did, indeed, Mrs. O'Connell.

He spoke.

He did, indeed.

He will rue the day, Miss Barry.

Rue he will, Mrs. O'Connell.

Mrs. O'Connell talks past me to the boys waiting on the bench for their telegrams, This is Frankie McCourt who thinks he's too good for the post office.

I don't think that, Mrs. O'Connell.

And who asked you to open your gob, Mr. High and Mighty? Too grand for us, isn't he, boys?

He is, Mrs. O'Connell.

And after all we did for him, giving him the telegrams with the good tips, sending him to the country on fine days, taking him back after his disgraceful behavior with Mr. Harrington, the Englishman, disrespecting the body of poor Mrs. Harrington, stuffing himself with ham sandwiches, getting fluthered drunk on sherry, jumping out the window and destroying every rosebush in sight, coming in here three sheets to the wind, and who knows what else he did delivering telegrams for two years, who knows indeed, though we have a good idea, don't we, Miss Barry?

We do, Mrs. O'Connell, though 'twouldn't be a fit subject to be talking about.

She whispers to Miss Barry and they look at me and shake their heads.

A disgrace he is to Ireland and his poor mother. I hope she never finds out. But what would you expect of one born in America and his father from the North. We put up with all that and still took him back.

She keeps talking past me again to the boys on the bench.

Going to work for Easons he is, working for that pack of freemasons and Protestants above in Dublin. Too good for the post office but ready and willing to deliver all kinds of filthy English magazines all over Limerick. Every magazine he touches will be a mortal sin. But he's leaving now, so he is, and a sorry day it is for his poor mother that prayed for a son with a pension to take care of her in her latter days. So here, take your wages and go from the sight of us.

Miss Barry says, He's a bad boy, isn't he, boys?

He is, Miss Barry.

I don't know what to say. I don't know what I did wrong. Should I say I'm sorry? Good-bye?

I lay my belt and pouch on Mrs. O'Connell's desk. She glares at me, Go on. Go to your job at Easons. Go from us. Next boy, come up for your telegrams.

They're back at work and I'm down the stairs to the next part of my life.

XVII

I don't know why Mrs. O'Connell had to shame me before the whole world, and I don't think I'm too good for the post office or anything else. How could I with my hair sticking up, pimples dotting my face, my eyes red and oozing yellow, my teeth crumbling with the rot, no shoulders, no flesh on my arse after cycling thirteen thousand miles to deliver twenty thousand telegrams to every door in Limerick and regions beyond?

Mrs. O'Connell said a long time ago she knew everything about every telegram boy. She must know about the times I went at myself on top of Carrigogunnell, milkmaids gawking, little boys looking up.

She must know about Theresa Carmody and the green sofa, how I got her into a state of sin and sent her to hell, the worst sin of all, worse than Carrigogunnell a thousand times. She must know I never went to confession after Theresa, that I'm doomed to hell myself.

A person that commits a sin like that is never too good for the post office or anything else.

The barman at South's remembers me from the time I sat with Mr. Hannon, Bill Galvin, Uncle Pa Keating, black white black. He remembers my father, how he spent his wages and his dole while singing patriotic songs and making speeches from the dock like a condemned rebel.

And what is it you'd like? says the barman.

I'm here to meet Uncle Pa Keating and have my first pint.

Oh, begod, is that a fact? He'll be here in a minute and

sure there's no reason why I shouldn't draw his pint and maybe draw your first pint, is there now?

There isn't, sir.

Uncle Pa comes in and tells me sit next to him against the wall. The barman brings the pints, Uncle Pa pays, lifts his glass, tells the men in the pub, This is my nephew, Frankie McCourt, son of Angela Sheehan, the sister of my wife, having his first pint, here's to your health and long life, Frankie, may you live to enjoy the pint but not too much.

The men lift their pints, nod, drink, and there are creamy lines on their lips and mustaches. I take a great gulp of my pint and Uncle Pa tells me, Slow down for the love o'Jasus, don't drink it all, there's more where that came from as long as the Guinness family stays strong and healthy.

I tell him I want to stand him a pint with my last wages from the post office but he says, No, take the money home to your mother and you can stand me a pint when you come home from America flushed with success and the heat from a blonde hanging on your arm.

The men in the pub are talking about the terrible state of the world and how in God's name Hermann Goering escaped the hangman an hour before the hanging. The Yanks are over there in Nuremberg declaring they don't know how the Nazi bastard hid that pill. Was it in his ear? Up his nostril? Up his arse? Surely the Yanks looked in every hole and cranny of every Nazi they captured and still Hermann wiped their eye. There you are. It shows you can sail across the Atlantic, land in Normandy, bomb Germany off the face of the earth, but when all's said and done they can't find a little pill planted in the far reaches of Goering's fat arse.

Uncle Pa buys me another pint. It's harder to drink because it fills me and makes my belly bulge. The men are talking about concentration camps and the poor Jews that never harmed a soul, men, women, children crammed into ovens, children, mind you, what harm could they do, little shoes scattered everywhere, crammed in, and the pub is misty and the voices fading in and out. Uncle Pa says, Are you all right? You're as white as a sheet. He takes me to the lavatory and the two of us have a good long piss against the wall which keeps moving back and forth. I can't go into the pub again, cigarette smoke, stale Guinness, Goering's fat arse, small shoes scattered, can't go in again, good night, Uncle Pa, thanks, and he tells me go straight home to my mother, straight home, oh, he doesn't know about the excitement in the loft or the excitement on the green sofa or me in such a state of doom that if I died now I'd be in hell in a wink.

Uncle Pa goes back to his pint. I'm out on O'Connell Street and why shouldn't I take the few steps to the Jesuits and tell all my sins this last night I'll be fifteen. I ring the bell at the priests' house and a big man answers, Yes? I tell him, I want to go to confession, Father. He says, I'm not a priest. Don't call me father. I'm a brother.

All right, Brother. I want to go to confession before I'm sixteen tomorrow. State o' grace on my birthday.

He says, Go away. You're drunk. Child like you drunk as a lord ringing for a priest at this hour. Go away or I'll call the guards.

Ah, don't. Ah, don't. I only want to go to confession. I'm doomed.

You're drunk and you're not in a proper spirit of repentance.

He closes the door in my face. Another door closed in the face, but I'm sixteen tomorrow and I ring again. The brother opens the door, swings me around, kicks my arse and sends me tripping down the steps.

He says, Ring this bell again and I'll break your hand.

Jesuit brothers are not supposed to talk like that. They're supposed to be like Our Lord, not walking the world threatening people's hands.

I'm dizzy. I'll go home to bed. I hold on to railings along Barrington Street and keep to the wall going down the lane. Mam is by the fire smoking a Woodbine, my brothers upstairs in the bed. She says, That's a nice state to come home in.

It's hard to talk but I tell her I had my first pint with Uncle Pa. No father to get me the first pint.

Your Uncle Pa should know better.

I stagger to a chair and she says, Just like your father.

I try to control the way my tongue moves in my mouth. I'd rather be, I'd rather, rather be like my father than Laman Griffin.

She turns away from me and looks into the ashes in the range but I won't leave her alone because I had my pint, two pints, and I'm sixteen tomorrow, a man.

Did you hear me? I'd rather be like my father than Laman Griffin.

She stands up and faces me. Mind your tongue, she says.

Mind your own bloody tongue.

Don't talk to me like that. I'm your mother.

I'll talk to you any bloody way I like.

You have a mouth like a messenger boy.

Do I? Do I? Well, I'd rather be a messenger boy than the likes of Laman Griffin oul' drunkard with the snotty nose and his loft and people climbing up there with him.

She walks away from me and I follow her upstairs to the small room. She turns, Leave me alone, leave me alone, and I keep barking at her, Laman Griffin, Laman Griffin, till she pushes me, Get out of this room, and I slap her on the cheek so that tears jump in her eyes and there's a small whimpering sound from her, You'll never have the chance to do that again, and I back away from her because there's another sin on my long list and I'm ashamed of myself.

I fall into my bed, clothes and all, and wake up in the middle of the night puking on my pillow, my brothers complaining of the stink, telling me clean up, I'm a disgrace. I hear my mother crying and I want to tell her I'm sorry but why should I after what she did with Laman Griffin.

In the morning my small brothers are gone to school, Malachy is out looking for a job, Mam is at the fire drinking tea. I place my wages on the table by her elbow and turn to go. She says, Do you want a cup of tea?

No.

'Tis your birthday.

I don't care.

She calls up the lane after me, You should have something in your stomach, but I give her my back and turn the corner without answering. I still want to tell her I'm sorry but if I do I'll want to tell her she's the cause of it all, that she should not have climbed to the loft that night and I don't give a fiddler's fart anyway because I'm still writing threatening letters for Mrs. Finucane and saving to go to America.

I have the whole day before I go to Mrs. Finucane to write the threatening letters and I wander down Henry Street till the rain drives me into the Franciscan church where St. Francis stands with his birds and lambs. I look at him and wonder why I ever prayed to him. No, I didn't pray, I begged.

I begged him to intercede for Theresa Carmody but he never did a thing, stood up there on his pedestal with the little smile, the birds, the lambs, and didn't give a fiddler's fart about Theresa or me.

I'm finished with you, St. Francis. Moving on. Francis. I don't know why they ever gave me that name. I'd be better off if they called me Malachy, one a king, the other a great saint. Why didn't you heal Theresa? Why did you let her go to hell? You let my mother climb to the loft. You let me get into a state of doom. Little children's shoes scattered in concentration camps. I have the abscess again. It's in my chest and I'm hungry.

St. Francis is no help, he won't stop the tears bursting out of my two eyes, the sniffling and choking and the God oh Gods that have me on my knees with my head on the back of the pew before me and I'm so weak with the hunger and the crying I could fall on the floor and would you please help me God or St. Francis because I'm sixteen today and I hit my mother and sent Theresa to hell and wanked all over Limerick and the county beyond and I dread the millstone around my neck.

There is an arm around my shoulders, a brown robe, click of black rosary beads, a Franciscan priest.

My child, my child, my child.

I'm a child and I lean against him, little Frankie on his father's lap, tell me all about Cuchulain, Dad, my story that Malachy can't have or Freddie Leibowitz on the swings.

My child, sit here with me. Tell me what troubles you. Only if you want to. I am Father Gregory.

I'm sixteen today, Father.

Oh, lovely, lovely, and why should that be a trouble to you?

I drank my first pint last night.

Yes?

I hit my mother.

God help us, my child. But He will forgive you. Is there anything else?

I can't tell you, Father.

Would you like to go to confession?

I can't, Father. I did terrible things.

God forgives all who repent. He sent His only Beloved Son to die for us.

I can't tell, Father. I can't.

But you could tell St. Francis, couldn't you?

He doesn't help me anymore.

But you love him, don't you?

I do. My name is Francis.

Then tell him. We'll sit here and you'll tell him the things that trouble you. If I sit and listen it will only be a pair of ears for St. Francis and Our Lord. Won't that help?

I talk to St. Francis and tell him about Margaret, Oliver, Eugene, my father singing Roddy McCorley and bringing home no money, my father sending no money from England, Theresa and the green sofa, my terrible sins on Carrigogun-

402

nell, why couldn't they hang Hermann Goering for what he did to the little children with shoes scattered around concentration camps, the Christian Brother who closed the door in my face, the time they wouldn't let me be an altar boy, my small brother Michael walking up the lane with the broken shoe clacking, my bad eyes that I'm ashamed of, the Jesuit brother who closed the door in my face, the tears in Mam's eyes when I slapped her.

Father Gregory says, Would you like to sit and be silent, perhaps pray a few minutes?

His brown robe is rough against my cheek and there's a smell of soap. He looks at St. Francis and the tabernacle and nods and I suppose he's talking to God. Then he tells me kneel, gives me absolution, tells me say three Hail Marys, three Our Fathers, three Glory Bes. He tells me God forgives me and I must forgive myself, that God loves me and I must love myself for only when you love God in yourself can you love all God's creatures.

But I want to know about Theresa Carmody in hell, Father.

No, my child. She is surely in heaven. She suffered like the martyrs in olden times and God knows that's penance enough. You can be sure the sisters in the hospital didn't let her die without a priest.

Are you sure, Father?

I am, my child.

He blesses me again, asks me to pray for him, and I'm happy trotting through the rainy streets of Limerick knowing Theresa is in heaven with the cough gone.

Monday morning and it's dawn in the railway station. Newspapers and magazines are piled in bundles along the platform wall. Mr. McCaffrey is there with another boy, Willie Harold, cutting the twine on the bundles, counting, entering the count in a ledger. English newspapers and *The Irish Times* have to be delivered early, magazines later in the morning. We count out the papers and label them for delivery to shops around the city.

Mr. McCaffrey drives the van and stays at the wheel while Willie and I run into shops with bundles and take orders for the next day, add or drop in the ledger. After the papers are delivered we unload the magazines at the office and go home to breakfast for fifty minutes.

When I return to the office there are two other boys, Eamon and Peter, already sorting magazines, counting and stuffing them into newsagents' boxes along the wall. Small orders are delivered by Gerry Halvey on his messenger bicycle, big orders in the van. Mr. McCaffrey tells me stay in the office so that I can learn to count magazines and enter them in the ledger. The minute Mr. McCaffrey leaves Eamon and Peter pull out a drawer where they hide cigarette butts and light up. They can't believe I don't smoke. They want to know if there's something wrong with me, the bad eyes or the consumption maybe. How can you go out with a girl if you don't smoke? Peter says, Wouldn't you be a right eejit if you were going out the road with the girl and she asked you for a fag and you said you didn't smoke, wouldn't you be a right eejit then? How would you ever get her into a field for a bit of a feel? Eamon says, 'Tis what my father says about men who don't drink, they're not to be trusted. Peter says if you find a man that won't drink or smoke that's a man that's not even interested in girls and you'd want to keep your hand over the hole of your arse, that's what you'd want to be doing.

They laugh and that brings on the cough and the more they laugh the more they cough till they're holding on to one another banging one another between the shoulder blades and wiping tears from their cheeks. When the fit passes we pick out English and American magazines and look at the advertisements for women's underwear, brassieres and panties and long nylon stockings. Eamon is looking at an

American magazine called *See* with pictures of Japanese girls who keep the soldiers happy so far away from home and Eamon says he has to go to the lavatory and when he does Peter gives me a wink, You know what he's up to in there, don't you? and sometimes Mr. McCaffrey gets into a state when boys linger in the lavatory interfering with themselves and wasting the valuable time for which Easons is paying them and on top of it putting their immortal souls in danger. Mr. McCaffrey won't come right out and say, Stop that wanking, because you can't accuse someone of a mortal sin unless you have proof. Sometimes he goes snooping in the lavatory when a boy comes out. He comes back himself with the threatening look and tells the boys, Ye are not to be looking at those dirty magazines from foreign parts. Ye are to count them and put them in the boxes and that's all.

Eamon comes back from the lavatory and Peter goes in with an American magazine, *Collier's*, that has pictures of girls in a beauty contest. Eamon says, Do you know what he's doing in there? At himself. Five times a day he goes in. Every time a new American magazine comes in with the women's underwear he goes in. Never done going at himself. Borrows magazines to take home unbeknownst to Mr. McCaffrey and God knows what he does with himself and the magazines all night. If he fell dead in there the jaws of hell would open wide.

I'd like to get into the lavatory myself when Peter comes out but I don't want them saying, There he goes, new boy, first day on the job, already at himself. Won't light up a fag oh no but wanks away like an oul' billygoat.

Mr. McCaffrey returns from van delivery and wants to know why all the magazines aren't counted out, bundled and ready to go. Peter tells him, We were busy teaching the new boy, McCourt. God help us, he was a bit slow with the bad eyes you know but we kept at him and now he's getting faster.

Gerry Halvey, the messenger boy, won't be in for a week

because he's entitled to his holidays and he wants to spend the time with his girlfriend, Rose, who's coming back from England. I'm the new boy and I have to be messenger boy while he's gone, cycling around Limerick on the bicycle with the big metal basket in front. He shows me how to balance papers and magazines so that the bicycle won't tip over with me in the saddle and a lorry passing by that will run over me and leave me like a piece of salmon in the road. He saw a soldier once that was run over by an army lorry and that's what he looked like, salmon.

Gerry is making a last delivery at Easons kiosk at the railway station at noon on Saturday and that's handy because I can meet him there to get the bicycle and he can meet Rose off the train. We stand at the gate waiting and he tells me he hasn't seen Rose in a year. She's over there working in a pub in Bristol and he doesn't like that one bit because the English are forever pawing the Irish girls, hands up under the skirts and worse, and the Irish girls are afraid to say anything for fear of losing their jobs. Everyone knows Irish girls keep themselves pure especially Limerick girls known the world over for their purity who have a man to come back to like Gerry Halvey himself. He'll be able to tell if she was true to him by her walk. If a girl comes back after a year with a certain class of a walk that's different from the one she went away with then you know she was up to no good with the Englishmen dirty horny bastards that they are.

The train hoots into the station and Gerry waves and points to Rose coming toward us from the far end of the train, Rose smiling away with her white teeth and lovely in a green dress. Gerry stops waving and mutters under his breath, Look at the walk on her, bitch, hoor, street-walker, flaghopper, trollop, and runs from the station. Rose walks up to me, Was that Gerry Halvey you were standing with?

'Twas.

Where is he?

Oh, he went out.

I know he went out. Where did he go?

I don't know. He didn't tell me. He just ran out.

Didn't say anything?

I didn't hear him say anything.

Do you work with him?

I do. I'm taking over the bike.

What bike?

The messenger bike.

Is he on a messenger bike?

He is.

He told me he worked in Easons office, clerk, inside job?

I feel desperate. I don't want to make a liar of Gerry Halvey, to get him into trouble with the lovely Rose. Oh, we all take turns on the messenger bike. An hour in the office, an hour on the bike. The manager says 'tis good to get out in the fresh air.

Well, I'll just go home and put my suitcase down and go to his house. I thought he'd carry this for me.

I have the bike here and you can stick the case in the basket and I'll walk you home.

We walk up to her house in Carey's Road and she tells me she's so excited about Gerry. She saved her money in England and now she wants to go back with him and get married even if he's only nineteen and she's only seventeen. What matter when you're in love. I lived like a nun in England and dreamt of him every night and thank you very much for carrying my case.

I turn away to jump on the bike and cycle back to Easons when Gerry comes at me from behind. His face is red and he's snorting like a bull. What were you doing with my girl, you little shite? Eh? What? If 'tis a thing I ever find out you did anything with my girl I'll kill you.

I didn't do anything. Carried her case because 'twas heavy.

Don't look at her again or you're dead.

I won't, Gerry. I don't want to look at her.

Oh, is that a fact? Is she ugly or what?

No, no, Gerry, she's yours and she loves you.

How do you know?

She told me.

She did?

She did, honest to God.

Jasus.

He bangs on her door, Rose, Rose, are you there? and she comes out, Of course, I'm here, and I ride away on the messenger bicycle with the sign on the basket that says Easons wondering about the way he's kissing her now and the terrible things he said about her in the station and wondering how Peter in the office could tell Mr. McCaffrey a barefaced lie about me and my eyes when all the time he and Eamon were looking at girls in their underwear and then going at themselves in the lavatory.

Mr. McCaffrey is in a terrible state in the office. Where were you? Great God above in heaven, does it take you all day to cycle from the railway station? We have an emergency here and we should have Halvey but he's gone off on his friggin' holidays, God forgive the language, and you'll have to cycle around as fast as you can, good thing you were a telegram boy that knows every inch of Limerick, and go to every bloody shop that's a customer and walk right in grab whatever copies you see of *John O'London's Weekly* tear out page sixteen and if anyone bothers you tell them 'tis government orders and they're not to interfere in government business and if they lay a finger on you they're liable to arrest, imprisonment and a large fine now go for God's sake and bring back every page sixteen you tear out so that we can burn them here in the fire.

Every shop, Mr. McCaffrey?

I'll do the big ones, you do the small ones all the way to Ballinacurra and out the Ennis Road and beyond, God help us. Go on, go.

I'm jumping on the bike and Eamon runs down the steps.

Hey, McCourt, wait. Listen. Don't give him all the page sixteens when you come back.

Why?

We can sell 'em, me an' Peter.

Why?

'Tis all about birth control and that's banned in Ireland.

What's birth control?

Aw, Christ above, don't you know anything? 'Tis condoms, you know, rubbers, French letters, things like that to stop the girls from getting up the pole.

Up the pole?

Pregnant. Sixteen years of age an' you're pure ignorant. Hurry up an' get the pages before everybody starts runnin' to the shop for *John O'London's Weekly*.

I'm about to push away on the bike when Mr. McCaffrey runs down the steps. Hold on, McCourt, we'll go in the van. Eamon, you come with us.

What about Peter?

Leave him. He'll wind up with a magazine in the lavatory anyway.

Mr. McCaffrey talks to himself in the van. Nice bloody how do you do ringing down here from Dublin on a fine Saturday to send us tearing around Limerick ripping pages out of an English magazine when I could be at home with a cup of tea and a nice bun and a read of *The Irish Press* with my feet up on a box under the picture of the Sacred Heart nice bloody how do you do entirely.

Mr. McCaffrey runs into every shop with us behind him. He grabs the magazines, hands each of us a pile and tells us start tearing. Shop owners scream at him, What are ye doing? Jesus, Mary and Holy St. Joseph, is it pure mad ye are? Put back them magazines or I'll call the guards.

Mr. McCaffrey tells them, Government orders, ma'am. There is filth in *John O'London* this week that's not fit for any Irish eyes and we are here to do God's work.

What filth? What filth? Show me the filth before ye go

mutilatin' the magazines. I won't pay Easons for these magazines, so I won't.

Ma'am, we don't care at Easons. We'd rather lose large amounts than have the people of Limerick and Ireland corrupted by this filth.

What filth?

Can't tell you. Come on, boys.

We throw the pages on the floor of the van and when Mr. McCaffrey is in a shop arguing we stuff some into our shirts. There are old magazines in the van and we tear and scatter them so that Mr. McCaffrey will think they're all page sixteen from *John O'London*.

The biggest customer for the magazine, Mr. Hutchinson, tells Mr. McCaffrey get to hell out of his shop or he'll brain him, get away from them magazines, and when Mr. McCaffrey keeps on tearing out pages Mr. Hutchinson throws him into the street, Mr. McCaffrey yelling that this is a Catholic country and just because Hutchinson is a Protestant that doesn't give him the right to sell filth in the holiest city in Ireland. Mr. Hutchinson says, Ah, kiss my arse, and Mr. McCaffrey says, See, boys? See what happens when you're not a member of the True Church?

Some shops says they've already sold all their copies of *John O'London* and Mr. McCaffrey says, Oh, Mother o' God, what's going to become of us all? Who did ye sell them to?

He demands the names and address of the customers who are in danger of losing their immortal souls from reading articles on birth control. He will go to their houses and rip out that filthy page but the shopkeepers say, 'Tis Saturday night, McCaffrey, and getting dark and would you ever take a good running jump for yourself.

On the way back to the office Eamon whispers to me in the back of the van, I have twenty-one pages. How many do you have? I tell him fourteen but I have over forty and I'm not telling him because you never have to tell the truth to people who lie about your bad eyes. Mr. McCaffrey tells us bring in the pages from the van. We scoop up everything on the floor and he's happy sitting at his desk at the other end of the office ringing Dublin to tell them how he stormed through shops like God's avenger and saved Limerick from the horrors of birth control while he watches a dancing fire of pages that have nothing to do with *John O'London's Weekly*.

Monday morning I cycle through the streets delivering magazines and people see the Easons sign on the bike and stop me to see if there's any chance they could get their hands on a copy of *John O'London's Weekly*. They're all rich-looking people, some in motor cars, men with hats, collars and ties, and two fountain pens in their pockets, women with hats and little bits of fur dangling from their shoulders, people who have tea at the Savoy or the Stella and stick out their little fingers to show how well bred they are and now want to read this page about birth control.

Eamon told me early in the day, Don't sell the bloody page for less than five shillings. I asked him if he was joking. No, he wasn't. Everyone in Limerick is talking about this page and they're dying to get their hands on it.

Five shillings or nothing, Frankie. If they're rich charge more but that's what I'm charging so don't be going around on your bicycle and puttin' me out of business with low prices. We have to give Peter something or he'll be running to McCaffrey and spilling the beans.

Some people are willing to pay seven shillings and sixpence and I'm rich in two days with over ten pounds in my pocket minus one for Peter the snake, who would betray us to McCaffrey. I put eight pounds in the post office for my fare to America and that night we have a big supper of ham, tomatoes, bread, butter, jam. Mam wants to know if I won the sweepstakes and I tell her people give me tips. She's not happy I'm a messenger boy because that's the lowest you can drop in Limerick but if it brings in ham like this we should light a candle in gratitude. She doesn't know the money for my fare is growing in the post office and she'd die if she knew what I was earning from writing threatening letters.

Malachy has a new job in the stockroom of a garage handing out parts to mechanics and Mam herself is taking care of an old man, Mr. Sliney, out in the South Circular Road while his two daughters go off to work every day. She tells me if I'm delivering papers out there to come to the house for tea and a sandwich. The daughters will never know and the old man won't mind because he's only half conscious most of the time worn out from all his years in the English army in India.

She looks peaceful in the kitchen of this house in her spotless apron, everything clean and polished around her, flowers bobbing in the garden beyond, birds chirping away, music from Radio Eireann on the wireless. She sits at the table with a pot of tea, cups and saucers, plenty of bread, butter, cold meats of all kinds. I can have any class of a sandwich but all I know is ham and brawn. She doesn't have any brawn because that's the kind of thing you'd find people eating in lanes not in a house on the South Circular Road. She says the rich won't eat brawn because it's what they scoop off floors and counters in bacon factories and you never know what you're getting. The rich are very particular about what they stick between two slices of bread. Over in America brawn is called head cheese and she doesn't know why.

She gives me a ham sandwich with juicy slices of tomato and tea in a cup with little pink angels flying around shooting arrows at other little flying angels who are blue and I wonder why they can't make teacups and chamber pots without all kinds of angels and maidens cavorting in the glen. Mam says that's the way the rich are, they love the bit of decoration and wouldn't we if we had the money. She'd give her two eyes to have a house like this with flowers and birds abroad in the garden and the wireless playing that lovely *Warsaw Concerto* or the *Dream of Olwyn* and no end of cups and saucers with angels shooting arrows.

She says she has to look in on Mr. Sliney he's so old and feeble he forgets to call for the chamber pot.

Chamber pot? You have to empty his chamber pot?

Of course I do.

There's a silence here because I think we're remembering the cause of all our troubles, Laman Griffin's chamber pot. But that was a long time ago and now it's Mr. Sliney's chamber pot, which is no harm because she's paid for this and he's harmless. When she comes back she tells me Mr. Slinley would like to see me, so come in while he's awake.

He's lying in a bed in the front parlor, the window blocked with a black sheet, no sign of light. He tells my mother, Lift me up a bit, missus, and pull back that bloody thing off the window so I can see the boy.

He has long white hair down to his shoulders. Mam whispers he won't let anyone cut it. He says, I have me own teeth, son. Would you credit that? Do you have your own teeth, son?

I do, Mr. Sliney.

Ah. I was in India you know. Me and Timoney up the road. Bunch of Limerick men in India. Do you know Timoney, son?

I did, Mr. Sliney.

He's dead, you know. Poor bugger went blind. I have me sight. I have me teeth. Keep your teeth, son.

I will, Mr. Sliney.

I'm getting tired, son, but there's one thing I want to tell you. Are you listening to me?

I am, Mr. Sliney.

Is he listening to me, missus?

Oh, he is, Mr. Sliney.

Good. Now here's what I want to tell you. Lean over here so I can whisper in your ear. What I want to tell you is, Never smoke another man's pipe.

*   *   *

413

Halvey goes off to England with Rose and I have to stay on the messenger bike all through the winter. It's a bitter winter, ice everywhere, and I never know when the bike will go out from under me and send me flying into the street or on to the pavement, magazines and papers scattered. Shops complain to Mr. McCaffrey that *The Irish Times* is coming in decorated with bits of ice and dog shit and he mutters to us that's the way that paper should be delivered, Protestant rag that it is.

Every day after my deliveries I take *The Irish Times* home and read it to see where the danger is. Mam says it's a good thing Dad isn't here. He'd say, Is this what the men of Ireland fought and died for that my own son is sitting there at the kitchen table reading the freemason paper?

There are letters to the editor from people all over Ireland claiming they heard the first cuckoo of the year and you can read between the lines that people are calling each other liars. There are reports about Protestant weddings and pictures and the women always look lovelier than the ones we know in the lanes. You can see Protestant women have perfect teeth although Halvey's Rose had lovely teeth.

I keep reading *The Irish Times* and wondering if it's an occasion of sin though I don't care. As long as Theresa Carmody is in heaven not coughing I don't go to confession anymore. I read *The Irish Times* and *The Times* of London because that tells me what the King is up to every day and what Elizabeth and Margaret are doing.

I read English women's magazines for all the food articles and the answers to women's questions. Peter and Eamon put on English accents and pretend they're reading from English women's magazines.

Peter says, Dear Miss Hope, I'm going out with a fellow from Ireland named McCaffrey and he has his hands all over me and his thing pushing against my belly button and I'm demented not knowing what to do. I remain, yours anxiously, Miss Lulu Smith, Yorkshire.

Eamon says, Dear Lulu, If this McCaffrey is that tall that he's pushing his yoke against your belly button I suggest you find a smaller man who will slip it between your thighs. Surely you can find a decent short man in Yorkshire.

Dear Miss Hope, I am thirteen years old with black hair and something terrible is happening and I can't tell anyone not even my mother. I'm bleeding every few weeks you know where and I'm afraid I'll be found out. Miss Agnes Tripple, Little Biddle-on-the-Twiddle, Devon.

Dear Agnes, You are to be congratulated. You are now a woman and you can get your hair permed because you are having your monthlies. Do not fear your monthlies for all Englishwomen have them. They are a gift of God to purify us so that we can have stronger children for the empire, soldiers to keep the Irish in their place. In some parts of the world a woman with a monthly is unclean but we British cherish our women with the monthlies, oh we do indeed.

In the springtime there's a new messenger boy and I'm back in the office. Peter and Eamon drift off to England. Peter is fed up with Limerick, no girls, and you're driven to yourself, wank wank wank, that's all we ever do in Limerick. There are new boys. I'm senior boy and the job is easier because I'm fast and when Mr. McCaffrey is out in the van and my work is done I read the English, Irish, American magazines and papers. Day and night I dream of America.

Malachy goes to England to work in a rich Catholic boys' boarding school and he walks around cheerful and smiling as if he's the equal of any boy in the school and everyone knows when you work in an English boarding school you're supposed to hang your head and shuffle like a proper Irish servant. They fire him for his ways and Malachy tells them they can kiss his royal Irish arse and they say that's the kind of foul language and behavior you'd expect. He gets a job in the gas works in Coventry shoveling coal into the furnaces like Uncle Pa Keating, shoveling coal and waiting for the day he can go to America after me.

XVIII

I'm seventeen, eighteen, going on nineteen, working away at Easons, writing threatening letters for Mrs. Finucane, who says she's not long for this world and the more Masses said for her soul the better she'll feel. She puts money in envelopes and sends me to churches around the city to knock on priests' doors, hand in the envelopes with the request for Masses. She wants prayers from all the priests but the Jesuits. She says, They're useless, all head and no heart. That's what they should have over their door in Latin and I won't give them a penny because every penny you give a Jesuit goes to a fancy book or a bottle of wine.

She sends the money, she hopes the Masses are said, but she's never sure and if she's not sure why should I be handing out all that money to priests when I need the money to go to America and if I keep back a few pounds for myself and put it in the post office who will ever know the difference and if I say a prayer for Mrs. Finucane and light candles for her soul when she dies won't God listen even if I'm a sinner long past my last confession.

I'll be nineteen in a month. All I need is a few pounds to make up the fare and a few pounds in my pocket when I land in America.

The Friday night before my nineteenth birthday Mrs. Finucane sends me for the sherry. When I return she is dead in the chair, her eyes wide open, and her purse on the floor wide open. I can't look at her but I help myself to a roll of money. Seventeen pounds. I take the key to the trunk upstairs. I take forty of the hundred pounds in the trunk and the ledger. I'll add this to what I have in the post office and I have enough to go to America. On my way out I take the sherry bottle to save it from being wasted.

I sit by the River Shannon near the dry docks sipping Mrs. Finucane's sherry. Aunt Aggie's name is in the ledger. She owes nine pounds. It might have been the money she spent on my clothes a long time ago but now she'll never have to pay it because I heave the ledger into the river. I'm sorry I'll never be able to tell Aunt Aggie I saved her nine pounds. I'm sorry I wrote threatening letters to the poor people in the lanes of Lamerick, my own people, but the ledger is gone, no one will ever know what they owe and they won't have to pay their balances. I wish I could tell them, I'm your Robin Hood.

Another sip of the sherry. I'll spare a pound or two for a Mass for Mrs. Finucane's soul. Her ledger is well on its way down the Shannon and out to the Atlantic and I know I'll follow it someday soon.

The man at O'Riordan's Travel Agency says he can't get me to America by air unless I travel to London first, which would cost a fortune. He can put me on a ship called the *Irish Oak*, which will be leaving Cork in a few weeks. He says, Nine days at sea, September October, best time of the year, your own cabin, thirteen passengers, best of food, bit of a holiday for yourself and that will cost fifty-five pounds, do you have it?

I do.

I tell Mam I'm going in a few weeks and she cries. Michael says, Will we all go some day?

We will.

Alphie says, Will you send me a cowboy hat and a thing you throw that comes back to you?

Michael tells him that's a boomerang and you'd have to go all the way to Australia to get the likes of that, you can't get it in America.

Alphie says you can get it in America yes you can and they argue about America and Australia and boomerangs till Mam says, For the love o' Jesus, yeer brother is leaving us and the two of ye are there squabbling over boomerangs. Will ye give over?

Mam says we'll have to have a bit of party the night before I go. They used to have parties in the old days when anyone would go to America, which was so far away the parties were called American wakes because the family never expected to see the departing one again in this life. She says 'tis a great pity Malachy can't come back from England but we'll be together in America someday with the help of God and His Blessed Mother.

On my days off from work I walk around Limerick and look at all the places we lived, the Windmill Street, Hartstonge Street, Roden Lane, Rosbrien Road, Little Barrington Street, which is really a lane. I stand looking at Theresa Carmody's house till her mother comes out and says, What do you want? I sit at the graves of Oliver and Eugene in the old St. Patrick's Burying Ground and cross the road to St. Lawrence's Cemetery where Theresa is buried. Wherever I go I hear voices of the dead and I wonder if they can follow you across the Atlantic Ocean.

I want to get pictures of Limerick stuck in my head in case I never come back. I sit in St. Joseph's Church and the Redemptorist church and tell myself take a good look because I might never see this again. I walk down Henry Street to say good-bye to St. Francis though I'm sure I'll be able to talk to him in America.

Now there are days I don't want to go to America. I'd like to go to O'Riordan's Travel Agency and get back my fifty-five pounds. I could wait till I'm twenty-one and Malachy can go with me so that I'll know at least one person in New York. I have strange feelings and sometimes when I'm sitting by the fire with Mam and my brothers I feel tears coming and I'm ashamed of myself for being weak. At first Mam laughs and tells me, Your bladder must be near your eye, but then Michael says, We'll all go to America, Dad will be there, Malachy will be there and we'll all be together, and she gets the tears herself and we sit there, the four of us, like weeping eejits.

Mam says this is the first time we ever had a party and isn't it a sad thing altogether that you have it when your children are slipping away one by one, Malachy to England, Frank to America. She saves a few shillings from her wages taking care of Mr. Sliney to buy bread, ham, brawn, cheese, lemonade and a few bottles of stout. Uncle Pa Keating brings stout, whiskey and a little sherry for Aunt Aggie's delicate stomach and she brings a cake loaded with currants and raisins she baked herself. The Abbot brings six bottles of stout and says, That's all right, Frankie, ye can all drink it as long as I have a bottle or two for meself to help me sing me song.

He sings "The Road to Rasheen." He holds his stout, closes his eyes, and song comes out in a high whine. The words make no sense and everyone wonders why tears are seeping from his shut eyes. Alphie whispers to me, Why is he crying over a song that makes no sense?

I don't know.

The Abbot ends his song, opens his eyes, wipes his cheeks and tells us that was a sad song about an Irish boy that went to America and got shot by gangsters and died before a priest could reach his side and he tells me don't be gettin' shot if you're not near a priest.

Uncle Pa says that's the saddest song he ever heard and is there any chance we could have something lively. He calls on Mam and she says, Ah, no, Pa, sure I don't have the wind.

Come on, Angela, come on. One voice now, one voice and one voice only.

All right. I'll try.

We all join in the chorus of her sad song,

> *A mother's love is a blessing*
> *No matter where you roam.*
> *Keep her while you have her,*
> *You'll miss her when she's gone.*

Uncle Pa says one song is worse than the one before and are we turning this night into a wake altogether, is there any chance someone would sing a song to liven up the proceedings or will he be driven to drink with the sadness.

Oh, God, says Aunt Aggie, I forgot. The moon is having an eclipse abroad this minute.

We stand out in the lane watching the moon disappear behind a round black shadow. Uncle Pa says, That's a very good sign for you going to America, Frankie.

No, says Aunt Aggie, 'tis a bad sign. I read in the paper that the moon is practicing for the end of the world.

Oh, end of the world my arse, says Uncle Pa. 'Tis the beginning for Frankie McCourt. He'll come back in a few years with a new suit and fat on his bones like any Yank and a lovely girl with white teeth hangin' from his arm.

Mam says, Ah, no, Pa, ah, no, and they take her inside and comfort her with a drop of sherry from Spain.

It's late in the day when the *Irish Oak* sails from Cork, past Kinsale and Cape Clear, and dark when lights twinkle on Mizen Head, the last of Ireland I'll see for God knows how long.

Surely I should have stayed, taken the post office examination, climbed in the world. I could have brought in enough money for Michael and Alphie to go to school with proper shoes and bellies well filled. We could have moved from the lane to a street or even an avenue where houses have gardens. I should have taken that examination and Mam would never again have to empty the chamber pots of Mr. Sliney or anyone else.

It's too late now. I'm on the ship and there goes Ireland into the night and it's foolish to be standing on this deck looking back and thinking of my family and Limerick and Malachy and my father in England and even more foolish that songs are going through my head Roddy McCorley goes to die and Mam gasping Oh the days of the Kerry dancing with poor Mr. Clohessy hacking away in the bed and now I want Ireland back at least I had Mam and my brothers and Aunt Aggie bad as she was and Uncle Pa, standing me my first pint, and my bladder is near my eye and here's a priest standing by me on the deck and you can see he's curious.

He's a Limerickman but he has an American accent from his years in Los Angeles. He knows how it is to leave Ireland, did it himself and never got over it. You live in Los Angeles with sun and palm trees day in day out and you ask God if there's any chance He could give you one soft rainy Limerick day.

The priest sits beside me at the table of the First Officer, who tells us ship's orders have been changed and instead of sailing to New York we're bound for Montreal.

Three days out and orders are changed again. We are going to New York after all.

Three American passengers complain, Goddam Irish. Can't they get it straight?

The day before we sail into New York orders are changed again. We are going to a place up the Hudson River called Albany.

The Americans say, Albany? Goddam Albany? Why the hell did we have to sail on a goddam Irish tub? Goddam.

The priest tells me pay no attention. All Americans are not like that.

I'm on deck the dawn we sail into New York. I'm sure I'm in a film, that it will end and lights will come up in the Lyric Cinema. The priest wants to point out things but he doesn't have to. I can pick out the Statue of Liberty, Ellis Island, the Empire State Building, the Chrysler Building, the Brooklyn Bridge. There are thousands of cars speeding along the roads and the sun turns everything to gold. Rich Americans in top hats white ties and tails must be going home to bed with the gorgeous women with white teeth. The rest are going to work in warm comfortable offices and no one has a care in the world.

The Americans are arguing with the captain and a man who climbed aboard from a tugboat. Why can't we get off here? Why do we have to sail all the goddam way to goddam Albany?

The man says, Because you're passengers on the vessel and the captain is the captain and we have no procedures for taking you ashore.

Oh, yeah. Well, this is a free country and we're American citizens.

Is that a fact? Well, you're on an Irish ship with an Irish captain and you'll do what he goddam tells you or swim ashore.

He climbs down the ladder, tugboat chugs away, and we sail up the Hudson past Manhattan, under the George Washington Bridge, past hundreds of Liberty ships that did their bit in the war, moored now and ready to rot.

The captain announces the tide will force us to drop anchor overnight opposite a place called, the priest spells it for me, Poughkeepsie. The priest says that's an Indian name and the Americans say goddam Poughkeepsie.

After dark a small boat put-puts to the ship and an Irish voice calls up, Hello, there. Bejasus, I saw the Irish flag, so I did. Couldn't believe me two eyes. Hello, there.

He invites the First Officer to go ashore for a drink and bring a friend and, You, too, Father. Bring a friend.

The priest invites me and we climb down a ladder to the small boat with the First Officer and the Wireless Officer. The man in the boat says his name is Tim Boyle from Mayo God help us and we docked there at the right time because there's a bit of a party and we're all invited. He takes us to a house with a lawn, a fountain and three pink birds standing on one leg. There are five women in a room called a living room. The women have stiff hair, spotless frocks. They have glasses in their hands and they're friendly and smile with perfect teeth. One says, Come right in. Just in time for the pawty.

Pawty. That's the way they talk and I suppose I'll be talking like that in a few years.

Tim Boyle tells us the girls are having a bit of a time while their husbands are away overnight hunting deer, and one woman, Betty, says, Yeah. Buddies from the war. That war is over nearly five years and they can't get over it so they shoot animals every weekend and drink Rheingold till they can't see. Goddam war, excuse the language, Fawder.

The priest whispers to me, These are bad women. We won't stay here long.

The bad women say, Whatcha like to drink? We got everything. What's your name, honey?

Frank McCourt.

Nice name. So you take a little drink. All the Irish take a little drink. You like a beer?

Yes, please.

Gee, so polite. I like the Irish. My grandmother was half Irish so that makes me half, quarter? I dunno. My name is Frieda. So here's your beer, honey.

The priest sits at the end of a sofa which they call a couch and two women talk to him. Betty asks the First Officer if he'd like to see the house and he says, Oh, I would, because we don't have houses like this in Ireland. Another woman tells the Wireless Officer he should see what they have growing in the garden, you wouldn't believe the flowers. Frieda asks me if I'm okay and I tell her yes but would she mind telling me where the lavatory is.

The what?

Lavatory.

Oh, you mean the bathroom. Right this way, honey, down the hall.

Thanks.

She pushes in the door, turns on the light, kisses my cheek and whispers she'll be right outside if I need anything.

I stand at the toilet bowl firing away and wonder what I'd need at a time like this and if this is a common thing in America, women waiting outside while you take a splash.

I finish, flush and go outside. She takes my hand and leads me into a bedroom, puts down her glass, locks the door, pushes me down on the bed. She's fumbling at my fly. Damn buttons. Don't you have zippers in Ireland? She pulls out my excitement climbs up on me slides up and down up and down Jesus I'm in heaven and there's a knock on the door the priest Frank are you in there Frieda putting her finger to her lips and her eyes rolling to heaven Frank are you in there Father would you ever take a good running jump for yourself and oh God oh Theresa do you see what's happening to me at long last I don't give a fiddler's fart if the Pope himself knocked on this door and the College of Cardinals gathered gawking at the windows oh God the whole inside of me is gone into her and she collapses on me and tells me I'm wonderful and would I ever consider settling in Poughkeepsie.

Frieda tells the priest I had a bit of a dizziness after going to the bathroom, that's what happens when you travel and you're drinking a strange beer like Rheingold, which she believes they don't have in Ireland. I can see the priest doesn't believe her and I can't stop the way the heat is coming and going in my face. He already wrote down my mother's name and address and now I'm afraid he'll write and say your fine son spent his first night in America in a bedroom in

Poughkeepsie romping with a woman whose husband was away shooting deer for a bit of relaxation after doing his bit for America in the war and isn't this a fine way to treat the men who fought for their country.

The First Officer and the Wireless Officer return from their tours of the house and the garden and they don't look at the priest. The women tell us we must be starving and they go into the kitchen. We sit in the living room saying nothing to each other and listening to the women whispering and laughing in the kitchen. The priest whispers to me again, Bad women, bad women, occasion of sin, and I don't know what to say to him.

The bad women bring out sandwiches and pour more beer and when we finish eating they put on Frank Sinatra records and ask if anyone would like to dance. No one says yes because you'd never get up and dance with bad women in the presence of a priest, so the women dance with each other and laugh as if they all had little secrets. Tim Boyle drinks whiskey and falls asleep in a corner till Frieda wakes him and tells him take us back to the ship. When we're leaving Frieda leans toward me as if she might kiss my cheek but the priest says good night in a very sharp way and no one shakes hands. As we walk down the street to the river we hear the women laughing, tinkling and bright in the night air.

We climb the ladder and Tim calls to us from his little boat, Mind yourselves going up that ladder. Oh, boys, oh, boys, wasn't that a grand night? Good night, boys, and good night, Father.

We watch his little boat till it disappears into the dark of the Poughkeepsie riverbank. The priest says good night and goes below and the First Officer follows him.

I stand on the deck with the Wireless Officer looking at the lights of America twinkling. He says, My God, that was a lovely night, Frank. Isn't this a great country altogether?

XIX

'Tis